John P. Murphy is the Philip and Lynn Straus Curator of
Prints and Drawings at the Frances Lehman Loeb Art Center,
Vassar College. He co-curated the award-winning exhibition
"The Left Front: Radical Art in the 'Red Decade,' 1929–1940"
(The Block Museum of Art, Northwestern University) and is
currently working with the Philadelphia Museum of Art on an
exhibition related to Depression-era prints and politics in the
United States.

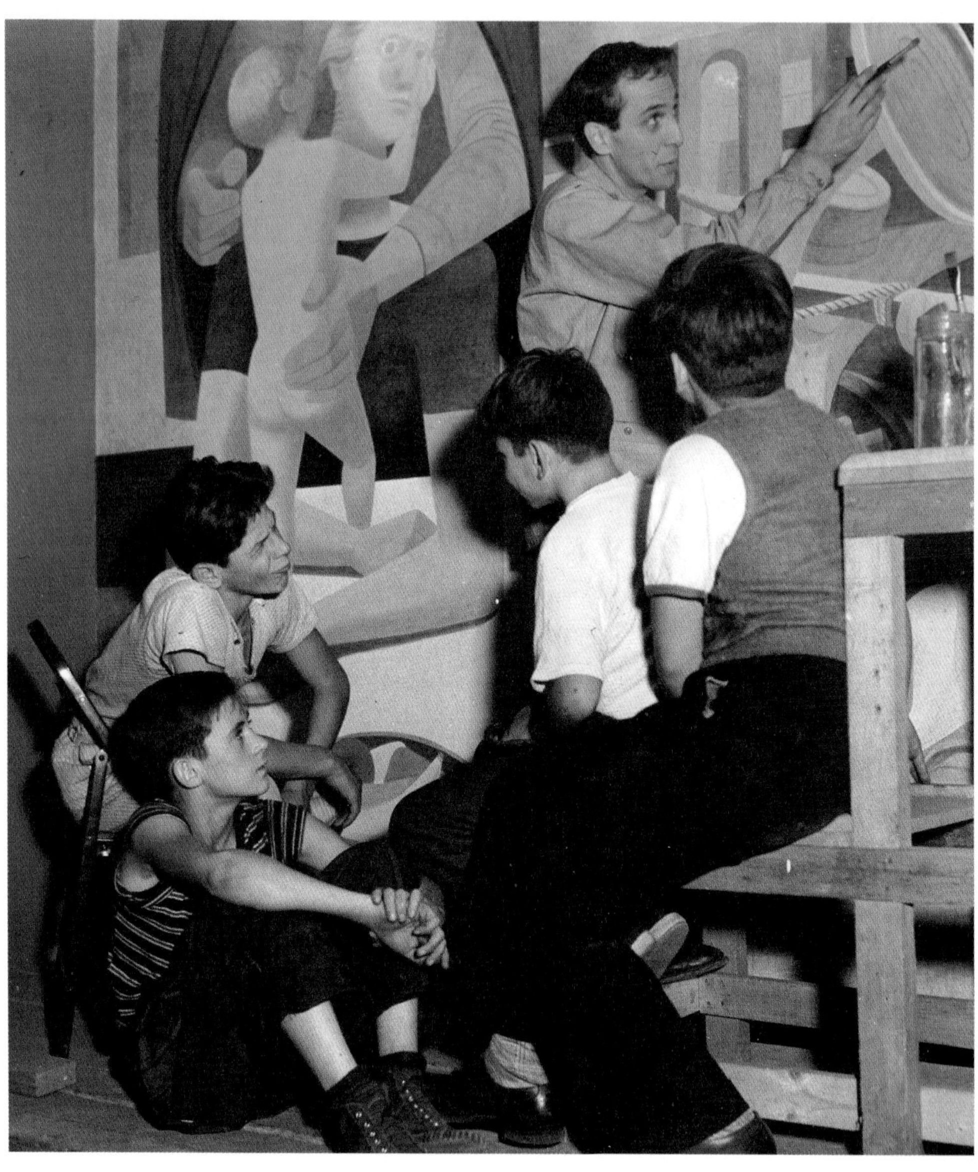

1 Sol Lisbohn, *Philip Guston Working on Mural*, 1940

World of Art

New Deal Art
Culture and Crisis in the Great Depression

John P. Murphy

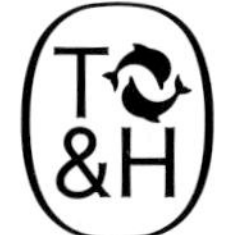

To Kristin, for making a world I want to be a part of

To my grandparents, for laying the foundation

Publication is made possible in part by a grant from
the Myers Foundations and a gift from Elizabeth Warnock
to the Department of Art History at Northwestern University.

Additional support is provided by the Philip and Lynn Straus
Endowment Fund through the Frances Lehman Loeb Art Center
at Vassar College.

First published in 2025 in the United Kingdom
by Thames & Hudson Ltd, 6–24 Britannia Street,
London WC1X 9JD

www.thamesandhudson.com

First published in 2025 in the United States
of America by Thames & Hudson Inc.,
500 Fifth Avenue, New York, New York 10110

www.thamesandhudsonusa.com

Art direction and series design by Kummer & Herrman
Layout by Adam Hay Studio

EU Authorized Representative: Interart S.A.R.L.
19 rue Charles Auray, 93500 Pantin, Paris, France
productsafety@thameshudson.co.uk
interart.fr

A CIP catalogue record for this book is available from the
British Library

Library of Congress Control Number 2025937257

ISBN 978-0-500-20502-0
01

Printed and bound in China through Asia Pacific
Offset Ltd

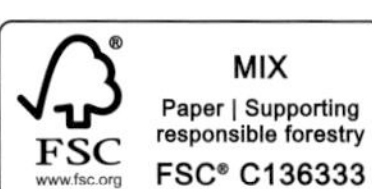

Contents

Acknowledgments

I might not be here without the New Deal. My grandpa was out of work during the Depression when the Works Progress Administration gave him a job (and the means to start a family) laying sidewalks in Urbana, Illinois. My parents instilled in me and my siblings a conviction, amounting to a creed, that culture is a necessity, not a luxury—a central theme of *New Deal Art*. Another theme is the strength of collective effort. I especially want to thank Bram and Sandy Dijkstra, champions of 1930s art, and the team at Thames & Hudson. The Dijkstras, Stephen Eisenman, Pat Hills, Alyx Raz, Ben Schacht, Tom Wolf, and six bright students in my 1930s seminar read and commented on early drafts—I'm grateful for their thoughts and feedback (mistakes and misjudgments, of course, remain my own). I'm grateful to friends and colleagues at the Loeb Art Center for their support, and for institutional support in the form of publication subsidies. The staff at the FDR Presidential Library in Hyde Park, New York, was immensely helpful, and the Living New Deal (livingnewdeal.org) is an indispensable online resource. The bibliography lists the cumulative work of scholars and curators, past and present, who have illuminated the promises and pitfalls of the New Deal art programs. I am particularly indebted to Andrew Hemingway, whose rigorous scholarship and critical insights into New Deal art and politics have been an abiding influence and inspiration.

Abbreviations

AAA – Agricultural Adjustment Administration
AAC – American Artists' Congress
ALA – Artists League of America
AU – Artists' Union
CAA – College Art Association
CAC – Community Art Center
CIO – Congress of Industrial Organizations
CPUSA – Communist Party USA
CWA – Civil Works Administration
DOI – Department of the Interior
FAP – Federal Art Project
FSA – Farm Security Administration
FTP – Federal Theatre Project
FWP – Federal Writers' Project
GSA – General Services Administration
HAG – Harlem Artists Guild
HCAC – Harlem Community Art Center
HUAC – House Un-American Activities Committee
JRC – John Reed Club
MHP – Milwaukee Handicraft Project
OWI – Office of War Information
PUAC – Public Use of Art Committee
PWAP – Public Works of Art Project
RA – Resettlement Administration
REA – Rural Electrification Administration
SSCAC – South Side Community Art Center
TRAP – Treasury Relief Art Project
TVA – Tennessee Valley Authority
UAG – Unemployed Artists Group
WPA – Works Progress / Projects Administration
WRA – War Relocation Authority

Introduction
Crisis and Opportunity

James N. Rosenberg (1874–1970) had a front-row seat to the end of the world. A bankruptcy lawyer by day, he was in Manhattan on "Black Tuesday," 29 October 1929, overcast and chilly, when the United States stock market collapsed. Stock prices plummeted, billions of dollars vanished, and thousands of investors were wiped out.

An artist by night, Rosenberg escaped from the "Wall Street inferno," as he recalled, to forge a hallucinatory lithograph in the heat of panic. Lightning splits the sky over buckling skyscrapers. A chaotic crowd rushes to escape the carnage. Birds of prey swoop in the air. The iconic steeple of Wall Street's Trinity Church cracks and bends. Silhouetted figures leap from rooftops in despair. The words *Dies Irae* hover in the storm clouds: Day of Wrath.

Shockwaves of financial panic radiated from Wall Street to Main Street. Banks failed, factories shuttered, businesses folded, and workers were handed the dreaded pink slip. Savings evaporated and there was no social safety net—no social security, unemployment benefits, or deposit insurance— to catch the falling. Millions of families faced eviction or foreclosure. Some ended up in shantytowns or went on the road in search of jobs that didn't exist. The unemployed, suffering hunger and malnutrition, queued up in breadlines and soup kitchens. Marriages disintegrated. Birth rates fell. Suicide rates skyrocketed.

When asked if anything like the Great Depression had happened before, the British economist John Maynard Keynes replied, "Yes. It was called the Dark Ages and it lasted four hundred years." Artists in the early 1930s made darkness visible.

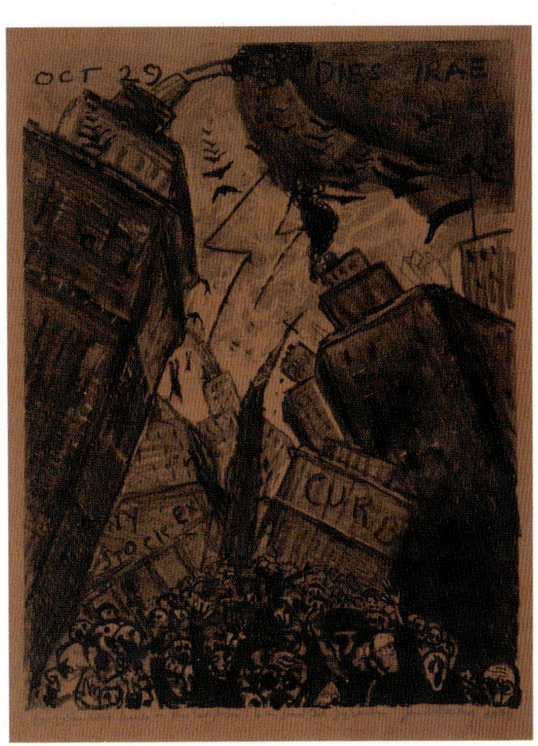

2 James N. Rosenberg,
October 29, Dies Irae, 1929

Clare Leighton (1898–1989) used dramatic perspective to stretch
the interminable length of a New York breadline. A huddled
group in the foreground warm their hands over a makeshift
fire. Above them, glowing advertisements and stair-stepped
skyscrapers rise like an inaccessible dream. Margaret Bourke-
White (1904–71) similarly measured the gap between illusion
and reality. On assignment for *Life* magazine, she photographed
a line of Black Americans seeking food from a relief agency—
bags, baskets, and buckets in tow—in the wake of catastrophic
flooding. A billboard of a grinning white nuclear family
announces, "There's no way like the American Way."

President Herbert Hoover's feeble response to the crash
failed to meet the scale of economic destruction. As the lights
blinked out in storefronts and breadlines stretched for blocks,
Hoover held fast to the conviction, expressed in a 1931 radio
address, that "the spread of government destroys initiative
and thus destroys character." He appealed instead to the tropes
of rugged individualism and the benevolence of corporate
leaders. Although he begrudgingly increased government
spending and approved some federal assistance to banks

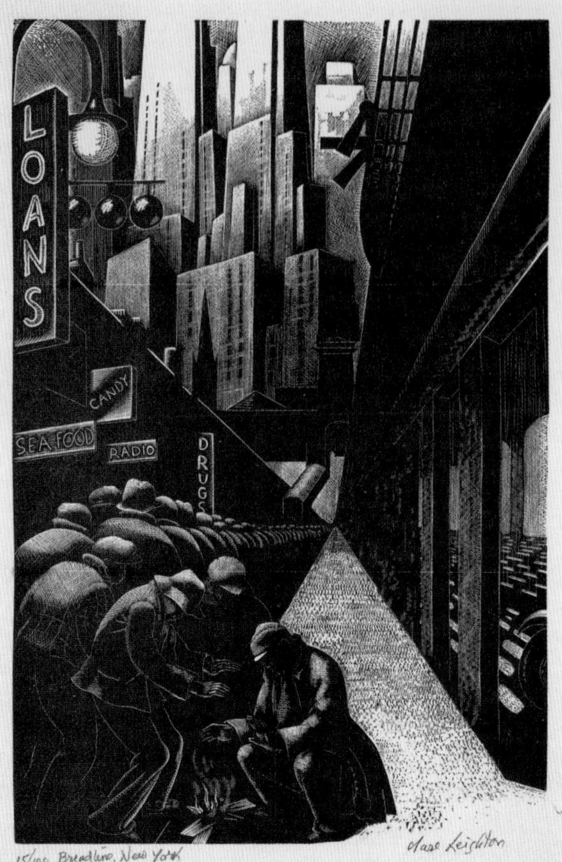

3 LEFT Clare Leighton, *Bread Line, New York,* 1932
4 BELOW Margaret Bourke-White, *At the Time of the Louisville Flood,* 1937

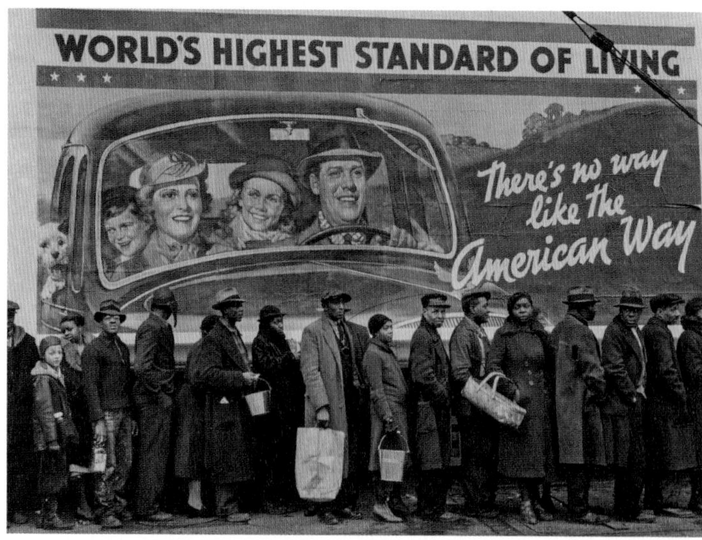

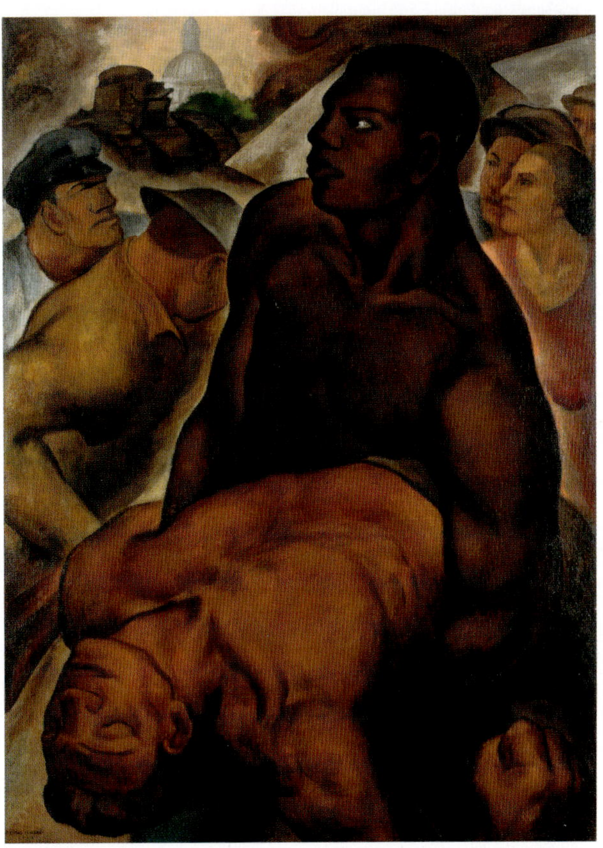

5 Eitaro Ishigaki, *The Bonus March,* 1932

and businesses, he helped defeat congressional relief bills that he considered handouts.

Inaction bred protest. In the summer of 1932, a twenty-thousand-strong "Bonus Army" of unemployed veterans of the First World War marched on the capital to demand advances on their war bonuses, which were not due to be paid out until 1945. The DC police and US Army routed the veterans from their encampments on the floodplains of the Anacostia River. In the ensuing melee, several unarmed demonstrators were killed and many more injured. Eitaro Ishigaki (1893–1958) painted a symbolic version of the event featuring a defiant Black marcher, stripped to the waist, cradling a fallen comrade who raises his fist in a final gesture of solidarity. In the distance rises the dome of the US Capitol, a beacon of democratic promise obscured by an armored tank and plumes of tear gas.

The New Deal

When the smoke cleared, a campaign song rang out: "Happy days are here again!" The 1932 presidential election served as a referendum on Hoover's weak response to the worsening crisis. Democratic candidate Franklin Delano Roosevelt (FDR), patrician governor of New York and fifth cousin to twenty-sixth president Theodore Roosevelt, had a broad smile and breezy manner in contrast to the dour Hoover. Stricken with polio in the early 1920s, Roosevelt embodied resilient optimism in the face of hardship, a quality that struck a chord in the depths of the Depression. In his speech accepting the party's nomination, he pledged "a new deal for the American people," and the phrase stuck. Voters handed Roosevelt and his New Deal a landslide victory.

Roosevelt took office amid cascading crises. The economic catastrophe, not confined to the US, undermined constitutional democracies across the globe. Adolf Hitler assumed power in Germany in 1933. Joseph Stalin tightened his grip on the Soviet Union. Commentators and policymakers, both liberal and conservative, wondered whether the US needed a strongman to muscle its way out of the Depression. Dictatorship could seem a viable, even preferable, alternative to democracy, able to move quickly without the checks of courts or Congress. Could liberal democracy survive the dual threat of depression at home and dictatorship abroad?

Roosevelt answered with assertive state intervention. Having promised on the campaign trail "bold, persistent experimentation" in pursuing solutions to the Depression, the newly elected President set in motion ambitious government programs to prop up the labor force and pump-prime the economy. His famous first hundred days in office saw a flurry of legislation to insure bank deposits, set up homeowner loans, reform industry and agriculture, stimulate regional development, and manage conservation efforts. "I think this would be a good time for beer," FDR announced after signing a bill to repeal Prohibition on the sale of alcohol.

At a time when American citizens expected little of the federal government besides protecting national borders and delivering the mail, the New Deal—the series of programs, policies, and reforms to mitigate the effects of the Great Depression—generated a profound and permanent shift in the state's role in American society. The government now took as its mandate the welfare of its citizens.

In his inaugural address, FDR asked Congress for "broad executive power to wage a war against the Emergency." He pressed out-of-work "foot soldiers" into service. Jacob Getlar

6

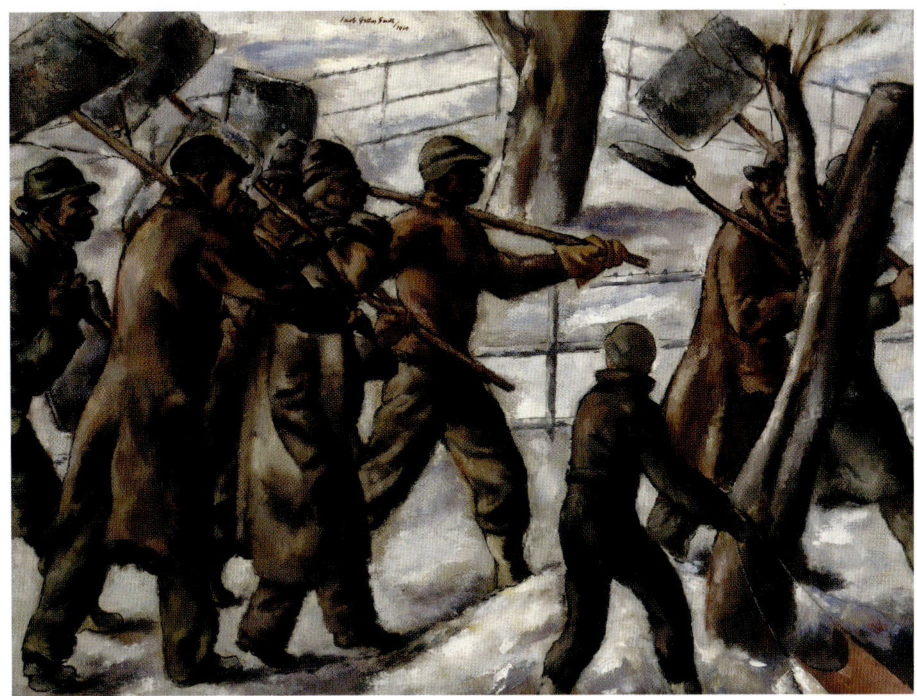

6 Jacob Getlar Smith, *Snow Shovellers*, 1934

Smith's (1898–1958) *Snow Shovellers* depicts a ragtag platoon
of workers on the march, shovels shouldered like rifles,
some dressed for outdoor work and others more suitably for
an office. Work groups such as these were part of New Deal
efforts to stanch economic hemorrhaging through work relief
(as opposed to direct relief or the "dole"), which, according
to Roosevelt, would "preserve not only the bodies of the
unemployed from destruction but also their self-respect,
their self-reliance, and courage and determination."

The most expansive job-creating agency was the Works
Progress Administration (WPA), a program now synonymous
with the New Deal. As part of the WPA, some eight million
workers undertook infrastructure projects between 1935
and 1943, building or renovating hospitals, schools, parks,
museums, libraries, courthouses, post offices, bridges, and
airports from coast to coast. It was the largest public works
initiative in the country's history, and art played a defining
role. So much so that FDR is supposed to have predicted,
"One hundred years from now, my administration will be
known for its art, not its relief."

A New Deal for Art

Professional artists were among the most vulnerable to the economic shock of 1929. Commercial galleries closed, private commissions dried up, and sources of patronage disappeared. A living based on the sale of artworks, precarious even in the best of times, proved untenable. Phil Bard's (1912–66) drawing for the journal *Art Front* finds an impoverished painter slumped in front of an easel beneath a dangling sword of Damocles, a symbol of the looming threat of hunger. Unsold canvases lean against the back wall.

"Long isolated from the rest of society," wrote painter George Biddle (1885–1973), "the artists joined their fellow men on the bread lines and in the relief stations." A schoolmate of FDR at both the exclusive preparatory school Groton and Harvard, Biddle encouraged the President in a 1933 letter to look to Mexico as a model for government-sponsored art. In Biddle's view, Mexican artists like Diego Rivera (1886–1957) had been able to express a "common social faith or purpose" in public murals representing the ideals of the revolutionary republic. "The younger artists of America," he wrote, "are conscious as they have never been of the social revolution that our country and civilization are going through; and they would be eager to express these ideals in a permanent art form if they were given the government's cooperation." (Biddle 1939, 268)

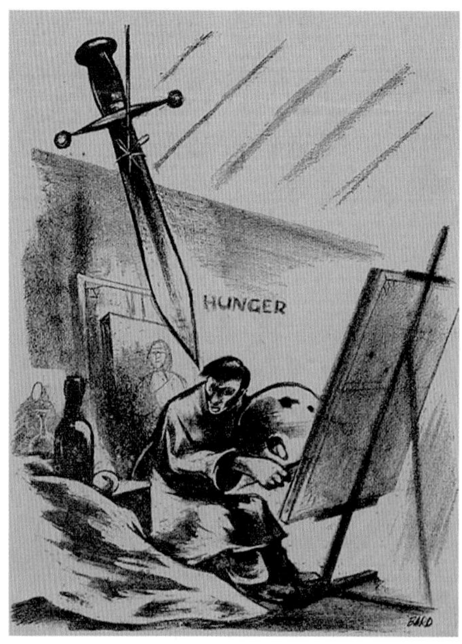

7 LEFT Phil Bard, "Hunger," *Art Front*, May 1935
8 OPPOSITE Diego Rivera, *In the Arsenal*, 1923–28

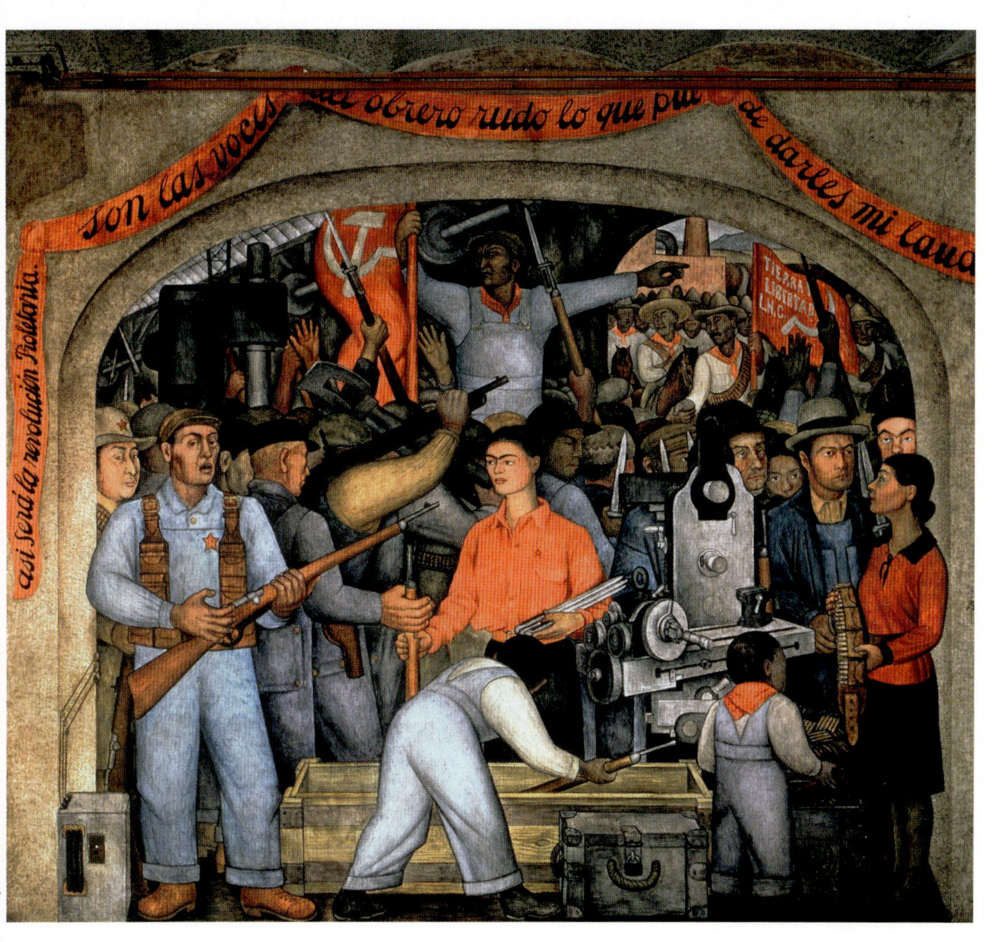
son las voces
del obrero rudo lo que pu
de darles mi laud
así será la revolución Proletaria.
TIERRA
LIBERTAD
L.N.C.

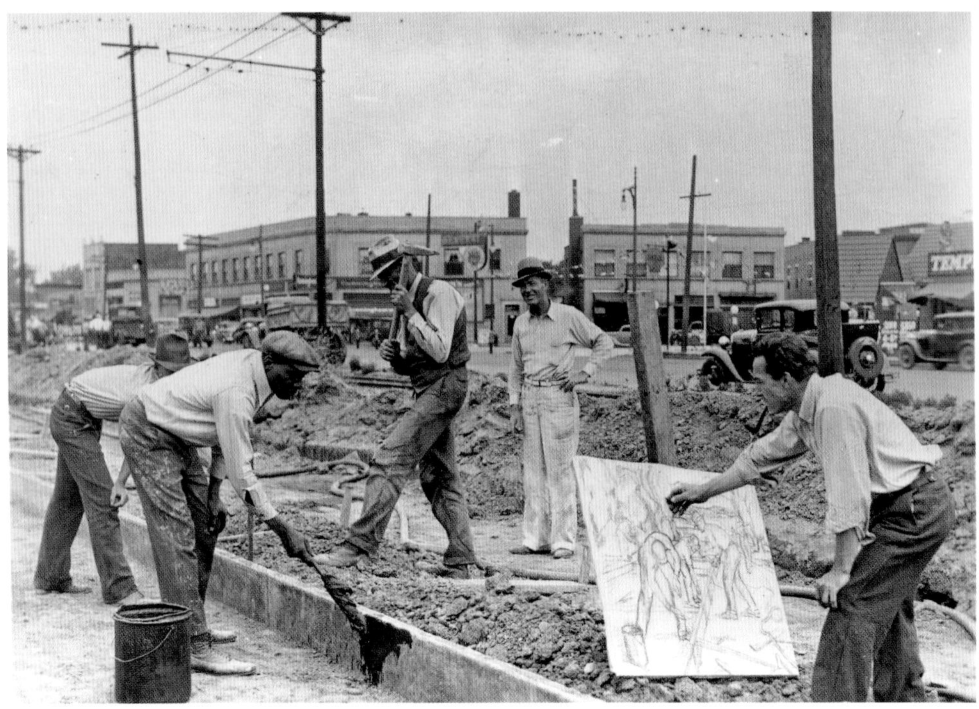

9 Artist sketching WPA construction workers, 1939

Roosevelt, in response, cautioned that he did not need "a lot of young enthusiasts painting Lenin's head on the Justice Building." (The same day Biddle wrote to FDR, Rivera's unfinished mural for the Rockefeller Center in New York was covered owing to its portrait of Bolshevik leader Vladimir Lenin.) But Biddle's letter expressed ideas in much wider circulation. That support for artists should be part of the economic recovery. That art could spiritually fortify a nation reeling from the Depression. That it could help restore public confidence in the state and the economy. These ideas—which underpinned state support for the arts in Europe, the Soviet Union, and Great Britain as well as Mexico—found sympathetic ears in the Treasury Department, which set up in late 1933 the first New Deal art program: the Public Works of Art Project.

So began an audacious experiment. Between 1933 and 1943 the US government, for the first and last time, subsidized art on a massive scale. A series of federal programs endorsed a public role for artists and opened the floodgates of creativity nationwide:

Public Works of Art Project (1933–34): The first federal art project operated as an emergency relief program from December 1933 to June 1934. It paid 3,750 artists a monthly wage to make some 15,000 artworks intended for tax-funded buildings.

Section of Fine Arts (1934–43): The Section, as it was known, sponsored competitions to hire artists to make murals and sculptures for federal buildings, mostly post offices and courthouses. The Section also ran the short-lived **Treasury Relief Art Project (1935–38)** with WPA funds.

Federal Art Project (1935–43): The WPA funded the largest cultural initiative of the New Deal, Federal Project One, which encompassed the Music, Theatre, Writers', and Art projects. At its height, the Federal Art Project employed over 5,000 artists, printmakers, artisans, and teachers.

Farm Security Administration (1935–43): The government agency charged with relieving the effects of drought and the depression on Dust Bowl farmers sent photographers like Walker Evans (1903–75) and Dorothea Lange (1895–1965) on assignment to help make their case to the public.

The sheer numbers are staggering. Ten thousand artists from coast to coast, in big cities and small towns, produced 3,500 murals, over 100,000 easel paintings, and 17,000 sculptures. Hundreds of thousands of affordable prints and eye-catching posters came off the presses. The Index of American Design documented over 18,000 decorative and folk-art objects. The Farm Security Administration amassed one of the world's most significant photography collections. Often lumped together as "WPA art," these initiatives put forward diverging, sometimes conflicting, goals for sustaining and mobilizing culture in the face of crisis.

Many artists who achieved postwar fame—Willem de Kooning (1904–97), Arshile Gorky (1904–48), Philip Guston (1913–80), Lee Krasner (1908–84), Jacob Lawrence (1917–2000), Alice Neel (1900–84), Louise Nevelson (1899–1988), Isamu Noguchi (1904–88), Jackson Pollock (1912–56), Mark Rothko (1903–70), Ben Shahn (1898–1969), David Smith (1906–65), and Charles White (1918–79), to name a few—cut their teeth on the easel, sculpture, or mural divisions of the government programs. Many were in their twenties with little or no professional experience. Most remembered their time on the projects as a golden age of camaraderie and optimism. A living wage meant they did not have to compete with one another for private patrons. Workshops and studios provided access to materials and the chance to experiment with new skills and techniques. They enjoyed a sense of shared purpose and the attention of the public, the press, and elected officials.

Russia-born Moses Soyer (1899–1974) remembered the WPA as giving artists a "feeling of belonging, of being useful members of society....It was a fine and hopeful period for American art." (Prelinger 2001, 94) His *Artists on WPA* captured this hopeful spirit. Artists and assistants work together on a mural scheme for the children's ward of a Brooklyn hospital. Artists sketch each other, consider their canvases, or add finishing touches. The sinuous rhythm generates a pleasing variety and cohesion, far from the stereotypical view of artists as isolated geniuses or antisocial bohemians. The artists appear relaxed and focused as they go about their work, which is also play, mirrored in the scenes of frolicking children.

Soyer's utopian vision, however, was hard-won, the product of organizing, protesting, and bargaining. Soyer belonged to the Artists' Union, formed in 1934 to advocate for better working conditions, increased pay, and freedom from censorship while lobbying to make the federal art programs permanent. Union members adopted militant tactics, including occupying government offices and holding administrators hostage.

10 BELOW Moses Soyer, *Artists on WPA*, 1935
11 OPPOSITE Ben Shahn, *Artists' Union Demonstrators*, 1935

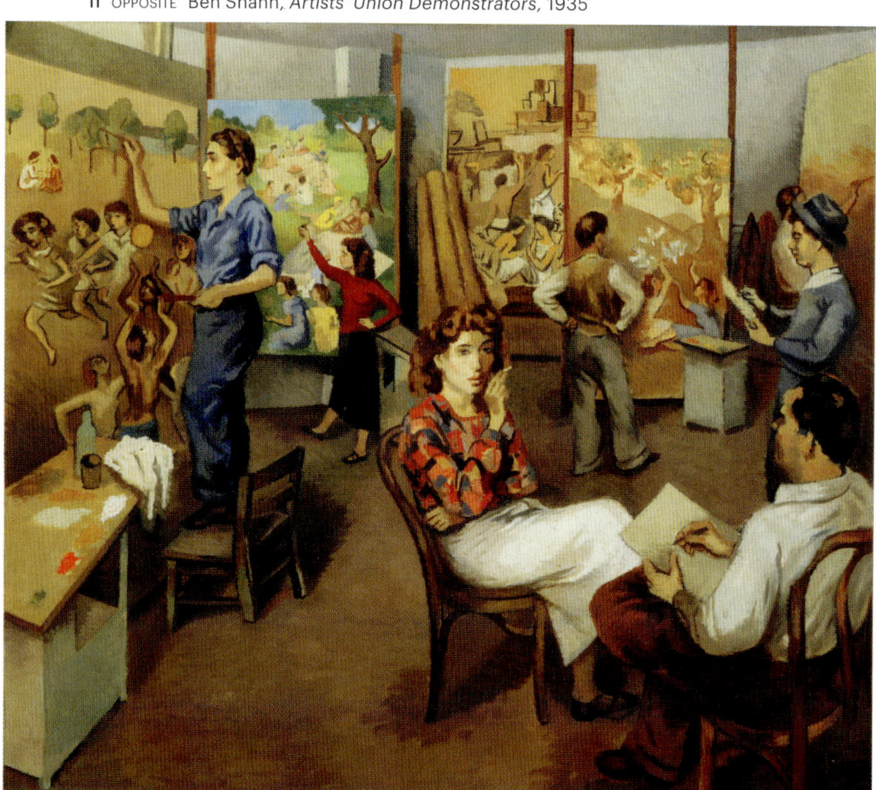

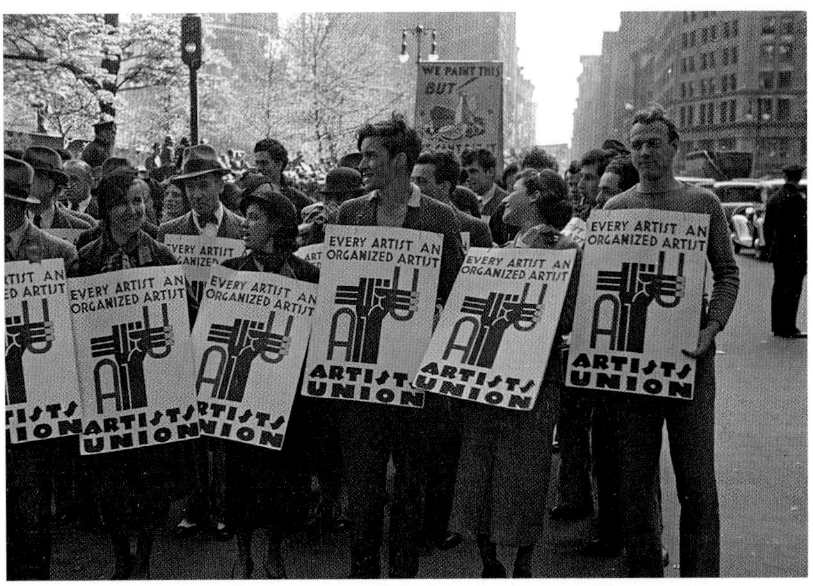

Although George Biddle's 1933 letter to FDR serves as a founding myth of New Deal art, efforts by organized artists pushed federal officials to act on behalf of the hard-hit culture sector. "It is directly due to the formation, existence and activities of the Artists' Union," argued its president Phil Bard (who drew that hungry artist for *Art Front*), "that government projects on a large scale were brought into being." (Bard 1935, 2)

Cultural Democracy

What role should the arts play in a democracy? New Deal art programs became a lightning rod in debates about culture, government patronage, national history and identity. Conservative lawmakers objected to wasteful spending on shiftless or subversive artists. Cultural elites, clinging to an ideal of art as the emanation of singular genius, bemoaned art degraded to public service. Communists and fellow travelers, if they overcame their suspicion of Roosevelt as a tool of corporate interests, seized on the projects as a chance to socialize culture. Debates, controversies, and compromises defined the New Deal's uneasy nexus of artists, administrators, politicians, media commentators, and the wider public.

The "public" was the critical ingredient; national director of the Federal Art Project Holger Cahill claimed that "an attempt to bridge the gap between the American artist and the American public" was the governing principle behind their

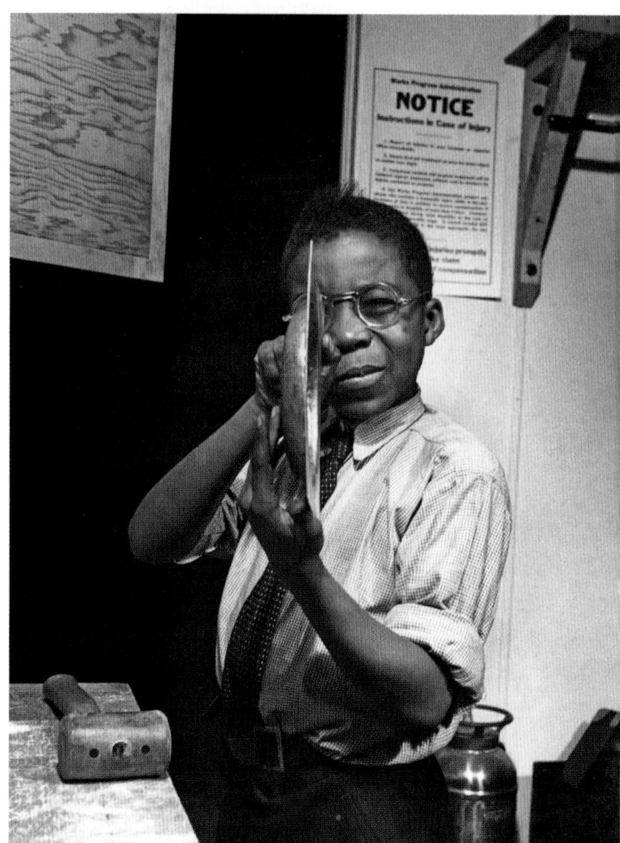

12 Genevieve Naylor,
A young boy inspects a
metal bowl he has crafted
in a Harlem Arts Center
workshop, 1938

entire program. Administrators like Cahill pegged the value of government-funded art to the idea of cultural democracy, the broadening of access to art and culture. Art, which had long catered to elite audiences in urban centers, should be widely accessible as a public good like electricity or clean water.

To this end, art spread beyond the private gallery or museum. It occupied alleyways, subways, and the walls of post offices, courthouses, prisons, orphanages, and hospitals. The FAP established over a hundred community art centers, notably the Harlem Community Art Center and Chicago's South Side Community Art Center, offering underserved communities the chance to make and see original art. The program spanned the country from cultural capitals to remote backwaters, from Cape Cod to the Oregon coast. Millions of Americans who had never set foot in a museum or gallery gained access to original art and art education through government funding.

Public murals, often sited in local post offices, broadcast
New Deal optimism. They were commissioned by the Section
of Fine Arts, whose administrators encouraged ennobling
views of the "American scene"—a strategically vague term
encompassing the country's history and landscapes, myths
and legends, prosperous industries, and rural folkways. Section
chiefs hoped that public art would be a resource for coping
with the Depression, renewing in everyday Americans a sense
of collective identity and belief in progress.

Visions of golden wheatfields, thriving factories, and
muscular workers can bear a resemblance to Soviet socialist
realism or the "blood and soil" nativism of Nazi propaganda.
The question in the US context of whether government support
for artists meant government *control* of art raises thorny issues
of agency and resistance. Mute artworks, not to mention unruly
artists, make unstable mediators between the state and its
citizens. Suffice to say, for now, that the New Deal art programs
were not top-down monoliths. They were jury-rigged on the
shifting sands of party politics and public opinion, subject to
criticism in the free press and budget cuts by anti-New Dealers
in Congress.

Consider Hale Woodruff's (1900–80) mural, *The Building of
Savery Library.* A racially integrated workforce of carpenters,
plumbers, and masons join in service to a common goal:
building a campus library for Talladega College in Alabama.
The mural's surface palpates with brilliant colors and
overlapping bodies in vigorous motion. It is a typical, almost

13 Hale Woodruff, *The Building of Savery Library*, 1942

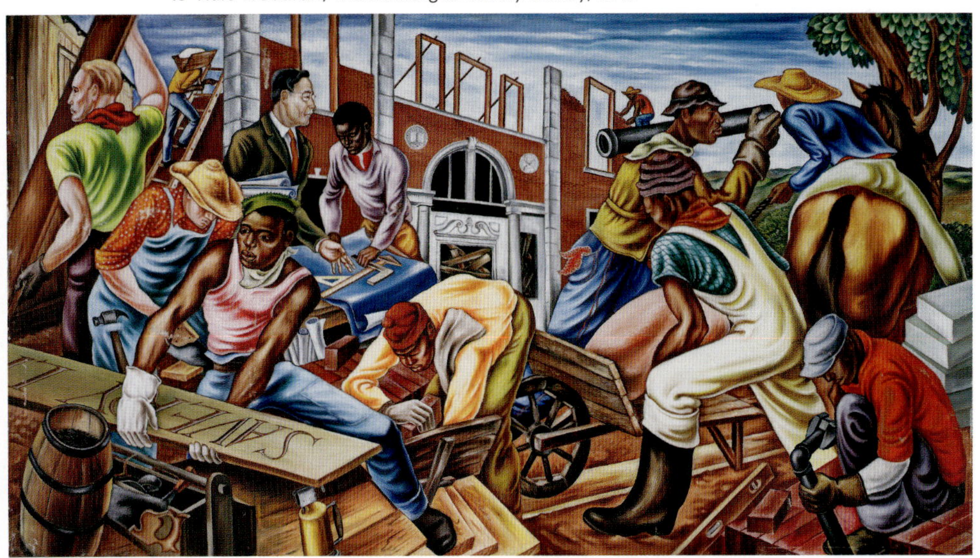

archetypal, New Deal mural. Yet Woodruff, a Black artist who had studied fresco painting in Mexico with Diego Rivera, did not take his scene of integrated labor for granted. *The Building of Savery Library* culminates a mural cycle that begins with a slave ship mutiny and continues through courtroom battles for human rights and the risks of the Underground Railroad. Freedom, progress, and racial harmony are not foregone conclusions; they are part of generations of struggle.

I Am an American

What does American art look like? Or an American artist? The government programs expanded the definition of art to include industrial design, folk art, and art by self-taught artists and children. The Federal Art Project's non-discrimination clause guaranteed, in principle if not in practice, equal opportunities for women artists and artists of color. Building on the momentum of the suffrage movement, women assumed key roles in New Deal arts administration, received coveted commissions, and earned equal pay for equal work.

Many artists hired on the programs, such as Moses Soyer, were themselves immigrants; others were the children of immigrants, a significant number from Jewish families fleeing violent antisemitism in the crumbling Russian empire. A third came from working-class backgrounds, and a number of New Deal artists embraced pro-labor subjects. The Artists' Union advocated for the rights of artists as workers, while the antifascist American Artists' Congress fought the rising tide of authoritarianism.

Advocacy groups and pressure campaigns led to greater opportunities and visibility for Black artists such as Selma Burke (1900–95), Jacob Lawrence, Norman Lewis (1909–79), and Raymond Steth (1917–97). (Though Steth's *I Am an American* comments bitterly on the supposed benefits of citizenship— a peddler in a stovepipe hat trundles a cart festooned with an American flag.) Indigenous artists Gerald Nailor (1917–52) and Pablita Velarde (1918–2006), among others, asserted Native sovereignty on the walls of federal buildings. Latino artists Pedro Cervántez (1915–87) and Patrociño Barela (1900–64) earned national praise as "discoveries" of the art programs. Asian American artists such as Fay Chong (1912–73), Miné Okubo (1912–2001), Yasuo Kuniyoshi (1889–1953), and Eitaro Ishigaki overcame prejudice to achieve recognition until, following the invasion of Pearl Harbor, FDR authorized the mass incarceration of those of Japanese ancestry living on the West Coast. Dorothea Lange, who was hired by the government to document the relocation process, photographed a sign hung

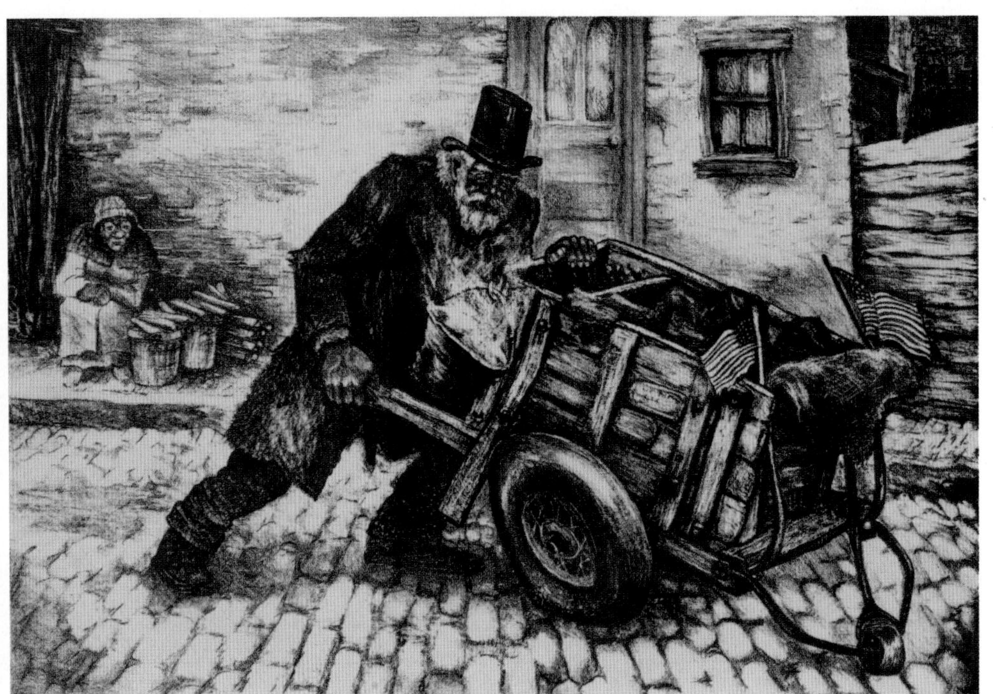

14 Raymond Steth, *I Am an American*, c. 1941

by a Japanese American outside his grocery store the day after
the Pearl Harbor attack: "I AM AN AMERICAN."

The experience of an artist like Okubo, who was incarcerated
in a wartime US internment camp, is a reminder that "democracy"
is not an abstract concept but an ongoing struggle. Nonwhite
artists, few of whom had supervisory roles, were often
treated by white administrators as ethnic artisans rather
than modern artists. New Deal art, especially public murals,
endorsed white settler visions of history while glossing over
or ignoring realities of conquest, slavery, or Native genocide.
They cast men as muscular breadwinners and women as
domestic caregivers. They exalted promethean power
over natural resources, complicit in a worldview that has
contributed to environmental devastation. Interpersonal
conflict and ideological inconsistency plagued the art
programs, which also suffered relentless criticism from
conservative media and cutbacks from Congress. The WPA
officially ended by presidential proclamation in 1943; part of
a national shift of resources toward a war economy.

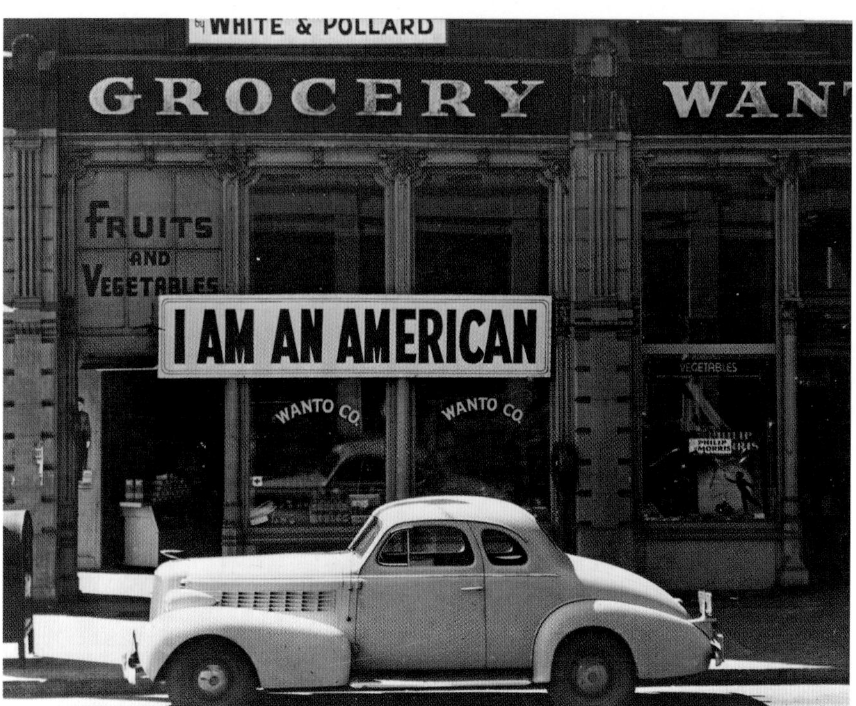

15 Dorothea Lange, *Japanese American-Owned Grocery Store, Oakland, California*, 1942

Art and Democracy

For all their flaws and contradictions, the New Deal art programs—to date the most significant federal investment in the arts in US history—broached a vision of art as essential to democracy. In a decade when democracy itself was at stake, and in an atmosphere of heightened fear and anxiety, New Deal artists confronted the twin crises of domestic depression and the global rise of fascism. The crises were linked, as FDR acknowledged in a 1938 speech: "The conditions for democracy and for art are one and the same," he said. "Nourish the conditions of a free life and you nourish the arts too."

The New Deal nourished the arts by broadening "New Horizons for American Art," the title of the first major exhibition of the Federal Art Project. New Deal artists, together with sympathetic administrators, championed the "new horizons" of cultural democracy: art by the people, for the people. Identifying as workers contributing to the common good, New Deal artists claimed their right to self-representation,

reinterpreted American history and identity, organized to
protect mutual interests, and participated in democracy
as a collective project.

"Art is a natural resource of this country," claimed *Art
Front*, the journal of the Artists' Union, "[it] is a living necessity
for both artists and audience, not a 'luxury' indulged in by
private connoisseurs." ("Organize Against Lay-Offs," 1936, 3)

Their argument resonates today. At a moment when public
arts funding is constantly under attack and fine art remains
largely the purview of the wealthy and well-educated, the view
that art—like clean water, education, or electricity—should be
accessible to all remains a radical proposition.

Rekindling the dream of cultural democracy, the belief in art
as a human right and a public good, begins with retracing steps
to the New Deal—when the depths of crisis opened new horizons
of unprecedented opportunity.

Chapter 1
The Public Works of Art Project

The hit 1932 song "Brother, Can You Spare a Dime?", made famous by Bing Crosby, gave plaintive voice to the down-on-their-luck. Albert Potter (1903–37) translated the refrain into a surreal scene of a ragged panhandler surrounded by faceless crowds. A colossal skeletal Death lies in wait among the skyscrapers, one bony hand gripping the Chrysler Building, grinning greedily at the spectacle of pain and suffering.

Death had much to smile about. The US economy hit its crushing nadir in March 1933, the month Franklin D. Roosevelt took office. In three years the economy had contracted by almost half. Factories stood silent and farms abandoned. Storefronts were empty and homeless shelters full. Herbert Hoover's ignominy lived on in so-called Hoovervilles—the shantytowns visible in urban outskirts and parks. Discarded newspapers ("Hoover blankets") covered the houseless curled up on park benches. The banking system was on the brink of total collapse, and at least fifteen million people—an estimated twenty-five percent of the workforce—were out of work.

Isaac Soyer's (1902–81) painting *Employment Agency* makes the emotional toll of the Depression palpable, depicting a row of dejected job seekers facing the interminable and likely futile wait for a prospect. The man in a fedora on the left buries his head in a newspaper, checking the wanted ads or keeping abreast of the grim headlines. A Black woman in a red hat and blouse (notes of defiant color in the drab surroundings), legs crossed in a blue skirt, props her head on her palm in pensive melancholy. (Black women faced disproportionately higher rates of unemployment than white men or women.) Next to her slumps a brown-suited man, staring at the floor in abject defeat.

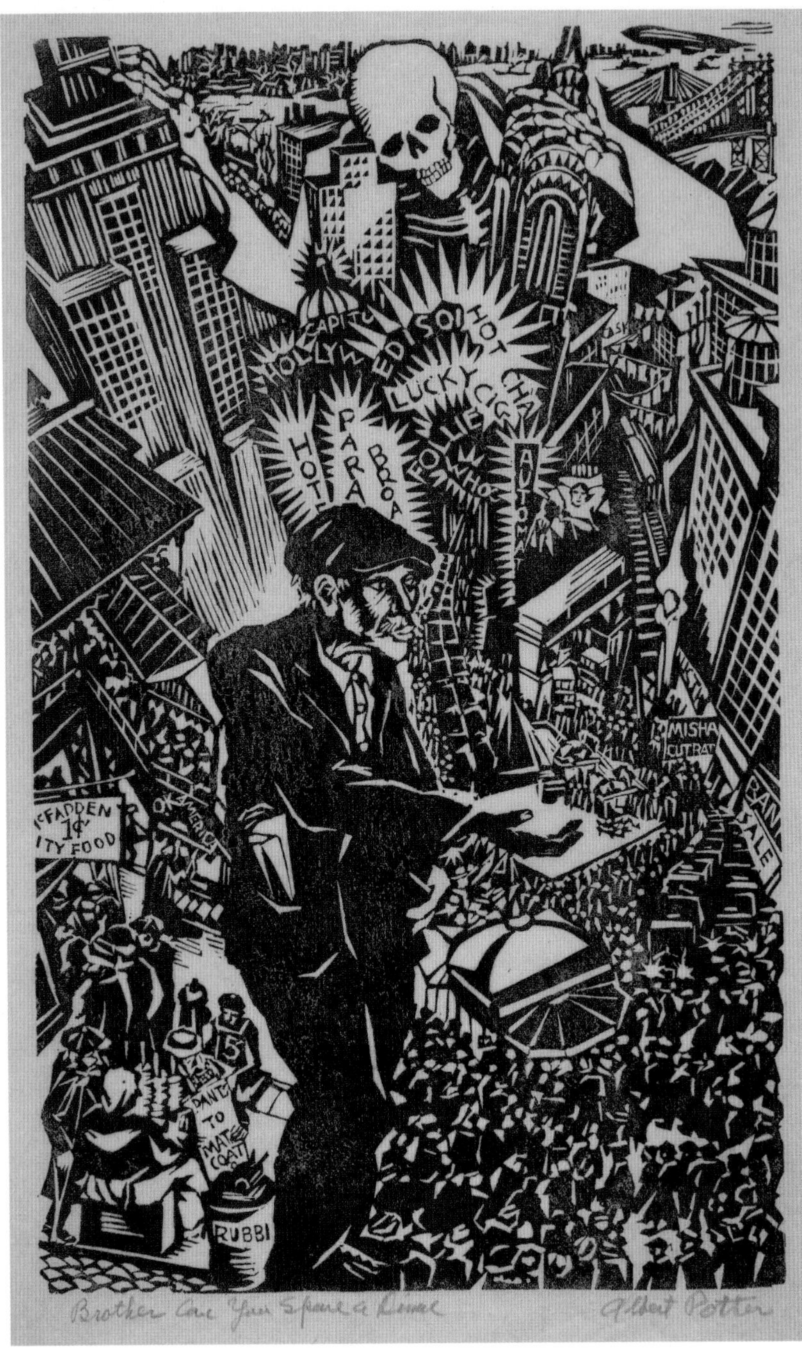

16 Albert Potter, *Brother Can You Spare a Dime?*, c. 1933–36

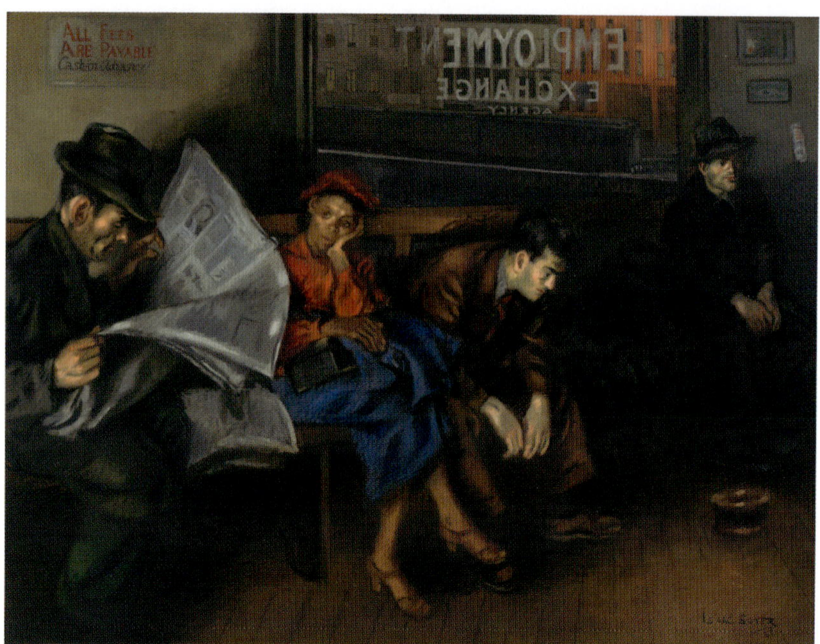

17 ABOVE Isaac Soyer, *Employment Agency*, 1937
18 OPPOSITE Grace Clements, *Winter, 1932*, 1933

The job seekers are physically proximate but emotionally and mentally distant, lost in their private worries in the limbo of the waiting room.

Others were less resigned. In Grace Clements's (1905–69) *Winter, 1932* a battalion of specters, hollowed out by hunger and rage, stride forward in a topsy-turvy world of fractured planes and stuttering architecture. Headlines clipped from newspapers advance alongside them: Hunger March, Against Hunger, Against Starvation. The word RELIEF is stenciled in red, the color repeated in the marching feet—aggressive notes in the earthy palette of ochres and browns. The dome of the chiaroscuro Capitol slants at an axis—a house divided.

As hunger marches descended on Washington, artists took desperate measures. Across the country, in places like Harlem, Chicago, Dallas, and Santa Barbara, they set up open-air markets to sell and barter their work. Alongside pushcart peddlers and pretzel vendors, they swapped paintings and pottery for food or medical services. A drawing for a trip to the dentist. A sculpture for a pair of shoes. A painting for a hot dog. "Broke or nearly so," wrote a visitor to a 1932 market in New York's Washington Square, "[artists] have come to offer their dreams in paint for vegetables, clothes, or luxuries they cannot afford." (Bustard 1997, 1)

In December 1932 Audrey McMahon (1898–1981) and Frances Pollack, administrators for professional organization the College Art Association (CAA), took matters into their own hands. Combining public and private funds, they hired a hundred out-of-work artists in New York at stonemasons' wages to teach art classes and decorate schools, churches, synagogues, and relief agencies. It was soon apparent, however, that these well-meaning efforts were woefully insufficient.

In her article "May the Artist Live?" published in October 1933 in the CAA journal *Parnassus*, McMahon urged the government to carry on the experiment she had begun. She lamented that "art has been kept remote from our daily lives," citing the talent of artists as a "national resource" that should be tapped to curtail unemployment, beautify public spaces, and widen art education. She ended with a clarion call: "Let us so conduct ourselves that it may be said of us by posterity that this was an era of cultural development. And let us help the American artist live."

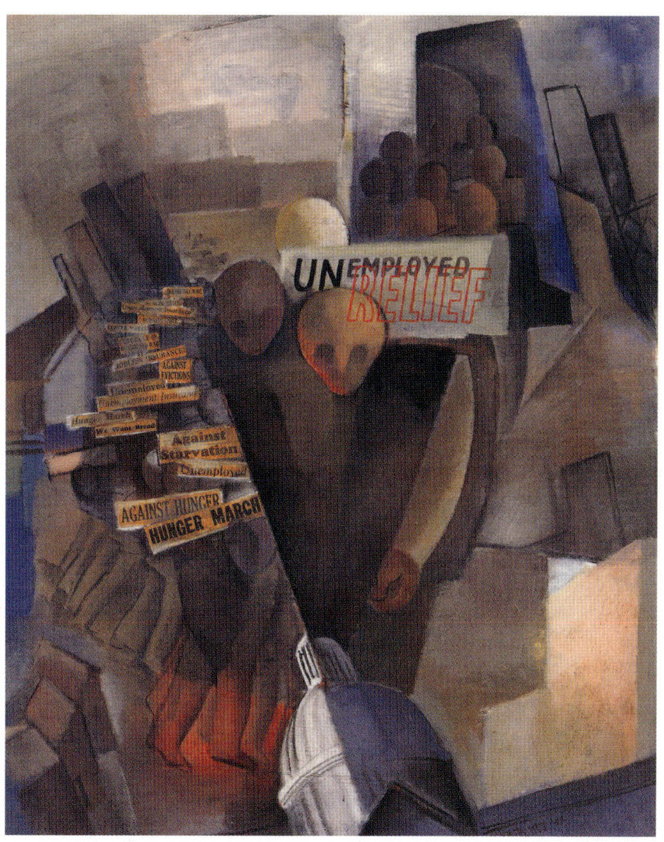

Public Works of Art Project

Plans were afoot to heed McMahon's call. Activist artists in New York had formed the Unemployed Artists Group to lobby for government aid to the culture sector (see Chapter 7). Journals like *Creative Art* and the *Magazine of Art* called for state-sponsored arts funding. Painter George Biddle had sent his famous letter to FDR, urging his former Groton and Harvard classmate to hire artists at "plumbers' wages" to paint murals for public buildings.

FDR passed the idea of a government art program on to the Treasury Department, custodian of federal buildings. The idea won the support of Treasury Secretary Henry Morgenthau Jr., prodded on by his wife, Elinor, an avid arts supporter, as well as another Eleanor: Roosevelt, who consistently championed public support for the arts.

Edward ("Ned") Bruce (1879–1943) was well-placed when the opportunity came to incubate a federal art program. After practicing law in New York, owning a newspaper in the Philippines, and trading in China, he gave up business at age forty-four to become an artist. It was an ill-timed career change. Despite early success and critical accolades, Bruce's prospects crashed on the rocks of the Depression, and he took a job as a Treasury Department advisor.

Remembered by a colleague as "heavy, humorous, loving to tease amiably," Bruce brought relevant skills and experience to bear leading the arts initiative: As a lawyer, navigating legalese and red tape; as a businessman, managing personnel; as a newspaper owner, finessing public relations; and as a painter, placating fellow artists.

In October 1933, at his rented home in northwest Washington DC, Bruce hammered out plans over long-distance phone calls

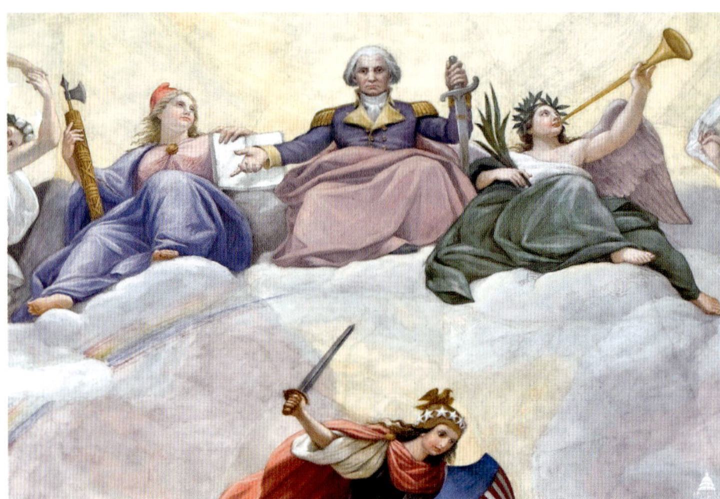

19 Constantino Brumidi, *Apotheosis of Washington*, 1865 (detail)

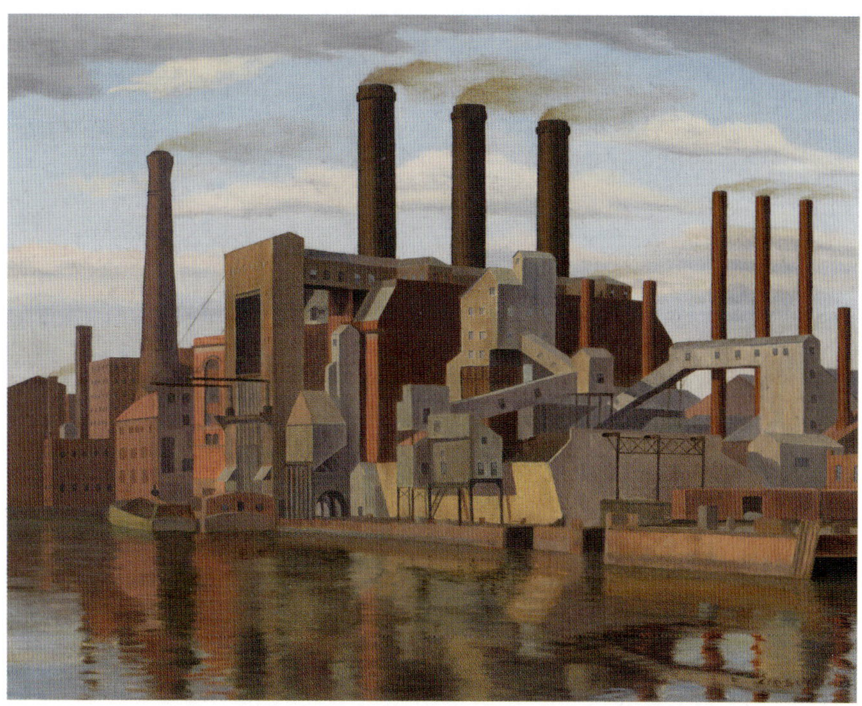

20 Edward Bruce, *Industry*, 1932

and in-person meetings with a revolving door of influential politicians, museum professionals, and civic leaders. The main question: How to organize a government art program to simultaneously employ artists, advance New Deal goals, and offer a return on taxpayer investment?

Bruce and his advisers had few precedents to follow. In 1910 Congress established a Commission of Fine Arts to advise on federal art and architecture. Its hidebound members dressed American history in classical garb. Bruce, for his part, disparaged "the sort of academic art that paints a lot of semi-nude ladies, draped in cheesecloth with a ribbon under their nipples, holding scales in one hand and a lamp in the other." (Musher 2015, 38) He could have been describing murals like Constantino Brumidi's *Apotheosis of Washington* painted in 1865 for the rotunda of the US Capitol, with George Washington enthroned on a cloud, flanked by Greco-Roman allegories of Victory and Liberty. Bruce rejected this fusty style in favor of something modern, populist, and progressive—like the New Deal.

In November, Bruce sent a memorandum to the Assistant Treasury Secretary outlining the basic premise: artists would

19

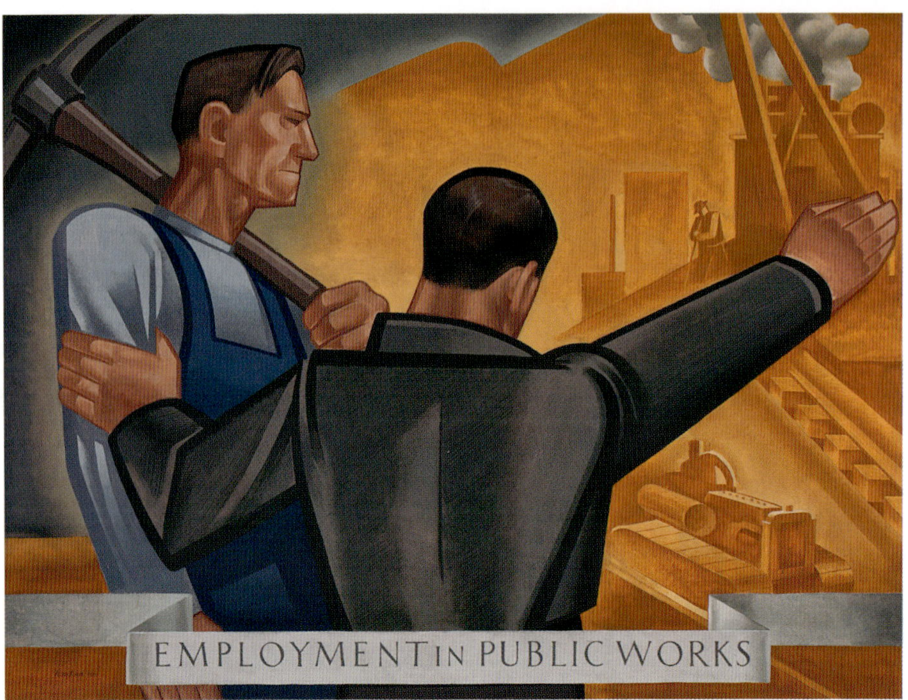

21 Tom Lea, *Employment in Public Works*, 1933–34

be hired to make works for tax-funded buildings inspired by American history, industries, and landscapes. (Bruce's own 1932 painting, *Industry,* suggested a template.) Too long isolated in ivory towers, artists would take their place alongside other productive workers. The "people" would be their patrons.

The message resonated. Harry Hopkins (1890–1946)—a sallow, sharp-witted relief administrator with a missionary zeal for the New Deal—approved the release of a little over one million dollars from the coffers of the Civil Works Administration (CWA) to underwrite the Public Works of Art Project (PWAP) in the Treasury Department. Bruce issued a press release: "In approving PWAP, Mr. Hopkins has recognized that the artist, like the laborer, capitalist, and the office worker, eats, drinks, has a family, and pays rent, thus contradicting the old superstition that the painter and sculptor live in attics and exist on inspiration." (FERA Press Release no. 464, 1933)

Bruce wasted no time. He staffed his Washington office with technical director Forbes Watson (1880–1960), urbane author and art critic, and assistant technical director Edward Rowan (1898–1946), a chain-smoking artist and gallerist. They were Ivy

Leaguers who threw themselves into the work with fervor and a certain noblesse oblige (for a time Bruce even refused a salary). European tours of the great Renaissance frescoes of Giotto, Masaccio, and Michelangelo fortified their belief in the power of public art to elevate and educate. All became ardent New Dealers who saw the US government as a benevolent patron and the PWAP as an extension of its public works. Tom Lea (1907–2001) distilled this idea in a semi-allegorical painting of a bureaucrat gripping a worker's arm and pointing to the promised land of a government job site.

The PWAP's stated objective was to "give artists employment at craftsmen's wages in the embellishment of public property with works of art." (McDonald 1969, 62) In a show of support from the executive branch, Eleanor Roosevelt attended an implementation meeting on 8 December along with an advisory committee of arts professionals and civic leaders. A week later, *Art News* reported on the "epoch-making" event of the PWAP's formation, which marked "the first official recognition in our history of the necessity of art and of its existence as a force in the life of this country." ("The Public Works of Art Project," 1933, 10)

American Scene

More immediate, however, was the PWAP's urgent goal to see artists and their families through the bleak winter months— the coldest on record. Headquartered in an untidy office in the Treasury Building, Bruce and his team oversaw sixteen regional centers nationwide, each staffed by a chairman and a volunteer committee of artists and arts professionals who reviewed applications and filled quotas.

They scaled up quickly. The PWAP hired nearly eight hundred artists before Christmas. By early January, fifteen hundred artists had been added to the payrolls, and another thousand were added a month later. They were paid between $26 and $42 per week based on experience, equivalent to CWA rates for skilled artisans. Their work became the property of the US government, meant for allocation to tax-funded buildings such as libraries, schools, and hospitals.

But what would artists make? "The subject matter assigned to them," wrote Bruce, "was the American scene in all its phases. Within this scope the artists were given the utmost freedom of expression." (Bruce 1934, 2) But that was a bit like Henry Ford saying his customers could have a car in any color so long as it was black. What, exactly, did the "American scene" look like?

Assistant director Rowan expected common sense to prevail, noting that "any artist who paints a nude for the Public Works of Art Project should have his head examined." One state

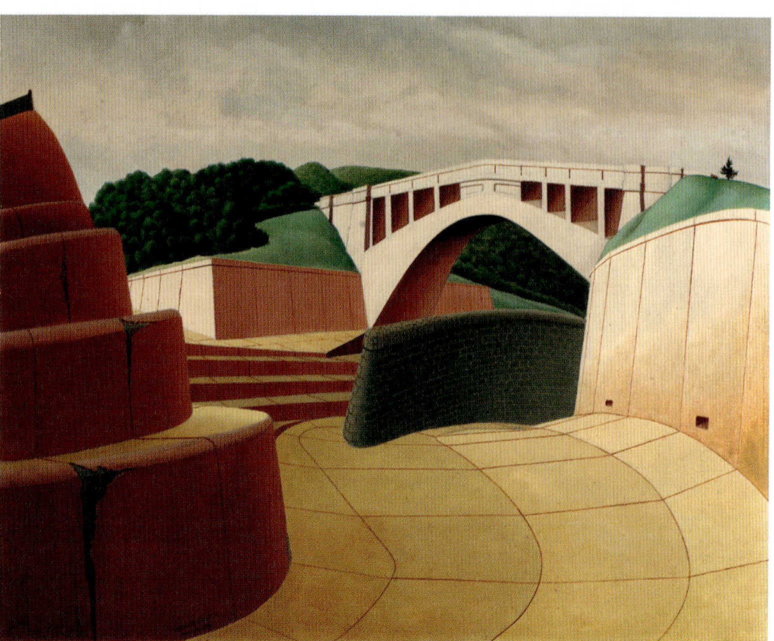

22 Arnold Wiltz, *Spillway, Ashokan Dam*, 1934

administrator put the matter bluntly: "No nudes, no dives, no
social propaganda." (Hills 1983, 24) They might have added:
no abstractions. Abstract artists—identified with Europe, political
dissent, and social nonconformity—struggled to get a foothold.
Anything inflammatory was discouraged. ("Conditions like
those existing today," Bruce warned Congress in January 1935
testimony, "breed the kind of spirit that revolutions are made
of.") PWAP-supported American scenes should help mollify
anger and discontent, in other words, not stoke the flames.

American was the watchword. It suited the isolationist mood
in the years following the First World War (1914–18) in which
over a hundred thousand US soldiers died in the battlefields
of France and Flanders. The 1920s saw restrictive immigration
policies and the resurgence of white terror organization, the Ku
Klux Klan. At the same time, the country's economic prosperity
and global clout bred a bullish sense of exceptionalism. A vogue
for American folk art and antiques swept up modernists and
wealthy collectors alike. Declaring aesthetic independence from
Europe, American artists, critics, and curators knit together a
national identity from regional influences.

One of those regions was upstate New York. The art colony
of Woodstock, a hamlet nestled in the Catskill Mountains,

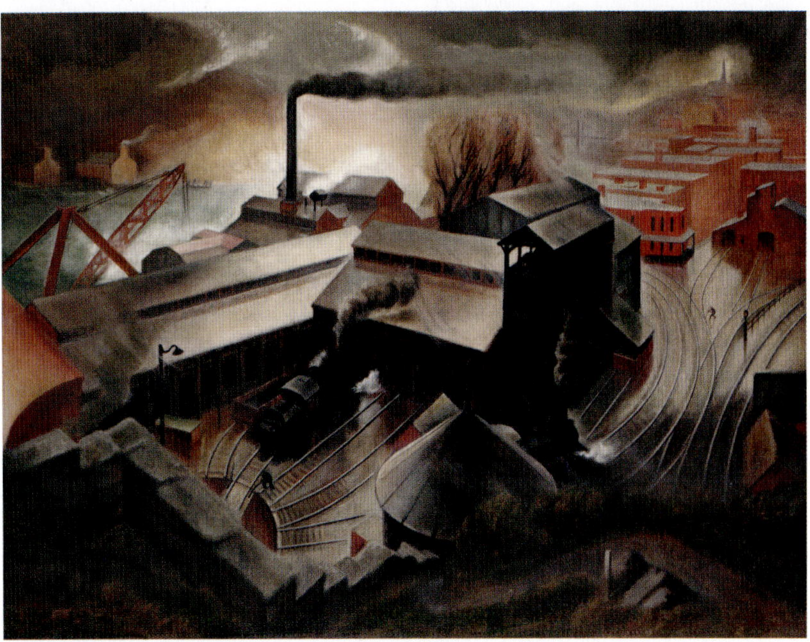

23 Austin Mecklem, *Engine House and Bunkers*, 1934

enrolled fifty artists on the PWAP while only seventy-two artists comprised the region encompassing Ohio, Michigan, Indiana, and Kentucky. This partially owed to favoritism: Juliana Force (1876–1942), cofounder of the Whitney Museum of American Art and New York's regional PWAP director, summered in Woodstock and knew the artists personally.

Style also played a role. Woodstock artists like Berlin-born Arnold Wiltz (1889–1937) and Austin Mecklem (1890–1951) painted in a modern but accessible style similar to that of Edward Bruce. Wiltz's *Spillway, Ashokan Dam* features his characteristic crisp, cool approach to infrastructure—in this case an upstate reservoir built in the early twentieth century to supply New York City with potable water. Mecklem, also on the PWAP, painted another point of contact between city and country: nearby Kingston's freight yard and port, one of the busiest on the Hudson River.

These paintings, combining urban and rural, landscape and industry, neatly conformed to Bruce's expectations for the American scene. From upstate New York to coastal California, a living tradition would be grounded in the country's skylines and rolling fields, harbors and railroads, mills and mines, labor and leisure, local lore and national history. Bruce believed such themes, treated with a painterly naturalism—not too modern, not too academic—would rally the nation's spirits and buff the tarnished American Dream.

Regionalism

The American scene bore a family resemblance to Regionalism, the nativist art movement identified with the Midwestern triad of Thomas Hart Benton (1889–1975), John Steuart Curry (1897–1946), and Grant Wood (1891–1942). The resemblance was no accident. PWAP official Edward Rowan was friends with Wood—they had founded a short-lived Iowa art residency together in 1932—and shared his vision of an authentically "American" art rooted in heartland virtues.

Born on a farm near Anamosa, Grant Wood spent most of his life in Iowa. It was a life of contradictions: A closeted gay man who studied modern art in Europe, Wood played up the persona of overall-wearing bumpkin ("All the really good ideas I ever had," he claimed, "came to me while I was milking a cow") and extolled in his paintings Iowa's fertile farmlands and stoic citizens—most famously in the instantly iconic *American Gothic*. He served as state chairman of the Iowa PWAP, convinced the program would help free artists from the corrupting influence of European modernism, the series of convulsive breaks with artistic tradition from Impressionism to Cubism radiating from cities like Paris and Berlin.

Wood's murals for Iowa State College, now University, in Ames evoke a golden age of yeoman farmers in the vein of Laura Ingalls Wilder's children's novel *Little House on the Prairie* (1935). The title of one such mural, completed in 1934, *When Tillage Begins, Other Arts Follow* signals a basic Regionalist belief: civilization springs from the soil. But this was increasingly untrue: in 1920, for the first time in American history, more people lived in cities than in the countryside. At the same time, a middle-class "back to the land" movement, spurred by bestsellers like Ralph Borsodi's *Flight from the City* (1933), vaunted the benefits of escaping the urban grind and reconnecting with nature.

Wood did not simply look backward, however; he brought the golden age up to date by showing advances in agricultural science taught at the College. An oil study for one of the murals, carefully transferred by assistants to canvas, divides the composition into thirds. On the left, a doctor readies to vaccinate a hog; in the center, a farmer stands atop a haybale operating a pulley system to transfer hay to the barn; on the right, a farmer unhitches draft horses from a wagon. Everything is in harmony—the X of the central farmer's

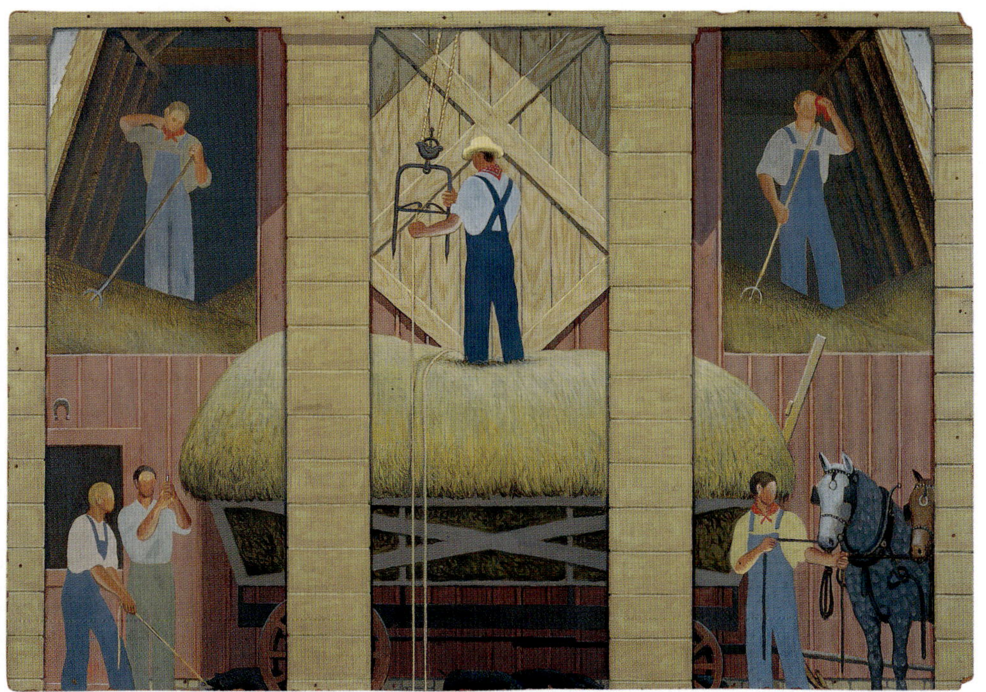

24 Grant Wood, *Study for Agricultural Science Mural*, 1934

overalls repeats the X-shaped crossboards of the barn door and haywagon. Everything is pristine—the farmers in the hayloft dabbing sweat is the only sign of toil.

Art Front, the journal of the Artists' Union, applauded Wood's technical gifts but chided him for ignoring contemporary realities: droughts, bad harvests, foreclosures, militant farmers' unions. The ideal of small-scale agriculture, calling back to Thomas Jefferson's forty-acre farm as the cornerstone of agrarian democracy, did not square with emerging agribusiness. In Iowa, as elsewhere, mechanized farming operations maximized profit at the expense of workers and the environment. Wood's paintings, from this perspective, were not regional *enough*. He treated Iowan farms and fields less with local accuracy than with the antiseptic reverence of religious painting.

Mean, Dirty, Avaricious

10 Moses Soyer (painter of *Artists on WPA*) cautioned his fellow artists to avoid the "chauvinism" of the American scene. "Yes, paint America," he wrote in *Art Front*, "but with your eyes open. Do not glorify Main Street. Paint it as it is—mean, dirty,

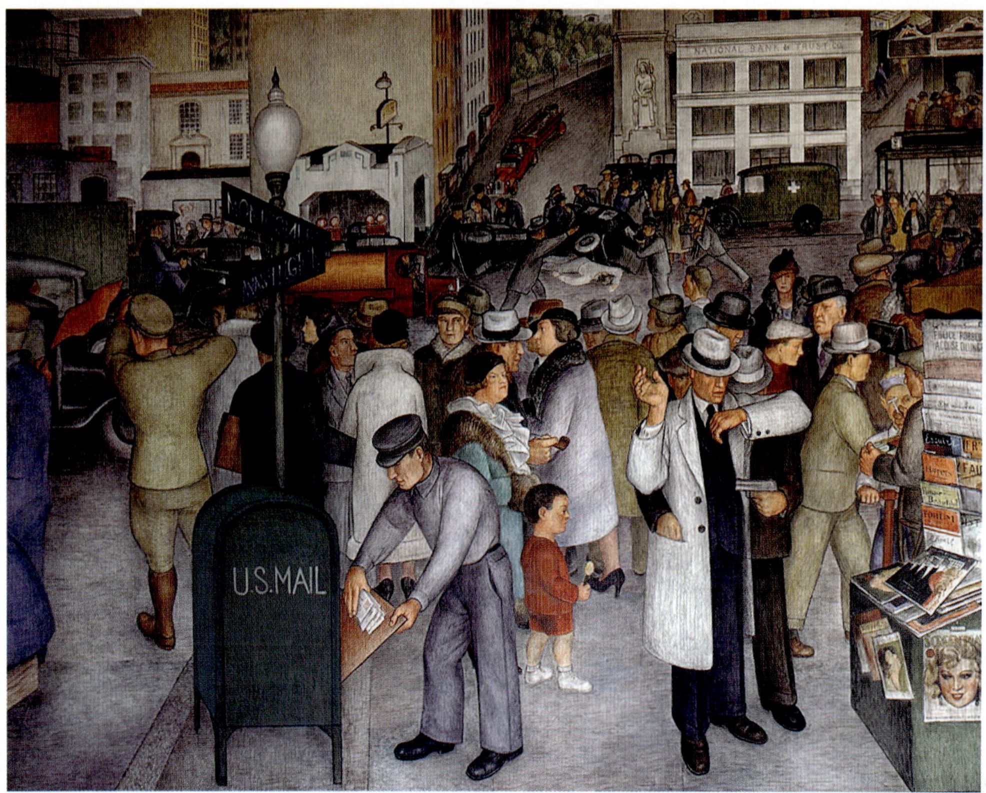

25 Victor Arnautoff, *City Life*, detail, Coit Tower, San Francisco, 1934

avaricious." (Soyer 1935, 7) That is how downtown San Francisco appears in Victor Arnautoff's (1896–1979) *City Life*. Painted as part of a large-scale PWAP program for the city's Coit Tower, a fluted concrete cylinder soaring two hundred feet above Telegraph Hill, the mural teems with unsavory vignettes, from a daylight mugging to a fatal car crash.

Arnautoff supervised two dozen artists working cheek-by-jowl in cold, cramped quarters in the tower's interior lobby, vestibule, and stairwells. They covered 3,700 square feet in true fresco, bonding paint chemically to the walls by applying it to wet plaster before it dried. It was the most ambitious PWAP project to date and the most controversial—an early test of the limits of artistic freedom on the government art programs.

Those limits were being tested globally. In charging artists not to glorify Main Street, Soyer continued: "Self-glorification is artistic suicide. Witness Nazi Germany." The Russia-born Soyer, from a family of Jewish refugees, reminded his readers that "self-glorification" of the *Volk*—blonde, blue-eyed peasants harvesting golden wheatfields—was the stock-in-trade of fascist art. As PWAP artists cashed their first government paychecks, their counterparts in Italy, Germany, and the Soviet Union were conscripted in the service of one-party rule. The Soviet Union disbanded independent and avant-garde groups in 1932 and two years later instituted socialist realism (scenes idealizing state leaders and policy) as the official style. Nazi Germany forced artists to join the Reich Chamber of Art, which controlled the flow of "racially pure" propaganda.

These developments had faint but audible echoes in New Deal art: a preference for heroic or romantic realism, general hostility to modernism, a mythic belief in folk nationalism, and the goal of propagandizing state policies. But the similarities should not be overstated. Hostility to modernism in the US, to put it mildly, never rose to the level of Nazi Germany's confiscation and destruction of "degenerate" modern art (or persecution of Jewish artists) or the Soviet Union's purge of writers and intellectuals during the 1936–38 Moscow show trials. Nor was there a US equivalent to the cult of the leader—considering FDR's broad popularity, it is surprising how rarely he shows up in New Deal art. The art programs in the US were temporary relief measures, not part of entrenched culture ministries imposing the party line. As such, they were subject to political jockeying, pressure from interest groups (including a vocal and influential Artists' Union—see Chapter 7), and attacks from the press and the public.

New Deal artists looked south for a model of state-sponsored art. The Republic of Mexico—established in 1920 after a bloody, decade-long civil war—hired artists to translate revolutionary ideals into rousing, action-packed murals. In the 1920s, a wave of US artists, including Victor Arnautoff and a handful of Coit Tower artists, flooded across the Rio Grande to bask in the Mexican Renaissance. They made pilgrimages to Mexico City's vast, strident public frescoes and genuflected before *los tres grandes* or "the Three Greats": José Clemente Orozco (1883–1949), Diego Rivera, and David Alfaro Siqueiros (1896–1974). In sweeping mural cycles like Rivera's *History of Mexico* (which Arnautoff worked on as an assistant), the Three Greats exalted peons and laborers, Indigenous history and folkways, revolutionary martyrs, and the overthrow of colonizers and capitalists.

Arnautoff and other enthralled New Deal artists adopted the Three Greats' vigorous style: vivid colors, dense massing of forms, and montage-like compositions. (By the early 1930s they could see examples closer to home, such as Rivera's 1931 murals in San Francisco for the Stock Exchange and California School

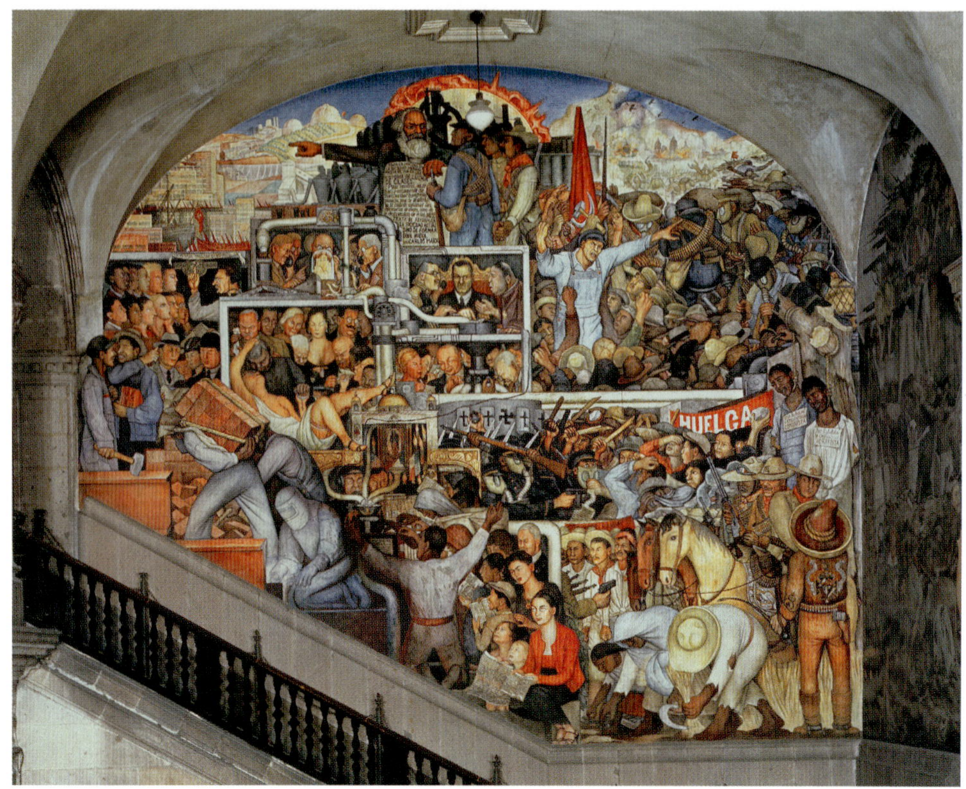

26 Diego Rivera, *History of Mexico*, Palacio Nacional, Mexico City, 1929–35

of Fine Arts.) More importantly, they embraced the Three Greats' zealous faith in art as a prime mover of social change. "Being with Rivera [in Mexico]," Arnautoff remembered, "confirmed me in the belief that the making of art is not a matter of idle contemplation, it cannot leave the viewer indifferent. Its goal is to move people." (Cherny 2017, 74)

Moving people could mean provoking them: Several Coit Tower muralists smuggled in Marxist iconography. They may have been inspired by the fresh controversy over Rivera's Rockefeller Center mural, *Man at the Crossroads*, destroyed when Rivera refused to paint out Bolshevik leader, Vladimir Lenin. Arnautoff portrayed himself lingering by a newsstand stocked with Communist publications *New Masses* and the *Daily Worker.* John Langley Howard (1902–99) painted an interracial picket of striking miners, one of whom carries a newspaper calling for a May Day demonstration supporting labor rights. Bernard Zakheim (1898–1985) painted Howard

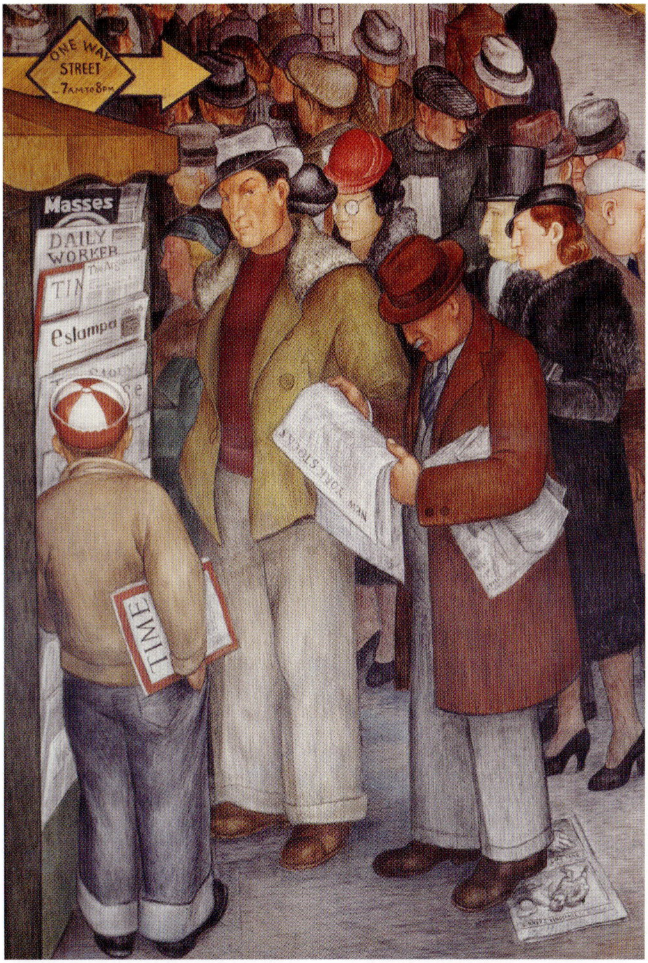

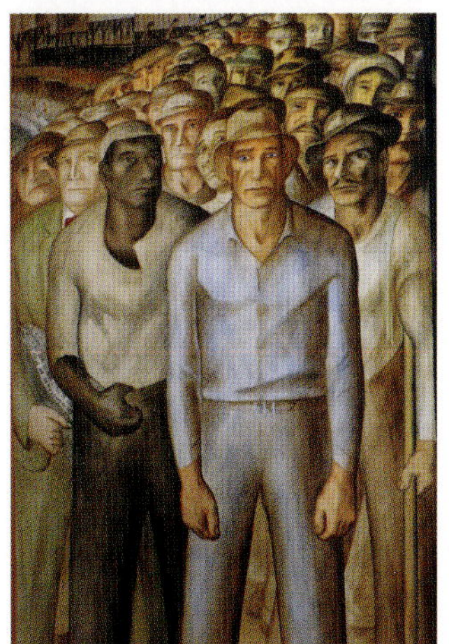

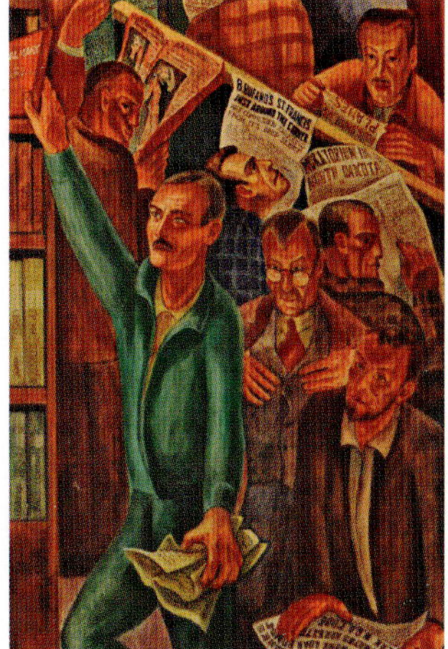

27 TOP Victor Arnautoff,
City Life, detail, 1934
28 NEAR RIGHT John Langley
Howard, *Striking Workers*, detail,
1934
29 FAR RIGHT Bernard Zakheim,
Library, detail, 1934

reaching for a copy of Karl Marx's *Capital* on a library shelf.
Three panels by Clifford Wight (*c.* 1900–60) outlined society's
progress from "Rugged Individualism" to "The New Deal" to
"Communism," complete with Soviet hammer and sickle.

The PWAP's regional chairman sent a desperate wire to
Edward Bruce in Washington:

*Certain difficulties concerning Coit Tower. Some artists have at
last minute incorporated in their murals details such as newspaper
headlines and certain symbols which might be interpreted as
communistic propaganda. These things not visible when design
approved.* (Marling 1982, 46)

Bruce fired back that "propaganda of this kind is hurtful to the
best interests of American art and is likely to discourage further
government patronage." The *San Francisco Examiner*, owned
by anti-New Dealer William Randolph Hearst, pounced on the
murals as evidence that taxpayer dollars were being wasted on
un-American propaganda. At the same time, a strike of the city's
longshoremen had escalated into street battles with the police

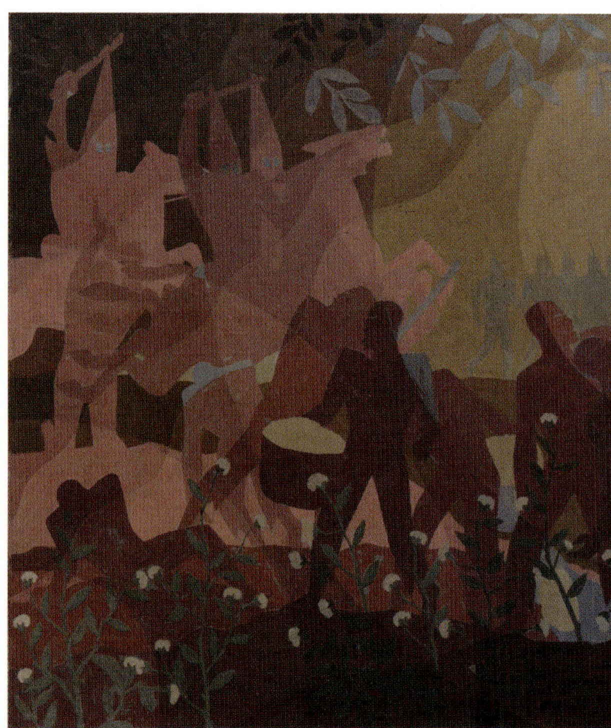

30 Aaron Douglas,
*Aspects of Negro Life:
From Slavery Through
Reconstruction*, 1934

and the National Guard, raising the stakes for tax-funded art with revolutionary overtones. The San Francisco Park Commission closed access to the tower and set up a police guard. In protest, the San Francisco Artists' and Writers' Union picketed.

The controversy ended with a whimper, not a bang—the only change to the murals was the removal of Wight's hammer and sickle. But it was the opening salvo in a protracted battle over art, censorship, and the American scene.

"Aspects of Negro Life"

On the other side of the country, Aaron Douglas (1899–1979) refocused the American scene on the Black experience. The PWAP sponsored his four-panel mural cycle, *Aspects of Negro Life,* for Harlem's 135th Street branch of the New York Public Library, now the Schomburg Center for Research in Black Culture. Featuring Douglas's signature silhouettes and radiating concentric circles—like water ripples disturbing the smooth surface of the past—the epic cycle traces African American history from Africa through enslavement, liberation, and the Great Migration to cities in the north.

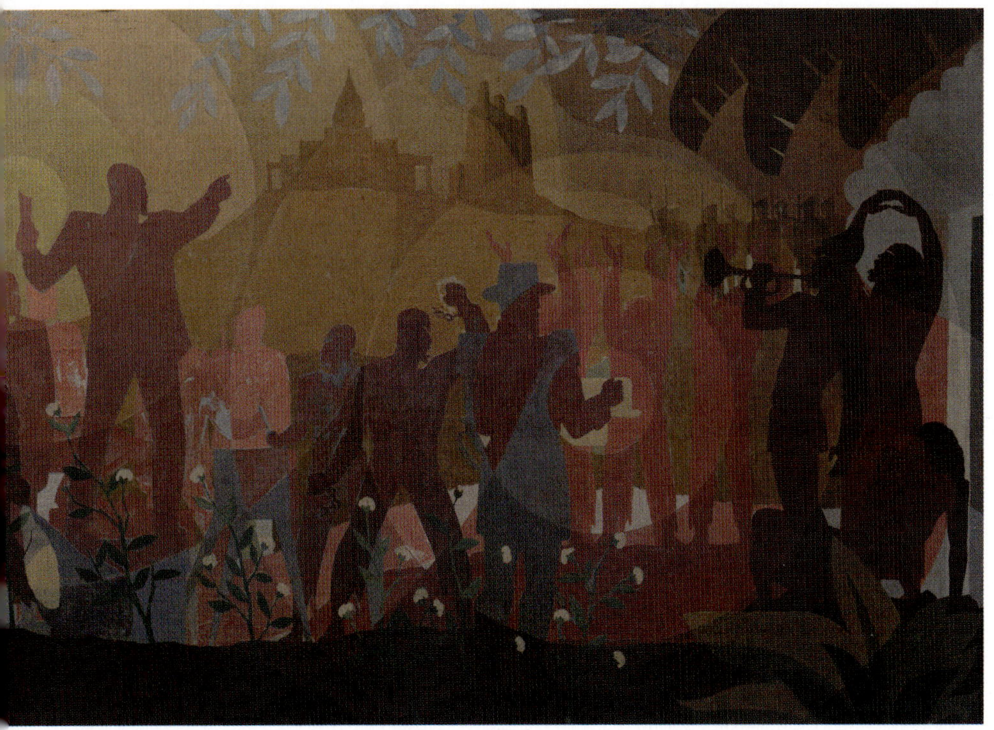

The PWAP required applicants to prove their professional
bona fides, a policy that tended to disqualify Black artists, the
vast majority of whom had been denied access to training and
education. Douglas, one of only about twenty Black artists hired
by the PWAP (out of nearly four thousand), was an exception.
After graduating as the first student of color in the fine arts
department of the University of Nebraska, Douglas joined the
1920s efflorescence of Black artists, writers, musicians, dancers,
and actors known as the Harlem Renaissance. Among them
was Arturo (Arthur) Schomburg (1874–1938), a Puerto Rican
immigrant of Afro-Caribbean and German descent who sold
his archive of African diasporic material to the Harlem branch
library. In an essay for the 1925 anthology *The New Negro*, edited
by Alain Locke (1885–1954), Schomburg declared, "The American
Negro must remake his past in order to make his future."

Douglas answered the call. Remaking the past began with
fusing the arts of Egypt and Africa with Cubism and Art
Deco to forge a race-conscious modernism. The first panel
of *Aspects of Negro Life* sources the headwaters of American
history to the ritual song and dance of Africa. The second
panel moves *From Slavery through Reconstruction* with cotton
plants, enslaved farmhands, and hooded Ku Klux Klansmen
on horseback. A Civil War soldier reads aloud the haloed
Emancipation Proclamation, declaring enslaved people free.
A towering orator, symbol of emboldened Black suffrage and
self-determination, points to a distant "city on the hill," the
unfulfilled promise of America's more perfect union.

In the third panel, *An Idyll of the Deep South,* the North
Star guides a fugitive to freedom from Jim Crow racial terror,
symbolized by the dangling feet of a lynching victim. *Song of
the Towers* completes the cycle with an allegory of the Great
Migration, the exodus of millions of Black Americans from
the rural South to industrial cities in the North in search of
jobs and a better life (though the painting's tendrils of smoke
and crumpled or terrified workers suggest dashed hopes). The
central jazz musician, perched on an industrial wheel, raises
his saxophone as if in praise. In the distance, between soaring
skyscrapers, the Statue of Liberty answers the gesture—the
promise of America undercut by the horrors registered in
the other panels. Douglas's American scene—riven by the
contradictions of freedom and slavery, suffrage and suffering—
gave visionary form to poet Langston Hughes's refrain "I, too,
sing America."

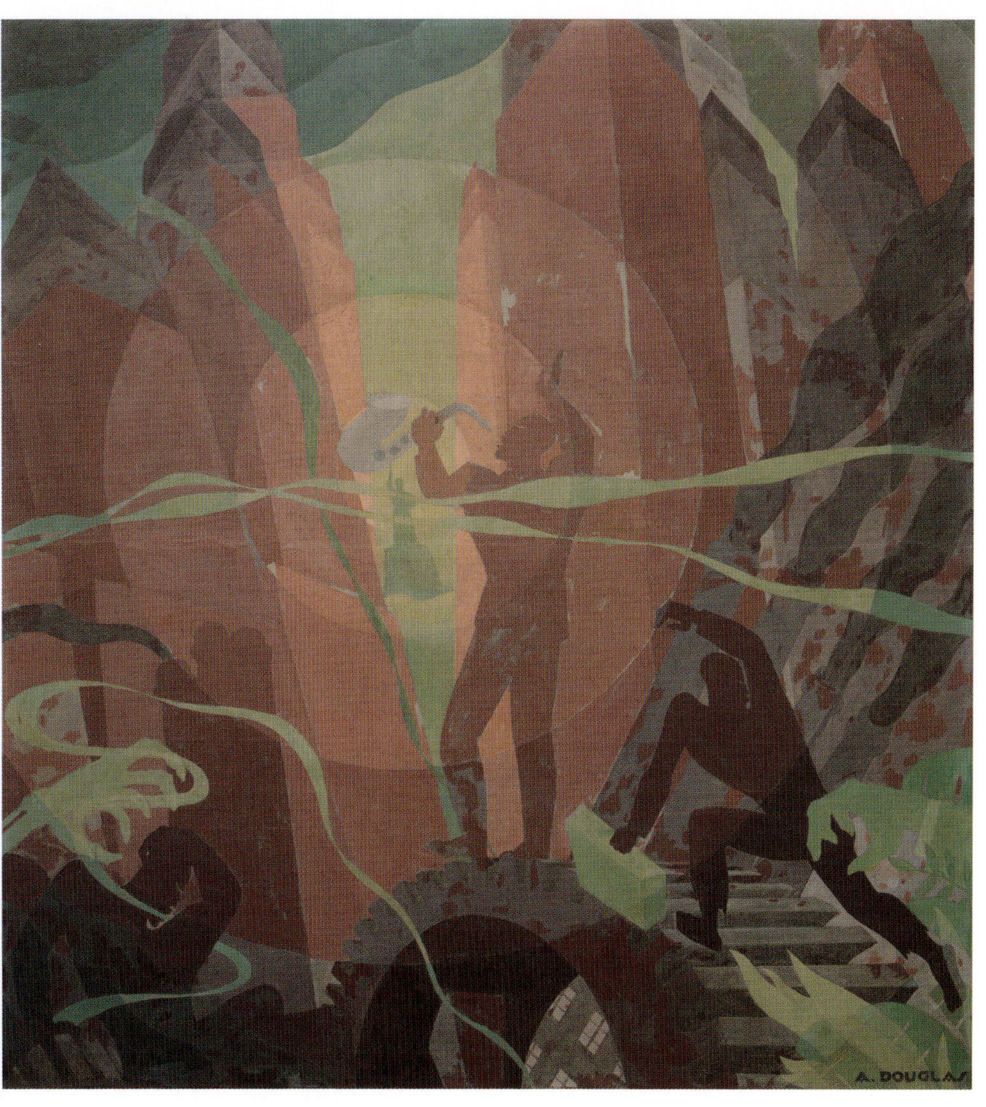

31 Aaron Douglas, *Aspects of Negro Life: Song of the Towers*, 1934

"A More Abundant Life"

In April 1934 the *National Exhibition of Art by the Public Works of Art Project* opened at the Corcoran Gallery of Art in Washington DC. Over five hundred works assembled from all sixteen regions packed the Corcoran's galleries, corridors, and stairwells. In the foreword to the exhibition catalog, Edward Bruce hailed the PWAP as a "significant example of the President's desire to give the people of this country 'a more abundant life.' It is the first completely democratic art movement in history." (Bruce 1934, 2)

What did a "democratic art movement" look like? A range of media, for starters: mural studies, paintings, prints, watercolors, textiles, ceramics, and sculpture. A quarter of the exhibited artists were first-generation immigrants. Nearly a third were still in their twenties. A gallery dedicated to Indigenous art made by the PWAP's Santa Fe-based Indian Division included Diné textiles, wood carvings, and mural panels by Pueblo artists Velino Shije Herrera (1902–73), Pablita Velarde, and Tonita Peña (1893–1949). Also on view were examples of Pueblo blackware pottery, a tradition recovered by two Tewa ceramicists Maria Martínez (*c.* 1887–1980) and her

32 Maria and Julián Martínez, *Black-on-Black Bowl*, 1934–36

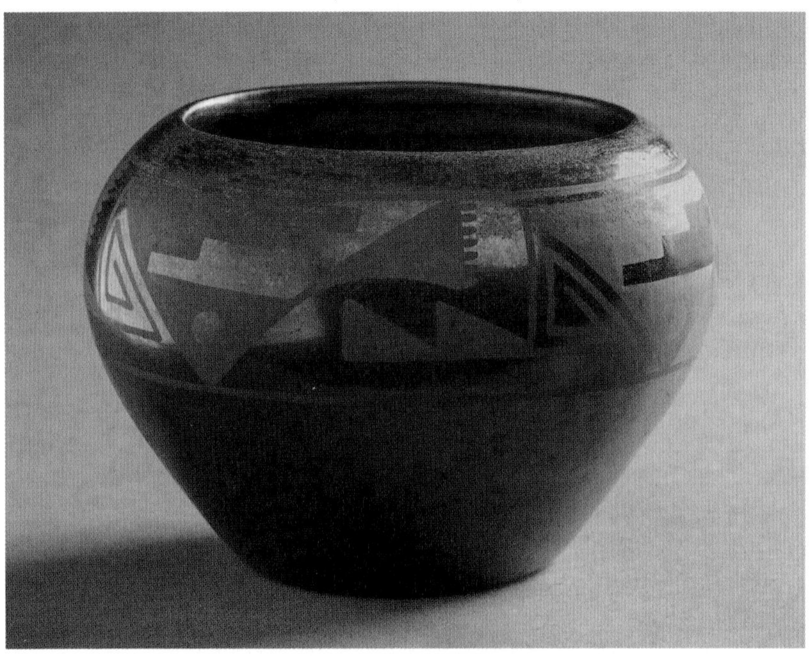

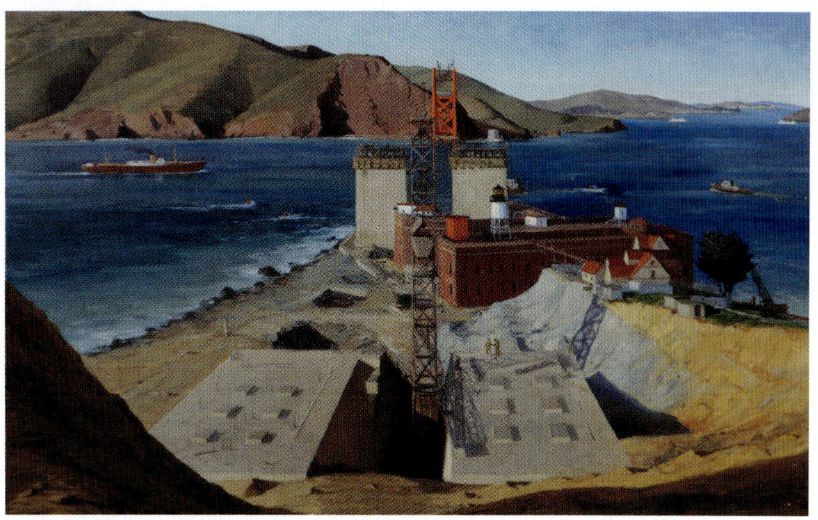

33 Ray Strong, *Golden Gate Bridge*, 1934

husband, Julián Martínez (1879–1943), who by 1935 had become
famous for their work. Maria went on to become in 1948 the
subject of the first full-length biography of a Native artist.

In a public show of support, the President and First Lady
attended the preview of the PWAP exhibition and selected, with
the aid of Bruce and his staff, over thirty paintings for display
in the White House staff offices. One was Ray Strong's (1905–
2006) *Golden Gate Bridge*, a large canvas of the highest-profile
engineering project on the West Coast, already a year underway
when Strong set up his easel on a promontory overlooking the
construction site. The chief engineer stands with a colleague at
the far edge of the right pylon, two ant-like specks swallowed
by the project's enormity. Beyond the blue-green Bay stands
the red northern tower of the iron-and-steel bridge and the
gently rising Marin County Headlands. The combination of
engineering marvel and majestic natural setting appealed
to FDR as the administration launched its nationwide public
works campaign.

The Roosevelts also selected *Subway* by Hungarian-born
Lily Furedi (1896–1969). In 1932 the Independent Subway System
opened in New York as the first city-owned and operated
subway, boasting ceiling fans, more seats, and spacious
interiors. Furedi's painting luxuriates in this new social space
of furtive looks and coded fashion, flickering between private
and public. Furedi's uncle, a concert violinist, may have
inspired the bow-tied musician nodding off, cradling a violin

case between his legs. He's surrounded by stylish commuters
absorbed in newspapers, magazines, conversation, and sidelong
glances (a man in a white fedora peeks at a woman applying
lipstick; a woman in green peers over the shoulder of a sharply
dressed Black man intent on his newspaper). In its unassuming
way, *Subway* paid tribute to New Deal-era progress, pluralism,
and modern convenience.

Another subterranean scene, Tyrone Comfort's (1909–39)
Gold Is Where You Find It, burrows underground to find a
shirtless prospector in shorts bracing one boot against the
recoil of a pneumatic drill. His hair bound in a stocking cap, his
face in shadow, the miner is all tension and sinew—his muscles
look sheared from the same rock as the mine wall. During the
Depression the price of gold increased, and miners reworked
old claims across the Western states of Utah, Colorado,
Nevada, and California. (Soon after becoming president, FDR
abandoned the gold standard to print more currency and
stimulate the economy.) Comfort's earthy palette and cropped

35

34 Lily Furedi, *Subway*, 1934

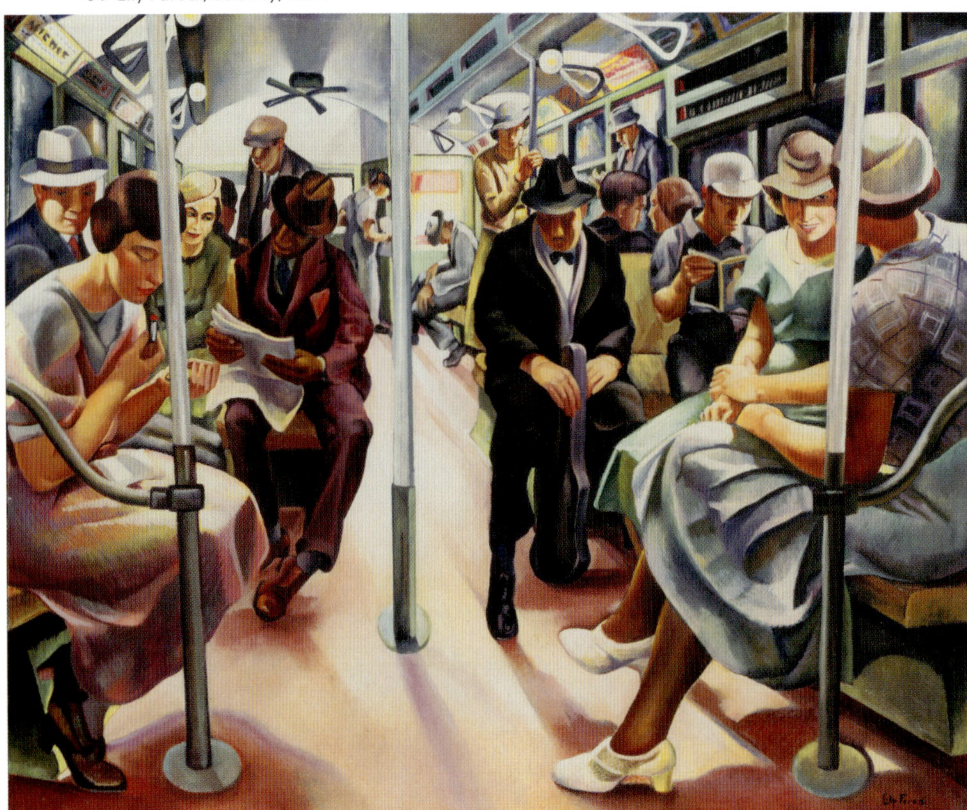

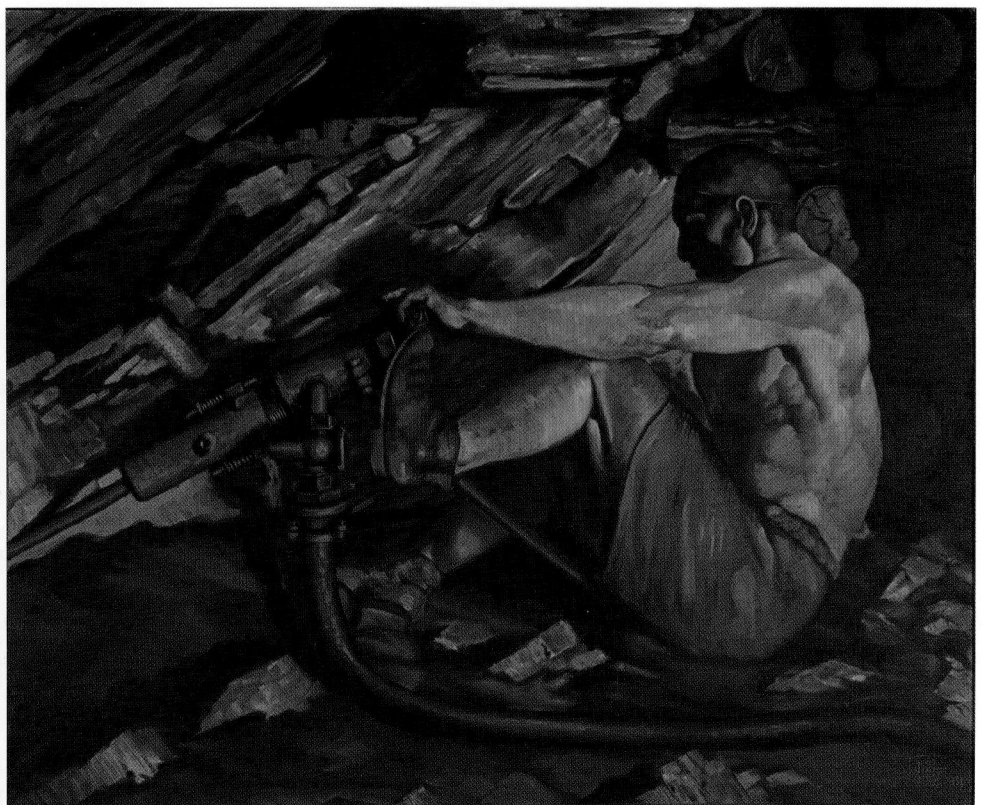

35 Tyrone Comfort, *Gold Is Where You Find It*, 1934

composition emphasize mining as a tough and risky venture.
But the Roosevelts, who acquired the painting for the White
House, likely saw an icon of New Deal virility: the bare-chested
male worker in the service of productive forces.

The exhibition featured relatively little sculpture, with only
eleven pieces out of over five hundred. The *New York Times*
singled out Maurice Glickman's *Negro Mother and Child* as the
exhibition's "one outstanding piece of sculpture...a work of
remarkable insight and plastic strength." (Jewell 1934, X7) The
barefooted figures stand tall and defiant, the mother's arms
crossed over her chest, the boy's arm raised and his other hand
balled in a fist. The plaster sculpture was later cast in bronze at
FDR's encouragement and now stands in the courtyard of the
Department of the Interior building.

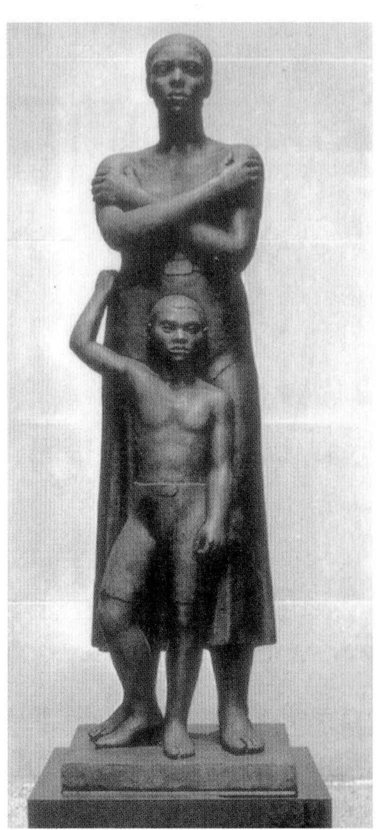

36 LEFT Maurice Glickman,
Negro Mother and Child, 1934
37 BELOW Isamu Noguchi,
Play Mountain, 1933, cast 1977
38 OPPOSITE Paul Cadmus,
The Fleet's In!, 1934

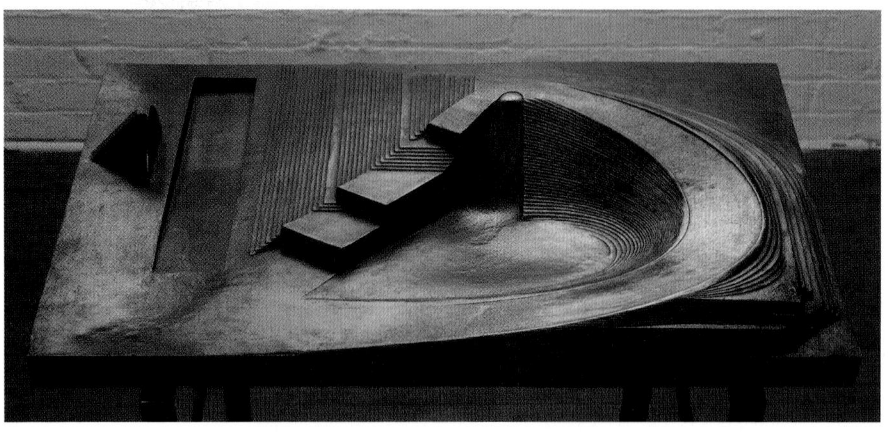

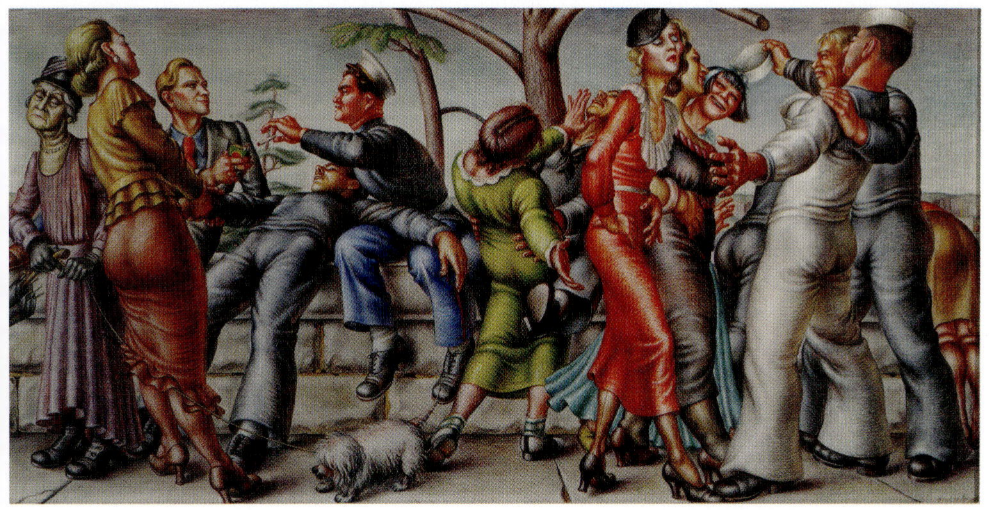

Censorship

The PWAP's pluralism only extended so far. Sculptor Isamu
Noguchi, a protege of Romanian modernist Constantin
Brâncuși, created a model for a Manhattan children's
playground as a proto-Earthwork molded into ramps, terraces,
steps, a pool, and slides. Forbes Watson reported that the PWAP
review board, expecting something more traditional, "turned
their thumbs down on [the design] so hard that they almost
broke their thumbnails." (Contreras 1983, 43) The board lacked
foresight; a playground design by Noguchi would be realized
decades later to great acclaim in Atlanta, Georgia's Piedmont
Park.

The most conspicuous absence from the exhibition, however,
was Paul Cadmus's (1904–99) *The Fleet's In!*, a ribald painting
of drunken servicemen on shore leave, consorting with sex
workers in Manhattan's Riverside Park. The frieze of tangled
limbs, clinging fabric, and shapely rear ends parodied classical
bacchanals. Scholars have pointed out coded signifiers of
queerness such as the rouged blonde civilian offering a Lucky
Strike cigarette to a seated marine. Retired Navy General
Admiral Hugh Rodman fumed that the painting "represents a
most disgraceful, sordid, disreputable, drunken brawl" and had
it spirited from the gallery. It found its way to Washington DC's
exclusive Alibi Club, where it hung for decades over a mantle for
an audience of senators and Supreme Court Justices.

The theft had the unintended effect of making the painting
a succès de scandale with media outlets giving the incident
breathy coverage. Cadmus took the scandal philosophically,

telling the *New York Times*: "I don't think admirals have much sense of humor if they are as deeply offended as reported. By attacking my painting, naval officials have only called attention to it, whereas if they had said nothing about it, it probably would have been noticed only by the art critics." (Meyer 2002, 39) In a fitting irony, the painting is now in the collection of the US Navy.

Artist as Worker

Controversy aside, the Corcoran exhibition met with a broad consensus that taxpayer money had been responsibly stewarded. ("Cost of Art Project Held Fully Justified" ran a headline in the *New York World-Telegram*.) Artworks went to schools, hospitals, courthouses, city halls, and congressional offices.

Secretary of Labor Frances Perkins, the first woman to hold a cabinet position and an early supporter of federal arts funding, selected a number of paintings from the exhibition for her department's building. She had plenty of topical art to choose from. The *Journal of Electrical Workers & Operators* noted that more than a fifth of the artworks on view dealt with labor and industry. A reproduction of Douglass Crockwell's (1904–68) PWAP painting of a paper mill in Glens Falls, New York, was included in the review. The painting features four blocky machine operators, styled as though they themselves were made out of wood, tending a massive paper roll.

According to the review, this newfound interest in the work of the working class (and the absence of "nudes, of night club subjects, of pretty women, of aristocratic looking men, of genteel houses") sprang from a recognition that the artist and tradesperson "are not so far apart as the world believes, and the unemployed artist is a good deal like the unemployed electrical worker or plumber." ("Doors Open on a Stale Tradition," 1934, 235)

And the specter of unemployment soon returned. The PWAP was designed and implemented as a crash jobs program to see a limited number of artists through the cold winter. It ended in June 1934, having employed 3,749 artists to make over 15,000 murals and mural sketches, oil paintings, watercolors, prints, and sculptures.

However short-lived, the PWAP laid the groundwork for subsequent New Deal art programs. It also exposed fault lines—race and representation, freedom and censorship, competing views of the American scene—that would widen over the decade.

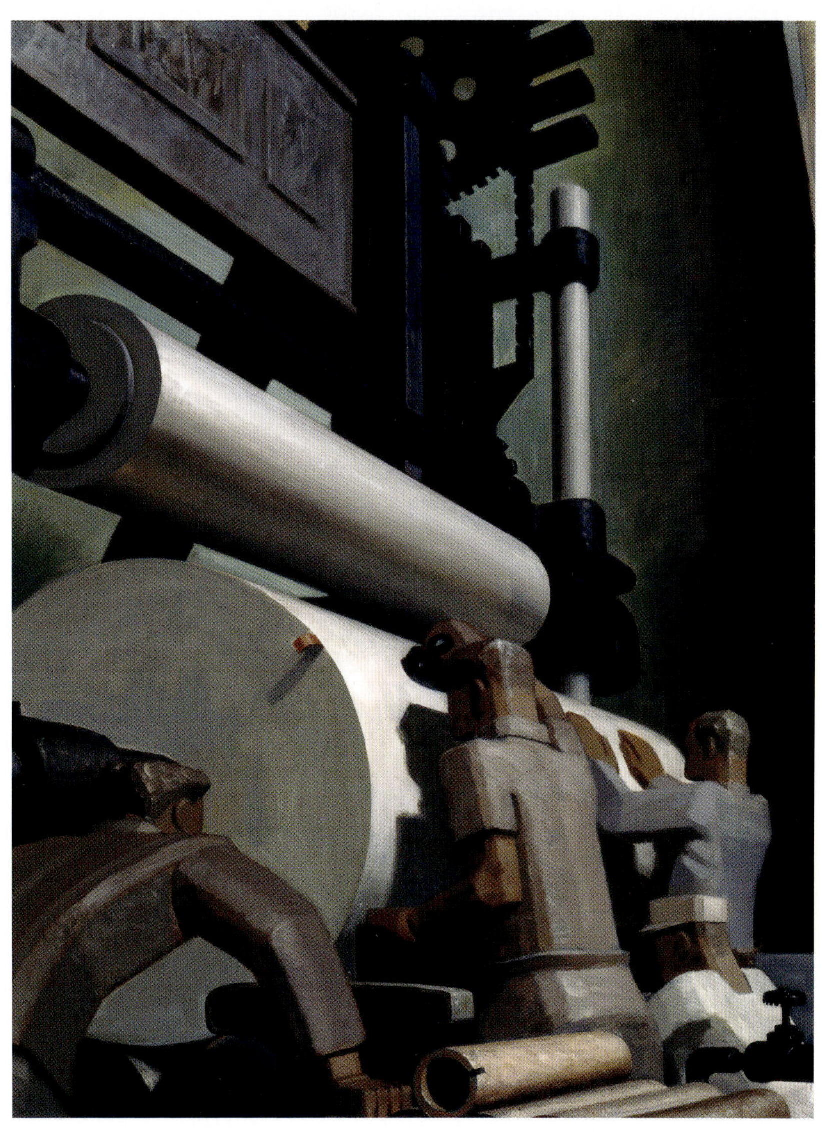

39 Douglass Crockwell, *Paper Workers*, 1934

PWAP artists and administrators looked to consolidate the win. George Biddle, who had first mooted the idea of state-sponsored art to his former classmate, FDR, happily reported in September 1934 in the *American Magazine of Art* that the PWAP "has made the artist conscious of the fact that he is of service to the community, that he fills a necessary function in our society."

The Roosevelt administration agreed. Within a few months of shuttering the PWAP, it would sponsor an even more ambitious public art program, the Section of Fine Arts. Many works commissioned by the Section are still on view today. And they are still liable to generate fierce controversy, debate, and even censorship.

Chapter 2
The Section of Fine Arts

Travel to any number of small towns in the continental
United States and you're likely to find a New Deal mural in the
local post office. You don't need to buy a ticket, go through
security, or make an appointment. You can stroll in and enjoy
a freely available work of original art, often installed over the
postmaster's door, while sending a package, picking up mail,
or chatting with neighbors. If you're from the area or know
its history, you might recognize portrayals of local industries,
popular tourist spots, or hometown heroes.

The mural may look something like Louise Emerson
Ronnebeck's (1901–80) *The Fertile Land Remembers*, painted in
1938 for the post office in Worland, Wyoming—a small town
along the Big Horn River in the state's northwest. Settlers sit
enthroned in an ox-driven covered wagon, resembling Christian
depictions of Mary and Joseph holding the baby Jesus. In the
sky above, Native bison hunters drift like fugitive storm clouds.
With its cinematic blurring of chronologies, the mural suggests
a double displacement: Native tribes displaced by white settlers,
whose homesteading gives way to the modern world of dams,
oil derricks, and transmission towers. As art historian Michaela
Rife has suggested, the ostensibly straightforward mural raises
more questions than it answers. Is the pioneer family the past or
future? Is modern industry to be celebrated or lamented? What
is it, exactly, that the fertile land (whose land?) remembers?
(Rife 2020, 21)

Murals like *The Fertile Land Remembers* are commonly thought
of as "WPA art," but in fact they had no official connection to the
Works Progress Administration. They were commissioned by
the Section of Fine Arts as part of the government's effort to
make art available to ordinary citizens while trumpeting New Deal
optimism. From the furthest reaches of northeastern Maine to
the southwestern corner of California, artists covered the walls of

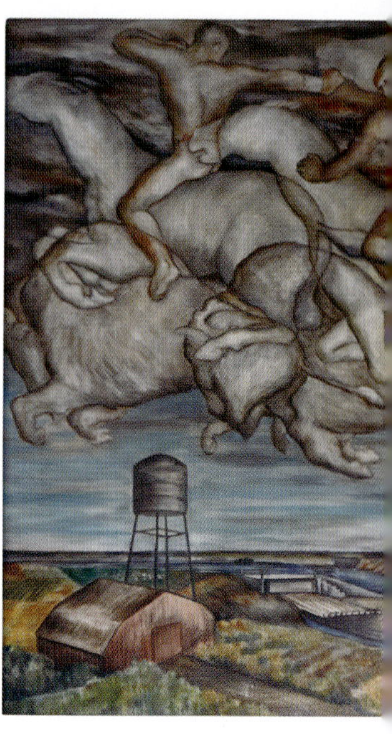

40 Louise Emerson Ronnebeck,
The Fertile Land Remembers, 1938

government buildings with murals meant to rekindle confidence in the state and the economy.

But look closer. Section muralists confronted the task of reconciling fundamental contradictions between the myths and realities of American history: peaceful settlement and violent conquest, freedom and slavery, prosperous industry and labor strife, progress and poverty. Complicated, contradictory arguments about American history, identity, and democracy are hiding in plain sight.

The Section

The success of the Public Works of Art Project (PWAP) opened the door to other government initiatives to support artists. As the PWAP wound down in the early summer of 1934, its director, Edward Bruce, proposed that the Treasury Department, the custodian of federal buildings, carry forward the PWAP's momentum.

With the support of Franklin and Eleanor Roosevelt, who had seen firsthand the fruits of the PWAP experiment, the Treasury Section of Painting and Sculpture (later the Section of Fine Arts, or the Section) was established in October 1934 with Bruce at the helm. Bruce, in turn, brought aboard his PWAP lieutenants, Edward Rowan and Forbes Watson, along with Olin Dows (1904–81)

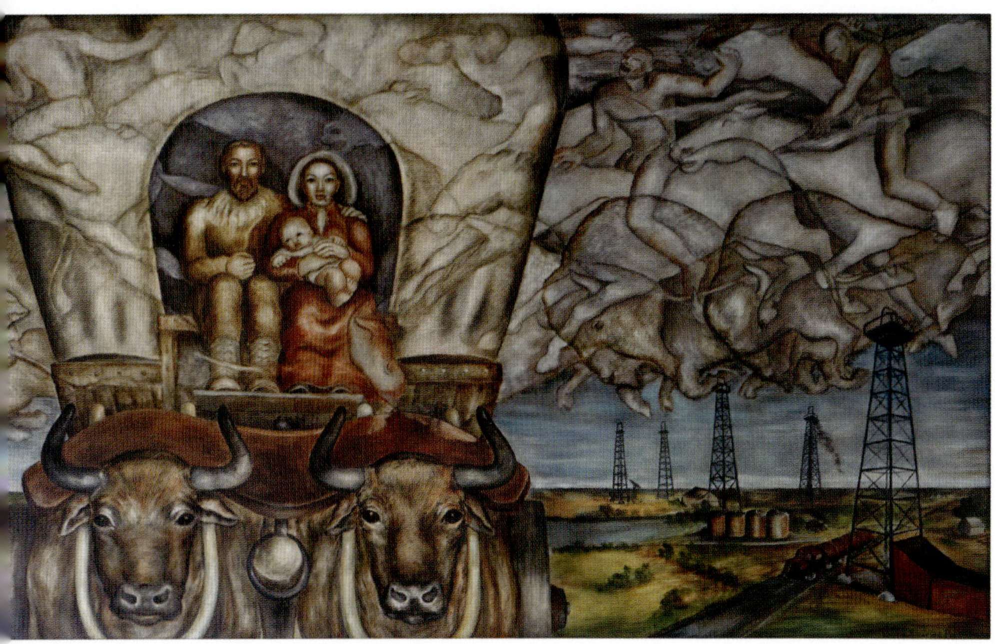

as his aides-de-camp, setting up in a row of offices in the Federal
Warehouse Building in Washington DC.

In an *Atlantic Monthly* article, "Art and Democracy," Bruce
outlined a program of federal art that would nurture regional
talent and place original paintings and sculptures in government
buildings nationwide:

*Our objective should be to enrich the lives of all our people by
making things of the spirit, the creation of beauty, part of their daily
experience; by giving them new hopes and sources of interest to
fill their leisure; by eradicating the ugliness of their surroundings;
by building with a sense of beauty as well as mere utility; and by
fostering all the simple pleasures of life which are not important in
terms of dollars spent, but are immensely important in terms of a
higher standard of living.*

Beyond the lofty rhetoric, the Section was essentially an arm of
the New Deal's public works. As part of the Treasury Department,
its funding came from money earmarked by Congress for the
construction of new federal buildings. Based on open design
competitions, artists were hired to embellish those new buildings
with murals or sculptures. The Section was not a jobs-creating
program, in other words; selected artists did not have to prove they

needed work. This emphasis on "quality"—granting commissions based on perceived merit—distinguished the Section from the later Federal Art Project's concern with quantity—giving jobs to as many unemployed artists as possible.

In other ways, however, the goals of the Section and the Federal Art Project were commensurate. Bruce believed art was vital to democracy and the people's representatives made the best patrons. "I want to take the snobbery out of art," Bruce said, "and make it part of the daily food of the average citizen." (Hemingway 2002, 81) At the same time, he wanted to refine the average citizen's palate. It was essential in his mind to maintain high aesthetic standards as part of a "higher standard of living" for American citizens.

The resulting program was unprecedented in scale and scope. Between 1934 and 1943, the Section commissioned over fourteen hundred murals and sculptures for federal buildings (mainly post offices) in cities big and small, urban and rural. The Section's free mimeographed *Bulletin*, edited by Forbes Watson, announced the terms and themes for upcoming competitions. Artists submitted scale designs to a Section-approved committee (school principals, postmasters, museum professionals, etc.), who relayed their winning selections to Washington. This process cloaked the Section in the guise of fairness. Still, less than a fifth of commissioned murals came about through actual competitions— the vast majority were awarded directly by Section chiefs to runners-up or artists who had otherwise impressed them.

Bruce and his team policed the process from design to execution. Where possible, they hired talent local to the region of the building. They urged non-local artists to visit communities in advance to gather material. "There he talks with the townspeople," Forbes Watson wrote, describing the ideal, "gathers their tales of folklore and history, visits the chief industries, and acquaints himself with the architecture and landscape peculiar to that region. From this material, he selects subject matter which typifies that community and which will lend itself to the creation of a vital design." (Park and Markowitz 1977, 37) Artists, however, rarely had the resources to cover out-of-pocket expenses for travel (they also had to pay for their materials and assistants), so few concept sketches incorporated actual fact-finding.

Most Section murals recycled generic American scenes— landscapes, historical vignettes, brawny workers, flourishing fields and factories—meant to be palatable to audiences of all ages and backgrounds. Section chiefs favored compositional clarity, good drawing, accurate details, and uncontroversial subject matter. Bruce liked designs that gave "the same feeling I get when I smell a sound, fresh ear of corn." (McKinzie 1973, 57)

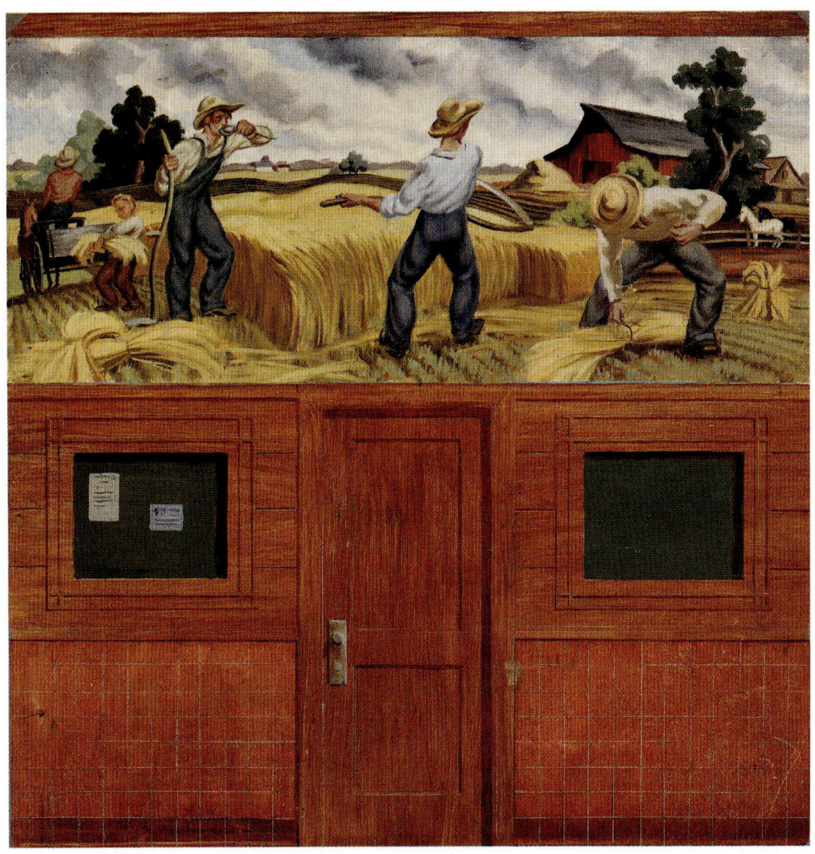

41 Joe Cox, *Study for Harvest*, 1939

The adjective "corny," in the sense of trite or mawkish, dates to the 1930s and could be applied to any number of Section murals. Joe Cox's (1915–97) *Harvest,* for example, is a nostalgic scene of grain harvested by hand designed for a post office in Alma, Michigan. A straw-hatted farmer at left sips water from a long-handled dipper; the central figure wields a scythe while a third bundles wheat into shocks, ready for loading into the buckboard.

Artists like Cox learned how to "paint Section," as the phrase went, submitting formulaic designs tailored to juries and Section officials. Even so, the finished study was Cox's *sixth* attempt to satisfy Section gatekeepers, who sanded the rough edges of proposals subject to final approval. However time-consuming and risk-averse, this process ensured the Section's survival as the longest-lived of the New Deal art programs.

"Pioneers"

The majority of Section murals went to small-town post offices. This was a logical place for Section art: Before the New Deal, the post office may have been a far-flung community's only direct encounter with the federal government. Post offices were hubs of community activity where people routinely visited and congregated. There were also a lot of blank walls to fill: three times as many post offices were built in the 1930s as in the previous fifty years.

The Postal Service also made a logical subject for Section art. For the post office in New Jersey's Haddon Heights, Isamu Noguchi sculpted a cloudlike bas-relief of a reclining woman dreamily composing a letter, setting the service's activities in motion.

Doris Lee (1905–83) painted *Country Post* for the new Post Office Department headquarters in Washington DC, appropriately among the first to receive Section-sponsored murals. Lee illustrated the excitement of rural mail delivery— even the terrier is eager to hear the news.

42 Isamu Noguchi, *The Letter*, 1939

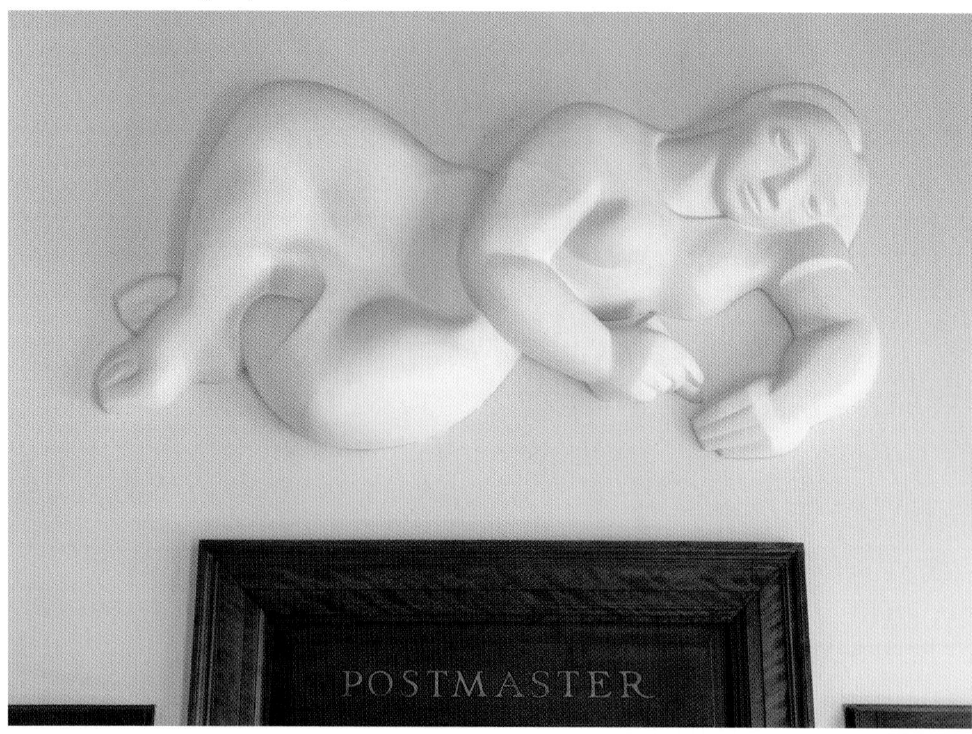

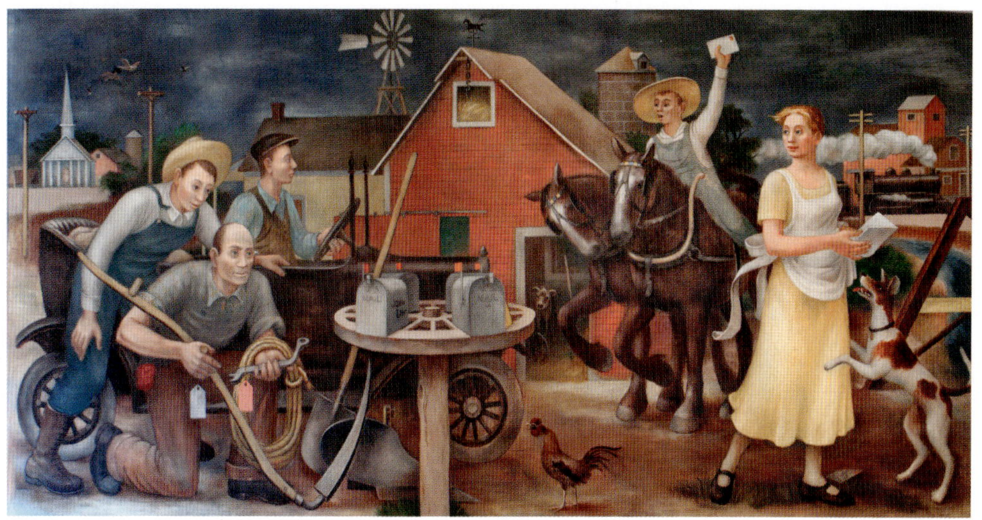

43 Doris Lee, *Country Post*, 1938

Farmers cluster around mailboxes mounted on a wagon wheel, greeting the arrival of new tools and farming equipment (the S-wrench and scythe still have their price tags attached). The Postal Service began offering free rural delivery in the late nineteenth century to relieve rural residents of picking up mail in a central post office or paying a private carrier. The service remained widely popular, a means of connecting, in Lee's interpretation, the modern world of trains and automobiles to the rural hallmarks of chickens, barns, and plow horses.

Following Lee's template, murals across the country portray the writing, sending, sorting, delivering, receiving, and reading of the mail. The postman (almost always a man—the Post Office didn't start hiring women mail carriers in significant numbers until the 1960s) regularly appears as a friendly and reliable civil servant braving the elements while making his rounds. Others depict the progress of mail delivery from horseback and stagecoaches to bicycle, rail, and airmail.

Where early settlers went, the Postal Service followed. Mail delivery linked frontier towns to the rest of the country via networks of cattle trails, Pony Express relay stations, stagecoaches, and railroads—all popular Section themes. Philip Guston—born Phillip Goldstein, the youngest son of Ukrainian Jewish immigrants and childhood friend of Jackson Pollock (they were expelled together from high school for distributing anti-faculty satire)—treated this entwined history in his study for a mural in Commerce, Georgia, *Early Mail Service and Construction of Railroads.* A trio of workers lay a line of track, their bodies rhyming with the three telegraph posts. The postman, arriving by horseback, unshoulders a mail sack. Town fathers busy themselves over the latest news while a woman in a shawl reads a letter—a gendered division of public and private spheres. Behind them the post office's classical pediment and portico suggest the post's civilizing influence.

Guston, in his mid-twenties, had already notched mural commissions in the US and Mexico (David Alfaro Siqueiros called him one of the most promising painters in either country). For artists accustomed to easel painting, however, murals posed distinct challenges. Few knew how to paint "true fresco," a challenging medium involving the application of water-based paint to wet plaster. Instead, most painted large oil-on-canvas panels in their studios that could be transported and installed on-site. Moreover, designing large-scale, multi-figure compositions that kept a sense of coherence and clarity was no easy task. Artists had to consider multiple viewpoints while contending with light pendants, ceiling fans, drab color schemes, and spaces cut up by windows, doors, clocks, and bulletin boards.

A sketch by Edward Chávez (1917–95) for a post office mural in Geneva, Nebraska, depicting settlers building a sod house (a shelter constructed using turf, usually to house livestock), tried a few solutions to the architectural challenges. The top of the door to the postmaster's office cutting into the composition (a frequent dilemma faced by artists), is cleverly incorporated

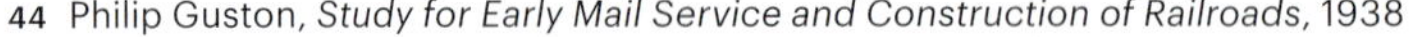

44 Philip Guston, *Study for Early Mail Service and Construction of Railroads*, 1938

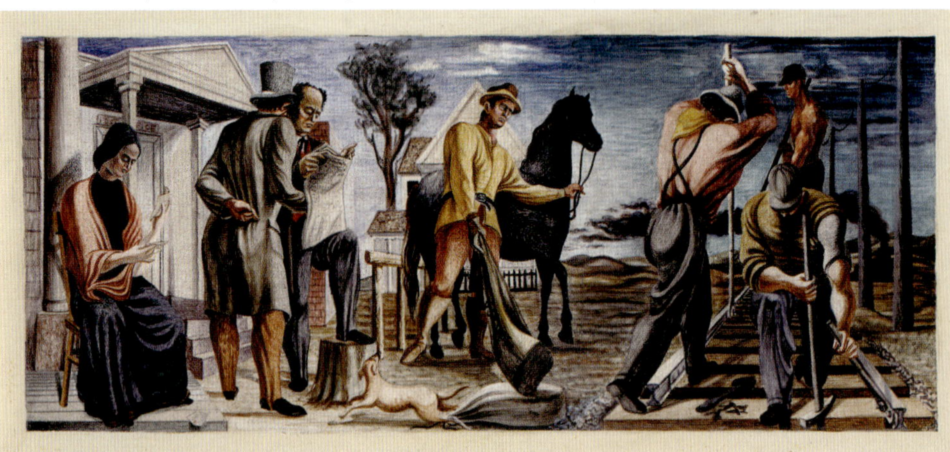

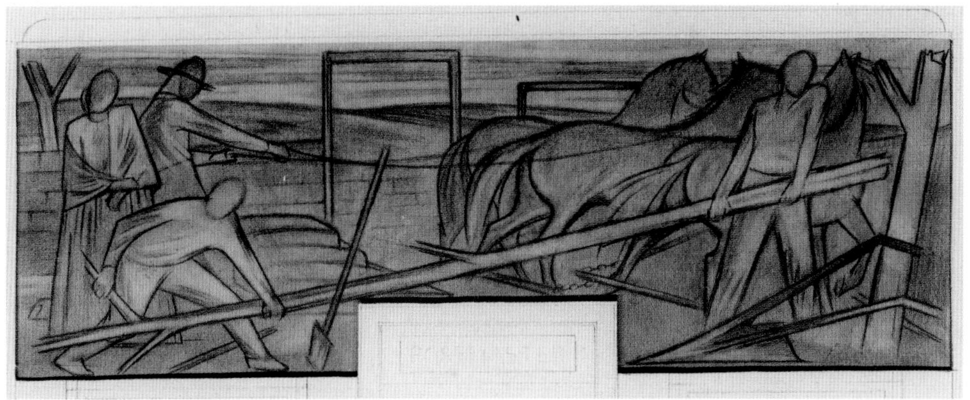

45 Edward Chávez, *Study for Building a Sod House*, 1941

by Chávez as a fulcrum for the length of post maneuvered by
two settlers. The beam's long diagonal ties the composition
together, bridging the horizontal span, a device repeated by
the swooping reins attached to a team of workhorses pulling
sod blocks. The frame of an unbuilt door adds a vertical accent
and repeats the shape of the postmaster's door, softening
its intrusion.

Social rather than aesthetic problems, however, soon
plagued the commission. Chávez—whose family of sheep
ranchers descended from early Spanish settlers—remembered
some Geneva residents complaining that the builders
(featureless in the sketch) looked more Chicano than Anglo in
the finished mural. This anxiety was likely part of a wave of
anti-Mexican xenophobia in the 1930s that led to immigration
quotas and deportations of seasonal workers.

Chávez's depiction of nonwhite settlers was an exception that
proved the rule. Edward Bruce considered Ward Lockwood's
(1894–1963) mural of *Daniel Boone's Arrival in Kentucky* for
the Lexington courthouse maybe the "best thing" painted
for the Section. As such, it distills the qualities of painterly
naturalism and whitewashed Americana prized by Bruce
and his colleagues. Broad-shouldered, square-jawed Boone—
mythologized for opening up the "Wilderness Road" beyond
the westward bounds of the thirteen colonies—appears as the
archetypal frontiersman in his coonskin cap and buckskin
jerkin. He stands ramrod straight, a frontier Moses at the apex
of a compositional pyramid with his companions arrayed below
to form the base. The composition is clear and uncluttered, as
simple and legible as its creed of frontier machismo.

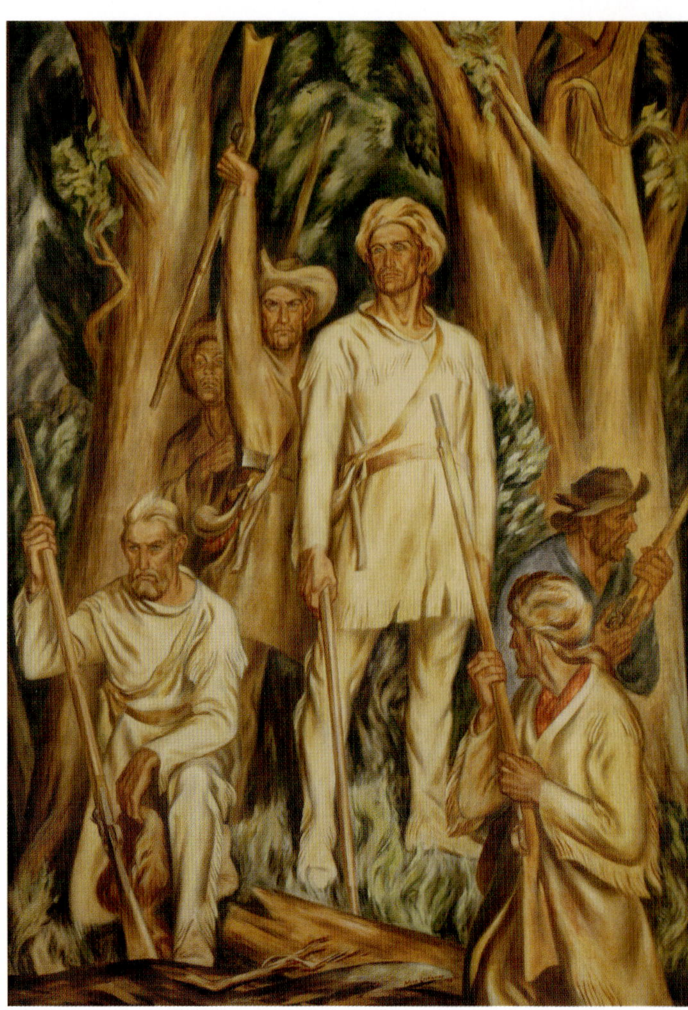

46 Ward Lockwood, *Daniel Boone's Arrival in Kentucky,* 1938

Boone joined a long list of real and fictional pioneers bestriding Section murals from Washington DC to Washington state: Lewis and Clark, Kit Carson, Davy Crockett, Natty Bumppo, Father Junipero Serra, Spanish gold hunters, French fur trappers, and "land run" settlers racing to claim allotments. Pioneers ford rivers, drive cattle, clear forests, build log cabins, and plant crops—scenes that gave ideological cover to white settler grabs for land and resources.

The "pioneer" figured regularly in FDR's rhetoric. "The period of geographical pioneering is largely finished," FDR said in a 1936 speech. "But, my friends, the period of social pioneering is only at its beginning." Section chief Edward Bruce expressed the same view when he testified before Congress in 1935 that the days of tapping "new territory with its vast natural resources is largely over." Instead, the US must "secure new frontiers," Bruce argued, which would come "in the field of art and science and literature." (Section *Bulletin*, June 1935, 6)

The new pioneers invoked by FDR and Bruce appear in Seymour Fogel's *Wealth of the Nation,* painted for the lobby of the Social Security Board Building (now the Wilbur J. Cohen Federal Building) in Washington DC. A shirtless Hercules operates the switch of a pair of giant cogwheels. The arc of his bare back repeats the curve of the blueprint draped over the architect's knee. The visual rhyme underscores the mutual necessity of manual and mental labor in service to a planned vision of progress. The central pair is flanked at the left by a suited scientist bent over a microscope, jotting notes; at the right by a pair of workers striding to a factory shift. The mural, painted in the heart of New Deal Washington, offers reassurance that the Depression's frightening uncertainties have been brought under control by new "pioneers" securing the frontiers of science, technology, and industry.

47 Seymour Fogel, *Wealth of the Nation*, 1942

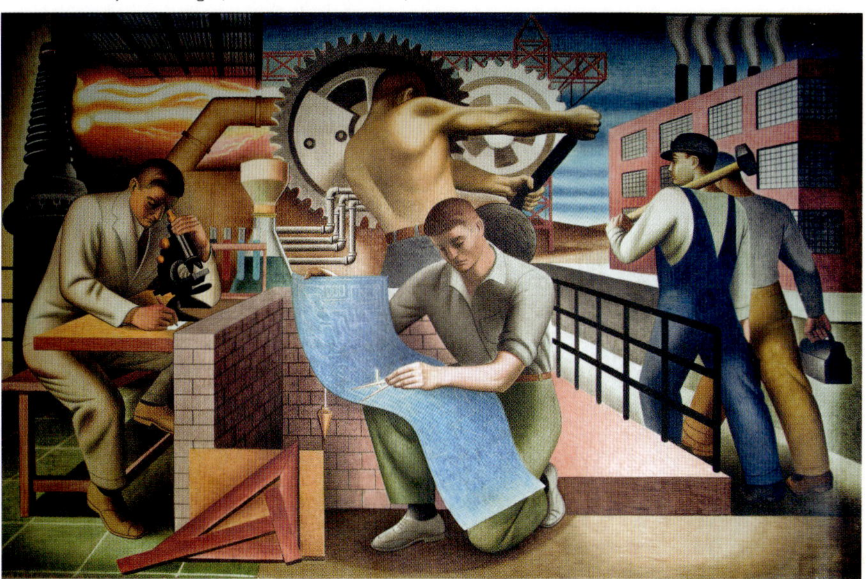

The Comradely Ideal

For Native Americans, the pioneer past romanticized in
Section murals meant the loss of lives, land, and sovereignty.
Over a quarter of Section murals depict Native Americans—
a clear indicator of their importance to the Section's vision of
national history and character. But that vision is complex and
contradictory. Portrayals of Native peoples by white artists
spanned crude caricature to cultural appreciation, but few
showed real intimacy with Indigenous history and lifeways.
Some murals glorify a prelapsarian world, as in Margaret
Martin's *Indian Hunters and Rice Gatherers,* painted for the
post office in St. James, Minnesota. Others show missionaries
converting Native peoples to Christianity. Mostly, artists
recycled stock subjects: peaceful first encounters, colonial or
pioneer settlement, trade and commerce, treaty-making or
negotiating (not breaking), conversion, and assimilation.

Section officials discouraged scenes of violence and warfare
as out of keeping with the program's goals of optimism and
uplift. They made exceptions, however, for violence directed
against Native Americans. Ethel V. Ashton (1896–1975) portrayed

48 BELOW Margaret Martin, *Study for Indian Hunters and Rice Gatherers,* 1939
49 BOTTOM Ethel V. Ashton, *Defenders of Wyoming Country–1778,* 1941

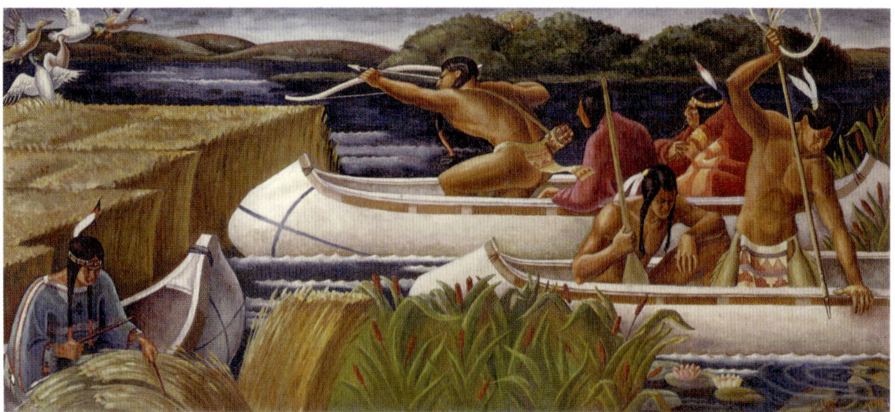

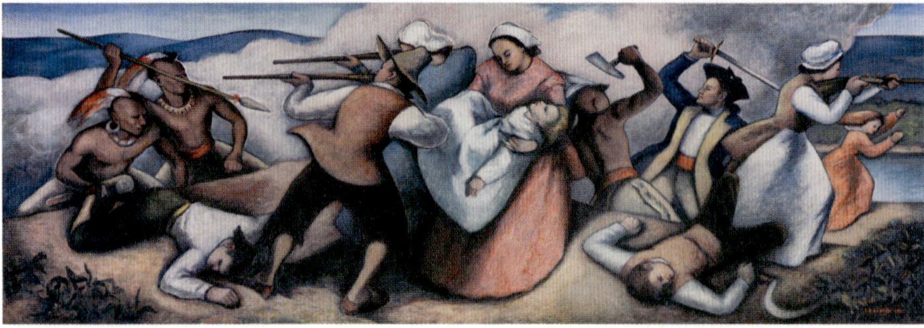

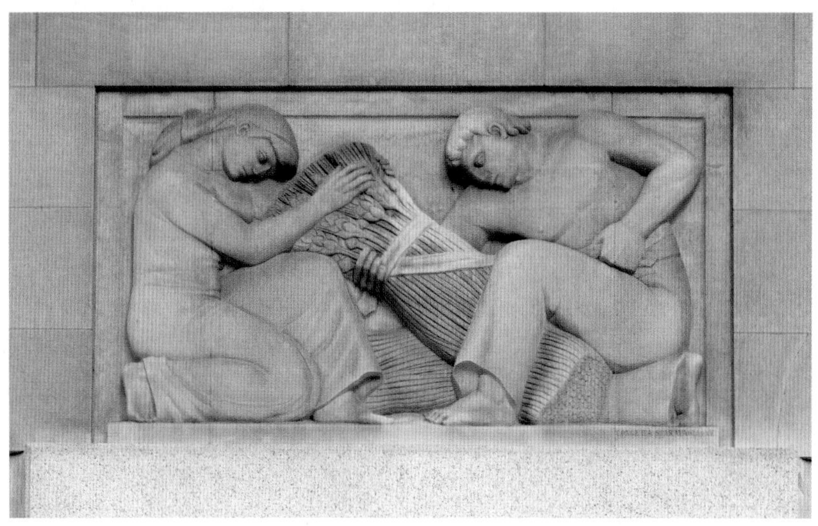

50 Concetta Scaravaglione, *Agriculture*, 1938

a Revolutionary War skirmish between patriot militia and forces loyal to the king, allied by the Haudenosaunee, a confederacy of northeastern tribes. Women in sunbonnets, standing shoulder-to-shoulder with male counterparts, aim their muskets at attacking warriors. The central mother holds her dead child in a pietà pose.

Ashton cast women in a heroic light at the expense of Native men reduced to cliché. Roughly nineteen percent of Section commissions were awarded to women, who dealt with structural sexism and an all-male upper administration, however sympathetic. Edward Rowan, the Section chief who worked most directly with artists, acknowledged in a letter that "a woman has to be twice as industrious and twice as conscientious as a man to hold the same position." (Melosh 1991, 227) While anonymous competitions theoretically made the selection process gender-blind, the highest-profile Section commissions went to male artists and privileged homosocial imagery.

Artists upheld what art historian Barbara Melosh called the "comradely ideal," a glossing of white men and women as allies domesticating the frontier. (This during a decade of rising divorce rates, fewer births, and gendered anxieties about work and its lack.) Concetta Scaravaglione (1900–75) symbolized Agriculture, sculpted for the southeast entrance of the Federal Trade Commission's headquarters in Washington DC, as a young couple binding grain. A latter-day Adam and

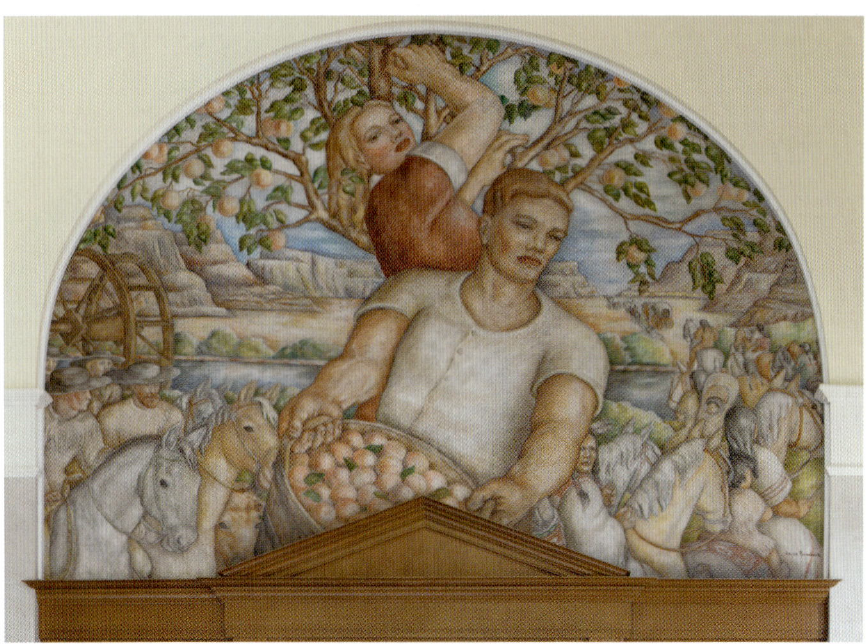

51 Louise Emerson Ronnebeck, *The Harvest*, 1940

51 Eve fill an arched lunette in Louise Emerson Ronnebeck's
The Harvest for a federal building in Grand Junction, Colorado.
Their overlapping Michelangelo-esque bodies look as pinkishly
ripe as the gathered peaches. In the background white settlers
arrive on horseback, displacing the Nuche people from their
homelands, who cross a river and vanish into the horizon.

Visual Sovereignty

Native artists resisted the trope of the "vanishing Indian" in
high-profile Section commissions. Kiowa artist Stephen Mopope
(1898–1974) painted sixteen panels on four walls of the Post
Office in Anadarko, Oklahoma, honoring Kiowa history and
traditions. Mopope grew up on the Kiowa Reservation where his
uncles trained him in the art of painting on hides for ceremonial
garments and tipis. (His Kiowa name, Qued Koi, means "Painted
Robe.") At the University of Oklahoma he banded with five other
Indigenous artists as the Kiowa Six, celebrated for paintings on
paper of everyday Native life. Mopope's skill as a graphic artist
suited mural designs, which need to be legible at a distance.
52 *Two Eagle Dancers*, performing a ritual adapted from Pueblo
tribes, form vivid silhouettes against a flat golden field in bold
celebration of ceremonial dance and song.

Mopope was one of six Native artists selected to paint murals for the new Department of the Interior (DOI) building in Washington DC, the first planned and built by the Roosevelt administration. The DOI, established in 1849 to manage the country's natural resources, by the 1930s oversaw national parks, hydroelectric dams, oil fields, public lands, mines, and waterways. It also ran the Bureau of Indian Affairs, and the murals appeared at an inflection point in the relationship between sovereign tribes and the federal government. In 1934 Congress passed the Indian Reorganization Act, the so-called "Indian New Deal," which restored a measure of sovereignty to Native tribes and prohibited land allotments, the policy of carving up tribal lands into indiviual parcels to break up large reservations.

Prickly, pugnacious, and outspokenly progressive Secretary of the Interior Harold Ickes, author of *The Autobiography of a Curmudgeon* (1943), closely supervised the mural program. A reform advocate who opposed the policy of forced assimilation, Ickes wanted the walls of the DOI building to reflect the "Indian New Deal." At the same time, Native artists were expected to deliver subjects—hunting, weaving, ceremonial dances and initiations—untroubled by the historical realities of dispossession or genocide. According to art historian Jennifer McLerran, the murals presented Native culture as a natural resource (like the rivers, lakes, and old-growth forests managed by the agency) for reconnecting urbanized whites to a more "authentic" culture grounded in unbroken traditions. (2009, 197)

52 Stephen Mopope, *Two Eagle Dancers*, 1936

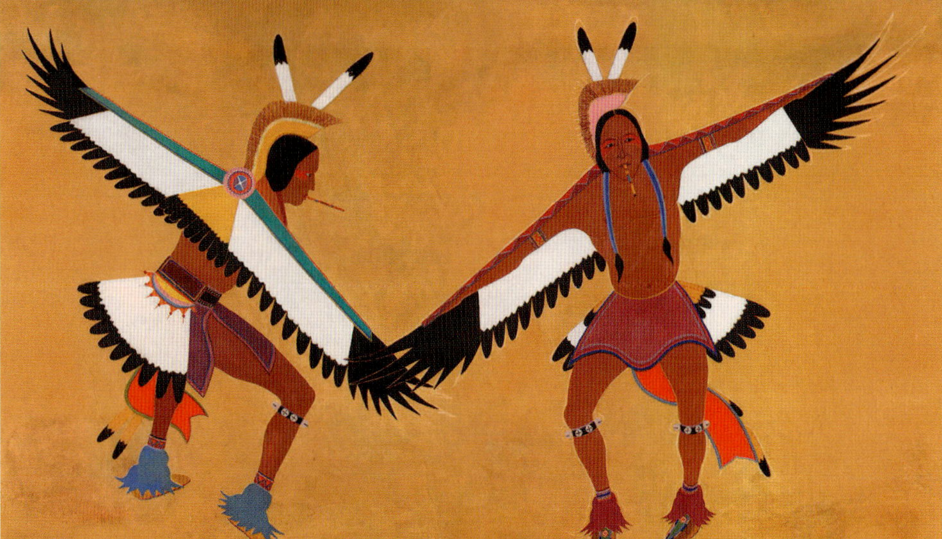

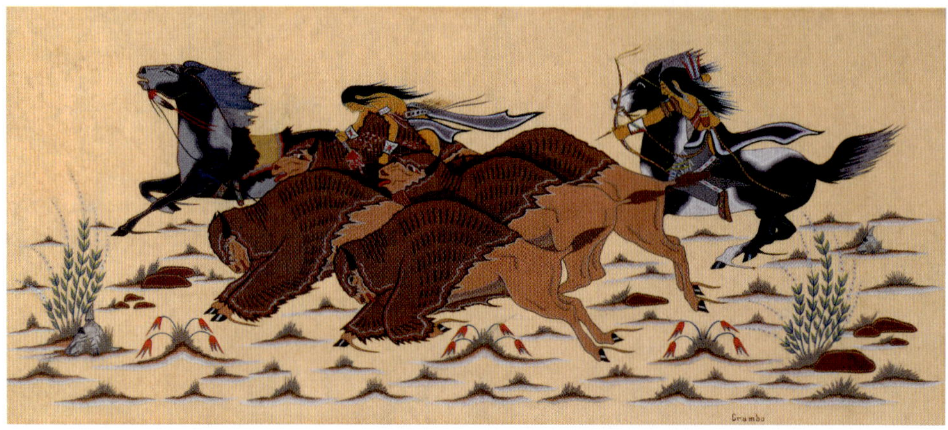

53 Woodrow Crumbo, *Study for Buffalo Hunt*, 1939

For Native artists, however, a simplistic division between
traditional and modern did not hold. Neshnabek artist
Woodrow "Woody" Crumbo (1912–89) painted a dynamic scene
of a buffalo hunt for the DOI's employees' lounge. Crumbo—
who played the cedar wood flute, danced ceremonially, and
learned Indigenous methods of silverwork, vegetable dyeing,
and weaving—saw the traditions portrayed on the DOI walls
as vital to contemporary Indigenous culture but under threat.
"I am attempting to record Indian customs and legends now,"
he said of his paintings, "while they are alive, to make them a
part of the great American culture before these, too, become
lost, only to be fragmentarily pieced together by fact and
supposition." (Mecklenburg 1979, 51) Crumbo's work, and that
of other Native New Deal artists, give form to what Anishinaabe
theorist Gerald Vizenor has called Indigenous survivance
(survival + resistance) in the face of genocide.

Government officials frowned on contemporary scenes of
Native and non-Native interaction. A rejected mural study by
Diné artist Gerald Nailor satirized a white bourgeois couple,
outfitted with a cigar and fur-lined collar, haggling over a woven
rug—a barbed comment on the equivalence of Indigenous
culture with the tourist market. Tewa artist Pablita Velarde,
working across the country in New Mexico, managed to sneak
in a similarly pointed scene showing a Pueblo guard turning
away a blue sedan carrying a nuclear family of white tourists.
Velarde had been commissioned by the National Park Service
to paint a cycle of over seventy paintings on Pueblo life for the
visitors' center at the Bandelier National Monument near Los
Alamos. The strong vertical of the Pueblo guard, reinforced by

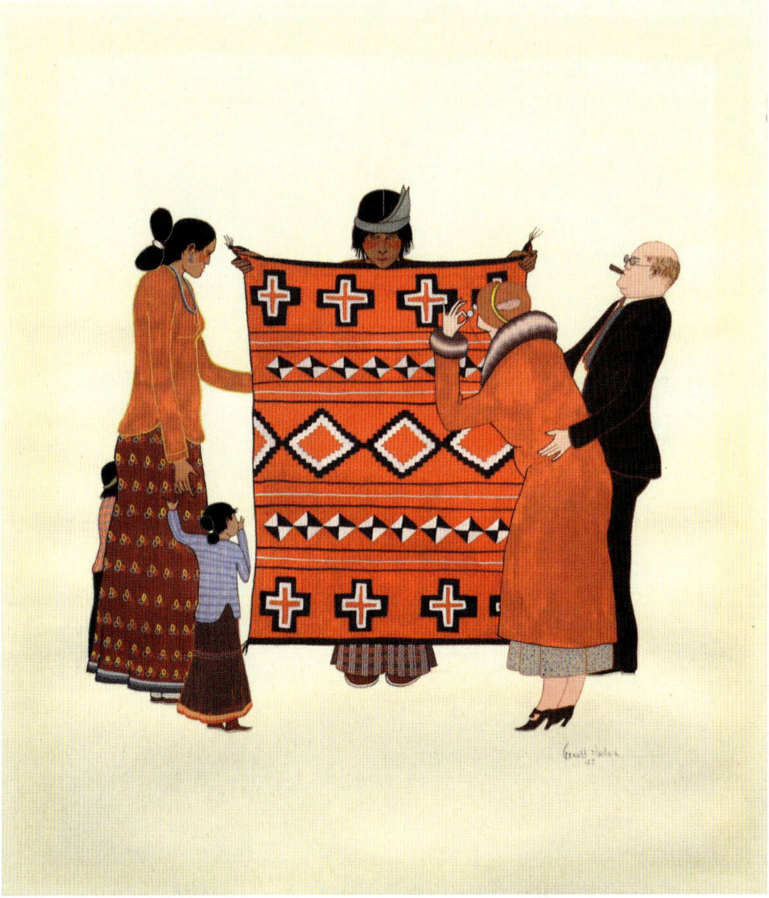

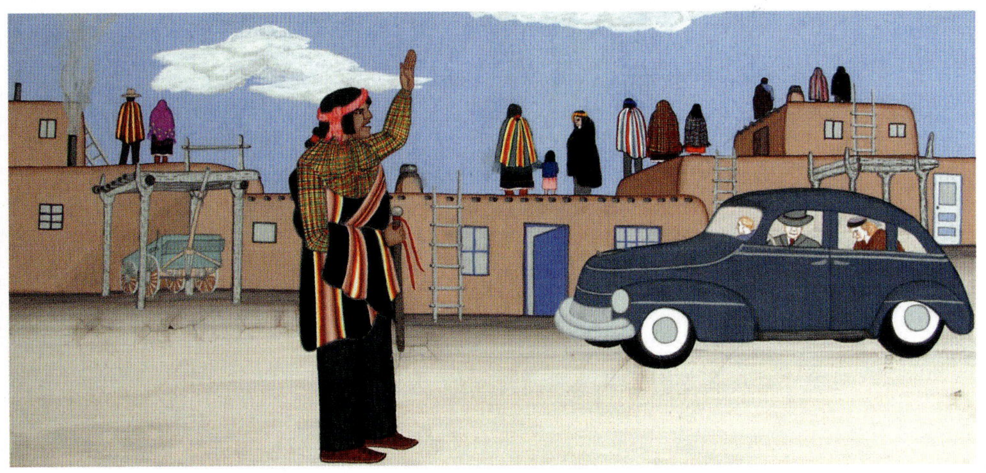

54 TOP Gerald Nailor, *Untitled (Tourists)*, 1937
55 ABOVE Pablita Velarde, *Guard Turning Tourists Away*, c. 1940

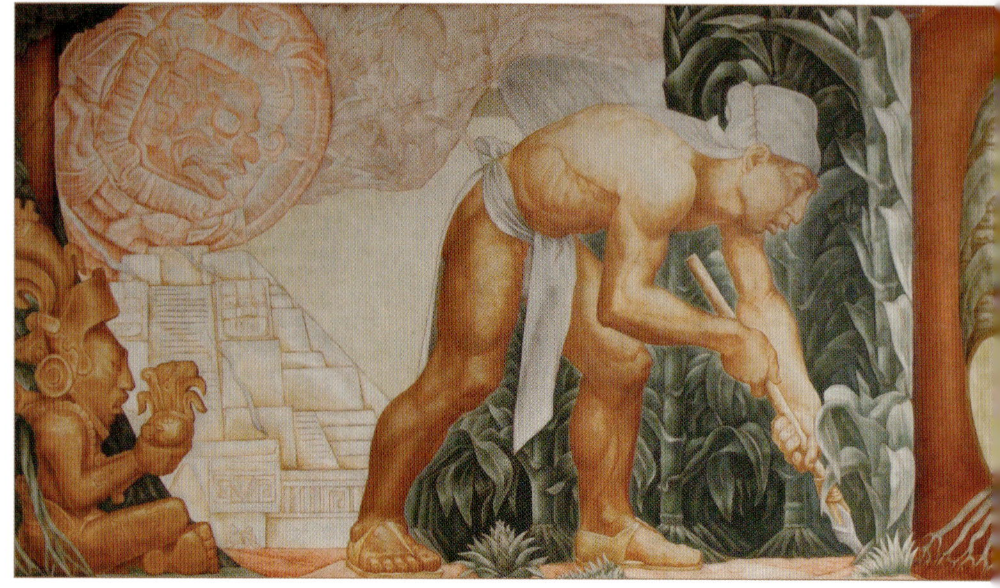

56 Lowell Houser, *The Evolution of Corn*, 1938

the ladder set against the adobe wall and his sarape's stripes,
asserts what Tuscarora scholar Jolene Rickard has called visual
sovereignty—an expression of Native autonomy especially
trenchant in a government building.

Cardinal Crops

Indigenous figures appear in Section murals dedicated to what
historian Charles Eldredge calls the cardinal crops—corn,
wheat, and cotton—that drove the United States's agricultural
economy. (2022, 4) Lowell Houser (1902–71) painted *The Evolution
of Corn* in 1938 for the post office in his hometown of Ames,
Iowa, in honor of the state's cash crop. (Houser had assisted
fellow Iowan Grant Wood on his PWAP mural cycle for Iowa State
University.) A talismanic cornstalk divides scenes of ancient
and modern cultivation. On the left a Maya farmer digs with
an obsidian-tipped hoe under the watchful eye of the rain and
sun gods. On the right a farmer picks corn from stalks under
an allegory of photosynthesis complete with evaporating water
molecules and an absorption spectrum. Houser aimed to "make
a sort of modern hieroglyph of the present," though with no
reference to Iowa's Indigenous tribes such as the Meskawi.

Joe Jones (1909–63), self-styled "Professor of Wheat," painted
a scene for the Seneca, Kansas, Post Office—the study shows
two farmers operating a combine and tractor with a harvester

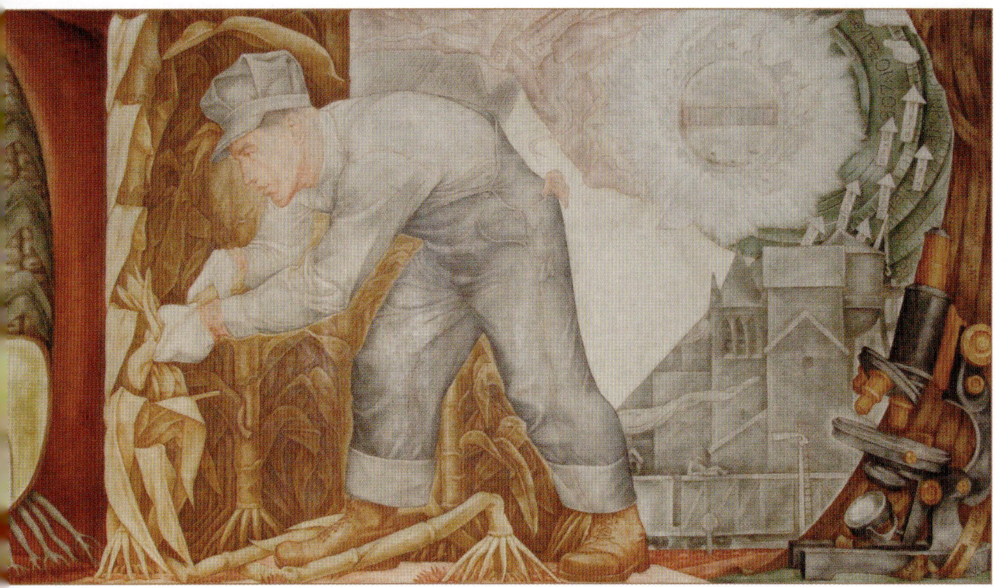

in the middle distance beneath a lowering sky. Jones, a communist firebrand, drew inspiration from the heartland and its hardworking farmers, and his career complicates tidy divisions between radical urban artists and conservative rural Regionalists. "I want the working people, the people producing useful things with their hands," wrote Jones to Section chief Edward Rowan, "to enjoy this painting for the understanding and strength of which part of their lives are reflected." (Hemingway 2002, 156)

Jones painted *Men and Wheat* amid controversies over government intervention in agriculture. The same year his mural was unveiled, Carey McWilliams published *Factories in the Field*, a farsighted analysis of emerging agribusiness colluding with the federal state following the Agricultural Adjustment Act of 1933. The act authorized the government to fix prices and regulate crop production by subsidizing farmers to reduce surpluses (a euphemism, in one case, for slaughtering six million piglets and pregnant sows) and limit the supply of crops like corn, wheat, and cotton. The AAA operated on the principle of rational state planning through a massive bureaucracy—a reality at odds with the Section's nostalgic scenes of small-scale family farms.

The South posed distinct challenges to the Section's uplifting vision of national unity. Federal aid generally went to large corporate farming operations or white landowners, who used funds to mechanize operations and fire sharecroppers. New Deal legislation excluded vulnerable farm workers from the benefits of social insurance and union protections. In 1930 over three-quarters of the country's Black population lived in the South, where the cash crop economy (cotton, sugar, rice, tobacco) depended on their labor. The Jim Crow system of legal segregation, backed by the threat of police or mob violence, limited or foreclosed opportunities for Black citizens in housing, education, and employment, while poll taxes and biased literacy tests suppressed the Black vote. The moral stain of slavery and the Cain-and-Abel fratricide of the Civil War remained in living memory.

Few of these contemporary realities appear in Section murals in the South. As art historian John Ott has shown, white artists upheld a system of white supremacy in portraying Black Americans as manual laborers policed by white overseers. (Ott 2025) During a period of agricultural crisis, particularly in the cotton industry, Section muralists resorted to a romanticized past. A 1938 mural for the Montevallo, Alabama, Post Office blithely ignored enslaved labor altogether in portraying *Early Settlers Weighing Cotton* as an all-white assembly. "They are a sturdy stock," reported the *Montevallo Times* in 1939, "healthy, intelligent looking people of Anglo-Saxon background." These rose-colored views of the antebellum South resembled those of Margaret Mitchell's novel *Gone with the Wind*, a bestseller in 1936 and an Oscar-winning film three years later.

Murals acknowledging slavery were likelier to appear, when they appeared at all, in the North than in the South—for example, white artist James Michael Newell's *The Underground*

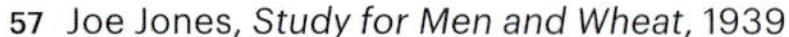

57 Joe Jones, *Study for Men and Wheat*, 1939

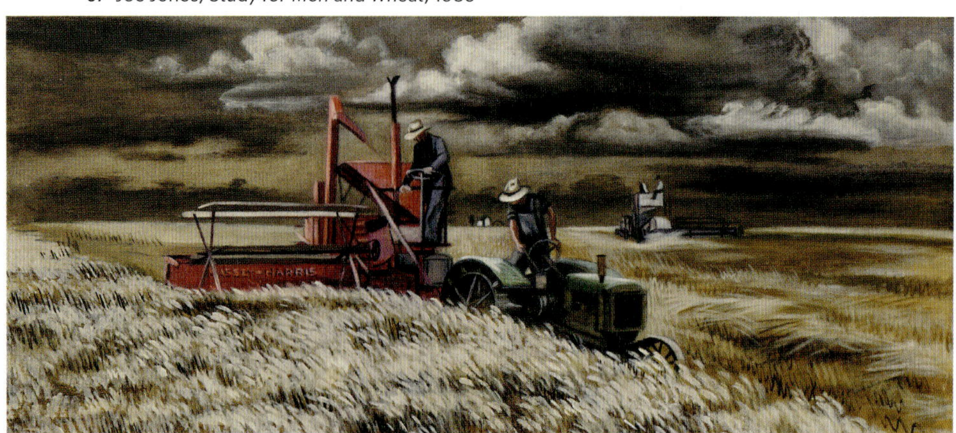

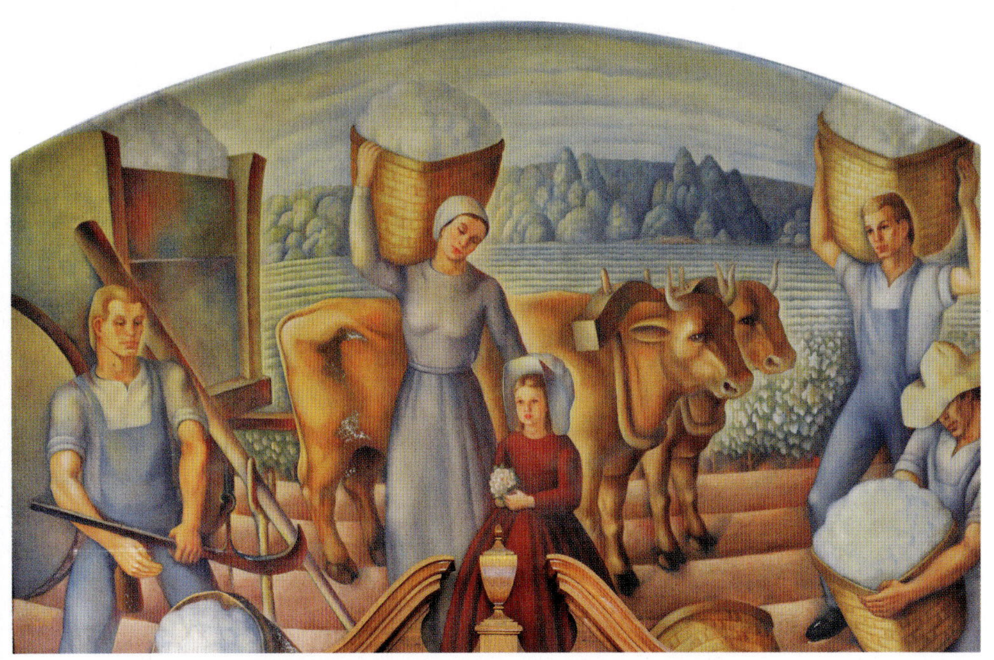

58 William Sherrod McCall, *Early Settlers Weighing Cotton*, 1938

Railroad painted for a post office in Dolgeville, New York. Historical scenes by Black artists related to slavery were even more uncommon. Black government official William J. Thompkins, the Recorder of Deeds in charge of public documents, shepherded an ambitious mural cycle for the agency's Washington DC building on the contribution of African Americans to the history and culture of the United States. William Edouard Scott (1884–1964) painted *Frederick Douglass Appealing to President Lincoln* for the building's foyer. Douglass, renowned abolitionist and the nation's first Black Recorder of Deeds, petitions Abraham Lincoln to let Black men enlist in the Union Army. Despite the mural cycle's theme, Scott was the only Black artist out of seven commissioned.

For a scene of agricultural labor by a Black artist we have to return to the Public Works of Art Project (PWAP). Earle Wilton Richardson (1912–35), a native New Yorker who trained at the National Academy of Design, painted for the PWAP the large canvas *Employment of Negroes in Agriculture*. Far from the stooped, anonymous cotton pickers typical of New Deal art, his quartet possesses monumental dignity. Richardson and his lover, Malvin Gray Johnson, had planned a series of murals celebrating "Negro Achievement" for a Harlem library. Johnson,

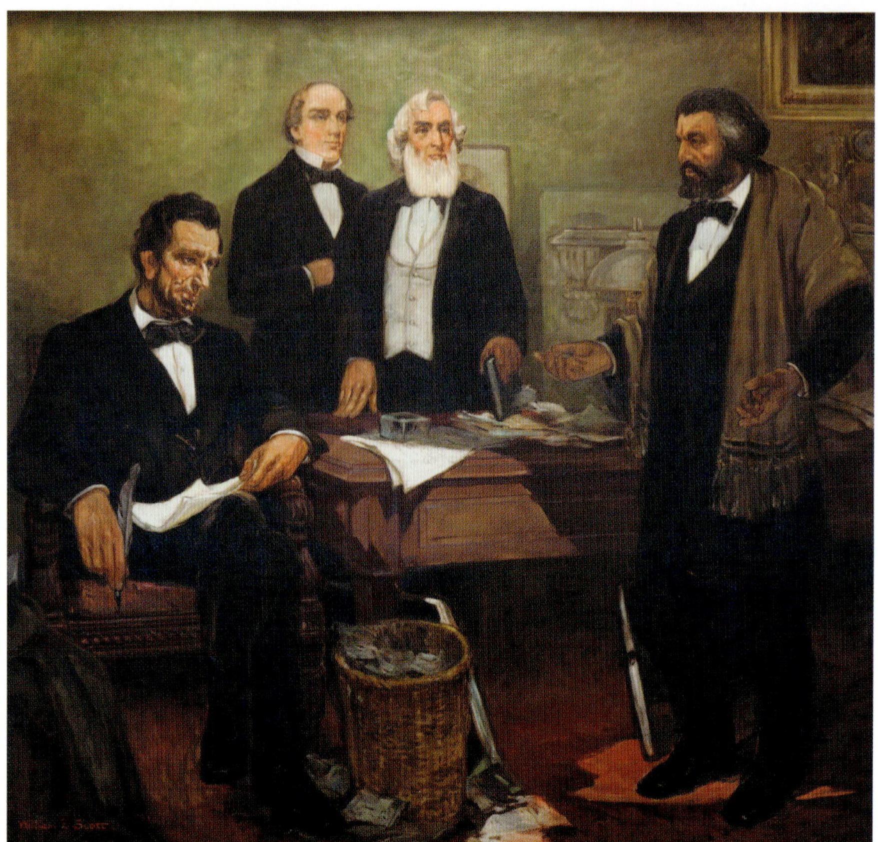

59 William Edouard Scott, *Frederick Douglass Appealing to President Lincoln*, 1943

however, took ill suddenly and passed away in November 1934. Richardson committed suicide a year later at age twenty-three, cutting short the life of one of the few New Deal artists tackling issues of race and identity from a Black perspective.

The Working Body

Several New Deal murals showed the meeting of agriculture and industry at the intersection of the traditional white family: male breadwinner, wife and caregiver, healthy baby. For a post office mural in Ambler, Pennsylvania, Harry Sternberg (1904–2001) portrayed himself with a wife and child as a "holy family" seated at the crossroads of the coal- and cornfields that drove the state's economy. He wears a pair of overalls, suitable to either farm or factory, and holds hands with his wife as their newborn lies enthralled by a buttercup. Sternberg, a leftist, had

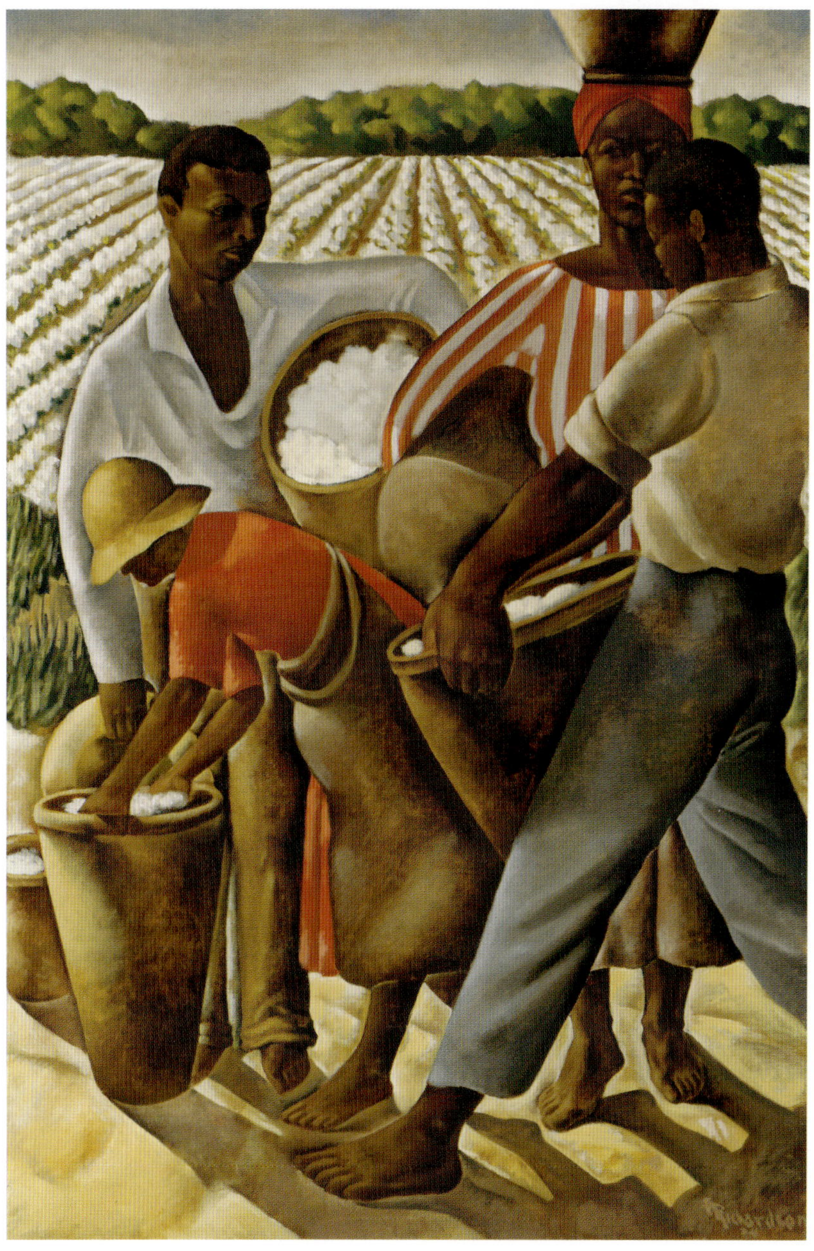

60 Earle Wilton Richardson, *Employment of Negroes in Agriculture*, 1934

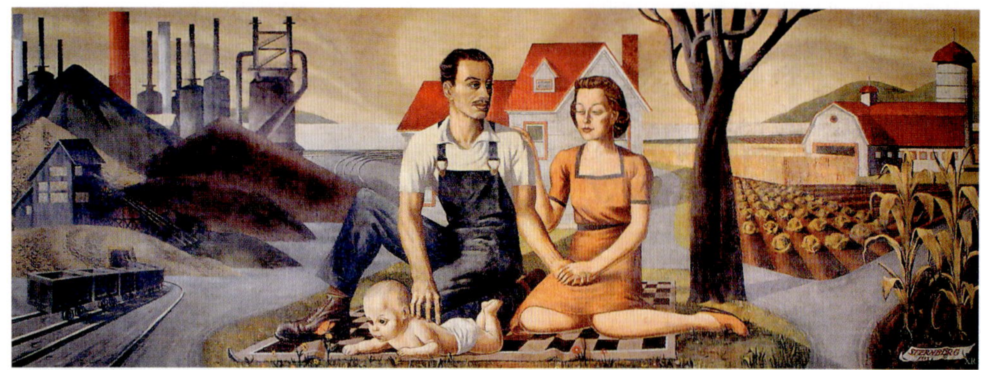

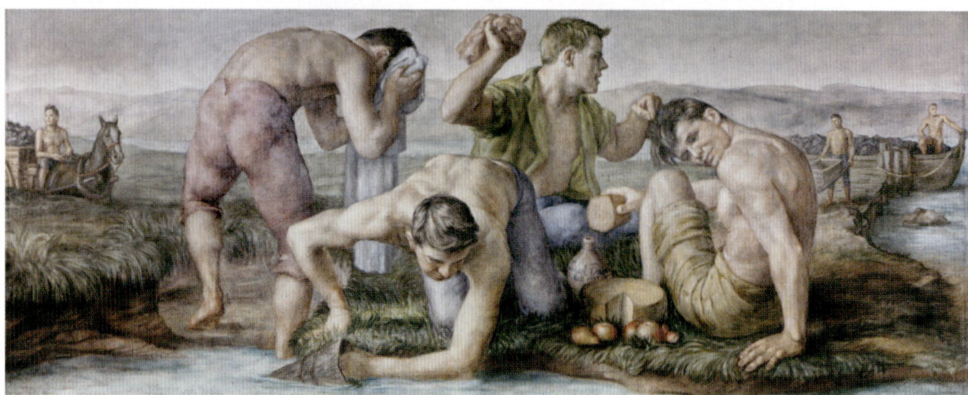

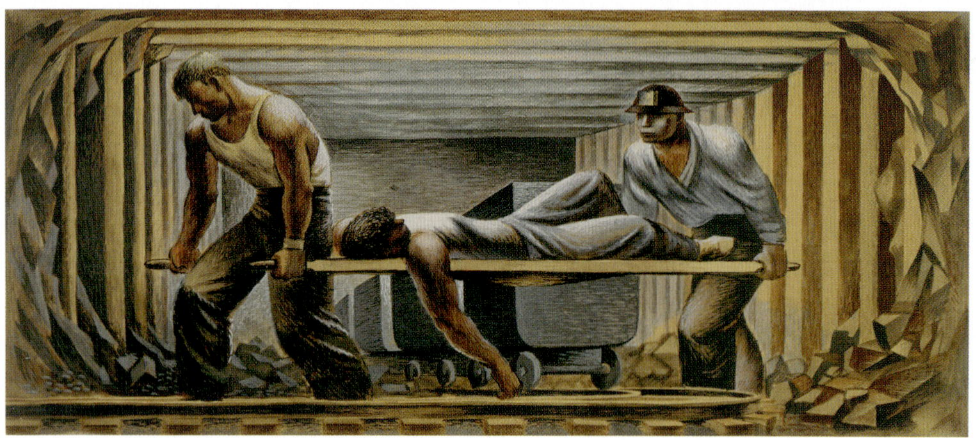

61 TOP Harry Sternberg, *The Family, Industry, and Agriculture*, 1939
62 CENTRE Jared French, *Mealtime, The Early Coal Miners*, 1936–38
63 BOTTOM Fletcher Martin, *Study for Mine Rescue*, 1939

made damning paintings and lithographs of Pennsylvania's coal and steel industries, and there is something incongruous in his attempt to reconcile heavy industry and homesteads, slag heaps and cabbage patches.

Other artists faced the same problem: how to exalt an industry as unpicturesque as coal mining? Jared French (1905–88) solved the problem by portraying a historical scene in *Mealtime, The Early Coal Miners,* made for the post office in Plymouth, a small town in northeastern Pennsylvania. French, a queer artist, interlaced a knot of lissome miners breaking for lunch on the banks of a stream. In the distance a coal boat approaches the shore piloted by an inexplicably naked male figure—the signature of an artist known for his classicizing nudes—who would have been too small for administrators to detect in the studies submitted for approval.

Fletcher Martin's (1904–79) *Mine Rescue* never made it past the approval stage. Designed for the post office in Kellogg, Idaho—home to a vast complex for the mining and smelting of lead, silver, and zinc—the mural study evokes biblical scenes of Christ entombed. The hewn rocks form a parenthesis around the central trio of two broad-shouldered miners carrying an injured miner on an improvised stretcher. Edward Rowan praised Martin's "distinguished" concept and composition, which also met with enthusiasm from the Mine, Mill and Smelter Workers Union. Other organizations, however, such as the Chamber of Commerce and the Idaho Art Association, objected to the negative portrayal of the mining industry and warned that the community would find it distressing to be reminded of personal loss. Administrators caved to pressure and instructed Martin to redesign the mural.

Promethean Power

In Washington DC, the Department of the Interior headquarters, along with its murals by Native artists, flaunted New Deal efforts to bring the country's natural resources under central state control. The agency ran the Public Works Administration (PWA), which undertook material- and labor-intensive infrastructure projects such as dams, bridges, and airports. William Gropper's (1897–1977) epic *Construction of a Dam,* inspired by sketching trips to the Grand Coulee Dam on the Columbia River (at the time the largest fabricated structure on earth), stretches twenty-nine feet across the DOI's second-floor lobby, dissolving the wall into a widescreen paean to labor power and technological progress.

The mural study breaks the composition into thirds (accounting for two marble pilasters) showing on the left

64 RIGHT William Gropper, *Study for Construction of a Dam*, 1938
65 BELOW Michael Lantz, *Man Controlling Trade*, 1942

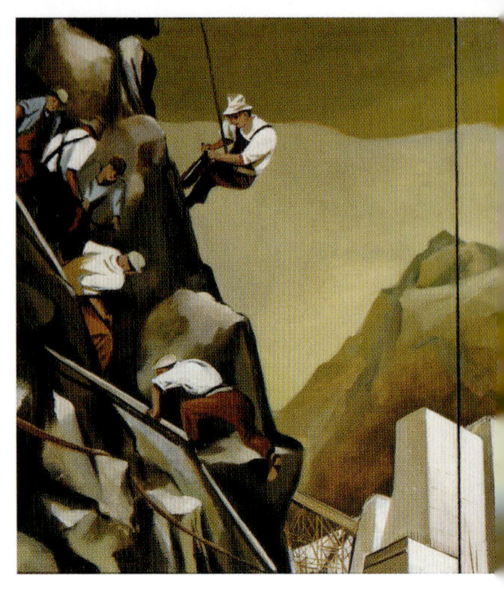

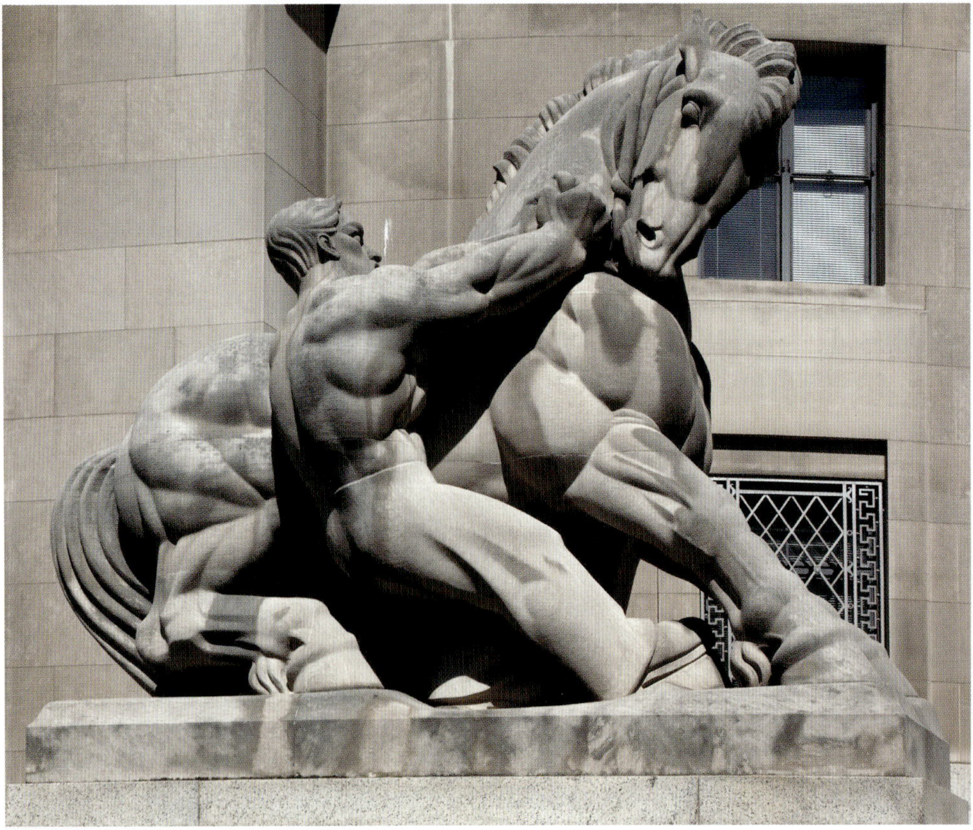

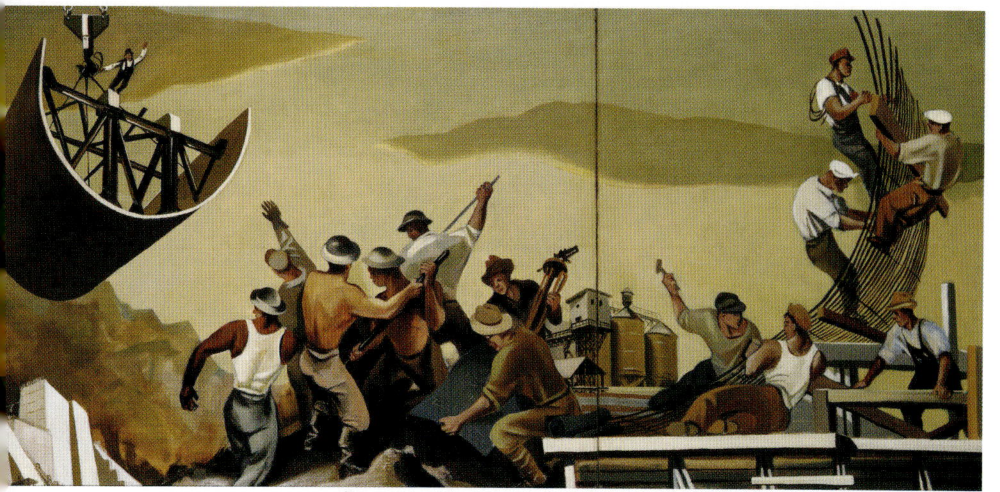

a team of so-called high scalers drilling holes into the side
of a sheer cliff to plant dynamite, a dangerous occupation
often performed by Native Americans. (Discriminatory
hiring practices assigned the relatively few Black and
Indigenous workers the most hazardous or menial jobs.)
In the dramatic central panel, a worker in hat and overalls
clings to a conduit suspended by a crane over a yawning
chasm. He signals to an (idealized) interracial group of
muscular workers and surveyors on the promontory below.
Their arched mass echoes the distant mountain peaks in
a sublime synthesis of nature, labor, and engineering.

Gropper paid tribute to the DOI's vision of skilled collective
labor and state control of public utilities. In sponsoring
major hydroelectric projects, the DOI went head-to-head with
commercial power companies in a check on the unregulated free
market. Michael Lantz (1908–88) allegorized this dynamic with
his limestone sculpture *Man Controlling Trade*, one of two on
pedestals flanking the Federal Trade Commission's Washington
DC headquarters. A shirtless colossus, symbol of the federal
government, strains to rein an untamed horse, symbol of the
unruly forces of trade and commerce.

Variations of Gropper's and Lantz's heroic workers flex in
Section murals from coast to coast. They drill for oil in Texas,
assemble cars in Detroit, mine for bauxite in Arkansas, puddle
steel in Pittsburgh, and hoist transmission towers in Tennessee.
Preindustrial economies based on horse- and muscle power
transformed into a fossil-fueled regime of automobiles, freight
trains, tankers, cranes, derricks, and pipelines. The men

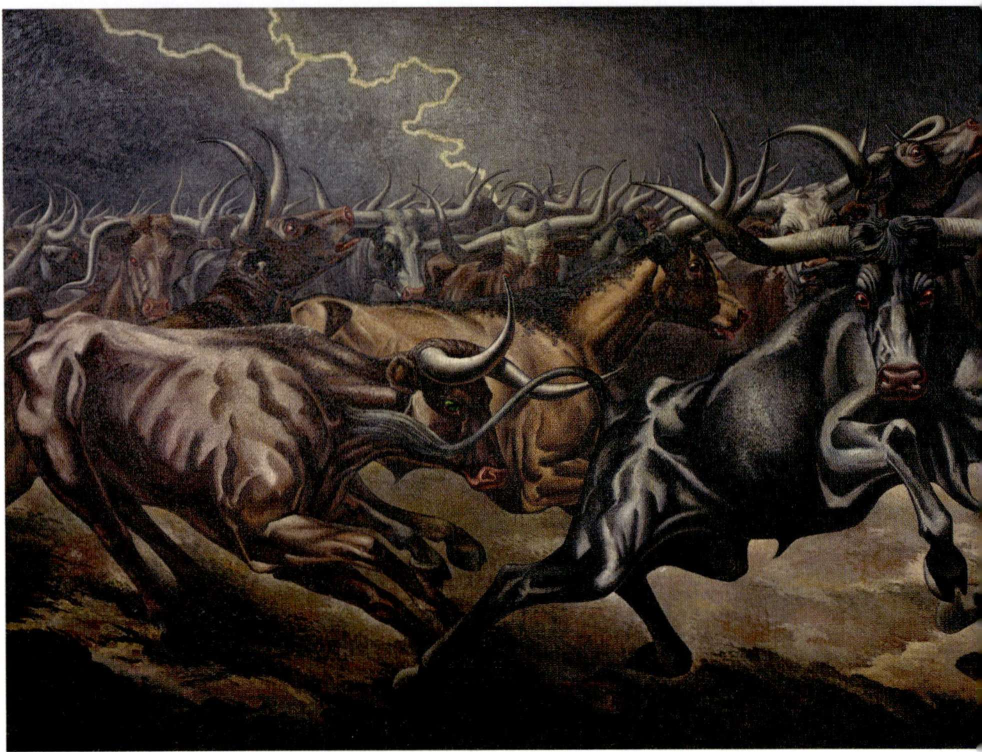

66 Tom Lea, *Stampede*, 1940

operating them are promethean figures, stealing fire from the gods, bending nature to the will of corporations and the state.

In rare cases, nature exacts revenge. The electricity harnessed and distributed by New Deal agencies like the Rural Electrification Administration could be a destructive force. Lightning flashes the dark sky of Tom Lea's *Stampede*, spooking a herd of cattle. A cowboy tumbles head-first over his horse, his body see-sawing with a lunging Texas longhorn. Painted for the post office in Odessa, Texas, a plains town near a cattle-driving trail, the mural undermines the Section trope of human power over the natural world. The longhorn's glistening flanks, flaring nostrils, and glittering red eyes embody furious nature refusing to be controlled.

The Public as Patron

Section murals shared qualities with the Federal Writers' Project's American Guide Series, state-by-state tour books brimming with lively accounts of American cities, towns, and

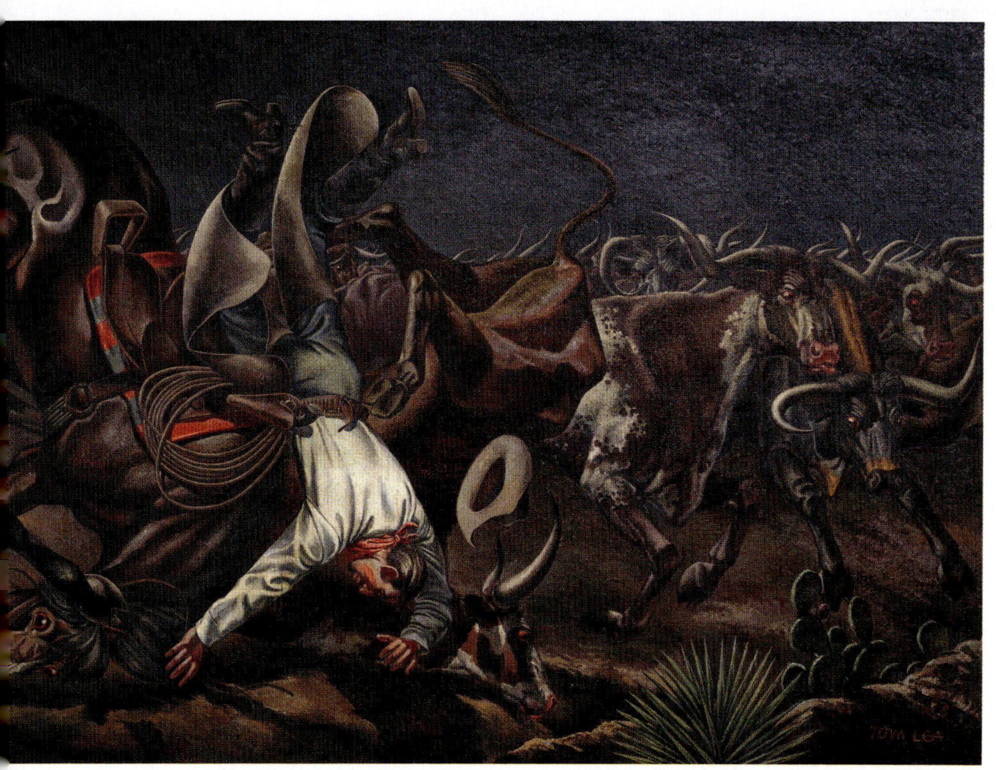

villages. Often relying on oral histories and folktales, FWP writers made vivid local history and legend, colorful characters and customs, regional industries and tourist attractions. Section muralists likewise portrayed American history in a folksy, favorable light, stressing the role of everyday people wresting a living through hard work, family bonds, and communal effort.

In many small towns a post office mural might be the only original public artwork the community could enjoy. Virginia Snedeker (1909–2000), herself a Section muralist, poked fun at the phenomenon with a 1941 *New Yorker* cover. A painter in a yellow smock stands on a ladder putting the finishing touches on a mural: An airmail pilot, goggles propped on his forehead, soars with angelic wings above a steamboat and a roaring train. Below him, a Pony Express rider rears back on a white charger, brandishing an envelope like a trophy. A humble crowd in aprons and overalls consider the grandiose mural with mild bemusement.

67

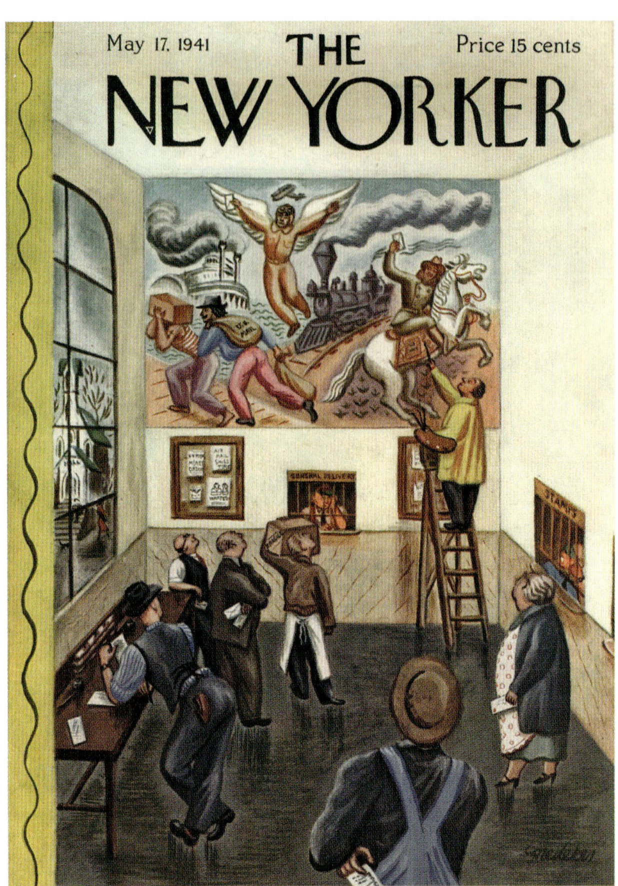

67 Virginia Snedeker,
New Yorker cover, 1941

Locals were not always happy about what they saw. Some viewed muralists as outsiders: urban, alien, and inattentive to local needs and interests. Citizens were alert for factual inaccuracies, communist propaganda, unflattering portrayals, and provocative or salacious content. Sometimes the objections were easily fixed: out-of-season crops, outdated plows or tractors, inaccurate historical costume, a liquor bottle in a dry state. In other cases, postmasters or civic leaders demanded wholesale changes or redesigns.

Such demands could also be forms of resistance. A post office mural in St. Joseph, Missouri, caricatured Black musicians singing and playing banjos on a levee. Black citizens organized a delegation to bring their objections to the local postmaster and wrote letters to the Section. Southern Cheyenne tribal members occupied public space outside the Watonga,

Oklahoma, post office over its mural's inaccurate portrayal of a Cheyenne Chief.

The Section preferred to advertise positive feedback. Its *Bulletin* reprinted letters from grateful postmasters and citizens expressing appreciation for a mural's decorative appeal or "civilizing" influence. On encountering a public mural, one letter-writer "felt that we were at last becoming a thoroughly civilized people." Another oft-quoted line came from a Texas postmaster: "How can we hope to make a finished citizen in an artless town?" (Marling 1982, 28)

Social Security

Cultural historian Michael Kammen defined nostalgia as "history without guilt," a phrase that might be the Section's epigraph. Section murals "make me feel very comfortable about America," Edward Bruce preened in a 1939 report to FDR: "There has been no sign of defeat or social unrest among them." (Hemingway 2002, 153) The able-bodied white pioneer in Section murals personified this spirit of guiltless conquest.

The central figure of *Child Labor*, a sad-eyed kid in a newsboy cap leaning on a pair of crutches, departs from the Section's ableist machismo. Viewers may have been reminded of polio-stricken FDR, reliant on steel braces, crutches, and a wheelchair for mobility. The boy was painted by Lithuania-born Ben Shahn as part of a mural cycle for the Social Security Administration in Washington DC. Scenes of child labor, old age, and unemployment give way on the opposite wall to panels celebrating public works and government assistance, reassuring

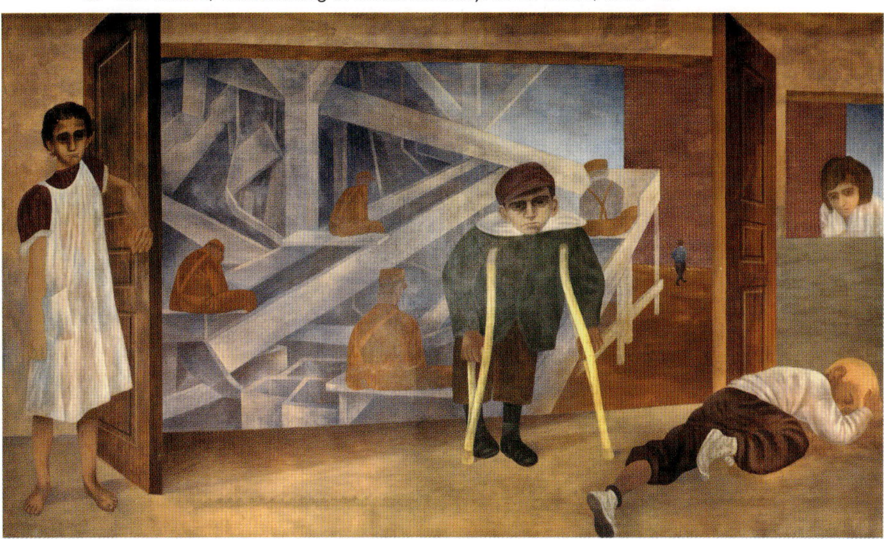

68 Ben Shahn, *The Meaning of Social Security: Child Labor*, 1940–42

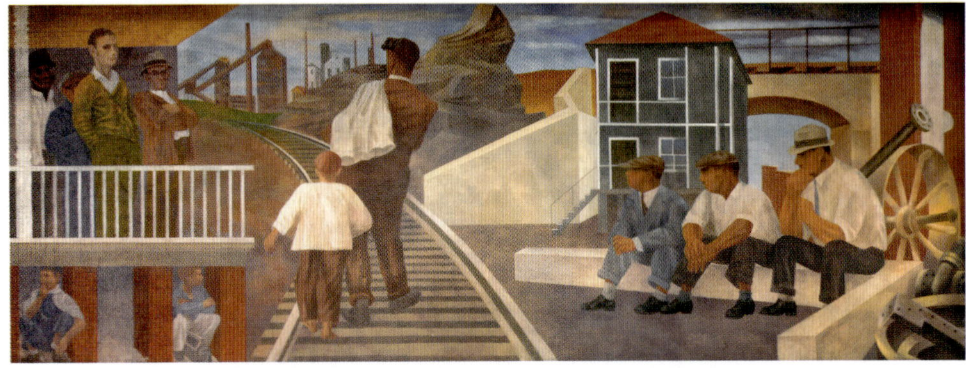

69 Ben Shahn, *The Meaning of Social Security: Unemployment*, 1940–42

audiences that the New Deal would relegate downbeat scenes such as *Child Labor* to history's proverbial dustbin.

But Shahn knew how precarious life in the US could be, especially for immigrants and the working class—his Jewish family arrived in 1906 after fleeing the crumbling Russian empire. At the time of the stock market crash the United States, alone among modern industrial nations, had no welfare program to insure against unemployment, old age, and infirmity. Several public figures stepped in to fill the void. Dr. Francis Townsend, a retired physician from California, amassed a sizable following for his Townsend Plan to provide a generous monthly stipend to citizens over sixty. Louisiana Senator Huey Long's populist Share Our Wealth campaign, which promised radical wealth redistribution through taxes on the rich, threatened Roosevelt's reelection chances until Long's assassination in September 1935.

Responding to these pressures, Roosevelt in 1935 signed into law the Social Security Act. The legislation funded benefits for retirees, the unemployed, and the disabled through payroll tax contributions. It was a compromise bill that established sixty-five as the retirement age at a time when over forty percent of the population would not live that long. The legislation did not cover farmworkers or domestic servants, leaving behind the predominantly Black and women workers in those jobs. Despite these compromises, the Social Security Act has endured as the most significant legislative achievement of the New Deal— considered today a "third rail" in politics, untouchable by either party.

As Roosevelt signed the Act into law, the unemployment rate hovered around twenty percent. In *Unemployment*, part of Shahn's Social Security cycle, a father and son walk down a receding set of tracks to an uncertain future, the father carrying their earthly possessions in a sack thrown over his shoulder. Three out-of-work men sit idly by on a curbstone in front of a vacant company house.

Roosevelt set up the Works Progress Administration to redress precisely this form of social insecurity. Artists would rank among those seeking work on the federal payroll. Through the WPA's Federal Art Project, thousands of artists, for the first and last time, would receive a living wage from the government for doing creative work. Poet Archibald MacLeish called it nothing short of a "cultural revolution in America."

Chapter 3
The Federal Art Project

When Alice Neel moved to New York's Greenwich Village
in the early 1930s she found evidence of the Depression all
around her. Long breadlines stretched around corners.
Evicted families shivered on sidewalks next to their piled-up
belongings. Hoovervilles multiplied in city parks and under
bridges. Neel, herself no stranger to hardship—by 1931 she
had lost her first child to diphtheria and survived two suicide
attempts and institutionalization—relied on free meals doled
out by sympathetic restaurant owners.

Before the New Deal, private charities stepped in to address
poverty. The Russell Sage Foundation, set up in 1907 to improve
living standards in poor neighborhoods, influenced social
policy by amassing research and data. Neel was unimpressed:
the Foundation "never gave a penny to the poor," she said,
"but they investigated the poor." Neel attended and then
painted such an investigation—or more of an inquisition.
A seated woman in a cloche hat and black dress, likely a
widow, hunches over and buries her hand in her hands. She
had been living with her seven children, Neel remembered,
under an overturned automobile. A semicircle of men in suits
and clerical collars sit in various shades of judgment, from
impassive to haughty. A red square sets the scene in a key of
wounded shame.

Artists on the government payroll, however grateful for
the lifeline thrown by the New Deal, came to know this scene
well and to identify with the woman under investigation. To
be eligible to work on the Federal Art Project (FAP) artists had
to prove they were really and truly destitute. An applicant
could have no assets or property—no savings, stocks or bonds,
insurance policies, real estate, or family money. They had to
disclose intimate details of their personal and financial lives

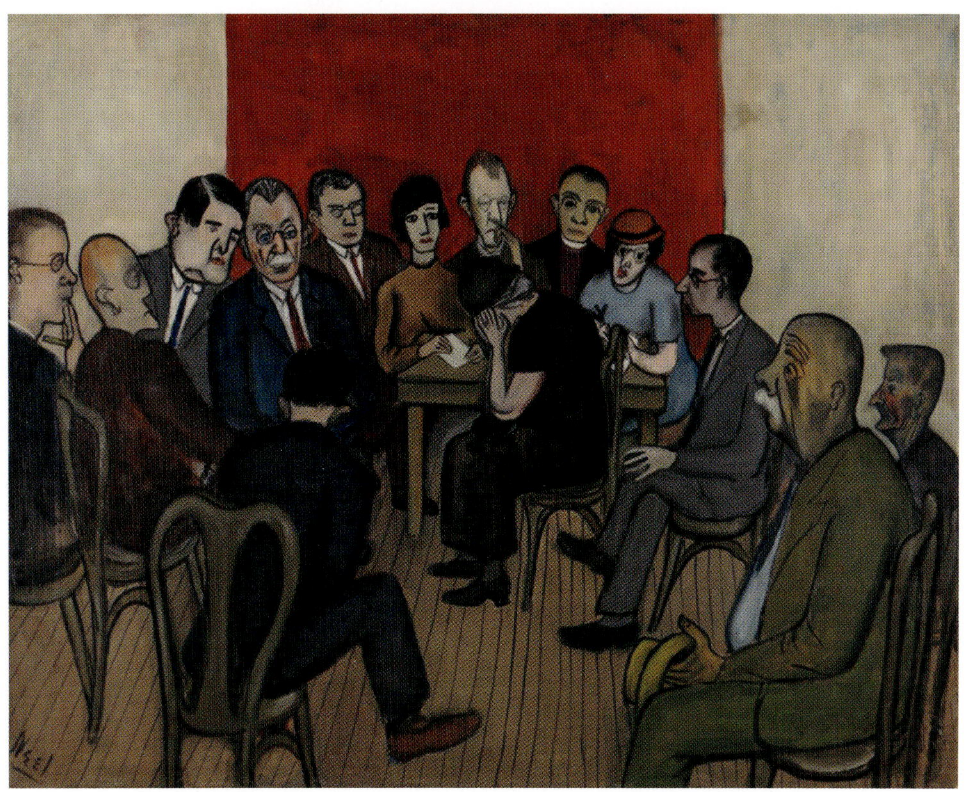

70 Alice Neel, *Investigation of Poverty at the Russell Sage Foundation*, 1933

and could expect home visits from social workers to confirm empty cupboards and iceboxes. The social stigma was real. For Ben Shahn, the FAP had an "aura of poverty about it," and Anton Refregier admitted that "we were all very conscious of the fact that we were part of millions of unemployed." (Greenfield 1998, 112)

Neel, among the first artists to join the government programs and the last to be dropped from the rolls, said simply, "I don't know how I would have eaten without [the WPA's] support." The Federal Art Project kept unemployed artists from starving—this is the essential fact. But Neel also called it "a great creative venture," acknowledging that the FAP went far beyond the mandate to put hungry artists to work. (Hoban 2010, 106)

The Federal Art Project transformed the artist's role in society. The very desperation that qualified artists for government aid also roused their sense of solidarity with the poor, fellow laborers, and each other. The stereotype of the artist as a dissolute bohemian, eccentric genius, or social malcontent gave way to a new concept: the artist as worker. Answering to taxpayers, they saw their art less as personal expression than public service, akin to bricklaying or road paving—a benefit to the whole community, not a narrow slice of wealthy patrons. Art by the people, for the people: cultural democracy in action.

Work Relief

The Depression had slogged on nearly six years when Congress passed the Emergency Relief Appropriation Act in 1935, the largest ever in peacetime. With these funds, Roosevelt established the Works Progress Administration (WPA) under the leadership of his friend and confidante, the tireless New Deal crusader Harry Hopkins.

The WPA's goal was to employ as many people as possible as quickly as possible in jobs reasonably aligned with their skills and training. Although it would have been cheaper to just send checks to the unemployed (less administrative oversight, for one thing), Roosevelt and Hopkins considered the cost of work relief, as opposed to direct relief or the "dole," justified. "First, in the saving of morale," Hopkins explained. "Second, in the preservation of human skills and talents. Third, in the material enrichment which the unemployed add to our national wealth through their labors." (Hopkins 1936, 1)

The WPA put people (mostly men, as the WPA only allowed one "breadwinner" on the government payroll per household) to work on the "material enrichment" of the country. They built schools, hospitals, bridges, airports, libraries, and community centers. They paved roads, laid sewer lines, cleared land, and planted trees. They shoveled snow, as in Charles Turzak's nocturnal scene of relief workers battling a Chicago blizzard. It may depict the winter of 1936 when northern Illinois endured historically heavy snowfall; schools and businesses closed, dairy farmers delivered milk by sleigh, and 2,500 WPA workers were called out to clear roads. The heroic central figure stands in classical contrapposto, braced against the swirling drifts. Come rain, sleet, or snow, the WPA worker would endure in their appointed task.

Treasury Relief Art Project

Before proceeding to the Federal Art Project, it is worth considering a short-lived program also funded by the WPA: the Treasury Relief Art Project (TRAP). In 1935 Edward Bruce, head of the Section of Fine Arts, applied for WPA funds and received

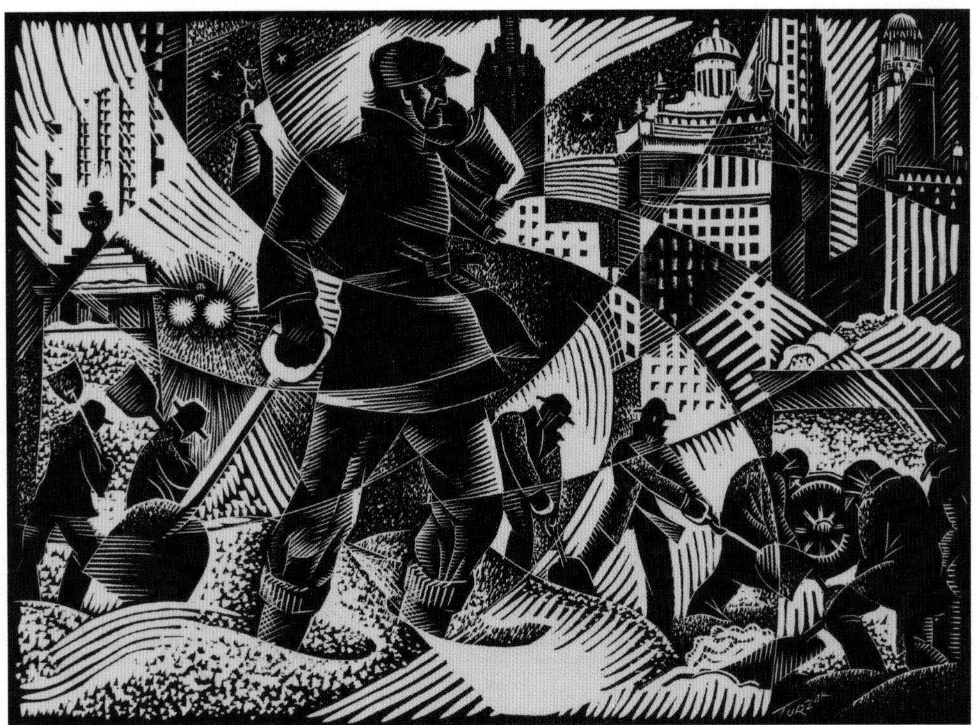

71 Charles Turzak, *Work Relief (Chicago Snowstorm)*, 1935–42

over half a million dollars to set up TRAP in the Treasury Department. TRAP operated from 1935 to 1938 under the directorship of Bruce's trusted lieutenant Olin Dows.

A comparison between TRAP and FAP is instructive. Both programs, drawing on WPA funds, were meant to give jobs to the unemployed. TRAP, however, operated more along the lines of the Section, prioritizing "quality" artists to make artwork for existing federal buildings. *Time* magazine called TRAP the "Ritz" of the programs—as such, it entered an unofficial competition with FAP (and awkwardly shared office space in New York) in securing talented artists.

One of those talented artists was Mark Rothko, famed postwar for his large, luminous bands of abstract color. In 1935 he was still Markus Rothkowitz, born in a shtetl to a Latvian Jewish family that had escaped czarist Russia's collapsing empire. Raised in Portland, Oregon, he earned a scholarship to Yale University but dropped out to try his luck in New York.

On the government programs, Rothko explored the theme of the New York subway in a suite of cryptic paintings.

72

Commuters crowd on a double-sided bench as if stranded in a netherworld. A sinister black-clad figure in a bowler hat and cane is sliced lengthwise by a column. Train tracks recede into a dark tunnel like a ladder plunging into an even deeper unconscious, evoking the fashionable writings of Sigmund Freud and Carl Jung. Rothko, who admitted to never feeling at home in his adopted country (and would die by his own hand in 1970), turned the subway platform into an alienated in-between space—subterranean and slightly menacing.

TRAP artists produced 90 murals, 65 sculptures, and over 10,000 paintings and prints meant for display in federal buildings. Reginald Marsh supervised a mural scheme for the domed rotunda of the US Custom House in Bowling Green, New York. Sisters Marion and Grace Greenwood, who had painted murals in Mexico under the aegis of Diego Rivera, collaborated on a mural for an affordable housing project in Camden, New Jersey. TRAP artworks made their way as far afield as a leprosarium in Carville, Louisiana, the country's only facility focused on treating leprosy, or Hansen's disease.

Yet in prioritizing "quality," TRAP filled only 356 spots out of its 450 quota. Struggling artists found this snobbery unconscionable in the depths of the Depression. In the meantime, the job of putting large numbers of unemployed artists to work fell to the Federal Art Project.

72 Mark Rothko, *Untitled (The Subway)*, 1937

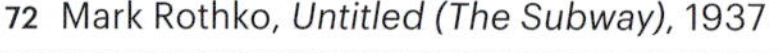

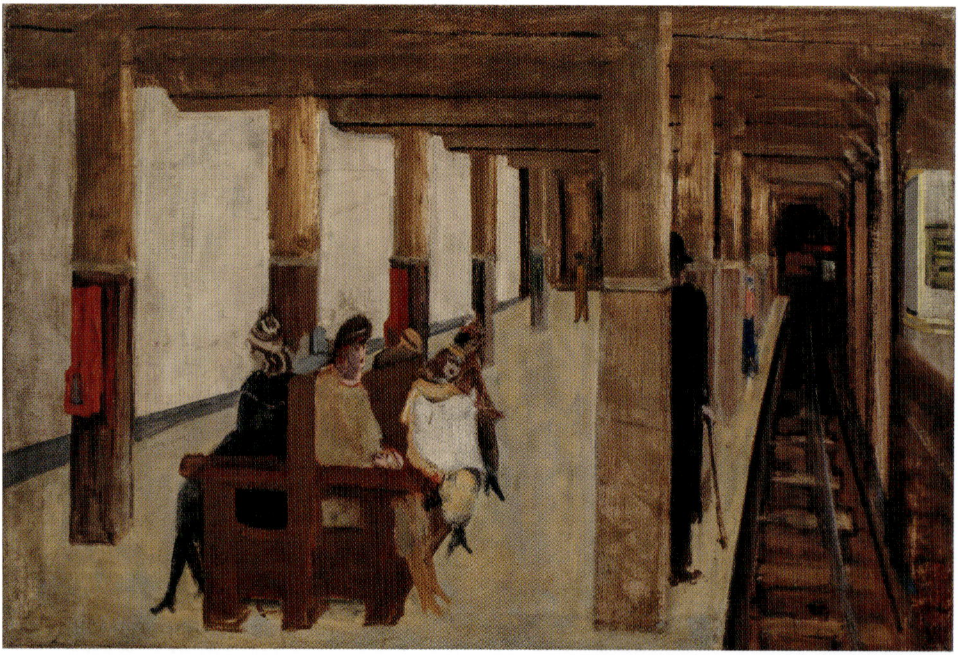

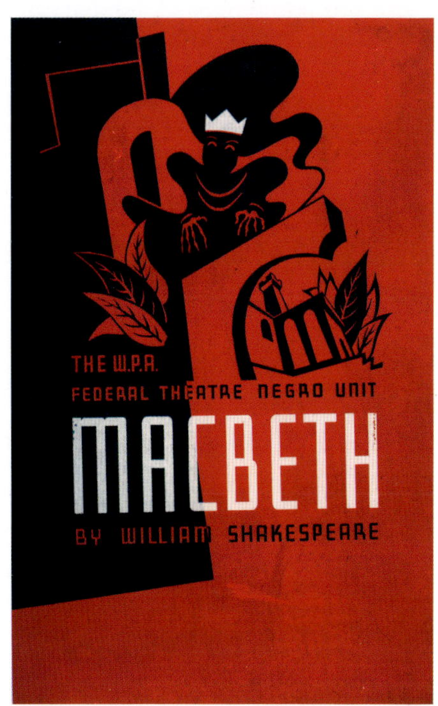

73 Anthony Velonis, poster
for *Macbeth, c.* 1936

Federal Art Project

The FAP began operating in October 1935 as part of the cultural arm of the WPA, along with the Theatre, Music, and Writers' Projects. These projects (later to include the Historical Records Survey) made up Federal Project Number One, or Federal One— the first and last time the US government subsidized culture on such a massive scale.

Support for artists was not a foregone conclusion. While few questioned the value of paying people to build roads, schools, and hospitals, what about making paintings or sculptures? When criticized for giving jobs to artists, WPA chief Harry Hopkins famously barked, "Hell, they've got to eat just like other people!" It wasn't a resounding endorsement.

Proving Federal One's worth fell to its administrators, headquartered in Washington DC, and the creative workers under their charge. The Writers' Project payroll included Saul Bellow, John Cheever, Ralph Ellison, Zora Neale Hurston, and Richard Wright. Hallie Flanagan directed the Theatre Project, which nurtured young talents like John Huston, Burt Lancaster, Arthur Miller, and wunderkind Orson Welles, who at age twenty directed a landmark adaptation of *Macbeth* set in Haiti and

73

starring an all-Black cast. The Music Project put on 225,000 performances for an audience of tens of millions, showcasing a range from classical composers like Bach and Beethoven to emerging talents like Florence Price and William Grant Still.

Harry Hopkins tapped Holger Cahill (1887–1960), a writer and curator with expertise in American folk art, to head the Federal Art Project. It was a canny choice. Cahill's background, which could not have been further from that of well-heeled Section chief Edward Bruce, sensitized him to cultural deprivation. Born Sveinn Kristján Bjarnason, the son of Icelandic immigrants, Cahill grew up in frostbitten North Dakota, traveled the world in his teens working odd jobs, and by his early twenties fell in with Greenwich Village artists and bohemians. He changed his name to Edgar Holger Cahill (friends called him "Eddie") and studied journalism and creative writing without taking a degree. He retained a folksy appeal; a journalist described his appearance—ruddy complexion, bristly mustache, and twinkling blue eyes—as that of a "healthy and jovial apple merchant." (Platt 1999, 180)

Two formative influences shaped Cahill's worldview. First, progressive educator and pragmatist philosopher John Dewey (1852–1952), who believed that art should be a vital part of lived experience, not cloistered in elitist galleries and museums. Second, his boss from 1922 to 1929 at the Newark Museum, John Cotton Dana (1856–1929), who introduced innovations such as expanded hours, reduced admission prices, and evening classes to improve accessibility. (Dana titled an article, "The Gloom of the Museum with Suggestions for Removing It.") Cahill's guiding principle, molded by Dewey and Dana, was to close the gap between art and life.

Closing that gap began with hiring artists. Lots of artists. Cahill never tired of repeating the mantra that the Federal Art Project's primary concern "was with the artist—not with art as such." In other words, the Project existed to provide jobs to the largest possible number of artists who needed them—ten thousand or so, ultimately. In the rush to fill quotas, many artists hired possessed little training or talent. Cahill considered this an acceptable price. Project art "wasn't always great quality," he admitted. "It wasn't always even good quality….But Congress didn't appropriate money for that. It appropriated money to preserve the skills of the unemployed." (McKinzie 1973, 94)

With this mandate in mind, the FAP swelled into a much more unwieldy, decentralized operation than Edward Bruce's Section of Fine Arts. Cahill hired state directors—typically artists, gallerists, or museum professionals—to administer

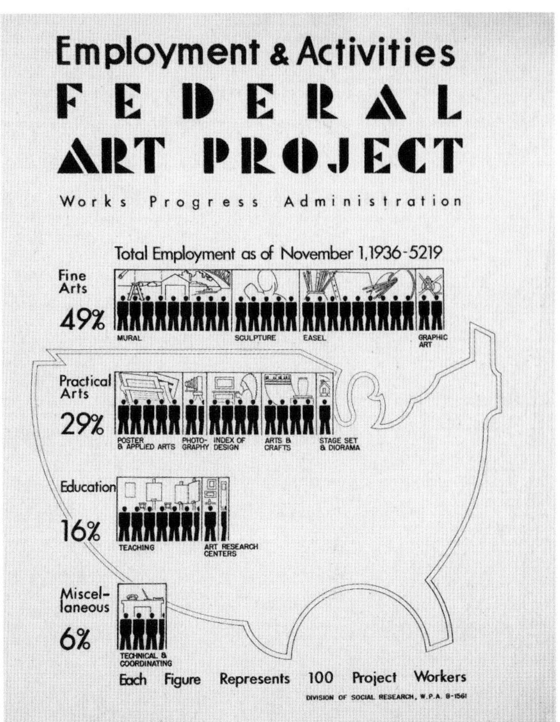

74 Federal
Art Project,
Employment &
Activities, 1936

the Project regionally. They classified artists on a scale
from A "professional" to D "unskilled" and assigned them
to separate divisions for murals, easel painting, sculpture,
prints, photography, posters, and applied arts.

In addition to artists, the FAP staffed clerical workers,
carpenters, models, teachers, and curators. An Exhibition
Division organized traveling shows and a Gallery Guide
department organized museum tours. The Index of American
Design cataloged the country's history of folk art. Community Art
Centers sprang up nationwide to offer art classes, lectures, and
exhibitions to rural and underserved communities (see Chapter 6).

Funding marked another significant difference between the
Section and the FAP. The Section had stable funding through
construction costs allocated for new federal buildings, whereas
the FAP relied on annual appropriations from Congress. This
meant that FAP administrators constantly had to justify the
program's existence to skeptical taxpayers and tightfisted
politicians. If they failed to prove the FAP's social benefits,
their funding would be cut or eliminated.

What did it look like for art to be socially beneficial?

Murals presented high-profile opportunities to prove art's social utility. The Federal Art Project ultimately oversaw the design and execution of some 2,500 murals for tax-supported nonfederal buildings such as schools, hospitals, libraries, airports, and prisons. (Federal buildings were the Section's purview.) While the Section's post office murals boosted local industries, FAP murals often had a specific role to play based on the character of the co-sponsoring institution. Murals in prisons might model social reentry; in hospitals, means of mollifying stress or anxiety; in schools, the orthodox interpretation of history.

75　　Lucienne Bloch (1909–99) painted *Cycle of a Woman's Life: Childhood* for the twelfth-floor recreation room of the Women's House of Detention in Greenwich Village. Built in 1932, the Women's House was held up as a model prison emphasizing reform rather than punishment—the mural joined other amenities such as a rooftop garden, basketball court, and library. During the planning stages, Bloch consulted staff psychiatrists and inmates; their feedback informed her utopian image of the life awaiting inmates beyond the prison walls.

Children in a public park play catch, build sandcastles, and take turns on a slide. Greenwich Village details garnish the scene: the flower vendor at his pushcart in the lower left, a kitten named Coconita perched on a windowsill. Two children share an apple, as if redeeming humanity's fall in the Garden of Eden. (Bloch recalled that women in the prison "adopted" various children in the mural and gave them names.) The racially integrated scene was itself aspirational in a recreation room designated for Black inmates. In a reflection titled "Murals for Use," Bloch expressed hope that the mural's "bright colors and bold curves" would help relieve the prison's monotony and ultimately "act as a healthy tonic." (Bloch 1973, 77)

Could surrealism, steeped in private dreams and fantasies, act as a healthy tonic? Walter Quirt's *The Growth of Medicine from Primitive Times,* installed in the lecture room of New York's Bellevue Hospital, tested the question. It was an exception among the dozen or so murals commissioned for the hospital's new psychiatric wing. (Where conditions could be challenging: "So many people, so much drama," one muralist recalled. "Life, death. Crying, screaming and also laughing.") Artists designed murals to speed patient recovery through tranquil scenes of woodworking, ceramics, and basket weaving—visual equivalents, as Jackson Davidow has shown, to occupational therapy. (2018, 85–88)

76　　By contrast, the study for Quirt's mural shows a Dalí-esque dreamscape of classical statuary and colonnades crowded with cavemen, Hippocrates, plague doctors, chemist Louis Pasteur,

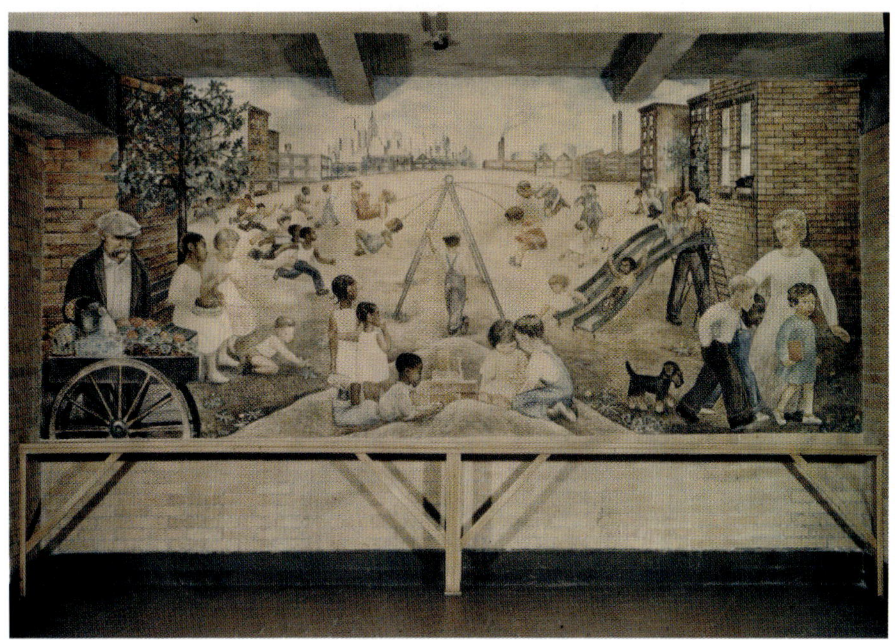

75 Lucienne Bloch, *Cycle of a Woman's Life: Childhood*, 1935

neurologist Ivan Pavlov, and Sigmund Freud. Quirt underwent psychoanalysis between 1935 and 1938 and came to the Jungian conclusion that "dreams and symbols are common to all even though individually we may hold opposing political or social views." (In 1936, Bellevue psychiatrists experimented with group psychoanalysis to accommodate patients otherwise unable to afford individual therapy—like the FAP, a means of broadening access to an elite resource.) By learning "to release his own fantasies," as Quirt put it, an artist might make the unconscious accessible to doctors for improved treatments toward collective wellbeing: A socially useful application of surrealism. (Quirt 1973, 81)

The Harlem Hospital Center, over a hundred blocks north of Bellevue, co-sponsored the first major government commission awarded to African American artists. It did not come easily. Despite the location in a predominantly Black neighborhood, the hospital's white superintendent objected to the mural program's emphasis on Black history and culture. Protests from organized artists forced the hospital to let the murals go forward as designed (see Chapter 6).

Charles Alston (1907–77), the first Black supervisor on a New Deal mural project, painted a diptych linking African healing

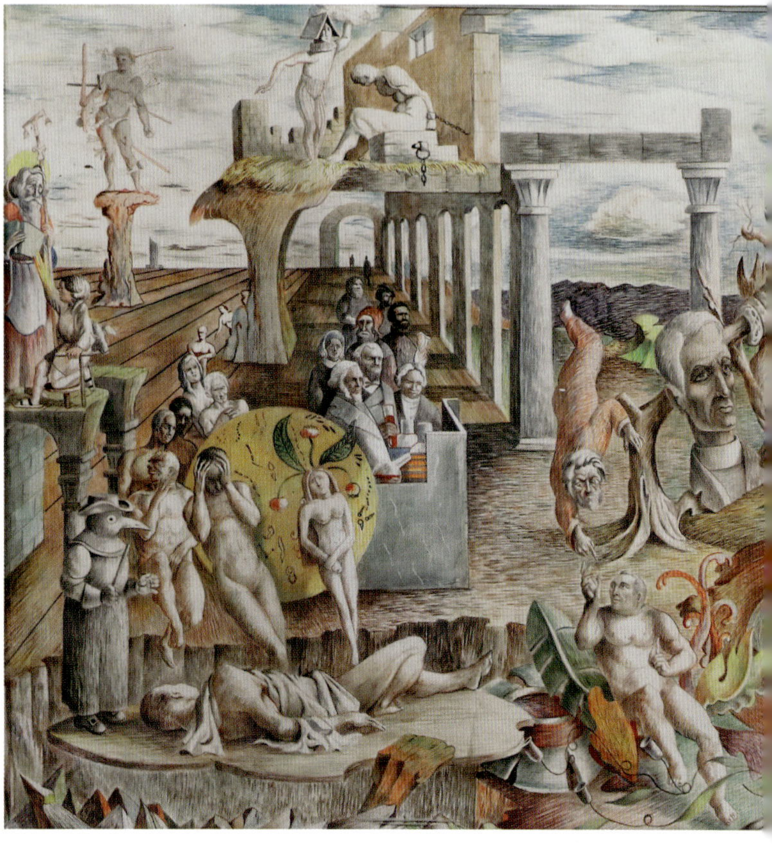

practices and modern medicine. Twenty-five-year-old Vertis Hayes (1911–2000) painted *The Pursuit of Happiness*, an eight-panel diasporic sweep from an African village to the modern metropolis. The youngest artist hired, Georgette Seabrooke (1916–2011), was not yet twenty when she painted *Recreation in Harlem*, keyed to its placement in a nurse's recreation room, a frieze of wholesome neighborhood vignettes: children study, a couple dance, the mail arrives, and women chat at a brownstone window.

Eitaro Ishigaki's mural for the nearby Harlem Courthouse, *Emancipation of Negro Slaves*, honored Civil War-era freedom fighters. John Brown, executed in 1859 for leading an abortive uprising against slavery, grips an anachronistic pump-action shotgun and stands shoulder-to-shoulder with Abraham Lincoln and abolitionist Frederick Douglass. They mass behind a shirtless Black man pressing forward with arm raised, shackles broken. The mural backed radical revisions of American

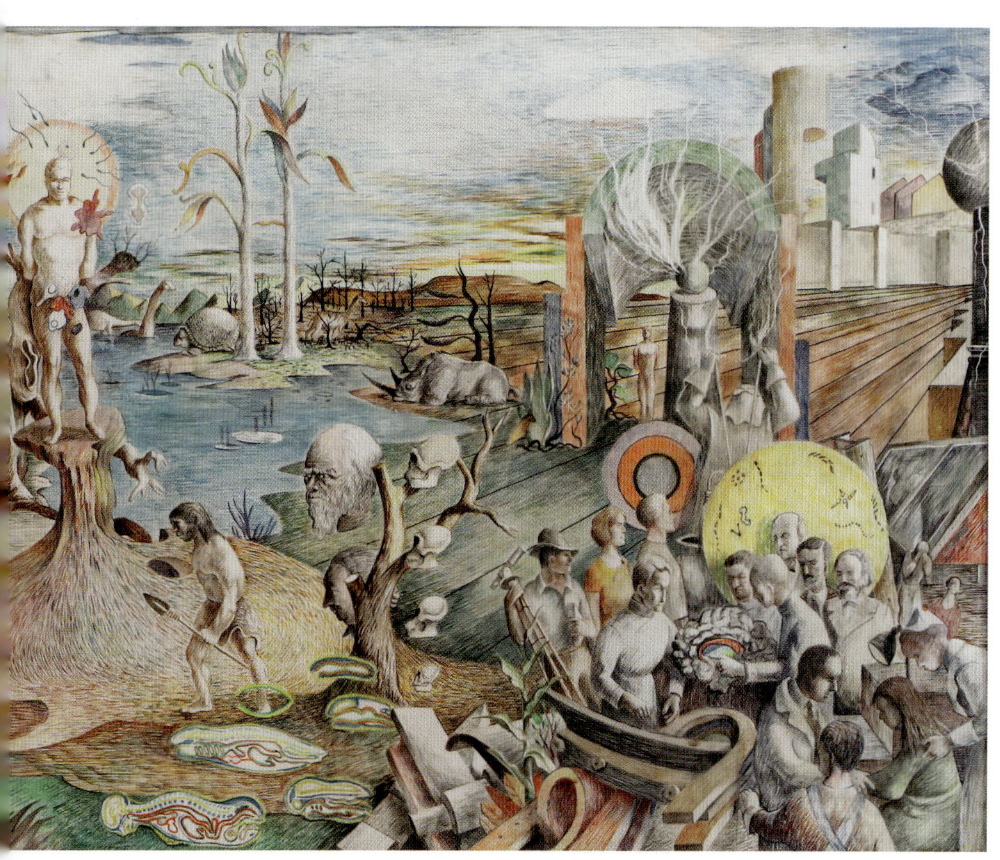

history: Marxist author Michael Gold enlisted Brown as a proto-revolutionary in his 1936 Federal Theatre Project play, *Battle Hymn*, and two years later Trinidadian scholar CLR James's *A History of Negro Revolt* placed enslaved Black people at the center of freedom struggles.

In 1938 a mayor-appointed arts committee deemed Ishigaki's murals offensive and ordered them removed. "They slander the murals because a Japanese artist painted these scenes of early American history," Ishigaki told Communist newspaper *Daily Worker*. "How can an alien understand the American struggle? they ask." (Wang 2017, 66–67) Of course, that was exactly his point: an "alien" could better understand the American struggle *as* struggle (a theme of Ishigaki's painting *The Bonus March*). Emancipation is something fought for, not bestowed—a resonant, if to some unacceptably provocative, message in a courthouse setting.

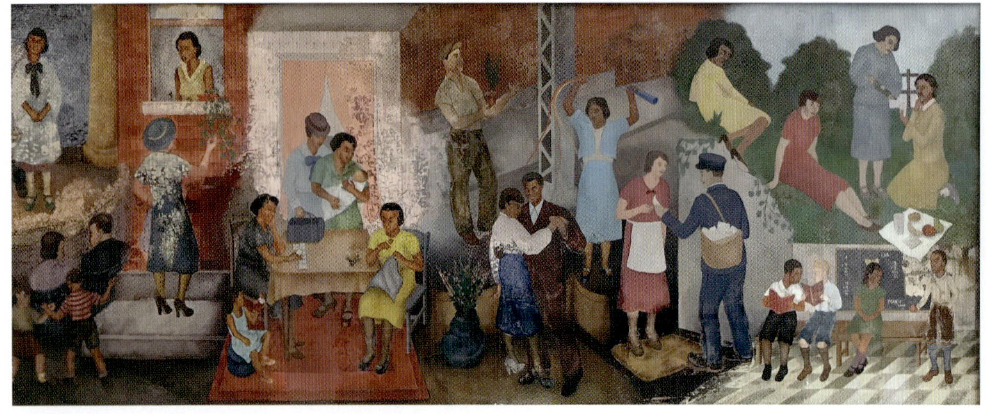

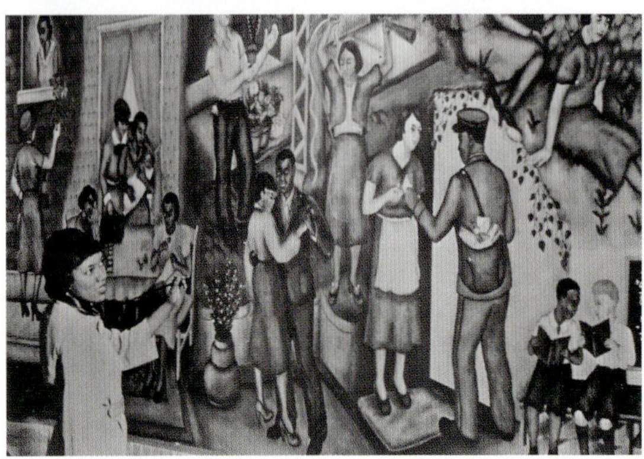

77 ABOVE Georgette Seabrooke, *Recreation in Harlem*, 1936
78 LEFT Georgette Seabrooke working on *Recreation in Harlem*, 1936

John Brown appears in another FAP mural that ran afoul of institutional censors. Charles White, in his early twenties, partially executed a two-part mural that would have connected the history of slavery in the South—with John Brown clutching a musket, a lynched figure hanging from a tree, a white overseer lording over a slumped man in shackles—to the current oppression of Black Americans in the North.

White knew that oppression firsthand. He was raised by a single mother on Chicago's South Side, where he was taught little about African American history in school. His mural, planned for a library in the predominantly Black neighborhood where he grew up, treated history as a "Struggle for Liberation" in the writhing, jampacked style of Mexican muralism. Part of that struggle was self-education: growing up, White spent countless hours in public libraries while his mom worked as a domestic. The white director of the city's library system deemed the mural "unfit" for a public space, and it was never installed.

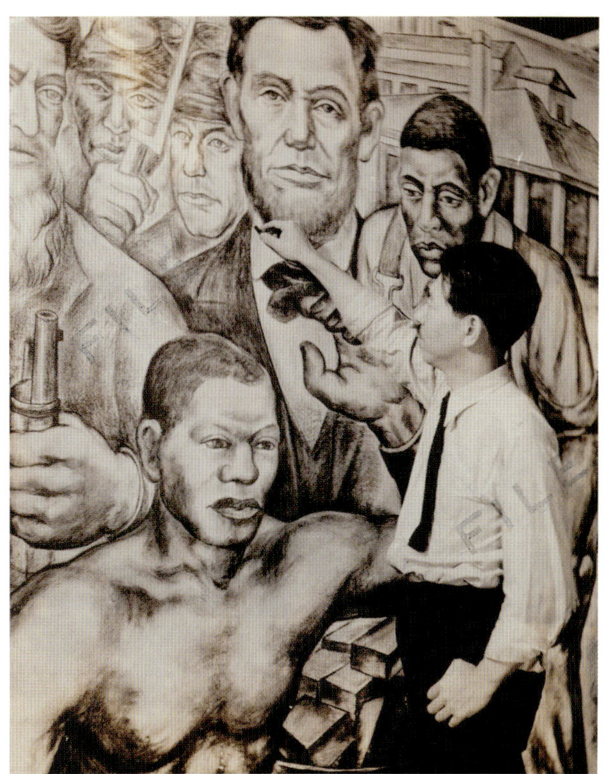

79 RIGHT Eitaro Ishigaki working on *Emancipation of Negro Slaves*, c. 1936

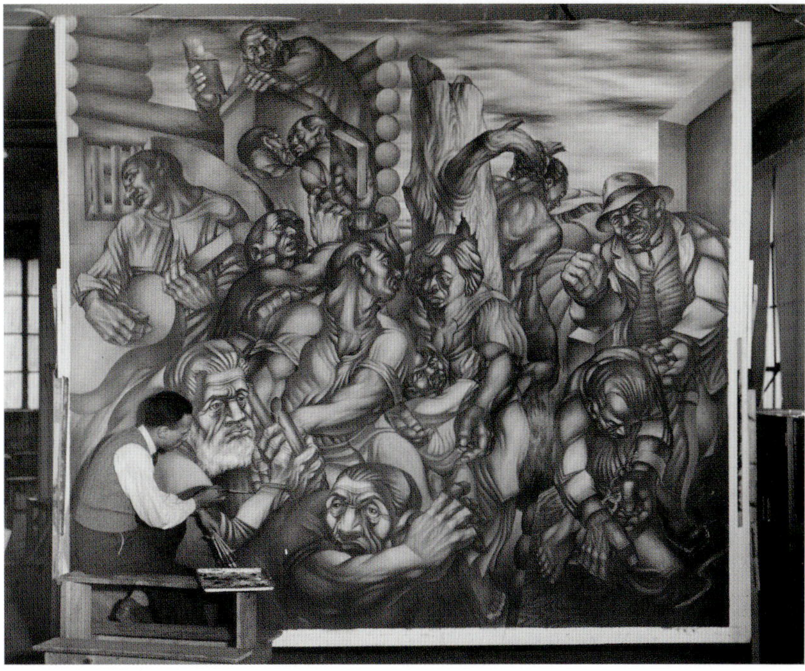

80 BELOW Charles White working on *Struggle for Liberation*, c. 1940

Murals and Modernism

Other forms of censorship were less overt. Project administrators generally frowned on modernism, for example, as derivative of European sources and potentially confusing to average viewers. In New York, however, a certain latitude allowed for notable exceptions. Arshile Gorky's series of ten oil-on-canvas panels for New Jersey's Newark Airport explored *Aviation: Evolution of Forms Under Aerodynamic Limitations*. The portentous title and abstracted forms—topographical maps and an airplane's mechanical parts, control panels, and instruments—signaled a modern style for modern air travel. Not all were convinced. On seeing the panels, New York City mayor Fiorello La Guardia is supposed to have exclaimed, "If this is art, then I'm a horse's ass."

La Guardia missed the deeper seriousness of Gorky's experiments. At age fifteen Gorky fled to the US from Armenia, where genocide claimed the life of his mother—she died starving in his arms. Photographer Alexander Alland (1902–89) survived a similar trauma; born in Crimea, he arrived at Ellis Island in 1923, in flight from the Russian pogroms that took the lives of his mother and brother. Both artists, having escaped terror, came to believe that art should transcend the past by keeping pace with the speed and dynamism of modern life— the "miraculous new vision of our time," as Gorky put it.

81 Arshile Gorky, *Aerial Map* (from *Aviation: Evolution of Forms Under Aerodynamic Limitations*), 1935–37

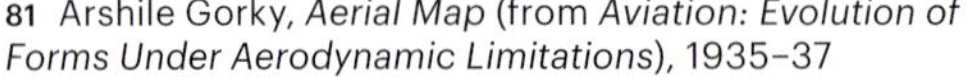

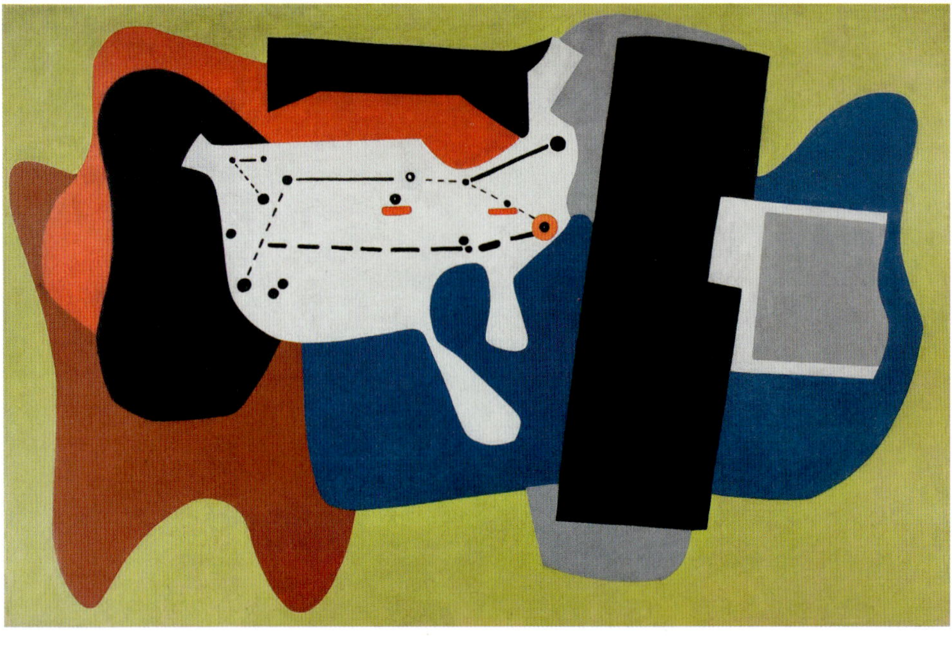

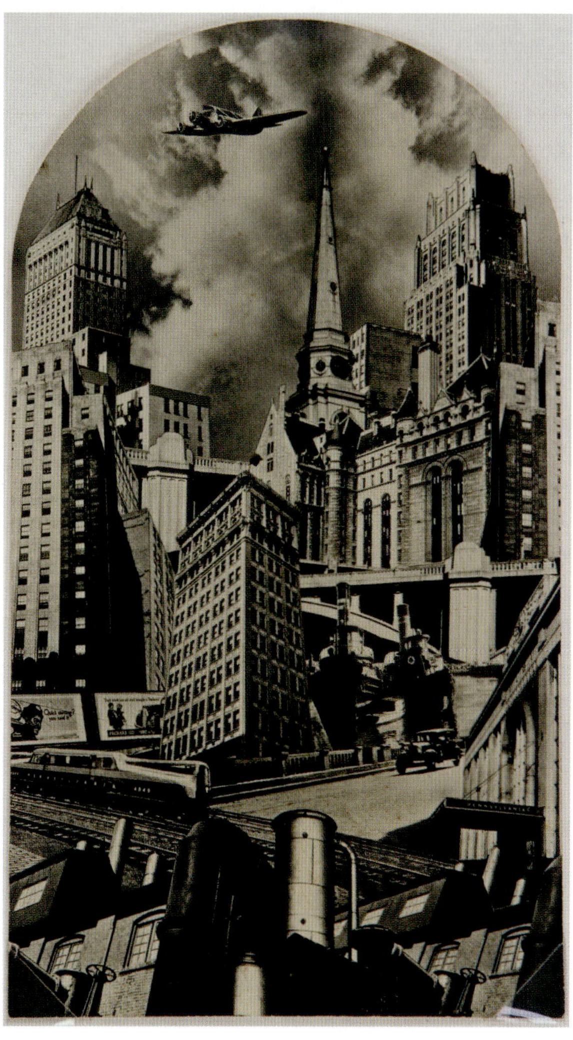

82   Alland's three-panel photomural for the Newark Public
Library drew on his early exposure to Russian montage. In the
central panel a trimotor aircraft soars above a jumbled pile-up
of billboards, water towers, rushing trains and automobiles,
and architectural landmarks. The elements collide like tectonic
plates, forcing upwards a new skyline. Photomurals—prints
enlarged from negatives and fixed to a canvas backing—were a
modern form par excellence. Cheaper and quicker than fresco
or oil-on-canvas, they could also be more readily switched out
and updated as prevailing tastes changed.

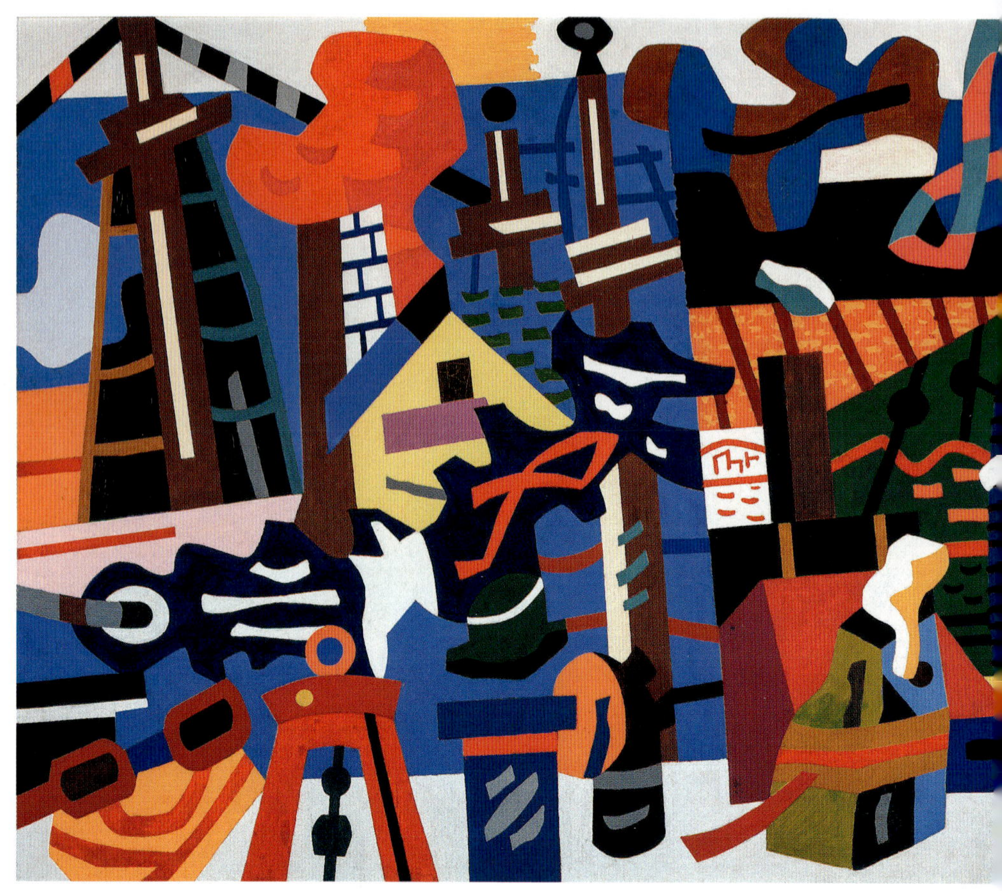

New York mural supervisor Burgoyne Diller, himself an abstract artist, persuaded the New York Housing Authority to hire a group of twelve modernists—among them Ilya Bolotowsky, Balcomb Greene, and Lee Krasner—for a mural program at the Williamsburg Housing Project, an affordable complex for low-income (whites only) tenants in ethnically diverse Brooklyn. "The decision to place abstract murals in these rooms," Diller wrote, "was made because these areas were intended to provide a place of relaxation and entertainment for the tenants." (Diller 1973, 69)

Stuart Davis (1892–1964) did not subscribe to the idea that abstract art appealed for its soothing decorative qualities. A tireless organizer and activist (he would play critical roles in the Artists' Union and the American Artists' Congress—see Chapters 7 and 9), Davis believed in abstract art as a progressive

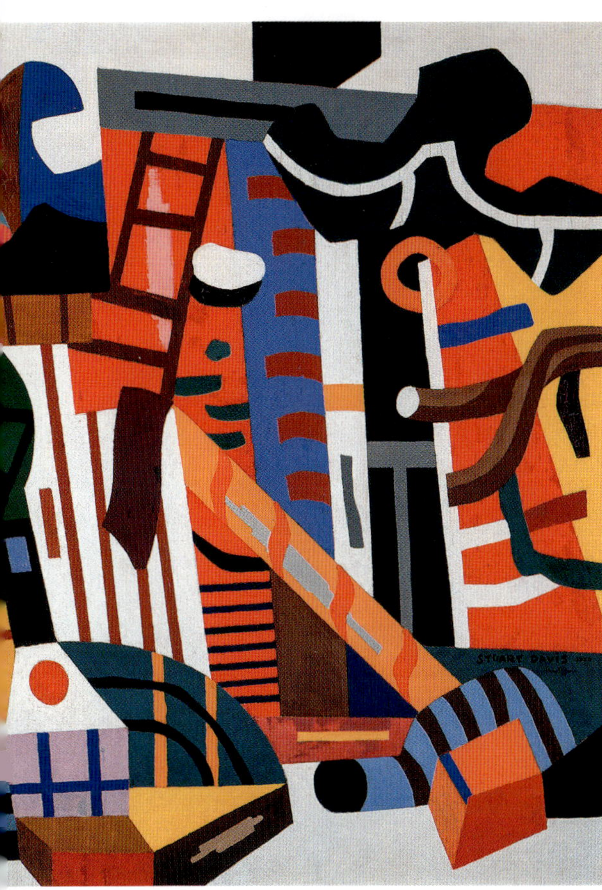

83 Stuart Davis, *Swing Landscape, 1937–38*

social force. He took inspiration from French modernist Fernand Léger (whom Davis unsuccessfully tried to get hired onto the FAP) in arguing for a "new realism" in art that paralleled rapid innovations in science and technology.

83   Davis's eye-popping *Swing Landscape* fused European modernism with the jazzy dynamism of American popular culture. The painting "swings" with its kaleidoscopic scrollwork and syncopated high-key colors, tuned to the hot jazz craze sweeping the country. The harbor iconography of boats and buoys, masts and rope ladders, suited Williamsburg's proximity to waterfront industries. The electrifying rhythms, unfixed from illusionistic realism, opened the visual world to a "new attitude" of chance and change, shock and sensation. Although *Swing Landscape* was never installed, it forecast the direction of abstract painting in the decades to come.

Easel Division

A contributor to *Art Front,* the journal of the Artists' Union, sardonically remarked in May 1937 that someone "had to be arrested, become seriously ill, or go insane to find there was a Federal Art Project" since the program's public art could be found almost exclusively in courthouses, prisons, and hospitals. To combat this perception, the project's Exhibition Division circulated traveling shows to museums, universities, community art centers, and department stores nationwide. The FAP also set up Federal Art Galleries in Boston, Chicago, New York, and Philadelphia, among other cities, to promote the Project's output.

The first high-profile showcase of the FAP's efforts, *New Horizons in American Art,* opened in mid-September 1936 at the Museum of Modern Art (MoMA) in New York. The museum devoted three-and-a-half floors to the first "visual report" of the FAP, an eye-straining display of over four hundred paintings, prints, and sculptures. *New Horizons* was meant to flex the "strength and vitality" of American art, in FAP director Holger Cahill's words, represented by works such as Charles Alston's studies for the Harlem Hospital, a photograph of Lucienne Bloch's *Childhood* panel, and studies for the Williamsburg Housing Project.

It was a homecoming for Cahill, who had served as interim MoMA director in 1932–33. His opening address, reprinted in the accompanying catalogue, amounted to a Project manifesto. He cited precedents for the FAP in the remote past—the ancient civilizations of Egypt, Rome, and China—as well as parallels in the global present—the culture ministries of France, Sweden, and Mexico. The FAP fulfilled the broader government goal of conserving natural resources: Trade skills, like old-growth forests, needed to be protected from the threat of extinction. At the same time, the Project nurtured young talent through training and exhibition opportunities. In MoMA, the temple of high modernism, Cahill provocatively argued that the FAP had rescued American artists from the "theoretical mazes" of modern art by reconnecting them with mainstream American life.

Easel painters, prominently featured in *New Horizons,* made up the majority of creative workers on the FAP. They earned about a hundred dollars a month in return for submitting a painting every four to six weeks, depending on size. Although wages were low, the demands were few (most supervisors were themselves artists), and artists benefited from materials, models, camaraderie, a measure of creative freedom, and a regular paycheck. (A "prudent couple could survive handily," one painter recalled, "if they ate with caution and watered down the gin.")

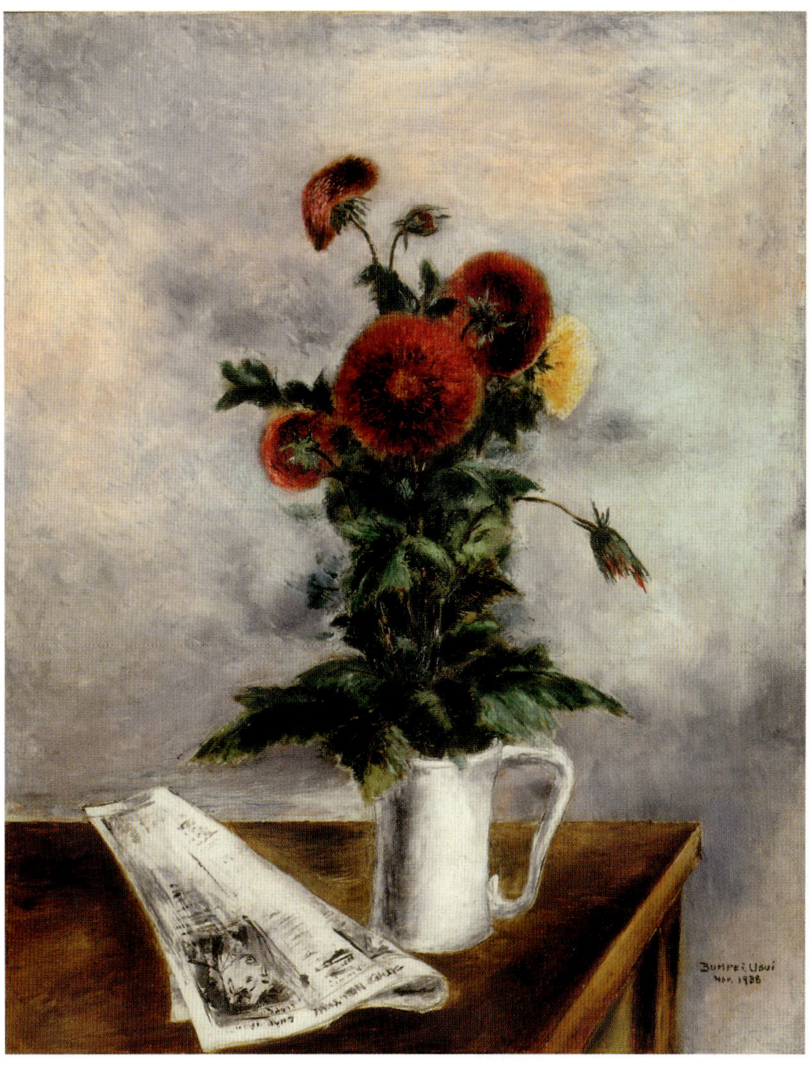

Artists delivered finished canvases to FAP headquarters, an
occasion to socialize and scout what other painters had been
doing. The paintings would, in turn, go on view in exhibitions or
to an institution that received full or partial government support.

84

The prohibition on nudity and overt politics remained,
so artists leaned on dependable genres such as still life and
landscape. Bumpei Usui's (1898–1994) *Dahlias*, with its feathery
brushwork and dappled color, traveled from New York to
San Francisco in FAP exhibitions as an exemplary still life.

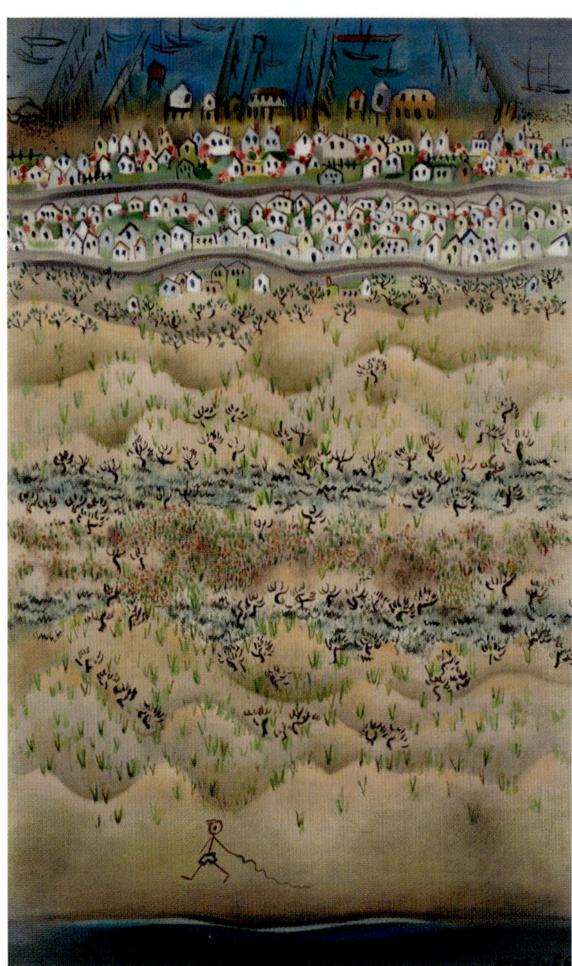

85 Loren MacIver,
Dune Landscape,
c. 1936

(One critic commended the "vitality with which old topics are newly endowed" in Usui's flower paintings.) Born in Japan, Usui emigrated to the US in 1921 where he soon became a sought-after picture framer while gaining recognition for his own paintings. In *Dahlias* the outside world, in the form of a folded newspaper, subtly intrudes in the otherwise timeless tableau.

Half the paintings reproduced in the *New Horizons* catalogue were landscapes, but they weren't all boilerplate American scenes. Loren MacIver's (1909–98) wiry, childlike *Dune Landscape,* for example, recalled Swiss modernist Paul Klee. A stick figure in swim trunks strolls along a Cape Cod shoreline trailing string. The middle ground of dune grass and scribbled seaweed rises in

stacked perspective to jostling beach houses and docks beyond.
MacIver and her poet husband counted among their friends
the writers Elizabeth Bishop, E.E. Cummings, and Marianne
Moore. The luminous dunescape, flattened like a sheet of paper
inscribed with stenographic shorthand, flickers between writing
and representation—a "sensitive, personalized expression," as
Cahill put it.

The relative freedom afforded Project artists could be
paralyzing. The WPA-era artworks of Jackson Pollock, still in
his twenties when he joined the FAP (and so poor he couldn't
afford to travel to his father's funeral), betray a certain restless
eclecticism. He struggled with the requirement, eventually
dropped, to punch a time clock at the beginning and end of
each working day. (A fellow artist remembered the late-sleeping
Pollock racing to Project headquarters in his pajamas.) Pollock
missed his monthly quotas, some of the paintings he turned
in were rejected, and he soon found himself despairing. "I'm
in a bog," he confessed to his Project supervisor. "I can't do
anything." (Solomon 1987, 83)

Cotton Pickers is one of Pollock's few surviving WPA-era
paintings. The style and subject are hand-me-downs from
Pollock's mentor, the Regionalist Thomas Hart Benton.
Sharecroppers harvest cotton by hand, wearing large hats

86 Jackson Pollock, *Cotton Pickers*, c. 1935

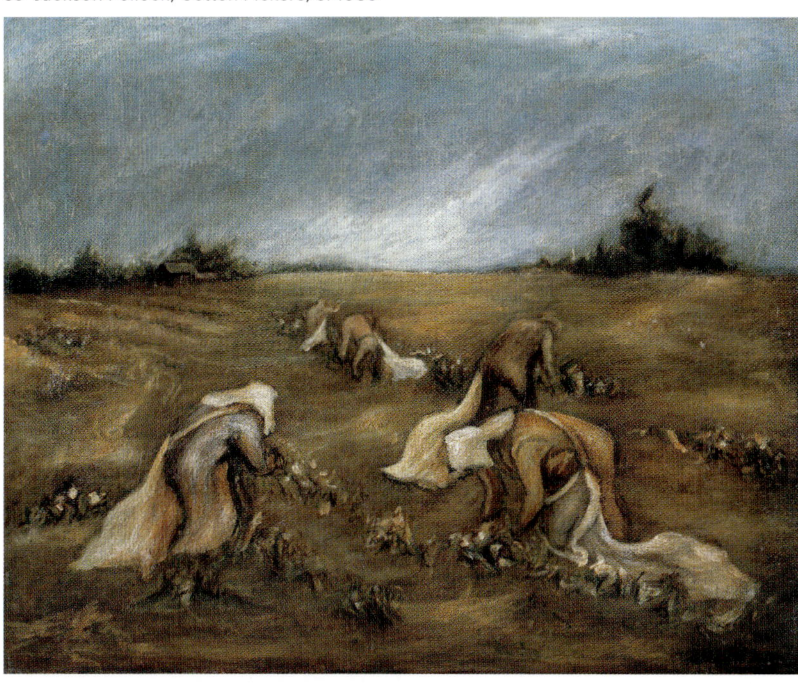

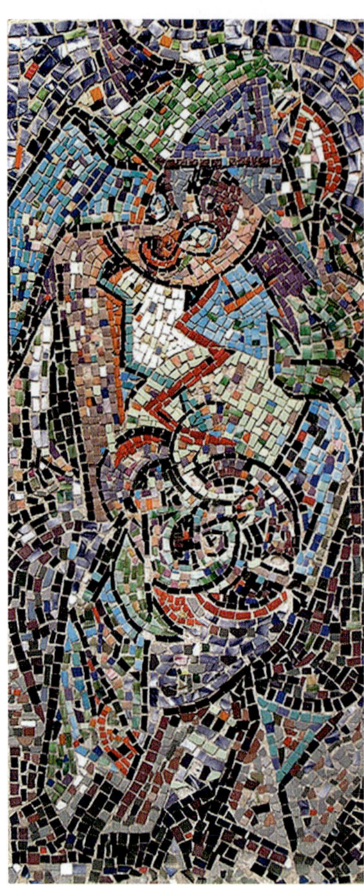

87 LEFT Jackson Pollock, *Untitled, c.* 1938–41
88 OPPOSITE Samuel Joseph Brown, Jr., *Mrs. Simmons, c.* 1936

and long sleeves to protect from the sun, weighed down by heavy, flowing sacks of cotton balls. The tentative composition, with its boneless fieldworkers, conveys little sense of heat or gravity. In search of an artistic identity, Pollock turned to other media. An untitled experiment in mosaic was never allocated to a public building. Mosaic's painstaking process of placing each tile by hand could hardly be further from the spontaneous drips and splatters of Pollock's postwar paintings, but there is a hint of their swirling lines and all-over compositions.

Pollock's shapeshifting characterized the project at large. "Our period in the fine arts has been a period of search rather than synthesis," Holger Cahill admitted in a letter to historian Mary Beard. "The most sincere, the most profound, artists of our day are searching, trying to find a way...and that, probably is true also of our most sincere political leaders." This homology between

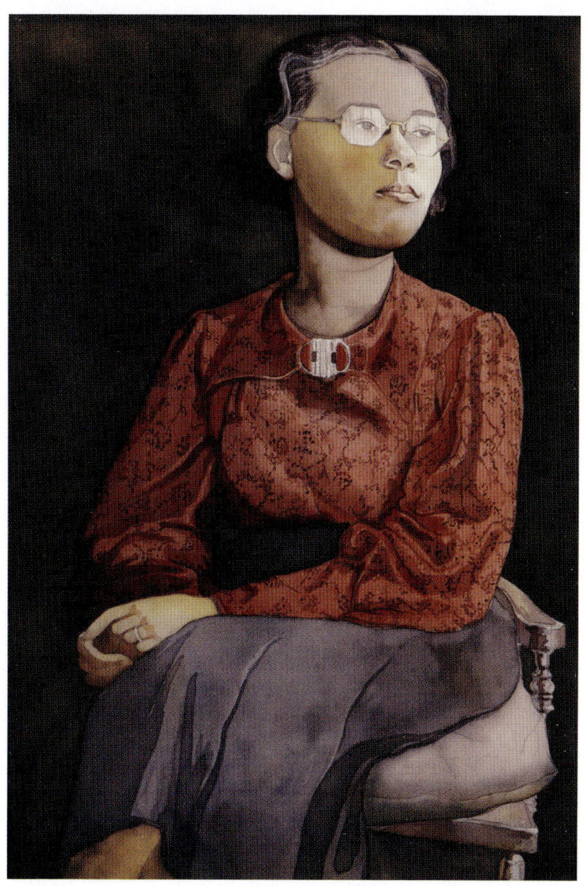

New Deal art and politics defined both in terms of pragmatic, open-ended experiment: search rather than synthesis. "It is common sense to take a method and try it," FDR said in a 1932 campaign speech. "If it fails, admit it frankly and try another. But above all, try something."

Even in the same medium an artist might test a range of subjects. Consider two watercolors by Philadelphia-based Samuel Joseph Brown, Jr. (1907–94), the first Black artist employed on the Public Works of Art Project. His facility earned Eleanor Roosevelt's admiration and national recognition—*Mrs. Simmons,* for example, exhibited in *New Horizons* and was reproduced in the catalogue. The subject poses with regal bearing, the picture of respectability in wire-framed glasses, a brooch pinned to her balloon-sleeved blouse, and legs crossed on a cushioned chair. In the challenging

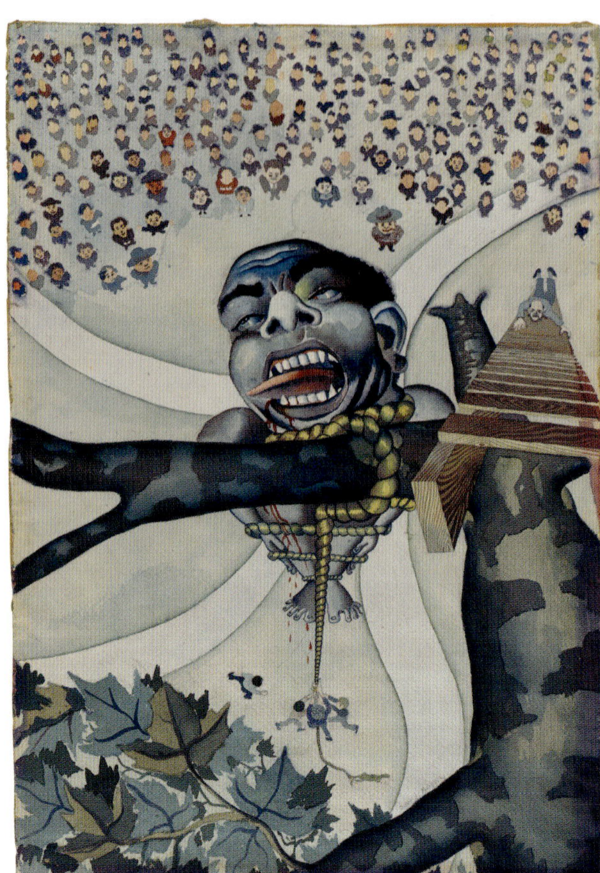

medium of watercolor, Brown mastered shimmering surface
textures and a glow of inner radiance.

89   *Mrs. Simmons* compares shockingly with *The Lynching,* a
watercolor painted by Brown for the PWAP and shown in an
NAACP-organized anti-lynching exhibition. We look down at
the tormented features of a bound victim, his sharp teeth bare
and tongue distended in a rictus of agony. The ground-level
paths twist like a pinwheel, where spectators crowd as if at
the foot of the cross. (Langston Hughes's 1930 poem "Christ in
Alabama" made the analogy between lynching and crucifixion
explicit.) The dizzying perspective intensifies the moral horror,
a blasphemy against Mrs. Simmons's dignity and self-possession.

Brown was not alone in tackling hard-hitting themes. The Depression shook artists out of the ivory tower—whatever their impulses or interests, many felt they could not ignore the miseries at their doorstep. To do so, artist Will Barnet said bluntly, "you had to be a jackass of some kind." (Hoban 2010, 103)

Artists who responded to current events—whether lynchings, breadlines, Hoovervilles, or labor strife—carried forward the urban realism of Ashcan School painters like George Bellows (1882–1925) and Robert Henri (1865–1929), known earlier in the century for gritty scenes of New York's rough Lower East Side and Bowery districts: dockworkers, smoky saloons, slum tenements, and blood-smeared boxing matches.

Socially conscious artists (among them Alice Neel, William Gropper, the Soyer brothers, and Ben Shahn) were retrospectively labeled social realists, but that was not a term used then. Holger Cahill called them the "social content" school, a combative group (often members of the Artists' Union—the subject of Chapter 7) critical of social injustice. Many were first- or second-generation immigrants and either members or partisans of the working class.

90 Jack Levine, *The Feast of Pure Reason*, 1937

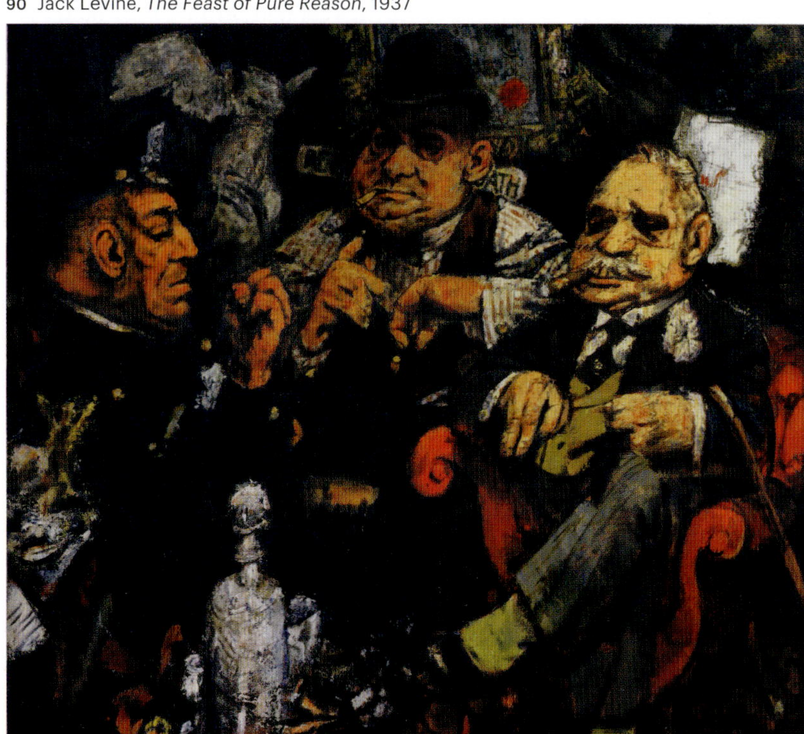

Jack Levine (1915–2010), the youngest artist on the Federal Art Project in Massachusetts, gained notoriety in 1937 for *The Feast of Pure Reason,* a scurrilous satire in the vein of German artist George Grosz. A clot of ghoulish power brokers conspires in a shadowy backroom: a "dirty" cop checking his fingernails, a crooked ward boss in a bowler hat and bow tie, and a cigar-chomping plutocrat in boutonniere and spats. The piece takes its title from a line from the "Circe" episode of James Joyce's *Ulysses,* set in Dublin's red-light district, drawing a parallel between Joyce's Dublin and Boston's rough-and-tumble South End where Levine grew up the son of Lithuanian Jewish immigrants.

Levine's satire targeted social evils, Holger Cahill noted in the aforementioned letter to Beard; it was not an outpouring of "personal hatreds and loathings and disgusts." This was an important distinction. While federal money should not subsidize personal bitterness, in Cahill's view, a caustic painting like Levine's could serve a social function. Levine, in his own words, "put these gentlemen on trial"—the painter as prosecutor.

Could surrealism, like satire, prosecute social evils? The movement came to American shores clouded in a heady perfume of sex, death, and dreams. In 1934 MoMA bought Salvador Dalí's (1904–89) *Persistence of Memory*, with its swarming ants and melting clocks, and displayed it two years later in the watershed exhibition, *Fantastic Art, Dada, Surrealism.*

Dalí's sleek dream symbolism influenced O. Louis Guglielmi (1906–56), who had two works in *New Horizons.* But Guglielmi dispensed with Dalí's hothouse sexuality and Freudian complexes. Instead, he yoked dream symbolism to social commentary, an uneasy marriage that came to be called social surrealism.

In *One Third of a Nation* a mourning wreath necklaces the cornice of a brick walk-up. Coffins strew empty streets and sidewalks as if washed up on a desolate shore. The title came from Roosevelt's second inaugural address, delivered in March 1937, in which he admitted the country's ongoing struggles: "I see one-third of a Nation ill-housed, ill-clad, ill-nourished." Guglielmi belonged to that "one-third"; he grew up in a tenement neighborhood where mostly immigrant families, exploited by slumlords and speculators, crowded into cramped, unsanitary, poorly-built dwellings. ("One Third of a Nation" was also the title of a Federal Theatre Project play, which opens with a fatal tenement fire and ends with a call to support legislation for affordable public housing.)

Roosevelt continued in the inaugural address: "The test of our progress is not whether we add more to the abundance of those

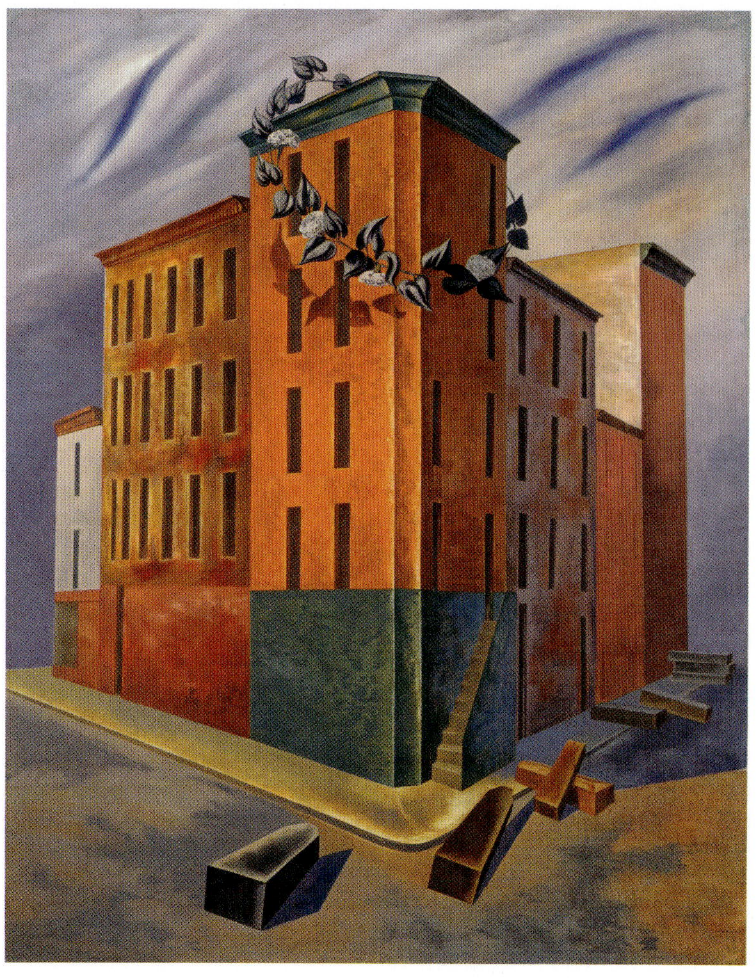

who have much; it is whether we provide enough for those who have too little." For Guglielmi this test also applied to culture. He felt the need, in his words, to create "a significant art and not merely some super-deluxe framed wallpaper to decorate the homes of the wealthy." (Guglielmi 1973, 114–15) The Project helped fulfill that need, in Guglielmi's view, by treating art as public rather than private property—a kind of collective dream.

Even public property could be highly personal, even hermetic. Chicago-based Gertrude Abercrombie (1909–77) painted dreamlike tableaux in a deadpan style—magic realism, as it was called. (The elusive term suggested ostensibly

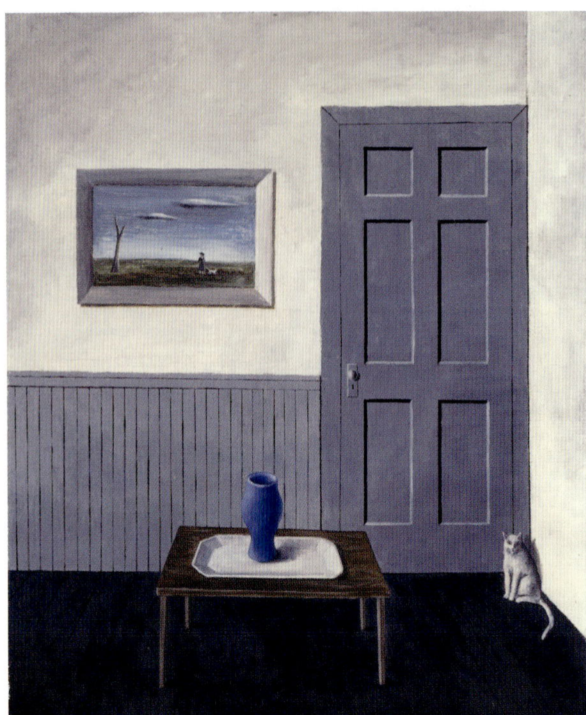

92 LEFT Gertrude Abercrombie, *White Cat*, c. 1935–38
93 OPPOSITE Josephine Joy, *CCC Camp Balboa Park*, c. 1933–37

realistic scenes estranged by hints of the weird or uncanny—
surrealism's more sober cousin.) An FAP salary allowed
Abercrombie, in her mid-twenties, to move out of her parent's
house and into the Hyde Park apartment that inspired her
paintings' bewitched interiors. The white cat of the title sits
watchfully at the corner of a closed door. A stoneware pitcher
rests on a tray on a low table. On the wall hangs a painting,
recognizably an Abercrombie, of a barren landscape with a
leafless tree and a wanderer with a cat. The strict palette and
austere composition heighten the sense of eerie anticipation,
as if the stage is set for an occult ritual.

"Poetry of the Soil"

The Federal Art Project's resources skewed to urban centers,
particularly New York. The city, boasting the major museums,
galleries, newspapers, art journals, and radio networks, sucked
up the country's cultural oxygen. At one point New York
employed almost half of all FAP artists, a reality at odds with
Cahill's ambition to redistribute cultural resources to all parts
of the country.

The Project's stated aim, however, partially achieved through exhibitions like *New Horizons*, was to promote talented artists working outside big cities. Several self-taught painters and sculptors (variously called folk, naive, or outsider artists—many from immigrant and working-class backgrounds) became standard bearers for a form of multicultural regionalism that Cahill called a "fresh poetry of the soil."

Josephine Joy (1869–1948) was in her mid-sixties, a generation or two older than many of her peers, when she joined the Southern California Art Project. *CCC Camp Balboa Park* honors a New Deal program close to President Roosevelt's heart, the Civilian Conservation Corps (CCC). The CCC put young, unmarried men to work building trails and campgrounds, roads and bridges, and planting hundreds of millions of trees, earning the nickname "Roosevelt's Tree Army." In Joy's painting a bald eagle soars over a billowing American flag, a stand of pepper trees, and a cluster of facilities in San Diego's Balboa Park. In the right corner, a small CCC crew hose a brush fire, a common duty in fire-prone Southern California.

Joy dispensed with "proper" perspective or scale (could any of the CCC crew members fit in one of the nearby buildings?) and instead used scale to lend symbolic heft to the patriotic eagle and flag. This lack of formal training—Joy did not pursue an art career until after her children had grown—aligned her with a period interest in self-taught artists like farmer

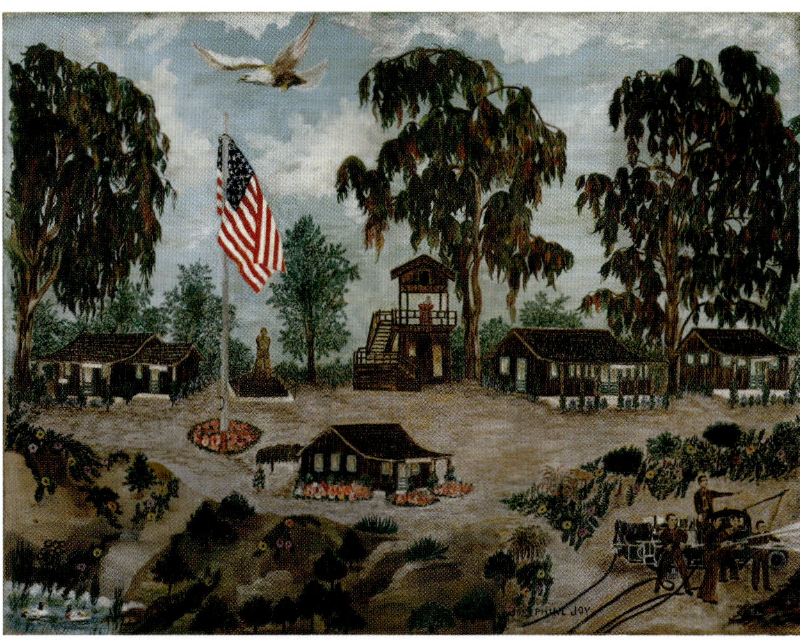

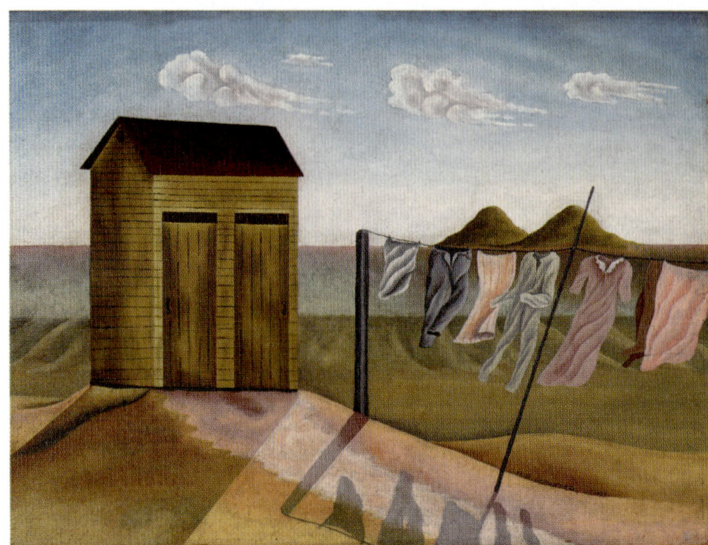

94 Pedro Cervántez, *Los Privados,* 1937

Anna Mary Robertson "Grandma" Moses (1860–1961), garment maker Morris Hirshfield (1872–1946), and house painter John Kane (1860–1934), as well as the FAP's promotion of folk art as "authentic" American culture (see Chapter 6). In 1942, collector and dealer Sidney Janis included Joy in his significant early study of non-academic art in the US, *They Taught Themselves,* and in the same year, the Museum of Modern Art presented *Josephine Joy: Romantic Painter,* a modest show of a dozen works, its first dedicated to a woman artist.

New Horizons vaulted two Southwestern artists to fame as paragons of the FAP's ethnic and regional diversity: Pedro Cervántez and Patrociño Barela. Born in Arizona to parents of Indigenous and Spanish descent, Cervántez lived most of his life in eastern New Mexico working for the railroad or picking cotton. His lapidary Project paintings treat deserted vistas of windmills, grain elevators, and railroad tracks. *Los Privados* is a view of an outhouse perched on a low-sloping hill. Clothes strung on a laundry line flap gently in the breeze, casting long shadows, their undulating folds echoing the landscape of the Llano Estacado, a Southwestern tableland. The sky's gradient blue complements the orange-tinted soil; the two hills on the horizon answer the privy's two doors. The painting's enigmatic intimacy—poignant with implied human presence—came from a democratic impulse: "My favorite subject is landscapes, direct from nature," Cervántez wrote, "because I feel that all this beauty and color should have a place in every home." (Nunn 2001, 55)

Cervántez was only twenty-three when ten of his works exhibited in the 1938 MoMA exhibition *Masters of Popular Painting*. Holger Cahill's catalogue essay, "Artists of the People," tied the display of non-academic artists, the majority first- or second-generation immigrants, to the FAP's goal of democratizing art. Cahill frequently cited Cervántez's paintings in his official FAP lectures, and they circulated widely in the agency's traveling exhibitions. Even so, Cervántez's short-lived career proved the limits of cultural democracy: After the programs ended, he worked as a sign painter and a school custodian, unable to sustain a livelihood as an artist absent government support.

Direct Carving

The breakout star of *New Horizons* was self-taught sculptor Patrociño Barela. His eight works on view, more than any other artist, prompted *Time* magazine to declare him the "discovery of the year." Barela belonged to the *santero* tradition of "saint making," carving statues and decorating altarpieces, imported by Spanish colonists to the Southwest in the seventeenth century. On the FAP, Barela carved *St. George*—the saint's upturned sword like a Christian cross planted on the decapitated head of the slain dragon—from a block of unpainted juniper pine whose natural color and grain interplays with rounded contours and shadowed hollows.

Barela had begun carving cedarwood *bultos,* small wood sculptures, in the early 1930s while working as a government teamster in Taos, New Mexico. Their compact power and sensitivity caught the eye of FAP's New Mexico state director Russell Vernon Hunter, who had also "discovered" Cervántez. Hunter romanticized Barela's poverty and lack of schooling. He is "free from our national passion for accumulating things," Hunter wrote in an appreciative but patronizing essay, and "knows more than most persons gain through formal degrees." (Hunter 1973, 96) This paternalism later extended to scuttling opportunities for Barela to exhibit in commercial art galleries, which Hunter feared would compromise the sculptor's integrity. (Barela would die in obscurity in 1964.)

Hunter's attitude was characteristic of the time; curators and critics described artists like Barela as "primitive" or "instinctive," a remnant from the preindustrial past. Art historian Stephanie Lewthwaite has pointed out that such romantic views ignored larger economic forces in the Southwest, where real estate speculation and large-scale ranching threw previously independent farmers and herders like Barela onto the wage labor market. (2015, 96) In other words, Barela was very much a modern artist, negotiating his ethnic identity vis-à-vis the commercial art market and the government art programs. For a brief time, he

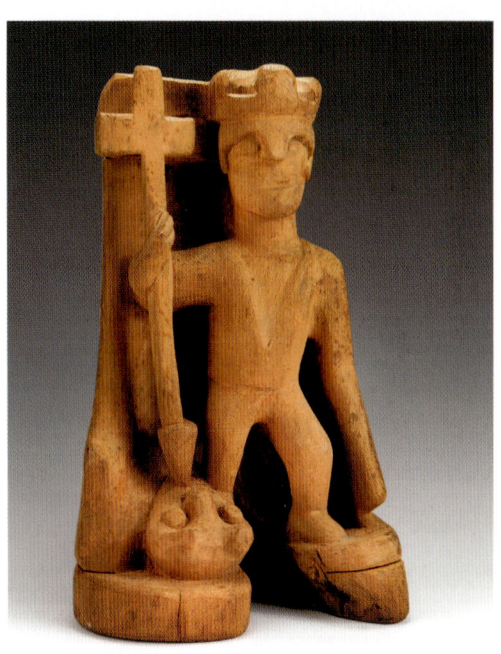

95 Patrociño Barela, *Saint George*, c. 1935–43

was arguably the most famous artist in the US—the "Teamster Art Sensation" according to MoMA publicity—and one of the first Mexican-American artists to achieve national celebrity.

Barela's sudden celebrity sprouted in well-prepared soil. His sculptures resonated with direct carving, the fashionable mode for modernist sculptors between the wars. In the United States, direct carvers such as John B. Flannagan (1895–1942) and William Zorach (1889–1966), following the European example of Constantin Brâncuși (1876–1957) and Amedeo Modigliani (1884–1920), worked with stone or wood instead of cast bronze, the main commercial method. Direct carvers self-identified as artisans and laborers, kin to the millennia-old tradition of Gothic masons, itinerant folk artists, or the unknown carvers of ancient Mesoamerica. Simple forms, unpainted surfaces, and archetypal themes expressed "truth to materials," a veritable credo.

One of the premier direct carvers of the 1930s was William Edmondson (1874–1951), the first Black artist (and the first sculptor) to receive a solo MoMA exhibition. The son of formerly enslaved Tennessee sharecroppers, he worked for nearly twenty-five years as a hospital janitor and orderly. At age fifty-seven Edmondson began salvaging curbstones and worked them with a short-handled hammer and railroad spike. He carved angels,

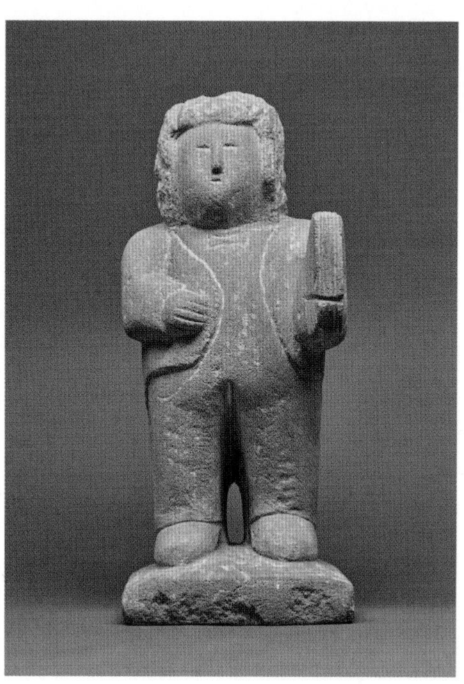

96 William Edmondson,
Preacher, c. 1940

animals, saints, teachers, boxers, nurses, biblical figures, and
First Lady Eleanor Roosevelt. Edmondson sculpted *Preacher* while
on the Nashville FAP. About a foot-and-a-half tall, the foursquare
preacher is firmly planted on a mound wearing a bow tie and a
long-tailed coat, a bible in one hand and the other folded across
his stomach. The vigorous carving honored the preacher's role as
a spiritual and often political leader in Black communities. There
may be a hint of self-portraiture: Edmondson considered himself
a maker of "sermons in stone."

Monumental outdoor sculpture could take on the character
of direct carving. In Southern California, Donal Hord (1902–66)
worked with obdurate stones such as diorite and obsidian.
"Respect your material," Hord wrote, citing a maxim of direct
carving, "It will probably outlast you, so don't betray it." (Hord
1973, 106) His *Guardian of the Water* is a sixteen-foot-tall granite
sculpture, volumetric and simplified, of a woman shouldering
an *olla*, or water jar—a theme appropriate to a fountain in
drought-prone California. She stands in front of the County
Administration Center (in 1939 the Civic Center), keeping a serene
watch over the bay.

San Diego residents at the time complained the "Guardian"
appeared too ethnic; Hord reassured them that he had indeed

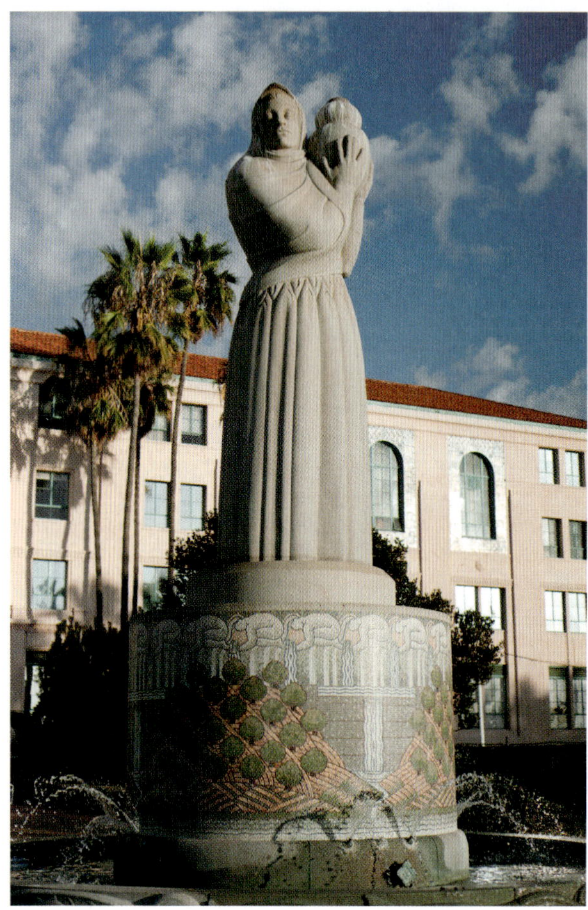

97 Donal Hord,
Guardian of the Water,
1939

used a white model. This racial anxiety was not uncommon
(recall the complaints that Edward Chávez's Nebraskan pioneers
did not look Anglo enough) and a reminder that democratic
pluralism, a threat to white power, did not go unchallenged.

New Horizons

The Federal Art Project's pluralism extended to making art for
the blind. Sargent Claude Johnson's (1888–1967) relief sculptures
for the California School for the Blind in Berkeley, California,
began under the auspices of the Public Works of Art Project.
A screen designed to cover a pipe organ in the auditorium's loft
is a hieratic composition of stylized gazelles, plants, birds, and
rabbits. In the central panel a boy claps cymbals at the base
of the Tree of Life, whose radiating branches suggest acoustic

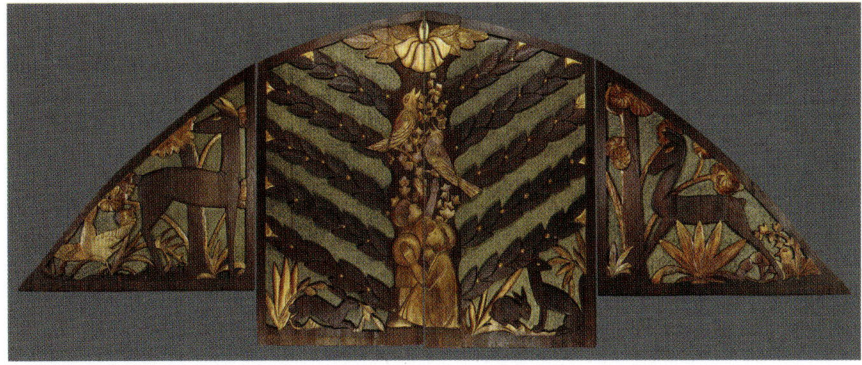

98 Sargent Claude Johnson, *Organ Screen*, 1933–34

vibrations. Johnson returned to the School years later for the FAP—he worked as a staff artist and then supervisor (one of the few Black artists to attain the rank) from 1936 until early 1943—to carve a proscenium arch above the auditorium stage. He later said of his FAP experience that it was "the best thing that ever happened to me." (LeFalle-Collins 1998, 18)

If the Federal Art Project was the best thing that ever happened to Johnson, a critic for *The Nation* wondered whether the Depression "may prove to have been the best thing that ever happened to American art." The counter-intuition was prompted by *New Horizons in American Art*, the major FAP survey. The show met with near-universal acclaim, a sense that it marked a sea change in American culture. "No one could have imagined in 1933," wrote historian and public intellectual Lewis Mumford, "that the first attempts to keep a few amiable souls from starving would broaden into a movement as solid in achievement and as encouraging to the younger painters and sculptors as the FAP has now become." (Mumford 1936, 206) The *New York Times* found that the FAP may serve as a blueprint "to indicate the function that art might and should perform in society."

What function might that be? The "new horizons" would open on to more artists, a wider audience, and a more equitable distribution of culture. Prints were at the center of debates about how to reach those horizons. They made original art accessible and affordable, the perfect medium for cultural democracy. They also proved some of the most subversive, even shocking, works of the federal art programs.

Chapter 4
The FAP Graphic Arts and Poster Divisions

Fred Becker (1913–2004) lived in a coldwater flat in the back of an East Village meat market known as Slaughterhouse Alley. He spent late nights drawing caricatures at jazz clubs, and woke to the death throes of chickens. When he applied for WPA work relief in 1935 the government home inspector "took one baleful look at the appalling decrepitude of the surroundings," he remembered, "and signed me on without a murmur." (Becker 1998, 76)

Becker, a printmaker, was hired onto the Graphic Arts Division of the Federal Art Project. He undertook a series of wood engravings on the life of Black folk hero John Henry, a railroad steel driver who won an apocryphal contest against a steam-powered rock drill at the cost of his life. (Henry was in the air: the subject of a popular folk ballad, an illustrated 1931 novel, and composer Lamar Stringfield's suite *The Legend of John Henry*.) In *John Henry's Hand* railroad tracks, eyeballs, root systems, and flora-fauna vein the life- and love-lines of a palmistry chart. The print's arresting strangeness earned it a spot on the walls, the only given to a Project printmaker, of the Museum of Modern Art's landmark 1936–37 exhibition *Fantastic Art, Dada, Surrealism*.

Affordable, portable, multiple—prints (or graphic arts) confused boundaries between fine art and mass media: books, posters, newspapers, even radio. Becker's John Henry engravings inspired a segment of the Federal Theatre Project's WNYC radio series, *What Good Is Art?* At the top of the program the announcer admitted, "To the vast majority of radio listeners, art, if it is not considered entirely useless, is something at all events for the select few to enjoy."

By "art" the announcer likely meant, and listeners likely pictured, paintings or sculptures—unique luxury objects only

99

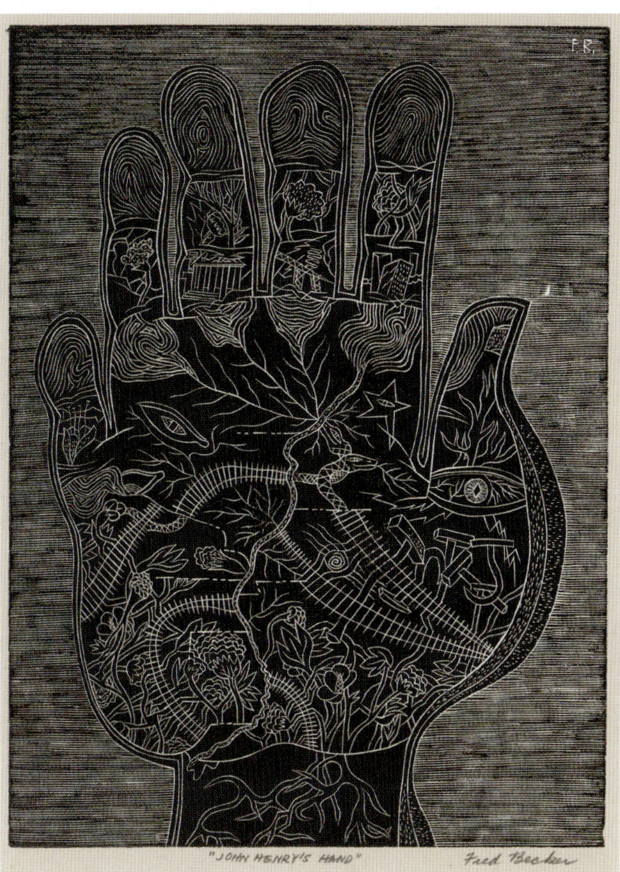

99 Fred Becker,
John Henry's Hand,
1935–39

the "select few" could afford. The accessible, audience-friendly radio program—and by extension the prints that inspired it—would break down those walls between the public and art.

Prints and Democracy

What, exactly, is a print? It might be a woodcut, etching, lithograph, or screenprint. Each consists of ink and paper, like a drawing, but adds an essential third element: a matrix. The matrix, whether a woodblock or a copper plate, "holds" or contains the artist's design (*matrix* is from the Latin for "womb"). By gouging into a woodblock or carving grooves into a copper plate, the artist creates, in effect, a template or cast. Inking the matrix and pressing it to a sheet of paper, either by hand or with a mechanical press, transfers the design. (Jacob Kainen's strapping artist-worker, in an apron and rolled-up

100

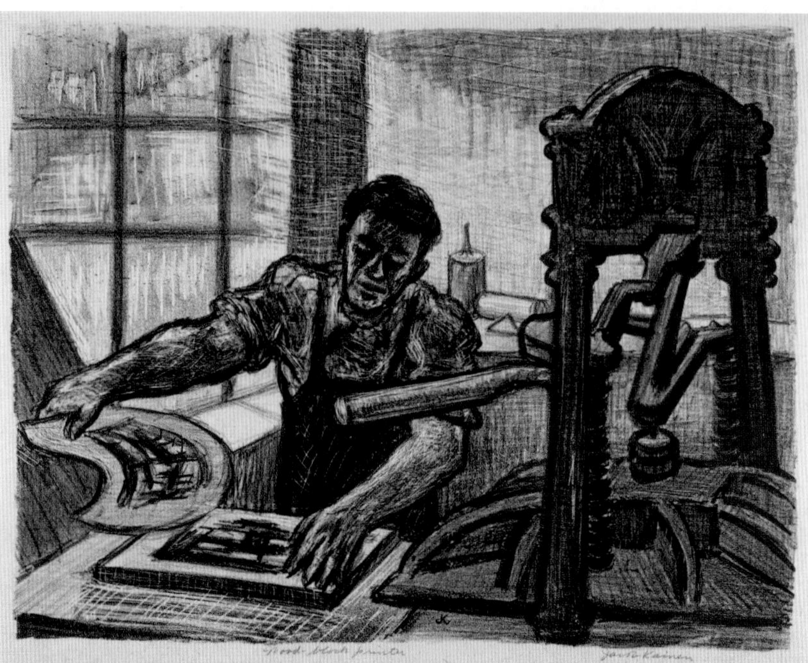

100 Jacob Kainen, *Wood-Block Printer*, 1940

shirtsleeves, is pulling a print from a woodblock.) Repeating
the process yields multiple prints or "impressions," and a set
number of impressions make up an edition.

Before the New Deal, etching dominated the small and
insular world of fine art prints, and printmakers tended to
work in isolation on private presses or one-on-one with a
master printer. Kainen was among a group of New York-based
artists who pressured FAP administrators to open a print
studio; they even volunteered to buy presses with their own
money. Administrators relented, and the Project's first print
workshop opened in February 1936 on the twelfth floor of FAP
headquarters in midtown Manhattan.

At its height, the Graphic Arts Division employed nearly
eight hundred artists across thirty-five cities. (Besides New
York, active workshops included Philadelphia, Cleveland,
San Francisco, and Los Angeles.) Roughly 200,000 prints
based on 11,000 designs went into circulation from Project
studios, dwarfing the output of paintings, sculptures, and
murals. Administrators quickly took to calling prints the most
"democratic" of all mediums, ideally suited to the New Deal
goal of cultural democracy.

Truth or Beauty

In the nineteenth century the New York City-based printmaking company Currier and Ives popularized affordable lithographs for the middle class. Their prints prefigured the 1930s American scene: nostalgic views of baseball games, horse-drawn sleighs, or Hudson River steamboats. Cahill hoped that printmakers could help restore the "popular appreciation of art" while upholding artisanal values of craft and quality. Blanche Lazzell's color woodcut *My Wharf Studio* was exhibited in *New Horizons for American Art,* the Federal Art Project's 1936 MoMA showcase, as a premier example of an American scene treated with the formal sophistication of a Japanese woodblock print. Such prints, administrators hoped, would flow into the homes of American citizens as part of the "practical pattern of their lives," as one Graphic Arts supervisor put it. (Harris 1995, 38)

A number of FAP printmakers held fast to another vision of democratic prints for the people. Prints belonged to the history of agitprop posters, broadsides, and political cartoons: urgent

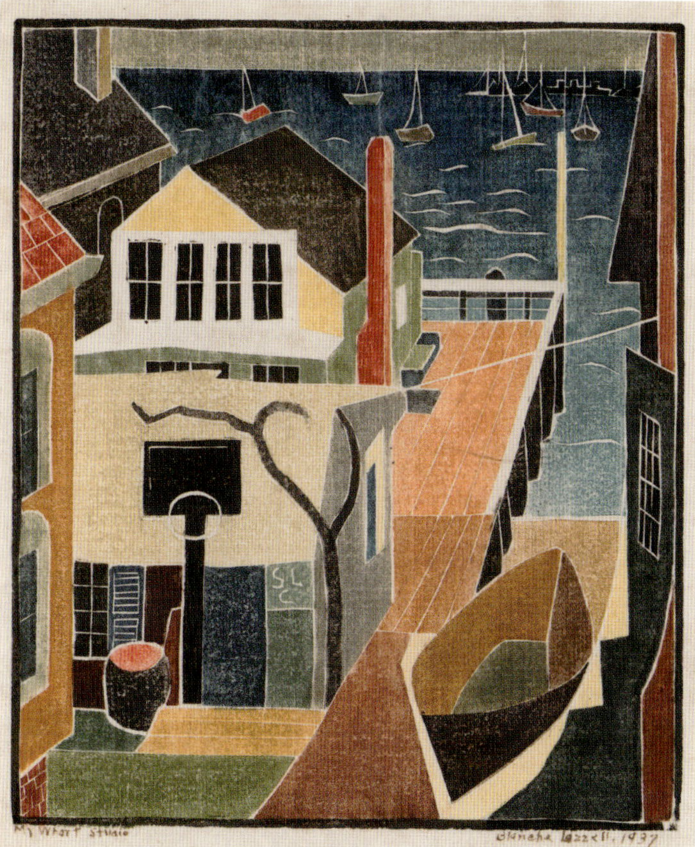

101

101 Blanche Lazzell,
My Wharf Studio,
1937

graphics designed for maximum visual and emotional impact. They looked to Francisco de Goya (1746–1828) and Honoré Daumier (1808–79) as artists who deployed prints to skewer the powerful and rouse indignation over social iniquities and inequities. German artist Käthe Kollwitz (1867–1945) modeled humanist sympathy for the working class, women, and the victims of war and oppression. In the first decades of the twentieth century, Ashcan School artists like John Sloan made gritty, topical prints indebted to their early careers as newspaper illustrators.

Project supervisors, many of them artists, subjected the Graphic Arts Division to less oversight than the Mural Division. Printmakers used their relative freedom to take on challenging, provocative, or subversive subjects. Nearly a quarter of the exhibited prints in *New Horizons* dealt with raw themes like unemployment, slum housing, and labor unrest. Eli Jacobi's (1898–1984) *All Night Mission* portrayed the rough Bowery district shelter shut down at various times as overcrowded, unsafe, and unsanitary. Anonymous masses huddle under the watchful eye of a crucifix and a sign that reads Jesus Sees. Government patronage, Jacobi wrote, afforded printmakers the freedom to explore "how far one can go to marry truth—ugly truth—to beauty." (Jacobi 1973, 157)

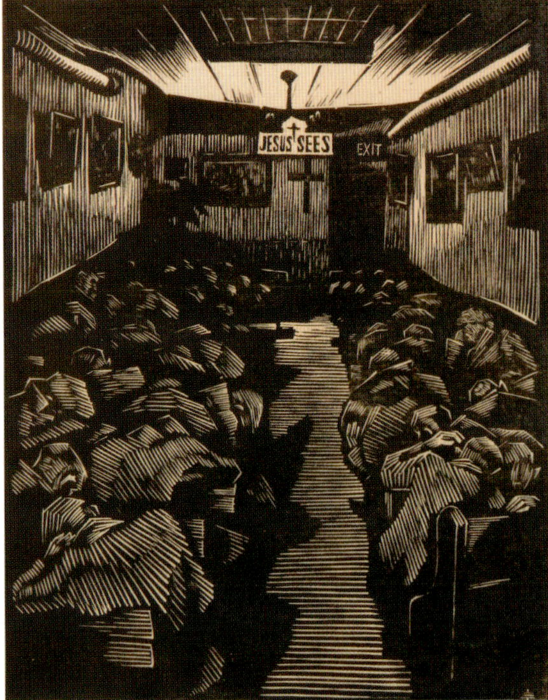

102 Eli Jacobi, *All Night Mission*, 1936

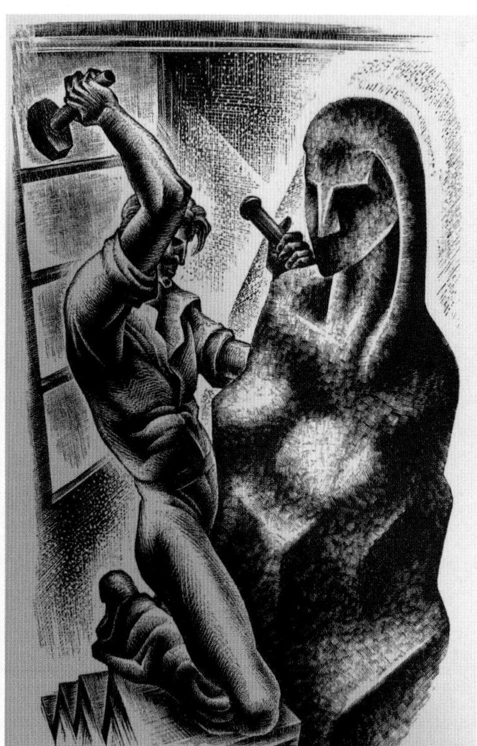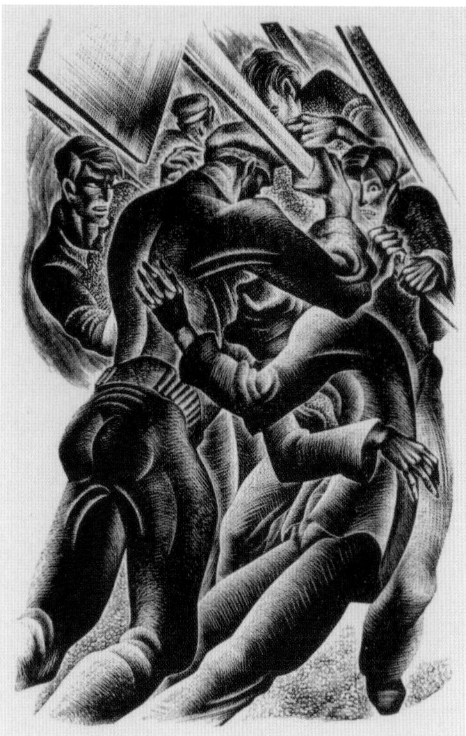

103 Lynd Ward, plates from *Prelude to a Million Years*, 1933

Truth or Beauty? Several FAP printmakers dramatized the choice. Fred Becker had been thrilled to discover that his idol Lynd Ward (1905–85), innovator of the graphic or "wordless" novel in the 1930s, ran the Project's New York printmaking division. Ward's 1933 wordless novel, *Prelude to a Million Years*, made vivid the inner conflict of the Depression-era artist. Should an artist follow their personal muse? Or should they make art in the service of progressive change? (This "Lady or the Tiger" choice continues to bedevil artists.)

103   *Prelude* opens with its sculptor protagonist carving a Venus de Milo-esque vision of idealized beauty. Over the course of the novel, he confronts a series of social realities—police brutality, domestic abuse, alcoholism, flag-waving chauvinism—that shock him out of his dreamy stupor. Artists, in Ward's view, should not retreat to airy aestheticism; they had an obligation to confront the social injustices of the day. Prints, like the book's wood engravings, suited that mandate: able to deliver bracing images quickly to large audiences.

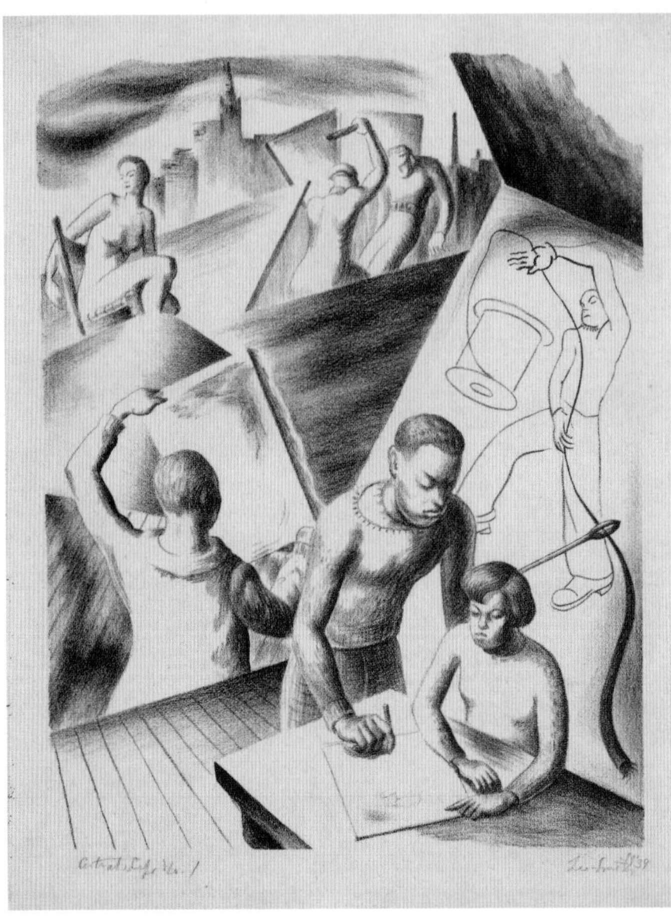

104 Hughie Lee-Smith, *The Artist's Life, No. 1*, 1939

Hughie Lee-Smith (1915–99) identified the same tension in his lithograph *The Artist's Life, No. 1*, made in Cleveland on the Ohio Art Project. He taught at Karamu House, one of the oldest Black theaters in the US, where Langston Hughes premiered several of his plays. Lee-Smith portrayed himself leaning over a table, offering guidance to a student. Behind them, in a fan of overlapping vignettes, he draws from a nude model, a policeman clubs a demonstrator, and a worker lassoes a needle and thread from a hovering spool.

Again the choice: Should an artist follow their muse? Or should they take sides in response to current events? (Only a few artists, like Stuart Davis, insisted on the autonomy of art as itself politically progressive.) Lee-Smith's firsthand experience with union activism and teaching disadvantaged youths made

the choice clear: The third print in the series found him fully
committed to the workers' movement.

Living Newspapers

Prints remained a close cousin in the 1930s to political
cartoons and newspaper illustrations. Many Federal Art Project
printmakers—Mabel Dwight (1875–1955), William Gropper,
Louis Lozowick (1892–1973), and Elizabeth Olds (1896–1991), to
name a few—contributed biting illustrations to *New Masses*
and *Daily Worker.* Leo J. Meissner (1895–1977) collapsed prints
and newspapers in his wood engraving *Civilization AD 1935.*
A newspaper called *The Daily Blast,* published from "Anywhere
1935," features a front page with slanted columns captioned
Lynching, Strikes, Breadlines, Intolerance—recurring topics
in Depression-era prints. A 1938 article in the *Magazine of Art*
described contemporary prints as "one with the people, as alive
to ground swells as the morning newspaper." (Grafly 1938, 32)

Prints relayed an urgency similar to the Federal Theatre
Project's Living Newspapers, short plays that dramatized

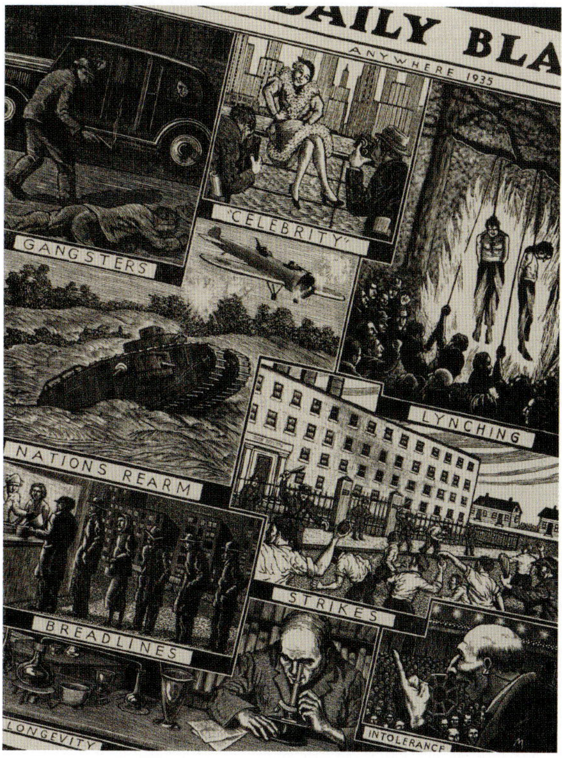

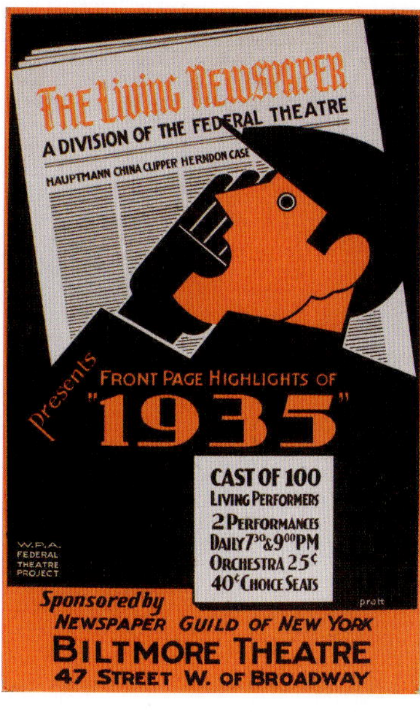

105 LEFT Leo J. Meissner,
Civilization AD 1935, 1935
106 ABOVE *Front Page
Highlights of 1935,* 1935

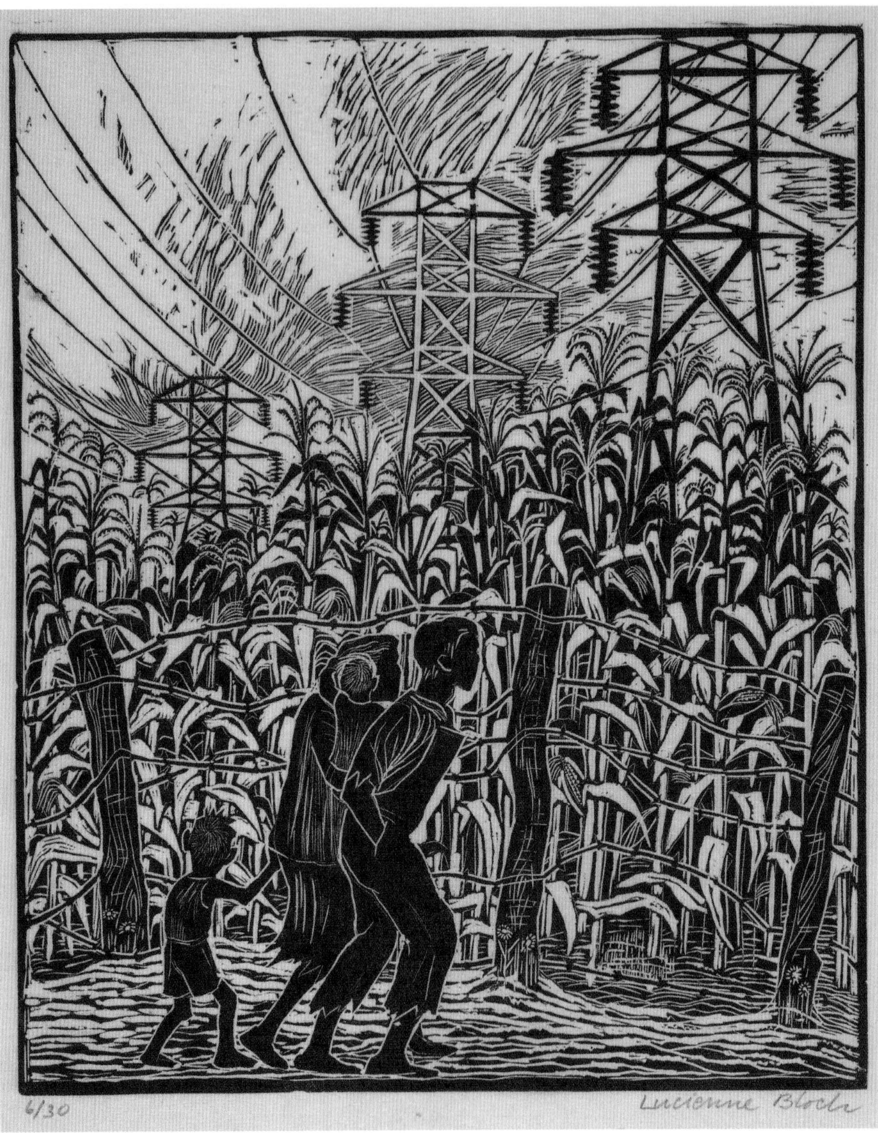

107 Lucienne Bloch, *Land of Plenty*, 1936

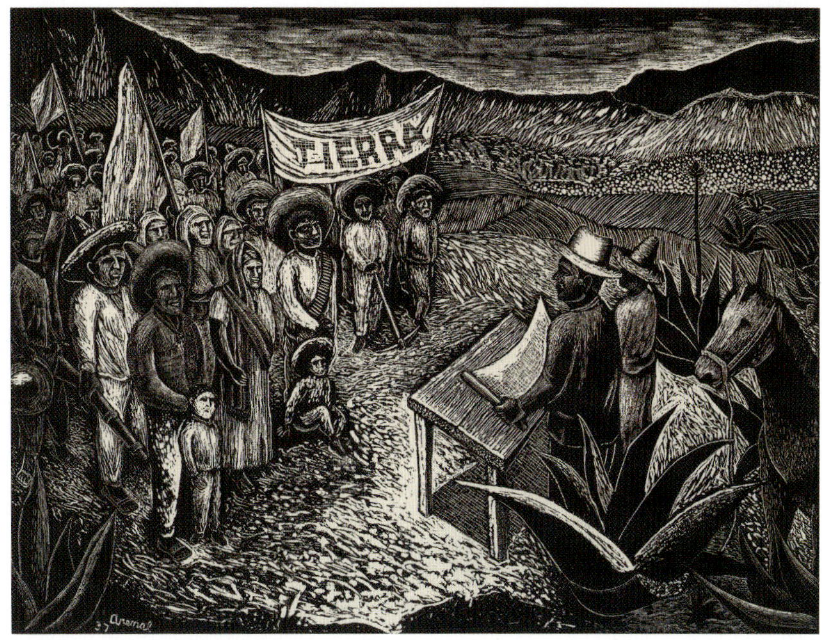

108 Luis Arenal, *Distribution of Land*, 1937

current events and hot-button issues: housing and healthcare, private versus public power, racism and fascism. The 1937 Living Newspaper *Power* made a case for publicly owned utility companies like the Tennessee Valley Authority (TVA), which expanded access to electricity in the rural South.

107   Lucienne Bloch's privately printed woodcut, *Land of Plenty*, comments sharply on these government initiatives. The choice of woodcut—a relief method where parts of the woodblock are cut away, leaving the design proud of the surface to receive ink—is deliberate. It is the oldest print medium in the Western tradition, long associated with books, broadsides, and political messaging. (Woodcuts, for example, spread Martin Luther's anti-papacy propaganda during the Protestant Reformation.) The medium's rough-hewn look fits the theme of bare survival: A barbed wire fence cordons off the promised "plenty" of the title from a barefooted family in tattered clothes trudging across the foreground. The trailing child turns longingly to the abundance on the other side of the fence.

108   Luis Arenal's (1908–85) wood engraving *Distribution of Land* treats a similar theme. Born in southern Mexico, Arenal had an active career in Mexico and the US. In New York he worked on the FAP's mural and print divisions, complicating, for a time,

definitions of "American artist" tied to citizenship. (Rufino Tamayo (1899–1991) was another Mexico-born artist active on the FAP; in 1937 the WPA updated its policies to exclude non-citizens.) Arenal's father died fighting in the Mexican Revolution, which saw land redistribution from wealthy estate owners to small-scale farmers. In *Distribution of Land* a crowd of campesinos hold flags and a banner emblazoned with the word Tierra. At the table stands Mexico's president Lázaro Cárdenas overseeing the redistribution process, a priority for his time in office. In 1937 Arenal decamped to Mexico City, where he co-founded El Taller de Gráfica Popular (The People's Graphic Workshop), soon to become the most progressive printmaking studio in the Americas and future destination for FAP artists like Charles White.

Machine Fodder

Where government-funded murals promised thriving workers and prosperous industries, FAP prints cast a dark, even dystopian, gaze over the machine age. Nan Lurie (1910–1985), who assisted Lucienne Bloch on her Women's House of Detention mural, sarcastically titled a Project lithograph *Technological Improvements*. A line of unemployed Black men, some barefoot, squeeze in a brick alleyway around the corner from a door marked No Help Wanted. Above them a steam shovel's mechanical maw disgorges a whirl of chewed-up workers. Lurie's theme was timely; she made the print the same year the government issued a nearly four-hundred-page report on *Technological Trends and National Policy*. Whatever their benefits, new technologies like diesel-powered tractors and the mechanical cotton-picker displaced agricultural workers, disproportionately Black. In Lurie's view, "technological improvements" threatened to make human workers obsolete.

Blanche Grambs's (1916–2010) *Design Steel* indicts the steel industry as a latter-day Mammon consuming souls and leaving death in its wake. Born in China to a missionary family, Grambs received a full scholarship to the Art Students League of New York. She was barely out of her teens when she joined her League instructor, Harry Sternberg (painter of Ambler, Pennsylvania, Post Office mural) on his Guggenheim-funded trip to Pennsylvania's coal and steel towns. In *Design Steel* a blast furnace towers like a monstrous deity. The gritty pitted surface of the aquatinted etching (heating powdered rosin on the copper plate to create tone and grain when inked and printed) suggests the blackish-gray coke consumed in the smelting process. Houses and cemetery crosses interlace in a nightmarish topography—the steel town as graveyard.

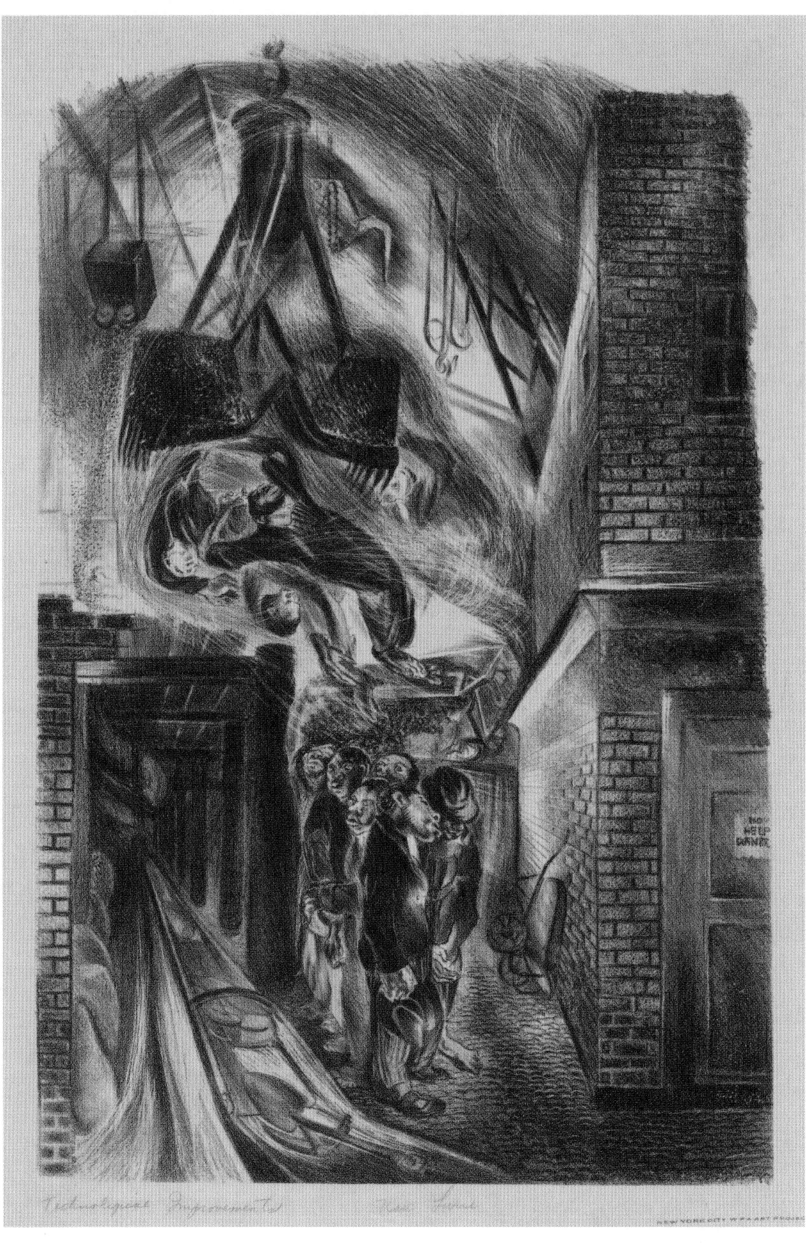

109 Nan Lurie, *Technological Improvements*, 1937

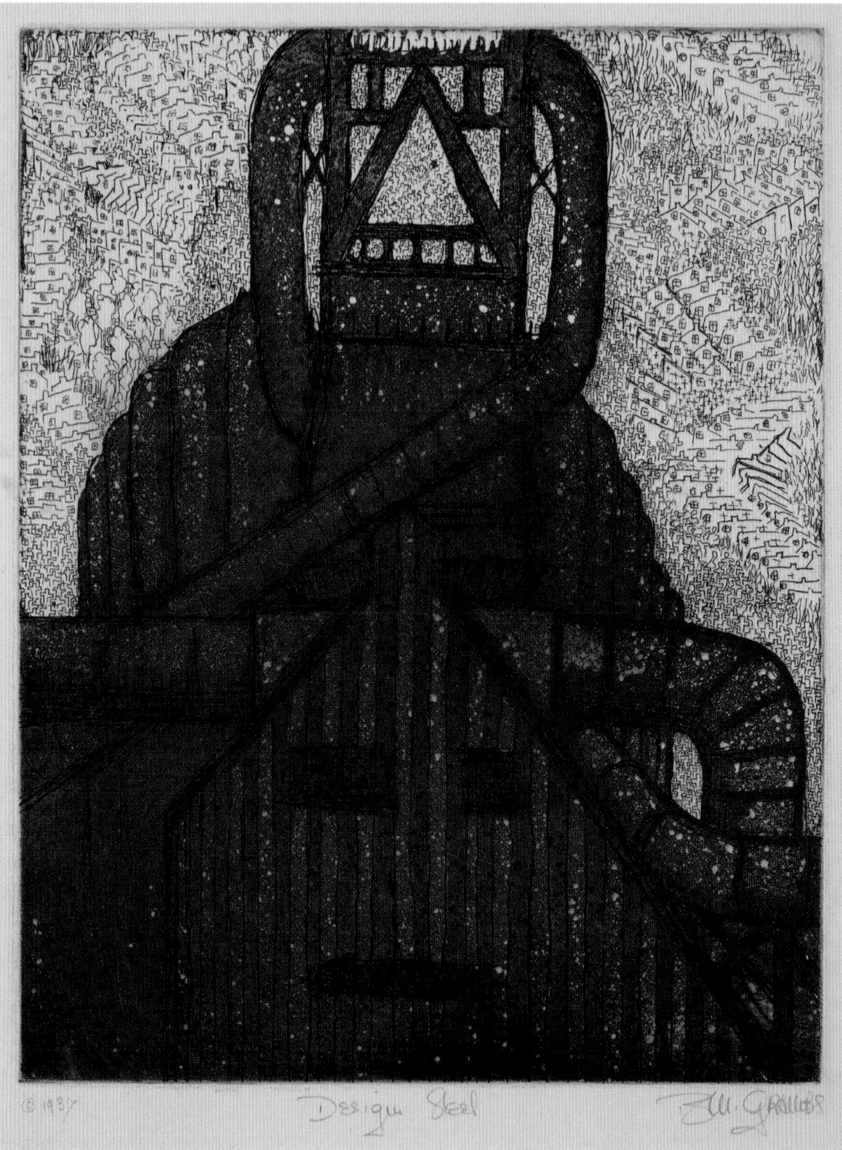

110 Blanche Grambs, *Design Steel*, 1937

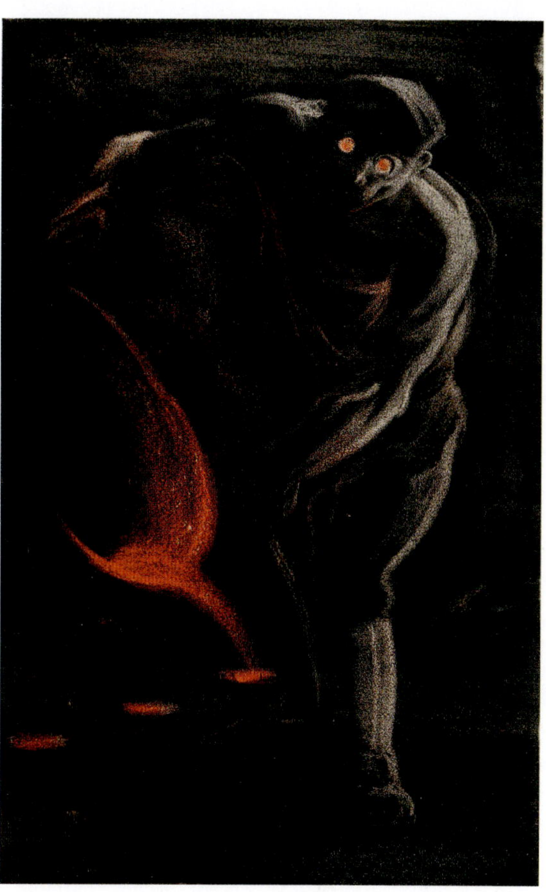

111 Lewis Rubenstein,
Foundry, c. 1938

111   From Grambs's forbidding furnace to the mill's dark
interior: in Lewis Rubenstein's *Foundry* a steelworker stands
over the narrow-gauge track pouring molten steel into an ingot
mold. Rubenstein based the print on sketches he made at a
Cleveland steel plant rocked by protests (he was hassled by
strikers who suspected him of being a company informant—
an occupational hazard for an artist making on-site sketches).
Reduced to a chalky outline and gleaming eye protection, the
steelworker is an underworld specter stripped of humanity—
a revenant from one of Grambs's cross-marked graves. Far
from the industrial sublime, *Foundry* is closer to poet William
Blake's "dark Satanic mills" where workers toil in infernal
heat and darkness.

Several Project printmakers turned inward, marrying truth and beauty through personal, if cryptic, prints. Dox Thrash (1893–1965), a veteran of the First World War, studied at the Art Institute of Chicago and worked as a commercial artist before joining Philadelphia's Fine Print Workshop in 1937 as its first Black printmaker. Thrash developed an innovative technique using carborundum, a commercial abrasive, to roughen the surface of copper plates. By smoothing and burnishing select areas of the roughened plate, a richly tonal image would emerge when inked and printed.

112 The process's rich shadows and velvety tones veil *Mary Lou* in mystery. Thrash confronted the crude stereotypes of Black Americans in popular culture—the caricatured Aunt Jemima brand, for example, or the minstrelsy of popular radio sitcom *Amos 'n' Andy*—with an enigmatic portrait that withholds as much as it reveals (a related print is called *Miss X*). It evokes what poet and essayist Édouard Glissant called "a right to opacity," to remain inaccessible to the possessive eyes of prejudice and power.

Enigmatic landscapes haunt the prints of Fay Chong. Born in Guangzhou (Canton), China, he moved with his family to Seattle in 1920 before the 1924 Immigration Act excluded all Chinese nationals. Chong picked up linoleum block printmaking (a variation of woodcuts using linoleum instead of wood as the matrix) in high school, where classmates included future sculptor George Tsutakawa (1910–97) and Northwest School painter Morris Graves (1910–2001), who helped Chong

113 gain a berth on the Seattle FAP. *At the Weird Pool*, in its swelling and tapering black lines, shows the fruits of Chong's trips to China in the mid-1930s to study traditional calligraphy. The weird pool's rippling lines encircle three figures canopied by a bending, leafless tree, the silhouetted branches like calligraphic strokes.

Chong worked alongside Nuche artist Julius Twohy (1902–

114 86). In *Blessed Pony,* horses patterned with triangles circle a central teepee shape. The schematic forms recall the painted pictographs and carved petroglyphs of the Uintah and Ouray Reservation in Utah where Twohy grew up. (The Nuche were among the first Native American tribes to acquire horses from colonists—they became adept riders and evolved a horse culture.) *Blessed Pony* also recalls the semi-abstract animism of German expressionists Wassily Kandinsky and Paul Klee, whose works exhibited at the University of Washington when Twohy was a student.

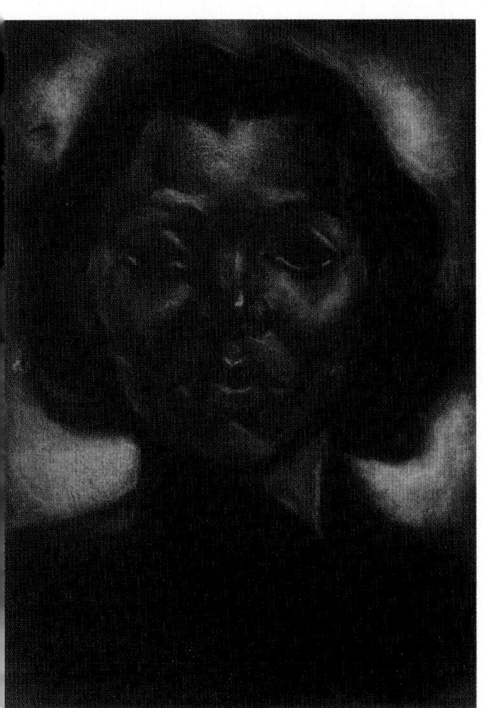

112 LEFT Dox Thrash,
Mary Lou, c. 1939–40
113 BELOW Fay Chong,
At the Weird Pool, 1938
114 BOTTOM Julius Twohy,
Blessed Pony, c. 1939

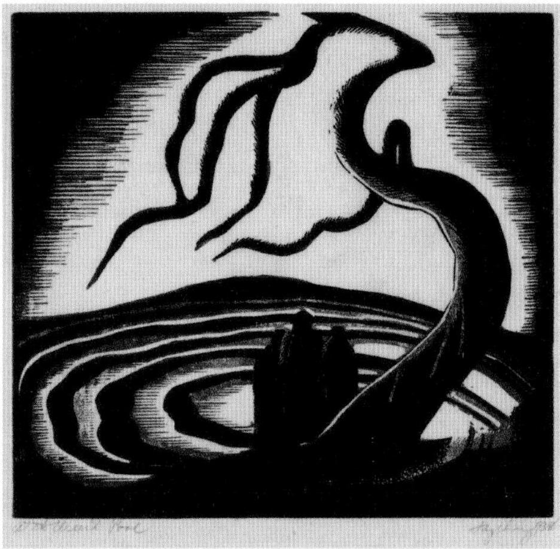

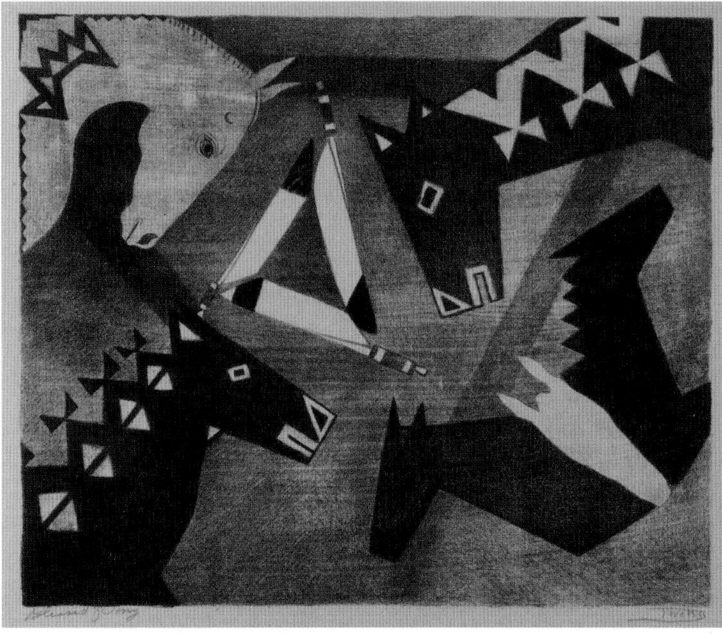

The FAP Graphic Arts and Poster Divisions

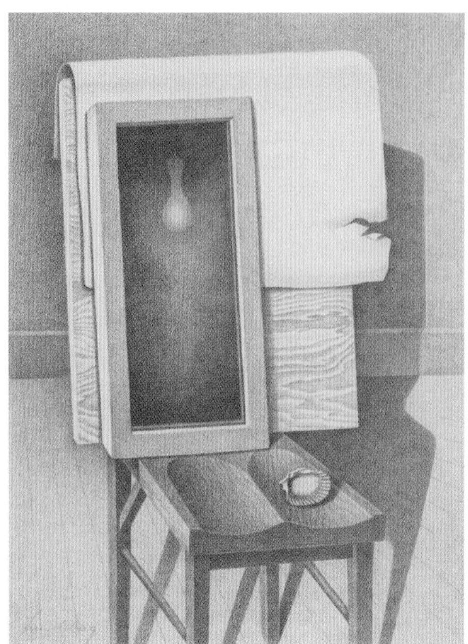

115 Helen Lundeberg,
Enigma, 1937

Twohy worked in lithography, a technically challenging medium popular with FAP artists given access to materials and the expertise of master printers. The medium is based on the premise that oil and water don't mix. The artist draws the design on limestone or a zinc plate with an oily pencil or crayon. The surface is treated with an acid solution and light water coating so that ink adheres to the drawn elements and is repelled by the water. Lithography enjoyed a nineteenth-century vogue, but by the early twentieth century had come to be tainted by commercial associations. The Federal Art Project revived in the US its widespread use.

Helen Lundeberg (1908–99) made lithographs on the Southern California FAP, where she was a guiding force behind postsurrealism, also known as the new classicism, the only surrealist group in the interwar United States. Lundeberg co-authored the movement's 1934 manifesto, announcing a cool, cerebral synthesis of dream symbolism and formal rigor. Instead of Freudian psychodrama, the lithograph *Enigma* exudes quiet introspection, even melancholy. Objects—a scalloped seashell, a chair, a mirror, a torn sheet of paper folded over a drawing board—appear in a carefully posed yet inexplicable arrangement. The mirror reflects an electric light, a symbol of artistic inspiration, realized in lithography's graphite-like sensitivity and precision.

115

Dream symbolism suffuses Jean Finlayson Holmes's (1910–87) *Ether*. On a moonlit night a cut-out view of a hospital finds a woman in labor attended by doctors and nurses. She has been given ether or chloroform to relieve the pain of childbirth. (By 1935 half of births in the US took place in hospitals, and three-quarters of urban births.) Holmes, who worked on the San Francisco FAP, drew on her own experience giving birth in summoning the anesthetic's "ethereal" hallucinations—an umbilically corded spirit in ascension—tethering the brightly lit hospital to the cosmic heavens.

Prints for the People

The title of the FAP's first major print exhibition, *Prints for the People* (1937), signaled its goal of cultural democracy.

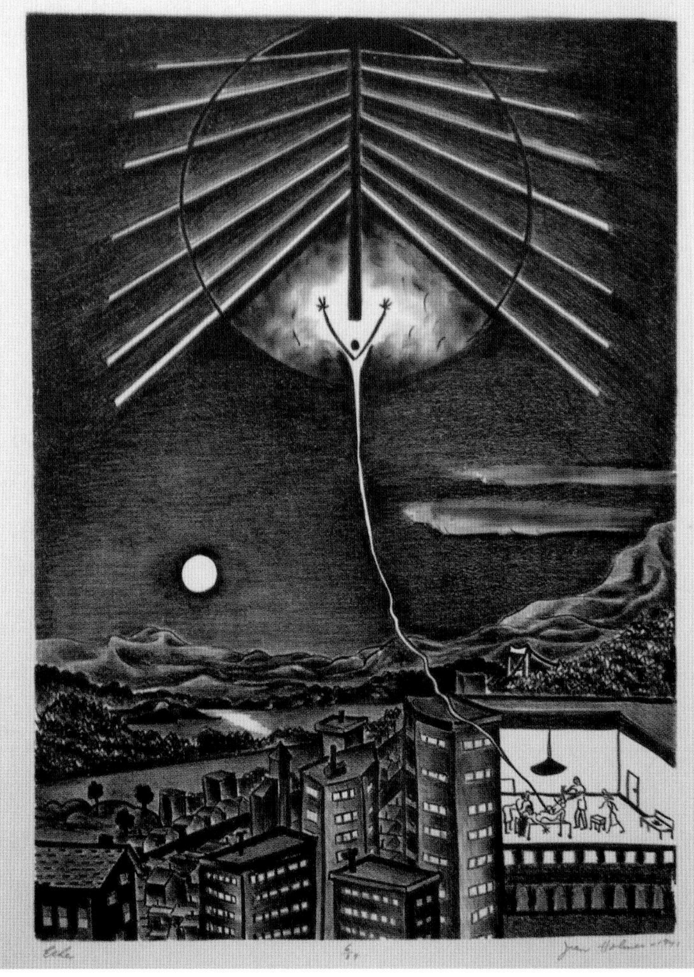

116 Jean Finlayson Holmes, *Ether*, 1941

Prints circulated in schools, colleges, settlement houses, and hospitals, and toured the country in exhibitions hosted by project galleries and community art centers. They could also be seen in WPA theaters, nonprofits like the YMCA and YWCA, and outdoor parks. Printmaking demonstrations often accompanied these exhibitions, along with tours put together by the teaching division, in keeping with the Project's educational priorities. The California division even loaned prints through the Berkeley Public Library.

Administrators highlighted technical innovations to shore up the idea that the FAP did socially useful work. In 1938, the Federal Art Gallery in New York on 57th Street hosted *Printmaking: A New Tradition*, which focused on developments in color lithography, a complex process requiring specialized equipment and a skilled printer.

New techniques could achieve arresting effects. In *Ku Kluxers* Chet La More (1908–80) used color lithography to create painterly splashes of blood red on the Klansmen's white robes. The three sheeted figures appear like tattered peaks against a blue backdrop smeared with scudding gray clouds. The central Klansman turns ominously to consider the viewer. The red, white, and blue color scheme placed white supremacy at the heart of American identity. This was more than symbolic; in the 1920s the KKK counted among its members US governors, senators, and judges. It is hard to imagine a mural or easel painting of the same subject receiving the government's stamp of approval, as this print did.

Screenprints

Color lithography was time-consuming and labor-intensive, requiring multiple heavy stones and the expertise of a master printer. Screenprinting, by contrast, was fast, cheap, and required little training or specialized equipment. In the early twentieth century commercial printers developed the medium to make designs on textiles, banners, and pennants. Ink is pushed with a squeegee through a fine mesh screen (traditionally silk, hence "silkscreen"), held taut by a frame, onto paper or canvas. A stencil blocks ink from passing through parts of the screen; the unblocked areas allow flat, saturated ink passages that create screenprints' distinct look. The Federal Art Project set up a special unit in 1938 to promote screenprinting as fine art, and advocates gave it a fancy name: serigraphy (silk + writing).

Miné Okubo, born in Riverside, California, experimented with screenprinting (the term serigraphy never quite stuck) on the San Francisco FAP. She likely took inspiration from

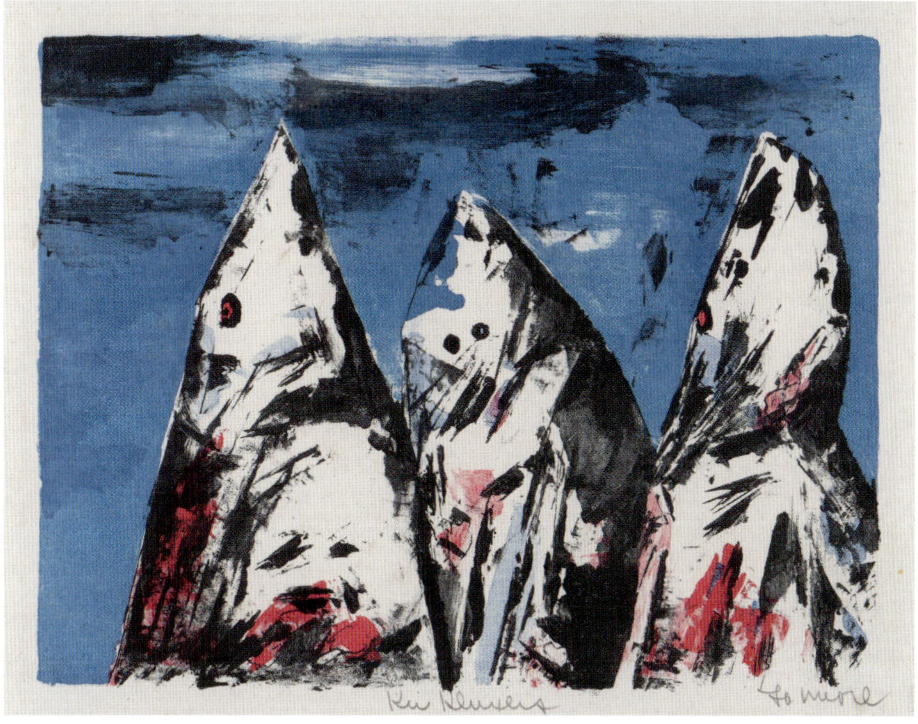

117 Chet La More, *Ku Kluxers*, 1939

Picasso: Forty Years of His Art, a blockbuster traveling exhibition on view at the San Francisco Museum of Modern Art in 1939. *Abstraction*, also titled *The Musician*, adopts Cubism's blocky jigsaw shapes and bright planes of color. The interlocking pieces assemble into a musician, a typical Picasso motif, playing an instrument near an open window.

Screenprinting's vibrant colors were readily adapted to whimsy and humor. Elizabeth Olds, the first woman artist awarded a Guggenheim Fellowship, gave FAP screenprints a comic twist. *Summer People* gently mocks the *plein-air* painter, sight-sizing a pair of fishermen mending nets, as no better than a gawking tourist. Olds, willing to join a miners' union to make studies on active job sites (see Chapter 7), presumably had little patience for such shallow rubbernecking. But there may have been a hint of self-deprecation—her FAP wood engraving *Mending Nets* depicts the same subject.

Prints had mass-market potential. In 1934 an entrepreneur set up the Associated American Artists to sell $5 prints by artists like Grant Wood and Thomas Hart Benton in

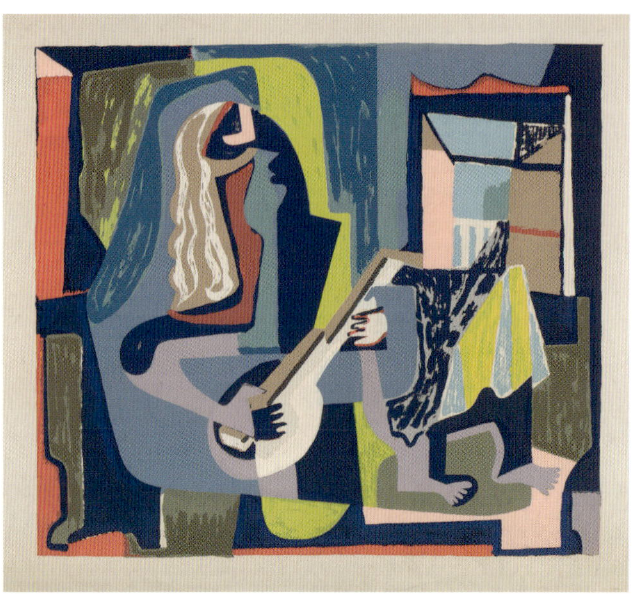

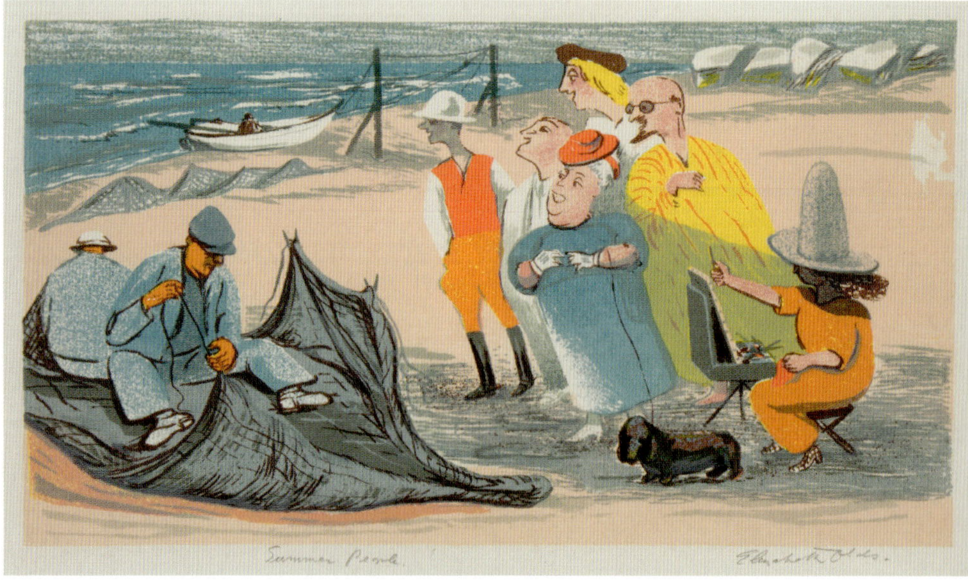

118 TOP Miné Okubo, *Abstraction,* c. 1935–43
119 ABOVE Elizabeth Olds, *Summer People,* c. 1938–39

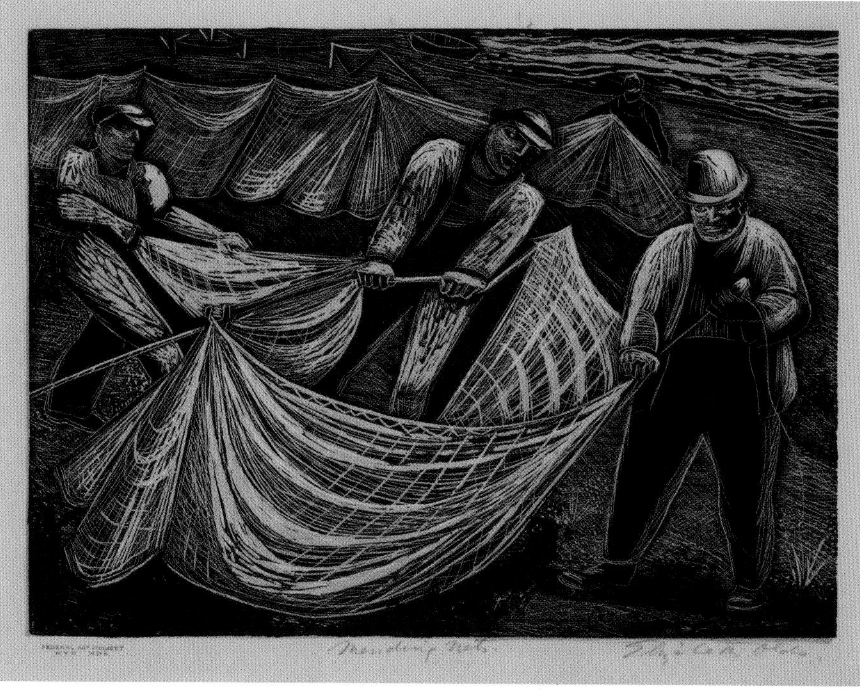

120 Elizabeth Olds, *Mending Nets*, 1935–42

department stores and through mail order. Even MoMA exhibited *American Color Prints Under Ten Dollars* in a bid to stimulate the art economy.

Olds, however, wanted prints to flow outside commercial channels. In a 1936 essay, "Prints for Mass Production," she vented her frustration over the FAP policy of limiting editions to between twenty-five and fifty impressions when many more could be printed. (A fellow printmaker compared this artificial scarcity to the controversial New Deal policy of driving up agricultural prices by culling livestock or plowing under fields.) Olds argued that large print editions could make art, like free public education, available to all.

Poster Division

In many ways, the Federal Art Project's Poster Division took up Olds's call. Anthony Velonis (1911–97), who worked with Olds and other artists to set up the screenprinting unit of the Graphic Arts Division, had first introduced the method to the Poster Division, where the process of painting and lettering posters by hand was laborious and inefficient. Screenprinting enabled the high-volume production of posters quickly at low cost. Operating across seventeen states, the five-hundred-strong division printed two million posters from over thirty thousand designs.

Richard Floethe (1901–88), director of the New York division, had trained at the Bauhaus and absorbed the German school's commitment to elevating the design of everyday objects through a harmony of form and function. (The Bauhaus also influenced the FAP's Design Laboratory; see Chapter 6). Floethe posted incoming jobs on a bulletin board and let the artists compete with concept sketches. He picked the most promising designs and sent them to the customer for approval.

Who were the customers? Government agencies, municipal departments, and tax-supported institutions commissioned posters for as little as a dime apiece. Subjects fell into several broad categories: housing, health, and safety; travel and tourism; cultural and educational programs; and posters for Federal One programs. Posters flew out of the workshops and onto the walls of libraries, hospitals, schools, post offices, and community centers. Commuters saw them on subways, buses, and trolley cars. FAP directors compared the posters to radio, movies, and newspapers as popular carriers of information with broad appeal.

Designers found creative visual solutions—asymmetry, abstraction, humor, inventive typography, bright colors—to get across New Deal policies. Posters for the Housing Authority, for example, promoted planned affordable housing as clean, modern, and streamlined—a "cure" for crime, infant mortality, and juvenile delinquency. Posters promoted workplace safety and professional development courses. Health and safety posters encouraged visits to doctors, outdoor activities like swimming, roller skating, or trips to the zoo and warned against quack cures and signs of disease. They reminded viewers to drink milk and to "Keep Your Teeth Clean."

WPA posters boosted tourism through its "See America" campaign. President Roosevelt had added millions of acres to the National Park System, and posters encouraged Americans to visit them for physical and spiritual nourishment. In elemental colors and dramatic compositions, posters celebrated the geysers, mountains, rivers, and redwoods of Yosemite, Yellowstone, the Grand Canyon, and Crater Lake. A dynamic poster featuring a deer and doe bounding across a road, caught in the headlights of an onrushing car, warns the viewer *Don't Kill Our Wild Life*—underscoring the tension between the administration's desire to preserve "wilderness" while opening it up to tourists.

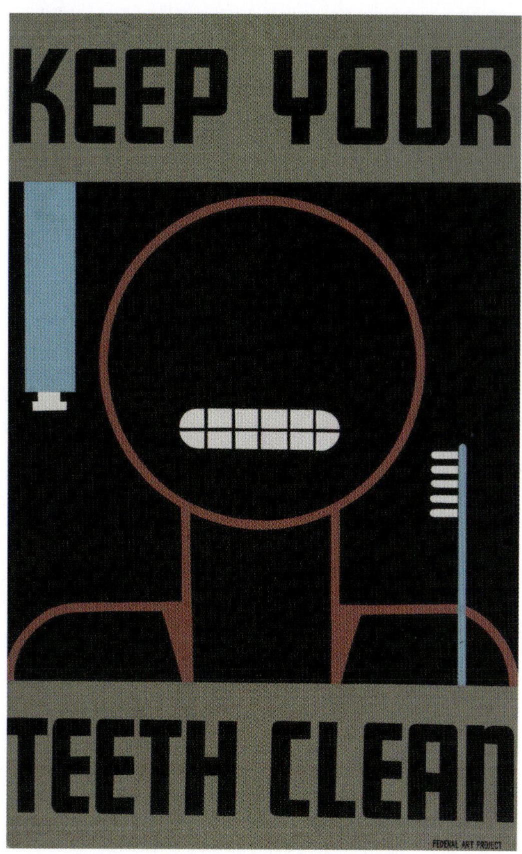

121 *Keep Your Teeth Clean,* 1938

Lester Beall (1903–69) designed modernist posters for the Rural Electrification Administration (REA), set up in 1935 to promote electricity's social and economic benefits—such as powering labor-saving appliances like vacuum cleaners and washing machines—to rural communities. In Beall's *Radio* design, principles of novelty and efficiency fuse with American patriotism (the red, white, and blue color scheme) and pioneer spirit. The diagonal arrows signaling radio waves relieve the homestead's isolation. By the end of the 1930s nearly every US household had a radio. Listeners could tune in to music, news, serials, soap operas, or one of Roosevelt's Sunday evening "fireside chats"—an early and masterful use of mass communication by a sitting president. Beall's posters were exhibited at the Museum of Modern Art in 1937, praised by director Alfred Barr as "worthy of serious consideration as works of art." (Golec 2013, 412)

123

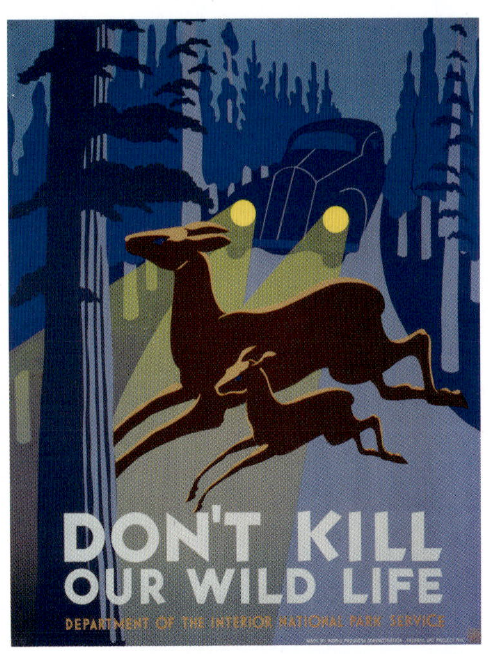

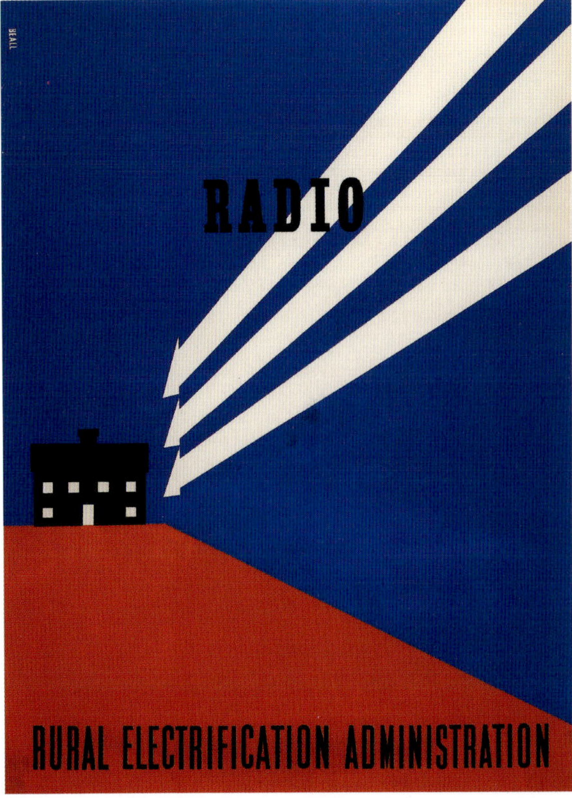

122 ABOVE LEFT *Don't Kill Our Wild Life*, 1940
123 LEFT Lester Beall, *Radio*, 1937

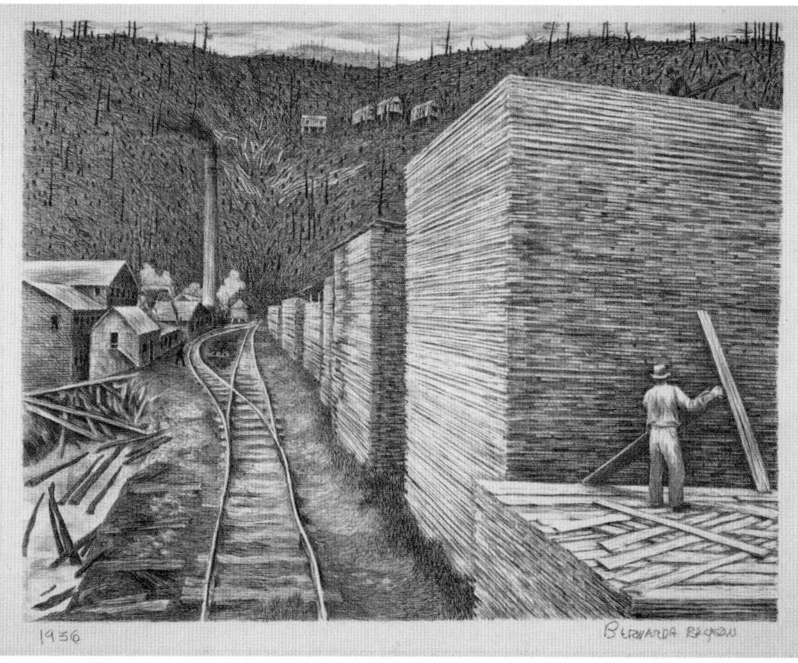

124 Bernarda Bryson, *Cut-Over Land*, 1936

The FAP was not the only government agency that sponsored printmaking. The Special Skills Section of the Resettlement Administration, established in 1935 to aid suffering farmers and sharecroppers, invited Bernarda Bryson (1903–2004) to set up a lithographic shop. There she began work on an ambitious print series, the *Vanishing American Frontier*, which condemned settlement as a series of human and ecological disasters, from slave markets to mining accidents to deforested hillsides. In *Cut-Over Land*, the denuded hills, dotted with stumps like grave markers, have been converted via heavy logging into rows of fungible stacked timber.

Bryson gathered material for the series on travels with her partner, Ben Shahn, who took photographs as they wound their way through the South and heartland states. Their creative partnership belonged to another chapter in New Deal art, one which saw the making of some of the most iconic images of the twentieth century.

Chapter 5
Farm Security Administration Photography

March 1936. Dorothea Lange speeds along a central California highway en route to Berkeley from Southern California. It's pouring rain. She's eager to get home, exhausted from weeks of travel and long days lugging around heavy equipment.

Somewhere outside Nipomo a sign catches her eye: Pea Pickers Camp. She ignores it—she's only seven hours away from a hot meal and a warm bed. She drives another twenty miles, but something compels her to turn back. "I was following instinct not reason," she recalled.

Lange parked her car and trudged through mud into the rain-sodden camp. She passed rows of canvas tents, scrapwood shacks, and corrugated metal lean-tos. No electricity or running water. Haggard transients unable to work because of an overnight freeze. One woman caught Lange's eye: dark hair cut in a bob, features creased and careworn. "I do not remember how I explained my presence or my camera to her," Lange remembered, "but I do remember she asked me no questions." (Lange 1960, 42)

Holding a Graflex camera at waist level, her head bowed, Lange took several exposures of the woman and her children in their tent. With the eye of a seasoned photographer, or a bird of prey, she slowly circled in on the subject, beginning with long shots that included the tent and an inventory of the family's meager possessions: a rocking chair, steamer trunk, a makeshift table, an oil lamp. She moved closer and, with a deft bit of stage direction, instructing the children to turn their heads, took the photograph known as *Migrant Mother*.

It remains the central icon of the Great Depression. Gazing into an uncertain future, "Migrant Mother" holds an infant swaddled in burlap as two children bury their heads on her shoulders. She is present in all her particularity: the strands of

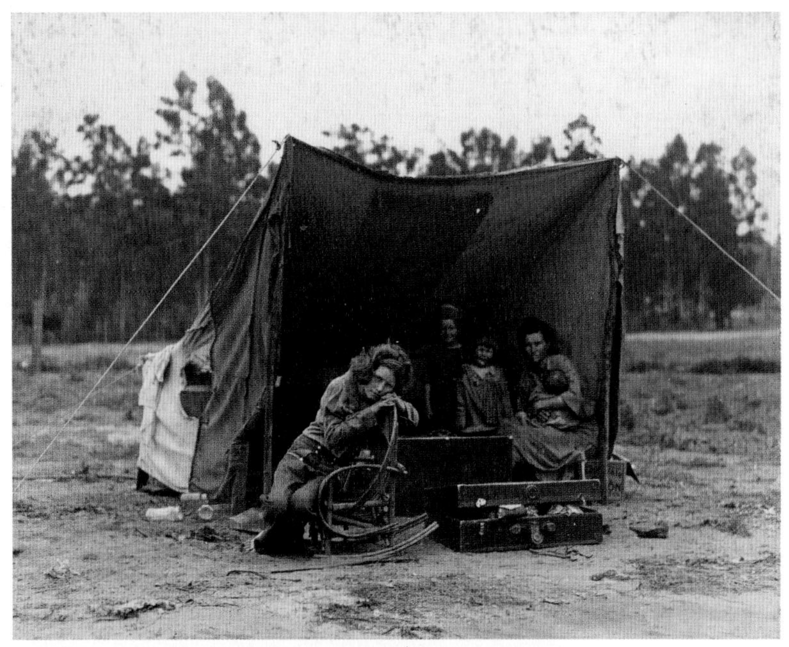

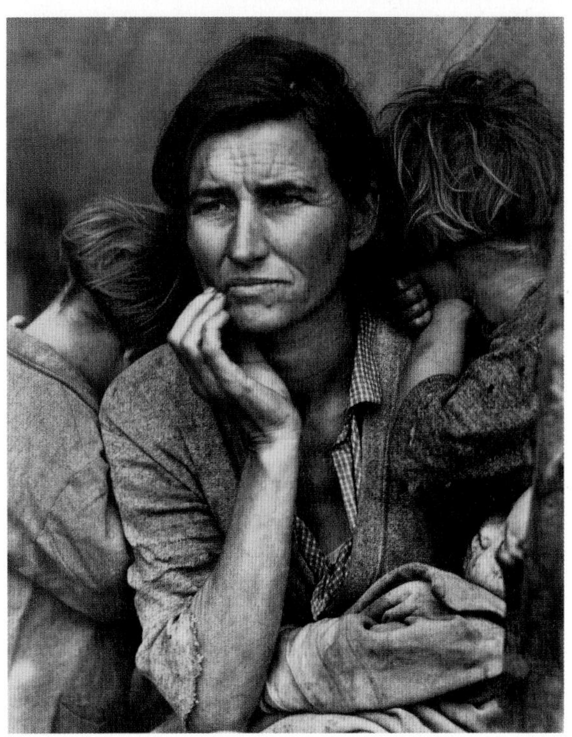

125 TOP Dorothea Lange, *Migrant Agricultural Worker's Family*, 1936
126 ABOVE Dorothea Lange, *Migrant Mother, Nipomo, California*, 1936

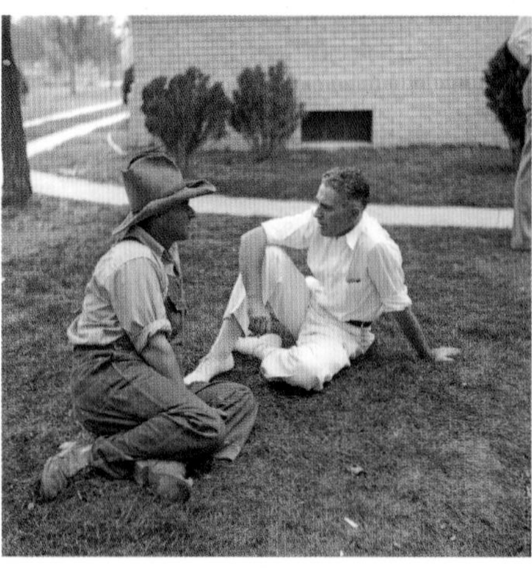

hair, deep worry lines, weave of fraying fabric, tattered gingham plaid blouse. She seems proud but confused: a question posed between the parentheses of her children. Her expression registers a note of bewilderment, a word used by novelist John Steinbeck in *The Grapes of Wrath* to capture the sense of pained confusion people felt at finding themselves in such dire circumstances: "I am alone and bewildered." Or perhaps, as Sally Stein has argued, it is the strain of a mother trying to hold a pose, to shoulder the burden and the myth of motherhood, to help her children the only way she can: by cooperating with this intrusive photographer.

Lange, usually meticulous with her notes, did not record the woman's name that day. Only decades later was her identity made public: Florence Owens Thompson. Details came out about her life: she was of Cherokee descent and had been an organizer for the Cannery and Agricultural Workers Industrial Union. That her first husband had died of tuberculosis years earlier. She wasn't a pea-picker; she was passing through and waiting while her partner went to get their car fixed. These details didn't matter. In the photograph she is not Florence Owens Thompson but *Migrant Mother*, a Depression-era Madonna. Lange herself said "I did not approach the tents and shelters of other stranded pea-pickers. It was not necessary; I knew I had recorded the essence of my assignment."

Farm Security Administration

What was that assignment? *Migrant Mother* came about through the sponsorship of an unlikely government agency: the Resettlement Administration (RA), created by Executive

Order in April 1935 and reorganized as the Farm Security Administration (FSA) two years later. Under the directorship of Rexford Tugwell (1891–1979), a leftwing economist and one of Roosevelt's "Brain Trust" of close advisers, the RA/FSA pursued a variety of state-driven solutions to rural poverty. The agency set up resettlement programs to move struggling farmers away from used-up fields. It also made low-interest loans, planted trees, conserved soil, and housed migrant workers. With his matinée-idol looks and impeccable white outfits, Tugwell could appear a starched contrast to the farmers he served (though, in fact, he grew up in rural New York). His belief in proactive government intervention earned him the nickname "Rex the Red" from anti-New Dealers, who smeared his efforts as Stalinist attacks on free enterprise.

Tugwell knew he would have to sway policymakers and public opinion to secure continued funding. He enlisted his former Columbia University associate, Roy Stryker (1893–1975), as head of the RA/FSA's Historical Section, in effect the agency's public relations arm. At Columbia they had worked together on an economics textbook packed with illustrations, enlivening dry facts through visual interest and emotional pull. The Historical Section would similarly deploy photographs to educate the public about the agency's programs and why they were desperately needed. Stryker considered it his mission to "tell the people of America that those in distressed areas are the same as everybody else except they need a better chance." (Musher 2015, 131)

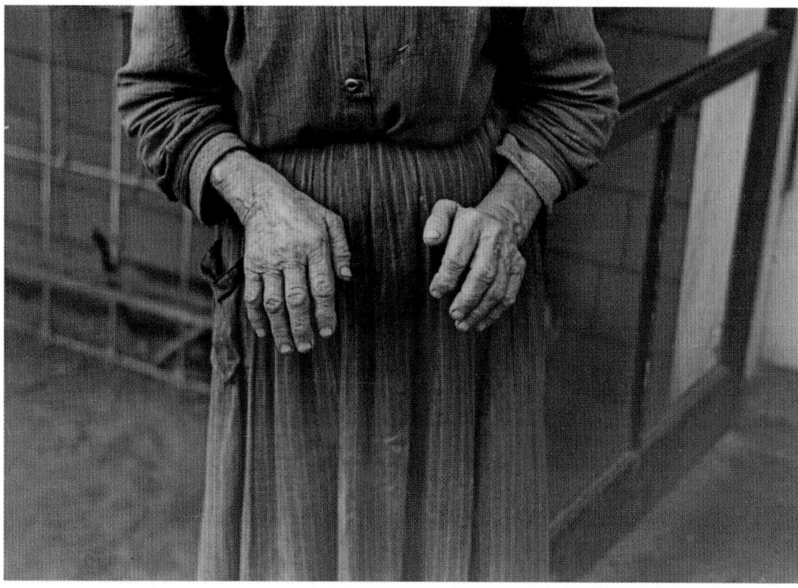

Consider the hands of Mrs. Ostermeyer. She holds
them up, wizened and swollen with arthritis, as if for our
inspection. The angles of the railing and the siding converge
on the hands, whose lighter tones stand out against the
darker pleating of her dress. Russell Lee (1903–86), trained
as a painter, took the picture on his first FSA assignment
in December 1936 to Woodbury County in western Iowa. He
made a series of photographs of the Ostermeyers, an elderly
couple who had recently lost their home to foreclosure.
Lee's cropping emphasized the vulnerable position of senior
citizens, especially farmworkers excluded from the Social
Security program passed the year before. Without other means
of support, the elderly often toiled until age or infirmity threw
them on the mercy of family or "old age homes." What could
be done? Lee fulfilled his brief: to show the need for direct
federal aid to people like the Ostermeyers.

The careworn face of Migrant Mother. The arthritic hands
of Mrs. Ostermeyer. Photographs like these by Lange and Lee
have shaped our collective memory of the 1930s: dust storms,
parched fields, abandoned farmhouses, migrant camps,
sunbeaten sharecroppers, broken-down jalopies, desolate
stretches of highway—all documented in stark, unsparing
black-and-white. They were taken as part of a concerted public
relations campaign. By humanizing the effects of economic
hardship, natural disasters, and poor land management, FSA
photographs worked to win the hearts and minds of the public
while encouraging the government to take action (and keep
the FSA funded). Behind every picture of overplowed fields
or overworked cotton pickers stood a battery of civil servants
ready to implement FSA policies. But the emotional appeal
had to come first.

Between 1935 and 1943 this modest goal—to document and
promote FSA efforts—snowballed into something far more
ambitious: nothing less than an attempt at a panoramic sweep
of American society. Stryker assembled for his Photo Unit an
astonishingly deep bench of talent—Jack Delano, Walker Evans,
Dorothea Lange, Russell Lee, Gordon Parks, Marion Post, Ben
Shahn, John Vachon, and others—to "introduce America to
Americans" by documenting virtually every facet of the country's
social and economic life. At the time, only Evans had a national
reputation, and some, like Shahn and Vachon, had little or no
formal photography training. They brought to their assignments
different priorities, politics, and visual sensibilities. But over
eight years, they all contributed to what Stryker came to call
"The File"—some 175,000 negatives that constitute arguably the
greatest photography collection in the world.

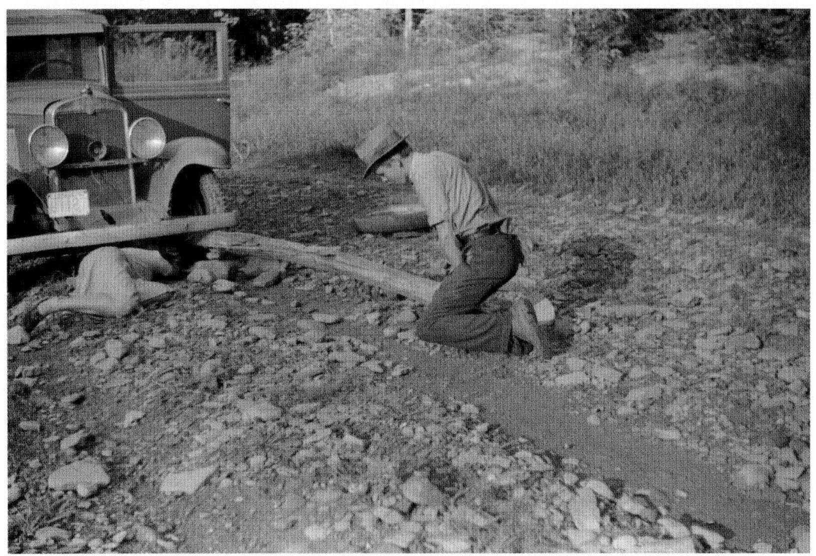

129 Marion Post Wolcott, *Mountaineer and Marion Post Wolcott Changing a Tire with a Fencepost as a Jack,* 1940

On the Road

From the central office in Washington, Stryker masterminded the far-reaching campaign. He issued a memorandum in 1936 prescribing "American Background," the FSA equivalent to the Section's American scene, as the agency's organizing principle. Like Section administrators, Stryker wanted his team to educate themselves about the history, habits, and circumstances of the people and places they would be documenting. He was always "throwing books at us," Marion Post (1910–90) remembered, a habit from his days teaching college seminars. Most importantly, he supplied "shooting scripts" for photographers to follow outlining keywords, themes, and subject matter.

129   Armed with this material (as well as a portable stove, coffee percolator, and shovel and axe in case of snow or fallen tree limbs), FSA photographers fanned out across the country in search of compelling material. The agency covered gas mileage, food, and lodging, and provided equipment—camera, film rolls, flashbulbs—for trips that could last months. Stryker penned long letters to photographers in the field offering instruction, course corrections, and morale boosters. Photographers shipped their negatives, the property of the US government, back to Washington (Lange locked horns with Stryker over this policy; she preferred to print her own negatives) where Stryker

"killed" images below his standard by punching holes through the negative or tossing out the sheet film. He oversaw a team of darkroom assistants and office administrators to print, catalog, and distribute the images to media outlets.

This efficient but top-down system did not sit well with Walker Evans, one of the first photographers hired onto the Historical Section. He claimed to not "give a damn about the office in Washington—or about the New Deal, really," and used FSA assignments to pursue his own aesthetic ends. Sent to Mississippi in 1936 to record soil erosion and architectural decay, Evans went "off script" and took pictures in the Black quarters of Vicksburg and Tupelo—one is a study in abstract lines, planes, and leaning bodies in exquisite tension. When in 1938 the Museum of Modern Art mounted *Walker Evans: American Photographs*, its first show dedicated to a single photographer, Evans issued a disclaimer in the accompanying catalog: "[The photographs] are presented without sponsorship or connection with the policies, aesthetic or political, of any of the institutions, publications or government agencies for which some of the work has been done."

Evans's studio mate, Ben Shahn, had no qualms about photography as a political tool. This attitude helped clarify the Historical Section's mission in its critical first year. "Look Roy," Shahn recalled explaining to Stryker, "you're not going to move anybody with this eroded soil—but the effect this eroded soil has on a kid who looks starved, this is going to move people." (Hurley 1972, 50)

Shahn applied this principle to photographs he took during a fall 1935 road trip with his partner, Bernarda Bryson. (Evans gave the untrained Shahn aperture advice: "F9 on the sunny side of the street, F4.5 on the shady side of the street.") One is captioned "Scotts Run, West Virginia, miner's sons," and depicts a trio of ragged barefooted boys scampering on a pile of discarded tires. A boy with a buzzcut and big ears turns to confront Shahn, more in curiosity it seems than anger.

His dad may have been part of the United Mine Workers strike for better wages and shorter hours. Shahn made his sympathies clear. On the same trip he snapped an irreverent photo of a sheriff's deputy leaning against a mailbox, jutting out his ample rear end. He's on hand to "keep the peace" during the miners' strike, but in Shahn's picture he's an emblem of faceless authority sustained by the threat of violence: the gun-and-holster slung low over his wide hips. With his lightweight 35mm Leica, outfitted with a right-angle viewfinder, Shahn could catch subjects unposed and unaware. Restless energy slants his pictures: skewed angles, blurred motion,

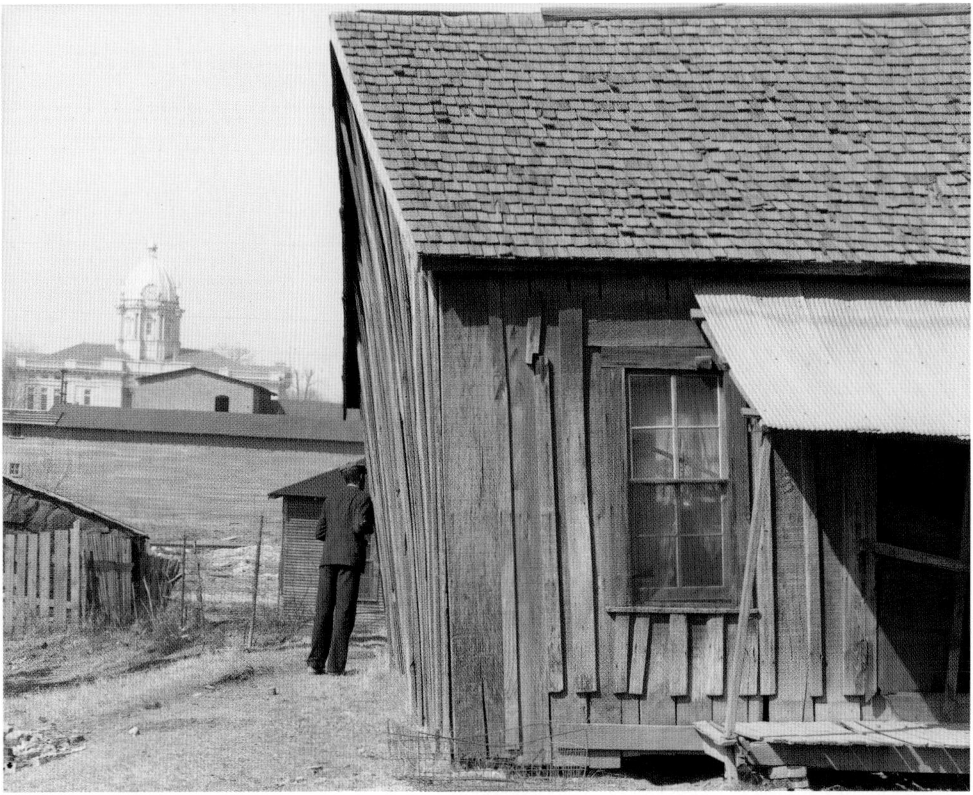

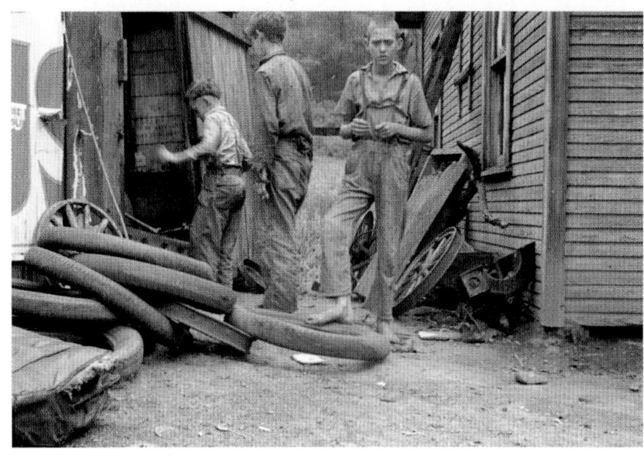

130 TOP Walker Evans, *Negro House, Tupelo, Mississippi*, 1936
131 ABOVE Ben Shahn, *Scotts Run, West Virginia, Miner's Sons*, 1935

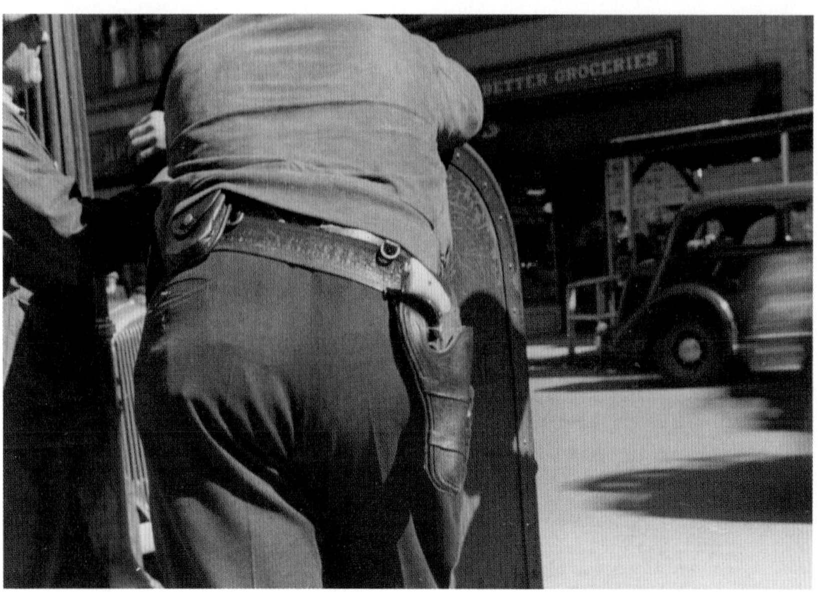

132 Ben Shahn, *A Deputy with a Gun on his Hip during the September 1935 Strike in Morgantown, West Virginia*, 1935

off-guard intimacy. They are more like sketches than meticulous compositions, the raw material of later prints and paintings.

Like most FSA photographers (Evans was the exception), Shahn believed evangelically in the power of images to instruct and influence. Few shied from the word propaganda. "Propaganda is to me a noble word," Shahn said. "Everything is propaganda for what you believe in," Dorothea Lange echoed in a 1968 interview. "I had deep sympathy for the underprivileged," Marion Post remembered, "[and] felt the need to contribute to a more equitable society." Post, Lange, Shahn, and their FSA colleagues documented the lives of the hungry and houseless, the downtrodden working poor: Pennsylvania coal miners, sharecroppers in the southern Black Belt, Mexican pecan shellers in Texas and carrot pullers in California, Filipino lettuce pickers and Japanese farmers in California. Some of their most indelible images came about through the suffering caused by the worst environmental catastrophe in US history.

Dust Bowl

"Black Sunday": April 14, 1935. The towering dust storm could be seen approaching from miles away. The air turned cold. Wind moaned through the trees and birds took flight in terror. Dust blinded cattle and suffocated chickens. The black cloud rolled east, blotting the sun across the Midwest all the way to the Atlantic. Woody Guthrie, the Oklahoman folk troubadour, sang in "Great Dust Storm" of the "deathlike" cloud filling the sky: *We thought it was our judgment, we thought it was our doom.*

In the 1930s, severe droughts combined with disastrous land-use policies—overplowing, overgrazing, and replacing native grasses with cash crops like corn and wheat—wreaked havoc across the Great Plains. Without stabilizing prairie grasses, wind eroded the loose topsoil and whipped up "black blizzards" of dust, darkening skies and destroying crops in Texas, Oklahoma, Kansas, the Dakotas, and nearby states. Newspapers called this region the "Dust Bowl."

Dust Bowl scenes conjured biblical plagues. In Cimarron County, Oklahoma, Arthur Rothstein (1915–85) snapped what Ben Shahn later called "the greatest picture of the whole period." A farmer and his two boys lean forward, heads bowed against the swirling dust and wind, passing a disused log-and-tarpaper shack. The smaller child trails behind, rubbing dust out of his eyes. Scholars have cast doubt on the veracity of the photograph, or at least the accuracy of the title. Could Rothstein have taken a picture *in* a dust storm? Would shadows cast so clearly with the sun obscured? Rothstein later admitted to at least partially staging the picture, defending the approach

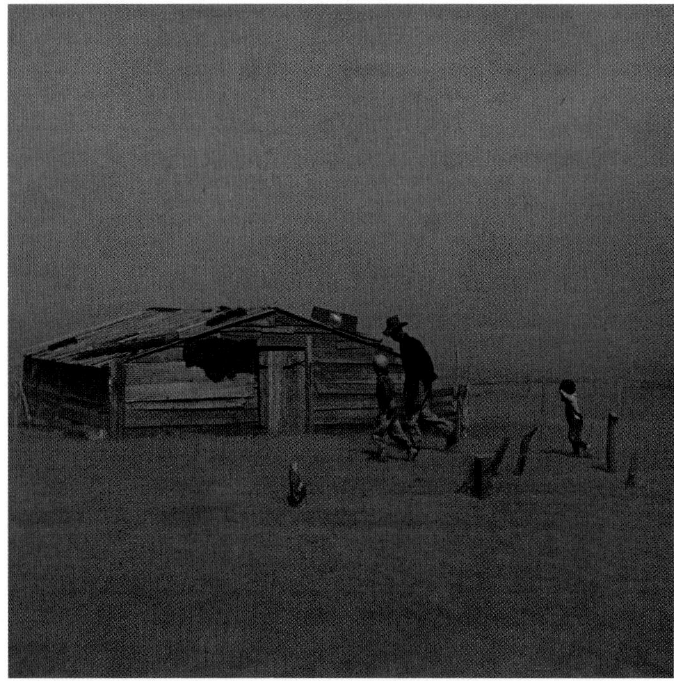

133 Arthur Rothstein, *Farmer and Sons in Dust Storm, Cimarron County, Oklahoma,* 1936

with the crafty argument: "Provided the results are a faithful reproduction of what the photographer believes he sees, whatever takes place in the making of the picture is justified." Other FSA photographers agreed. A documentary photograph "isn't something you happen to see," Jack Delano said, it is "an expression of the essence of what you are seeing." (Appel 2021, 75)

The "essence" of Rothstein's scene is the human struggle against a pitiless environment and the desperate need for government aid. Over the course of the decade a hundred million acres dried up, forcing the internal migration of two and a half million farmers, field workers, and their families. These "Okies" or "Exodusters" of Americana lore loaded up jalopies and drove west across Route 66 to the promised land of California.

John Steinbeck's bestselling novel *The Grapes of Wrath*, published in the spring of 1939 and adapted into an Oscar-winning film the following year, immortalized this Dust Bowl exodus through the Joad family's cross-country trek. The FSA

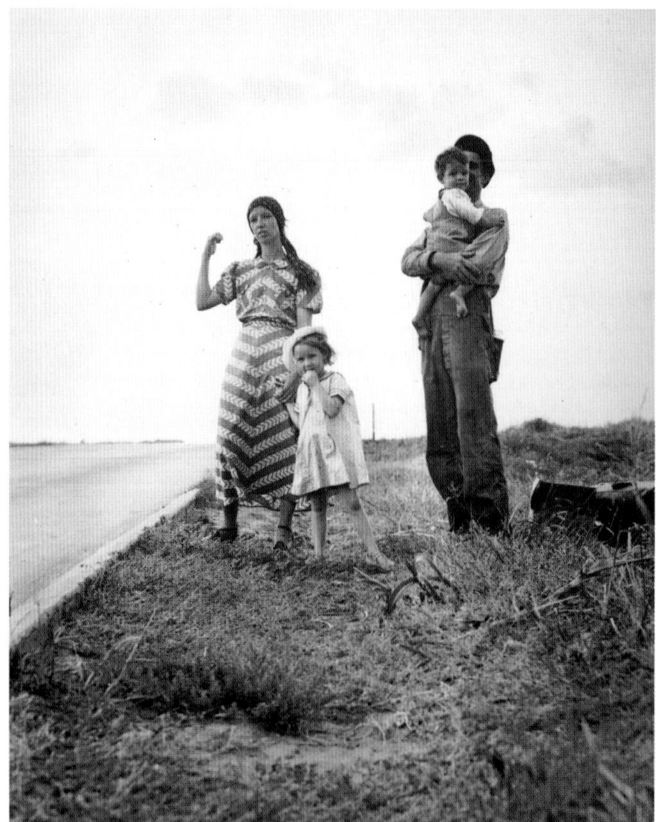

134 Dorothea Lange, *Hitch-hiking from Joplin, Missouri, to a sawmill job in Arizona. On US 66 near Weatherford, western Oklahoma, 1938*

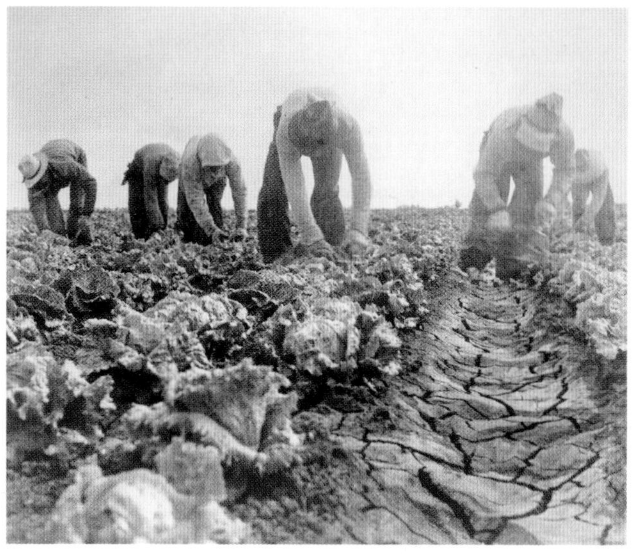

set up federal camps to provide basic shelter and facilities, but it was insufficient. Many ended up camping along irrigation ditches or in muddy fields near the large ranches where sanitation was poor and diseases like smallpox and typhoid spread. Few migrants found the work they sought, and the work to be had was low-paying, backbreaking, and seasonal.

Steinbeck treated the white midwestern Joad family as Dust Bowl archetypes, obscuring the fact that white migrants to California displaced Mexican and Filipino farmworkers. In many cases the newly arrived Okies undermined union efforts by crossing picket lines and taking jobs for less pay. The big commercial farms, often subsidized by the government, benefited from the labor strife and competition. Legislators targeted immigrants as contributing to an "oversupply" of labor, passing laws that halted immigration and led to the deportation of hundreds of thousands of Mexican and Chicano workers and their families. Dorothea Lange—whose economist husband, Paul Taylor (1895–1984), authored one of the first studies of migrant labor in California—documented some of these realities: a Mexican family marooned on the side of the road, for example, or a row of Filipino lettuce pickers stooped against the vast expanse of sky.

These were not the images that circulated more widely. A June 1937 article in *Life* magazine reproduced Lange's portrait of a white migrant farmer with the title "Dust Bowl Farmer Is New Pioneer." Beneath a battered soft-brimmed hat, he gazes

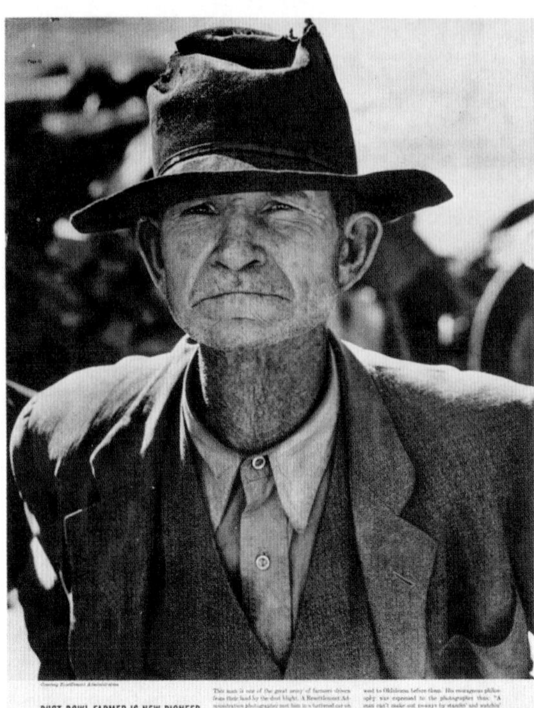

136 Dorothea Lange, "Dust Bowl Farmer Is New Pioneer," *Life*, 21 June 1937

outwards from weathered features, his neck too scrawny for a soiled shirt buttoned to the top. The caption reads, in part: "This man is one of the great army of farmers driven from their land by the dust blight....He has joined the pioneers who are seeking new lives on the Pacific Coast, as their fathers trekked west to Oklahoma before them." This optimistic recasting of the desperate farmer as a "new pioneer" evoked the Treasury Section's glorifying gloss on America's frontier past.

Lange's rawboned "Pioneer" came straight out of Dust Bowl central casting. FSA photographers had to strike a balance between exposing poverty and showing the victims as worthy of taxpayer dollars. Film critic and documentarian Pare Lorentz (director of the RA-funded masterpiece *The Plow That Broke the Plains*) noticed that "You do not find in [Lange's] portrait gallery the bindle-stiffs, the drifters, the tramps, the unfortunate, aimless dregs of a country." (Stott 1973, 58)

Black and White

In 1937 Lange asked Stryker whether she should focus more on Black or white sharecroppers. "Take both black and white,"

Stryker replied, "but place the emphasis upon the white tenants, since we know they will receive much wider use." (Appel 2021, 152) The emphasis Lange placed on a white overseer, rather than tenant, in a 1936 photograph taken in the Mississippi Delta is not what Stryker had in mind. When the *US Camera Annual* reproduced the photograph in 1939 it carried the provocative caption, "Did or didn't you know slavery was abolished?"

The stocky white overseer (not, in fact, the overseer of this particular plantation) in a brimmed hat, suspenders, and rolled-up sleeves and cuffs props a proprietary leg on the hub of a gleaming Chevrolet coupe. Behind him five Black men sit and stand on the porch of the plantation store. With his hand like a talon gripping his knee, the car owner addresses Lange's husband, a bespectacled sliver on the left margin of the composition. (Taylor often accompanied Lange on her field assignments, conducting interviews with subjects while she took photographs.) The low-angled framing stresses the relations of domination and dependence, ownership and debt that defined the sharecropper economy.

137 Dorothea Lange, *Plantation Overseer and his Field Hands, Mississippi Delta,* 1936

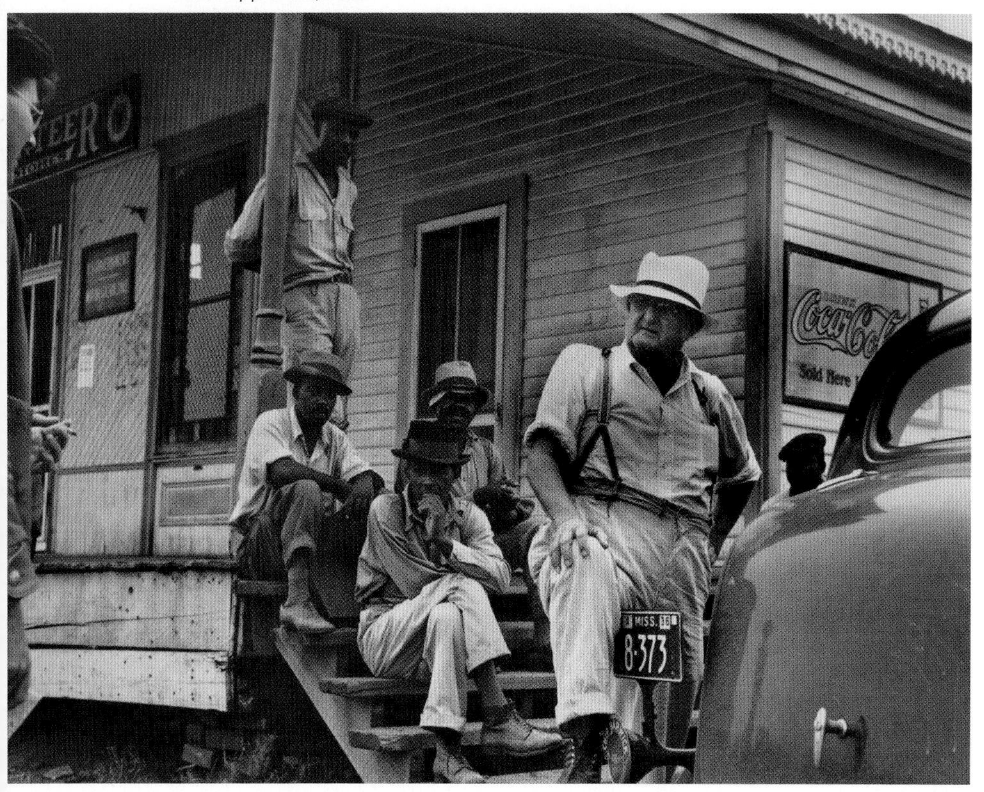

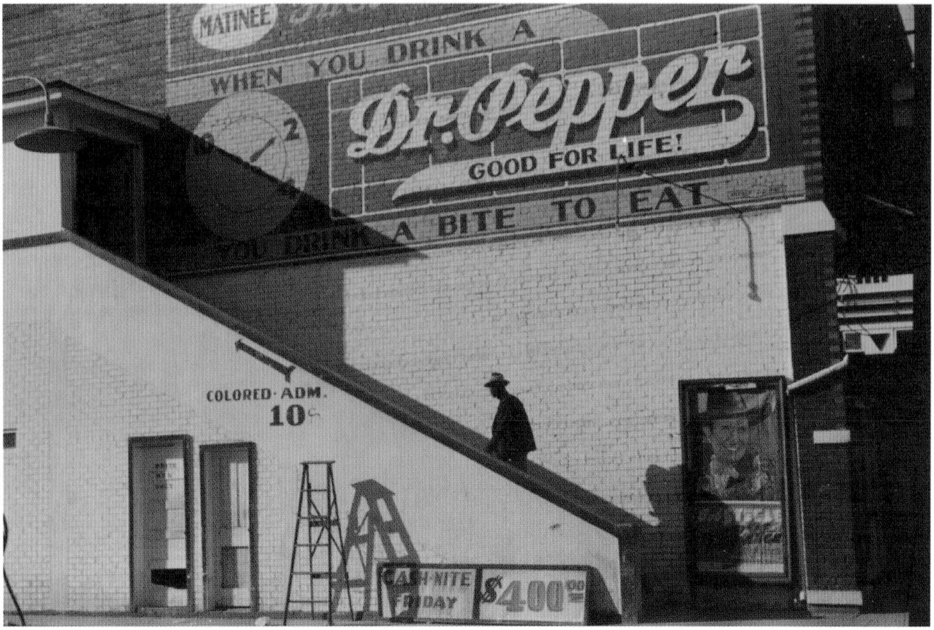

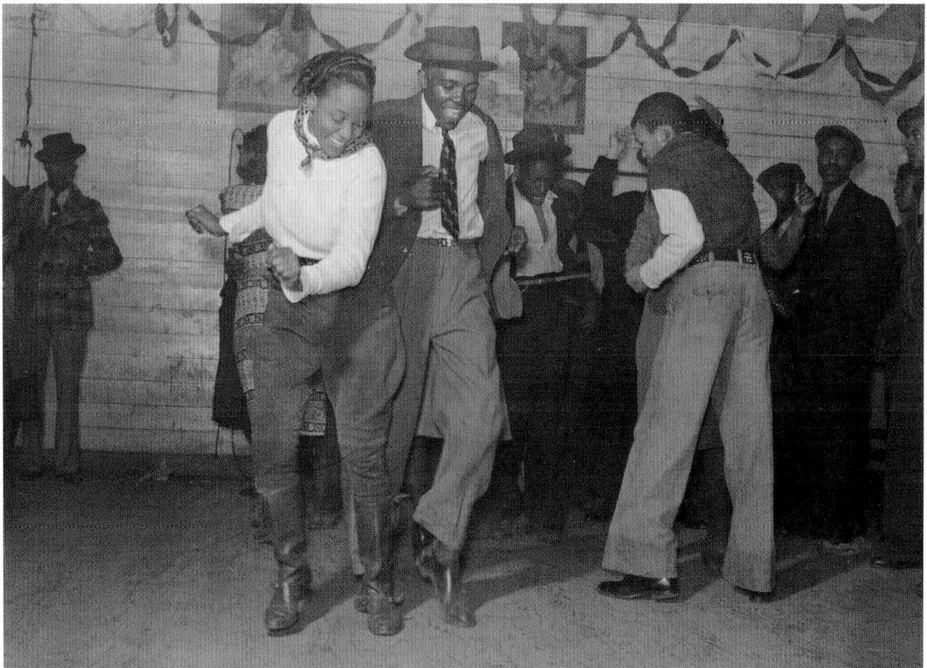

138 TOP Marion Post Wolcott, *Man Entering a Theater, Belzoni, Mississippi*, 1939
139 ABOVE Marion Post Wolcott, *Jitterbugging in Negro Juke Joint, Saturday Evening, Outside Clarksdale, Mississippi*, 1939

Stryker was wary of publishing images that exposed Jim Crow racism or argued for racial equality. Roosevelt relied on southern Democrats as swing votes in Congress, and their support enabled his New Deal agenda. The Southern bloc, though a legislative minority, wielded disproportionate influence in thwarting policies that threatened the Southern "way of life," a euphemism for segregation. Southern politicians, part of the ruling white elite in the former Confederacy, attracted investment to their regions with the promise of cheap, non-unionized labor. Stryker emphasized white suffering in FSA photography to appeal to the Dixiecrats who held the purse strings.

138 Photographers in the field had more license. One image in particular, taken by Marion Post in Belzoni, Mississippi, has become an icon of the Jim Crow South. A Black man in a fedora walks up the steps of a movie theater's segregated entrance, silhouetted against the painted brick, pulled upward by an arrow: "Colored Adm. 10¢." (By 1930 three out of five Americans went to the movies every week.) The clamoring type and chirpy slogans of modern advertising surround him: *Good for Life! A Bite to Eat. Cash-Nite $400.* A restroom door in the bottom left corner is designated for "White Men Only," a white man like the cowboy hero grinning from beneath his Stetson in a poster for horse opera *Feud of the Range.*

The photograph is almost expressionist: the raking afternoon shadows cleave a clock in two and heighten the sense of isolation and dread. Everything is doubled, shadowed, slanted, suggesting two worlds: one for whites and one for 133 Blacks. Like Rothstein's farmer struggling against the dust storm, Post's protagonist struggles against an environmental threat: the Jim Crow South, where virtually all public spaces— schools, hotels, trains, buses, restaurants—designated separate sections for Black patrons.

The stark geometries and brooding isolation of *Man Entering* 139 *a Theater* give way to the youthful *joie de vivre* of a juke joint on a Saturday night in Clarksdale, Mississippi. Post, who had studied dance with modernist innovator Ruth St. Denis, felt this photo "says the most about me," she later claimed, "what I was trying to do and trying to say." Post had been taking pictures at a Mississippi Delta plantation all week and convinced the owner's son to take her to a Saturday night dance. The foreground couple beams, mid-swing on bare floors beneath swagging streamers. But in the background a man in a cap, hands in pockets, regards Post's camera warily. Consciously or not, she had put the Black men in the room in danger: socializing with white women was the common pretext for lynching.

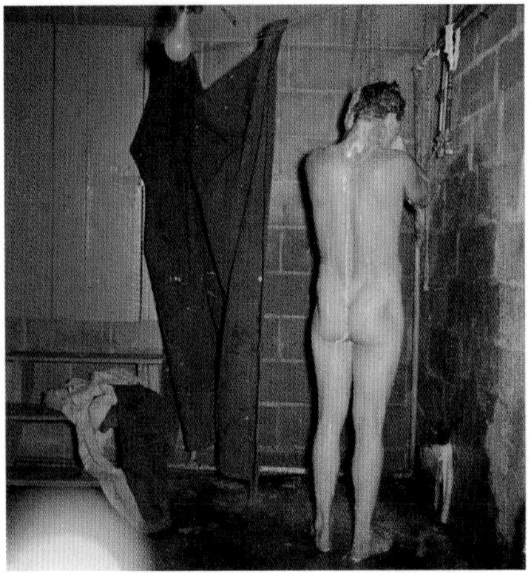

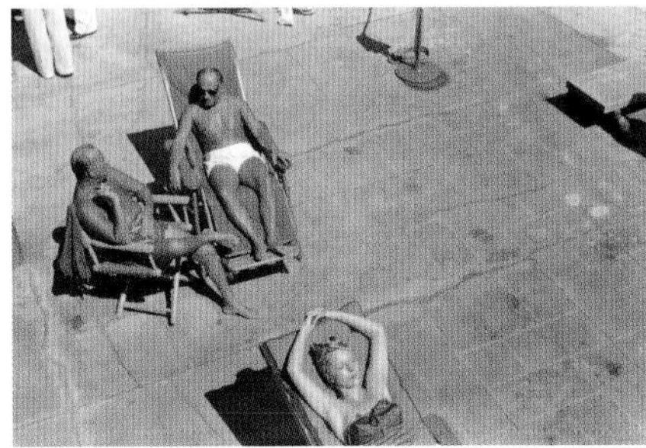

140 ABOVE LEFT Marion Post Wolcott,
*Miner Takes Shower, Which he Built
in the Cellar of his Home, Westover,
West Virginia,* 1938
141 LEFT Marion Post Wolcott.
June in January, Miami Beach, Florida,
1939

140

141

Post was a risk-taker. A young unmarried woman traveling back roads alone in a Plymouth Six, on assignment for weeks and months on end, defied social conventions. She was run out of one small town as a "gypsy" for her bronzed skin, jangly earrings, and colorful headscarf. On her first assignment to a West Virginia coal mining town, she photographed a miner taking a shower in the concrete cellar of his home. His clothes are piled on a low bench. A blanket strung along a rope for privacy is pulled to the side. Soap runs down his back. It is a moment of startling intimacy—the miner's exposed body flashbulb-carved in outline on the cinderblock wall.

Semi-nude bodies flaunt "how the other half lives" in Post's photos from Miami and Palm Beach, Florida. On assignment in the winter of 1938–39, Post took pictures of race tracks, resort hotels, beaches, and pleasure boats. At a private beach club, looking down from a height, she photographed a trio of sunbathers. Reclining in lounge chairs, oiled and bronzed, they exude ease and comfort, basking in sunshine. Post took

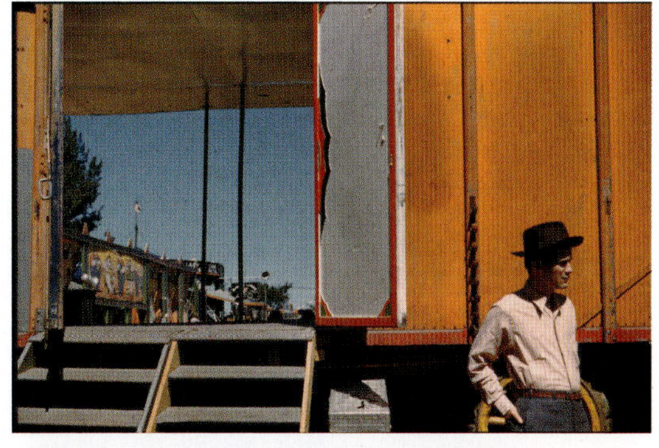

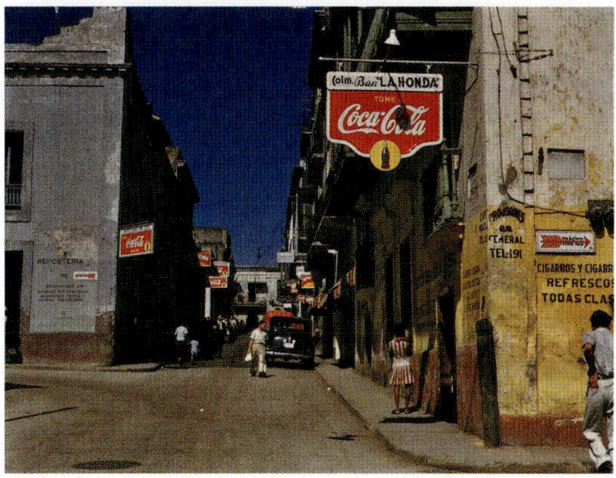

the photo, in her words, to contrast Florida's wealthy and "complacent" tourists with the "appalling conditions" of nearby migrant camps and citrus farms. (McEuen 2000, 151)

Post was among the FSA photographers who experimented with color. Kodachrome began selling color film in 1935, and the novel technology (dismissed by Walker Evans as "garish and vulgar") quickly became associated with advertising in glossy magazines. Stryker, however, saw its potential to attract publishers and encouraged his team to experiment with the medium.

Although the cost and complications of developing Kodachrome film prohibited its widespread use, there remains a small but vivid FSA record of the period in color. The Vermont State Fair blazes in Jack Delano's (1914–97) saturated compositions, exploiting the complementary blue sky and orange boxcar siding. Between late 1941 and the spring of 1942 Delano made trips to Puerto Rico, an unincorporated territory of the United States, where he took pictures of the coffee, tobacco, and sugar

142

plantations that drove the economies. They show the US as an imperial soft power, exporting brands like Coca-Cola and implementing FSA policies as an extension of mainland welfare.

How American People Live

Introducing "America to Americans" required publicity. The FSA mounted the exhibition *How American People Live* in New York in the spring of 1938 as part of an international photography exposition. (The "American People" of the title were, in fact, mostly a thin demographic slice of white rural farmers and sharecroppers.) Over a hundred thousand visitors came through the exhibition and were invited to record their reactions on comment cards. "Your pictures demonstrate clearly that one half of the people do not know how the other half lives," one person wrote. Another dismissed the display as "subversive propaganda." A writer for *Survey Graphic* noted that nine out of ten comment cards demanded a response to the plight of the people photographed—a sign that the photographers had achieved their goal of raising awareness—but disagreed on what that response should be. (Finnegan 2015, 164)

Most people encountered FSA photographs in books and magazines, not exhibitions. The FSA made its growing archive available free of charge to publications like *Life, Look*, and *US Camera* to ensure their wide circulation. (*Life* magazine alone reached around 23 million readers each week.) Published photographs typically appeared surrounded by explanatory text. Photographers made field notes and observations, the basis for sometimes lengthy captions that remained on file in the FSA's Washington DC office. This 1930s documentary impulse found writers, social workers, filmmakers, and sociologists conducting fieldwork and generating findings based on direct observation. Beyond FSA photos, examples include the *March of Time* newsreels, Living Newspaper dramatizations of current events, magazine photojournalism, or undercover reports in books and newspapers.

This impulse reached its zenith in the documentary photo book. Novelist Erskine Caldwell (1903–87) and photographer Margaret Bourke-White collaborated on *You Have Seen their Faces* (1937), a melodramatic account of Southern sharecroppers and tenant farmers with fabricated quotes. Dorothea Lange and Paul Taylor responded with *An American Exodus: A Record of Human Erosion* (1939), using direct quotes from their subjects. Novelist Sherwood Anderson (1876–1941) reproduced some of the FSA's more idyllic images for his 1940 tribute to what he called the "smaller scenes," *Home Town: The Face of America.* Marion's sister Helen Post (1907–79) took pictures for *As Long as*

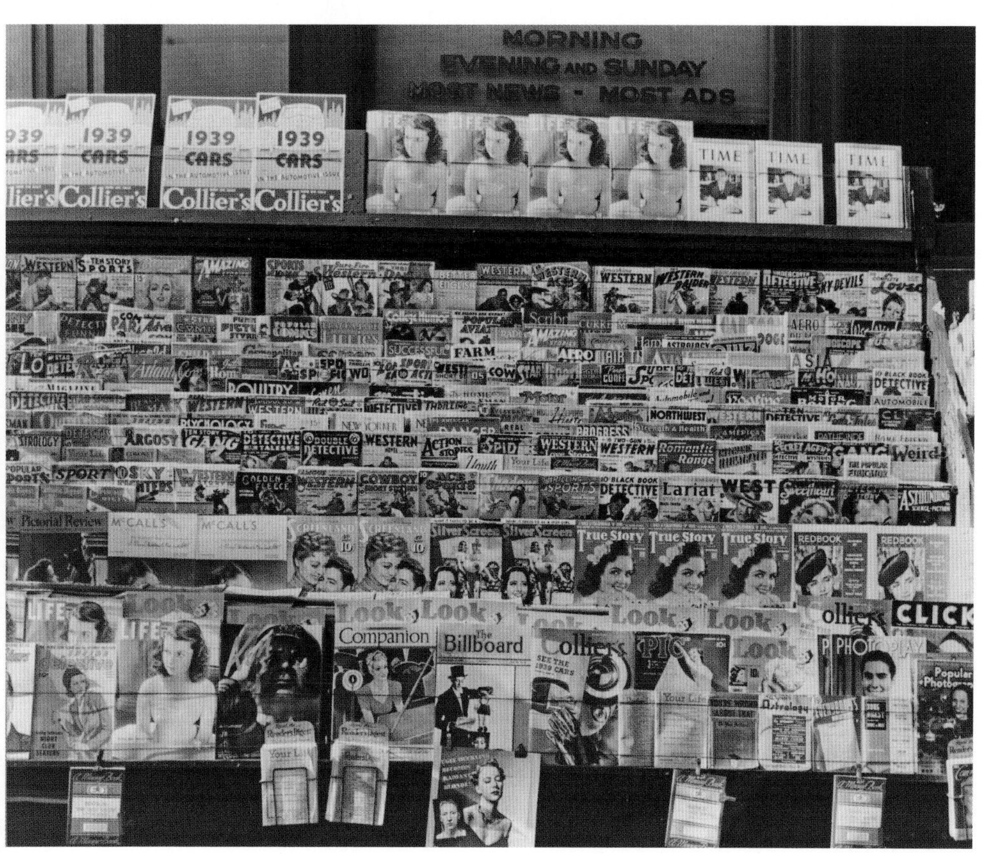

144 John Vachon, *Newsstand, Omaha, Nebraska*, 1938

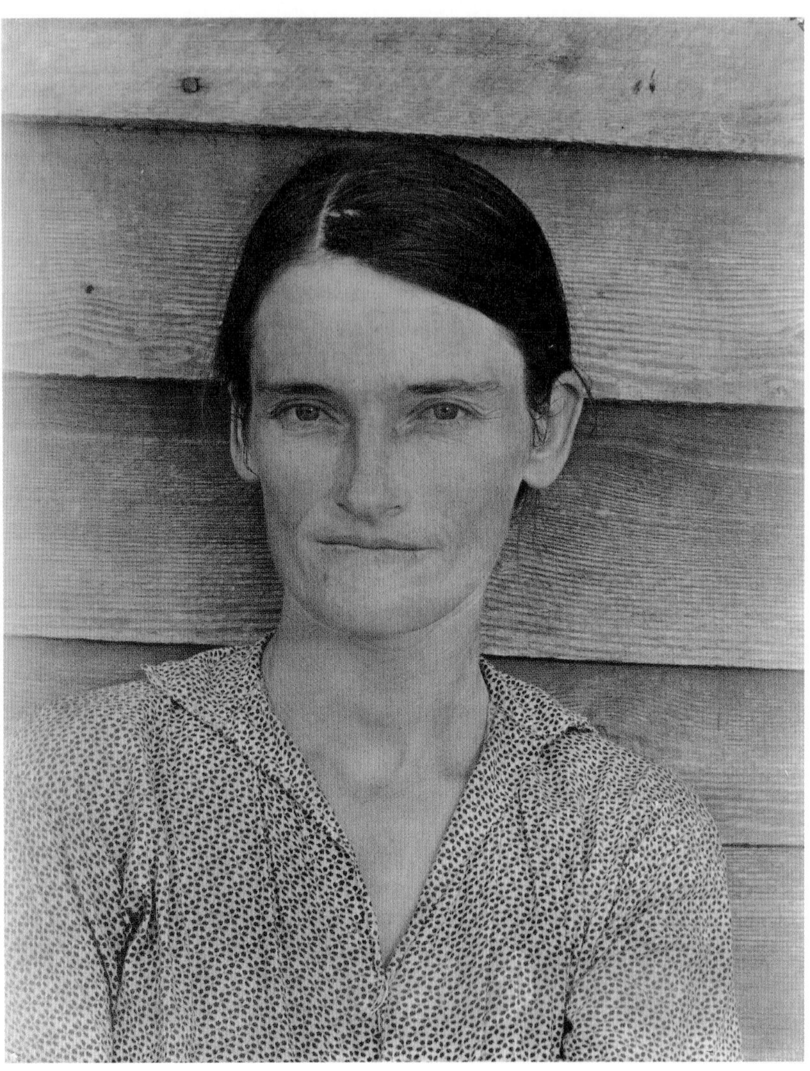

145 Walker Evans, *Allie Mae Burroughs, Wife of Cotton Sharecropper, Hale County, Alabama*, 1936

the Grass Shall Grow (1940), a sociological account of Indigenous life sponsored by the Bureau of Indian Affairs. In 1941 Edwin Rosskam (1903–85) compiled an anthology of FSA photographs called *12 Million Black Voices: A Folk History of the Negro in the United States* with blistering text by novelist Richard Wright (1908–60).

The era's most celebrated photobook—the still-strange and daunting 500-page *Let Us Now Praise Famous Men* (1941)—came about through an assignment from *Fortune* magazine. In the summer of 1936, on leave from the Resettlement Administration, Walker Evans traveled with writer James Agee (1909–55) to Hale County in rural Alabama to gather material for a photo essay on the lives of three tenant farmer families. Evans took a series of formally rigorous, unsentimental portraits—detailing every worry line, patterned dot, parallel lines of parted hair and woodgrain—of twenty-seven-year-old Allie Mae Burroughs ("Annie Mae Gudger" in the book) standing against the cabin's wood siding. The mutual withholding of photographer and subject, a kind of charged reticence, yields a "single, holy, unrepeatable individual," as Agee wrote. Like *Migrant Mother,* the portrait's iconic status (this variant from the series exhibited in MoMA's *American Photographs* and was reproduced in the catalogue) owes something to its art historical echoes: Burroughs is a sharecropper Mona Lisa with a secretive half-smile.

Gordon Parks (1912–2006), like Evans, subverted the traditional portrait. A grant from the philanthropic Rosenwald Fund secured a spot for Parks on the FSA; he arrived in January 1942 as the agency's only Black photographer. Determined to fight racism with his camera, Parks did not have to go far. Late one evening, when the building had emptied for the day, Parks introduced himself to Ella Watson, the woman who cleaned the FSA offices. At the time, nine out of ten Black Americans employed by the federal government did custodial work.

Parks' portrait of Watson undercut Grant Wood's *American Gothic*—which he knew well from years in Chicago—with bitter irony. Parks replaced the bald farmer gripping his pitchfork, an emblem of stern American rectitude, with Watson holding a broom, a symbol of women's labor. Echoes remain: the frontal pose, the round, wire-rimmed glasses, the thin ascetic features. The house's pointed arch window and board and batten siding become the stars and stripes, like prison bars, of a draped American flag. The slightly blurred flag, which decorated the office of a white woman whose desk job Watson had applied for, suggests the promise of an American Dream more mirage than reality. Stryker had encouraged Parks to "put a face on racism,"

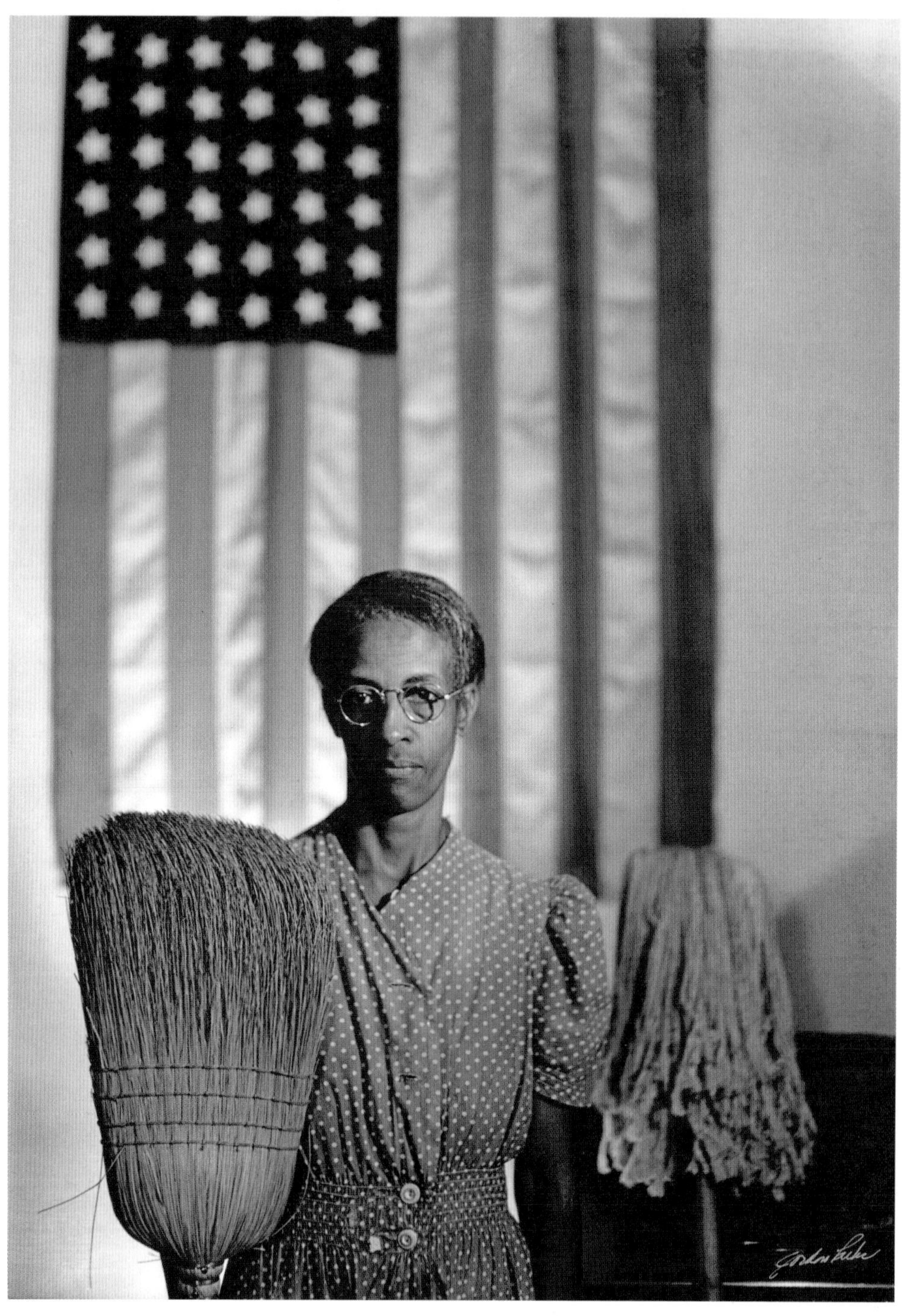

146 ABOVE Gordon Parks, *American Gothic, Washington DC*, 1942
147 OPPOSITE Grant Wood, *American Gothic*, 1930

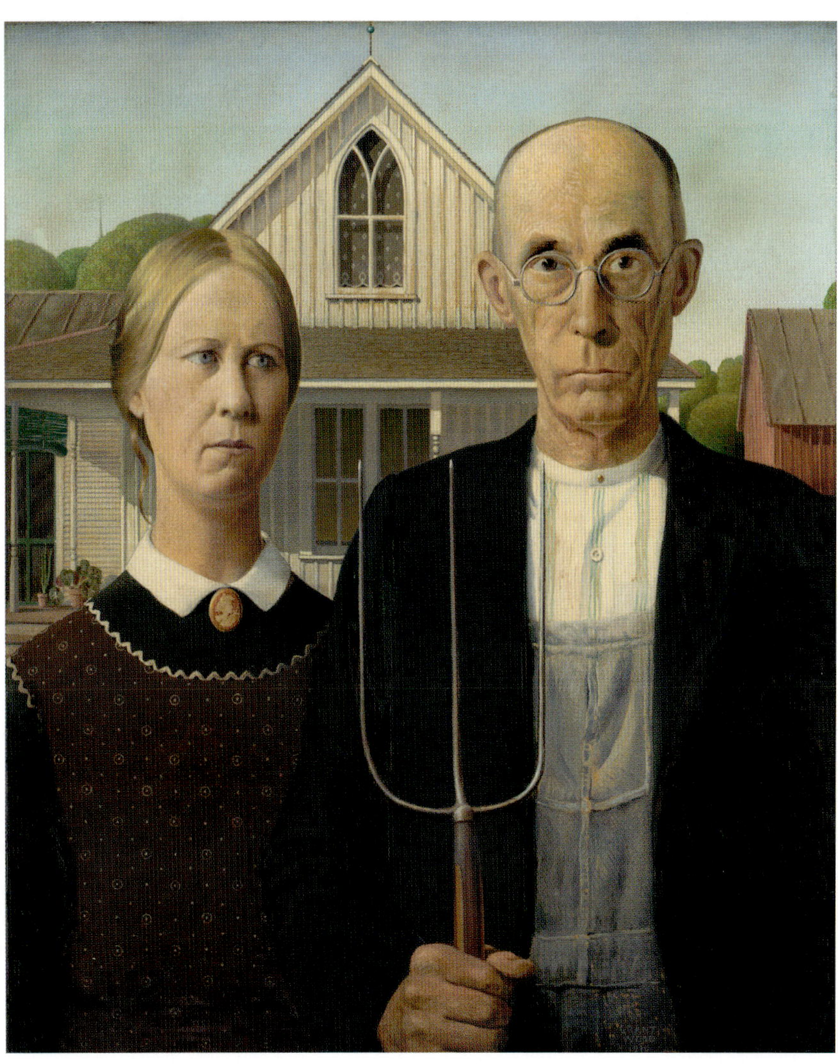

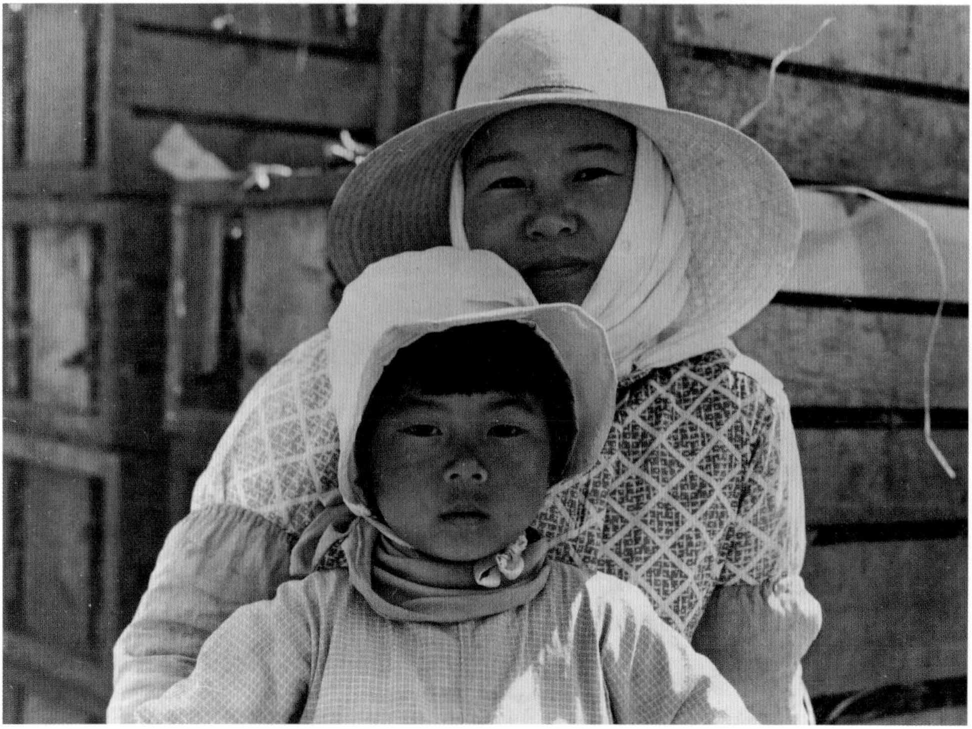

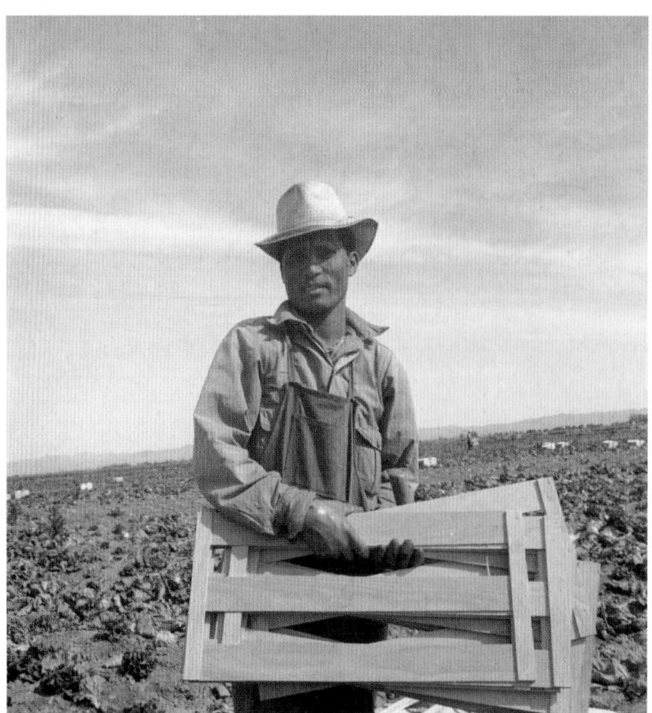

148 TOP Dorothea Lange, *Japanese Mother and Daughter, Agricultural Workers near Guadalupe, California*, 1937
149 LEFT Dorothea Lange, *Filipino Lettuce Field Laborer, Imperial Valley, California*, 1939

but when he saw *American Gothic* he said to him, "Well, you're getting the idea, but you're likely to get us all fired." (Parks 2005, 66)

The Face and The File

By the time Parks arrived in Washington, Stryker felt pressure to offer evidence of the federal programs' successes rather than the economy's failures. The FSA had shifted emphasis from the plight of the marginalized towards a more idealized vision of small-town life. When Russell Lee insisted on photographing impoverished Mexican pecan shellers in San Antonio, Stryker complained, "I must say that I can't do much glorifying out of anything you've taken." (Appel 2021, 187–88)

What remains are the faces. In their 1939 book, *American Exodus,* Lange and Taylor declared their intention to let the "living participants" of the time "speak to you face to face." Whether we're looking at a sharecropper's wife in Alabama, a cleaning woman in Washington DC, a Cincinnati kid in a hat and overalls, a Japanese mother and daughter in California, or a Filipino lettuce worker, FSA photographs generate intimacy through eye-level, head-on framing. French philosopher Emmanuel Levinas based ethical responsibility on the "face of the Other" which compels us beyond narrow self-interest to

150 John Vachon, *Negro Boy near Cincinnati, Ohio,* c. 1942

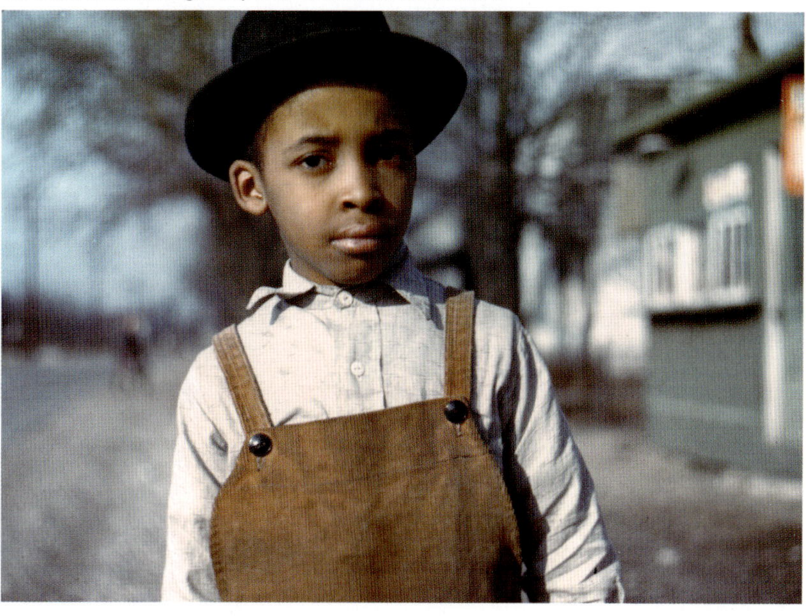

honor their transcendent value—what Agee called the "single, holy, unrepeatable individual." FSA photographers humanized social problems, inviting a politics based on imaginative sympathy and emotional appeal.

The Library of Congress holds some 175,000 negatives in its FSA archives. Stryker called his ever-growing pictorial record of American life The File. The File pictures a system, a world of social and economic processes. It is both a taxonomy of human faces and a sweeping record of the labor—plowing, picking, shucking, sorting, packing, delivering, selling, and so on—that went into producing the nation's goods and services. The File documents infrastructure: cars and trucks, trains and tractors, oil wells and coal mines, warehouses, and machine shops. Consumption and leisure: general stores and department stores, fruit stalls and newsstands, movie houses, and square dances. The unglamorous grind of democracy: town meetings, county elections, ballot counting.

The cumulative achievement of the FSA Photography Unit, for all its blind spots, is its record of "the most permanent and the most fleeting," as FSA art director Edwin Rosskam said, "the most gay and the most tragic—the cow barn, the migrant's tent, the tractor in the field and the jalopy on the road, the weathered faces of men...the faces of children and the faces of animals.... In rows of filing cabinets, they wait for today's planner and tomorrow's historian." (Natanson 1992, 4)

Chapter 6
The FAP Index of American Design and Community Art Centers

A bitterly cold morning in early November 1935 found hundreds of careworn women lined up outside the Veterans Administration building in Milwaukee, Wisconsin. "Many were poorly clothed, even unkempt," an observer recalled, "and some appeared physically weak from the lack of nourishment, medical attention, and insecurity suffered for so long a time." Young and old, immigrant and native-born, some with little or no English and few with any job training or experience, "They all had one thing in common, however, the NEED for work."

The observer was Elsa Ulbricht (1885–1980), a skilled artisan and educator newly hired by the Works Progress Administration (WPA) to lead the Milwaukee Handicraft Project (MHP). She remembered that morning vividly: the palpable sense of fear, anxiety, desperation. But beneath the fear she sensed another pulse: a desire to be useful, to have meaningful work, to be part of a greater good. Ulbricht resolved to contribute "to the cultural development of the individual and the community," as she put it, and not simply to offer busy work to the unemployed. (Ulbricht 1944, 6–7)

The MHP accomplished this goal by making jobs available to two groups otherwise discriminated against by the WPA: women and Black Americans. Women had been as hard-hit by the Depression as men yet represented fewer than twenty percent of WPA personnel. (Policy dictated that only one household member, usually the male breadwinner, could hold a WPA job.) The WPA jobs that *were* available for women and Black women, in particular, mostly reinforced traditional gendered roles: cooking, cleaning, canning, and sewing.

Between 1935 and 1942 the MHP employed a racially integrated workforce of over five thousand women to handcraft a variety of household articles—books, quilts, curtains, toys,

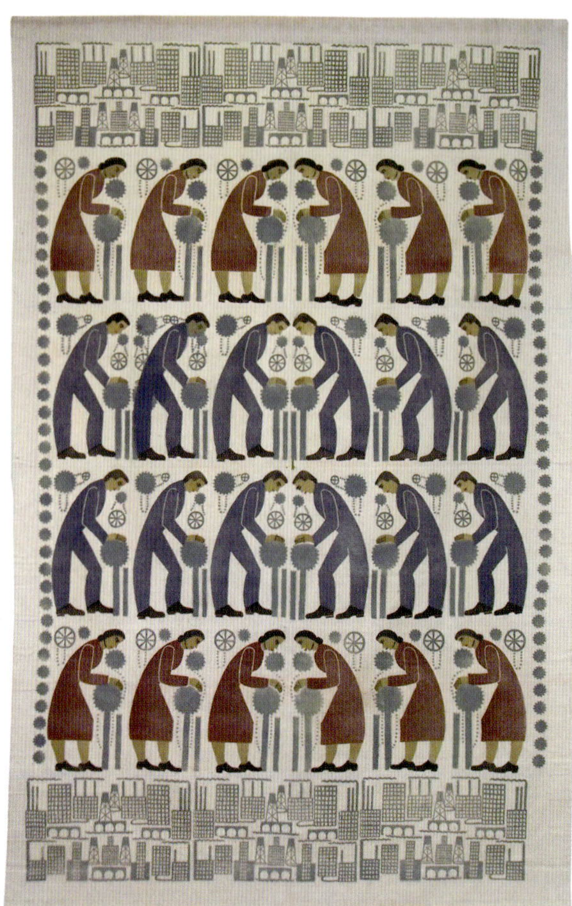

151 Florence Kawa,
The Workers, c. 1935

rugs, weavings—donated to Milwaukee public schools,
nurseries, and libraries, or sold at cost.

As MHP's reputation for beautifully designed, resourceful
products grew, orders poured in from all over the country.
Visitors included architect Frank Lloyd Wright and First Lady
Eleanor Roosevelt, who praised the MHP in her syndicated
newspaper column "My Day." *The Workers,* gifted to the First
Lady and possibly meant as a decorative wall hanging, featured
a design by Florence Kawa (1912–2008) of rows of factory workers
bent over their tasks. Those workers symbolized the triumph
of machine manufacturing, but the MHP, like other New Deal
initiatives, touted the benefits of making things by hand.

Craft and community were pillars of the Federal Art Project's
goal to build a cultural democracy. Craft bound communities

together; it was the art of everyday life, a grassroots alternative to the "genteel" tradition of fine art painting and sculpture. "An integration between the fine arts and the practical arts has been one of the avowed purposes of the [Federal Art Project]," wrote Constance Rourke, influential historian of American folk culture, "and likewise an integration of the arts with the life of the community." (Rourke 1936, 287) Two FAP initiatives aimed to fulfill those purposes: the Index of American Design and Community Art Centers.

Index of American Design

Constance Rourke (1885–1941) was an editor on the Federal Art Project's ambitious attempt to preserve and promote a national craft heritage: the Index of American Design. Between 1935 and 1942, around four hundred artists made over eighteen thousand watercolors representing functional and decorative art objects— furniture, ceramics, textiles, metalwork, and so on—from every region of the country dating back to the colonial period.

Textile designer Ruth Reeves (1892–1966) and New York Public Library archivist Romana Javitz (1903–80) conceived the Index as a visual encyclopedia of American folk culture. Their proposal found a receptive audience in Holger Cahill, who had organized groundbreaking surveys of American folk art at the Newark Museum and the Museum of Modern Art before becoming the Federal Art Project's national director. (A journalist reported that his "blue eyes get bluer when talking about his real love—early American art.") (Platt 1999, 180)

For Cahill, folk art expressed the lives of the "common people" in a preindustrial age when artists were more organically linked to the lives of those around them. The Index, Cahill hoped, would be a healthy reminder of art rooted in the soil of life, not withered in gloomy museums or stranded on the walls of the idle rich.

Rourke and Reeves went on the road in search of raw material. They scoured dusty attics and flea markets, antique shops and auction houses, dealer inventories and storerooms. What they found knit together various ethnic and regional traditions: wrought-iron farm tools of the Pennsylvania Dutch, weavings and woodcarvings of the Spanish Southwest, textiles of the Utah Mormons, shovels and pickaxes of North Californian miners, face jugs by enslaved and free Black potters in South Carolina. The Index's recovery of folk art—everyday objects crafted by anonymous artists with skill and ingenuity—challenged the cherished myth of an individual (white, male) genius creating masterpieces for elite audiences.

Whenever possible Index artists, primarily women drawn from the rolls of unemployed commercial artists and illustrators, worked

152

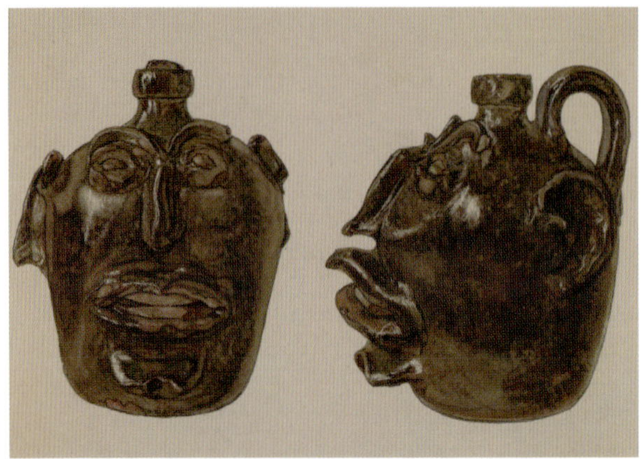

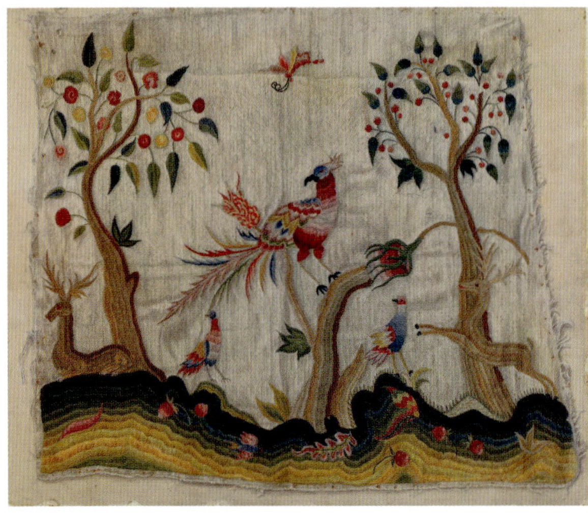

directly from the object, whether on-site in a museum, a collector's home, or a Project studio. With meticulous care they rendered a dazzling variety of items, materials, and textures: ship figureheads, iron stoves and weathervanes, patchwork quilts, hooked rugs, piggy banks, carousels, scrimshaws, saddles, spurs, ceramics, ox-carts, candle sconces, cornhusk dolls. The results, with the objects stark against the paper's negative space, could have an astonishing trompe l'oeil effect, as in the embroidered chair seat painted by Suzanne Chapman (1904–90), a master watercolorist who outlined her techniques in a manual shared with all Index employees.

Shaker Modern

Shaker design emerged as a key part of the Index's inventory. It could be reclaimed as uniquely "American" since the Shakers, a communitarian sect escaping persecution abroad, landed in upstate New York in the late eighteenth century. So-called for their "shaking" communal dances, the Shakers practiced pacifism, celibacy, and equality of the sexes. The spare elegance of their furniture and household items—whether chests, clocks, or chairs—expressed spiritual values: simplicity, humility, hard work. In Shaker design "the consciousness of the community was always uppermost," Constance Rourke wrote, "where the individual lost himself in the sense of the whole." (Rourke 1973, 166) A message of social cohesion rather than rugged individualism resonated in the Depression.

The stripped-down Shaker aesthetic also chimed with the hard-edged contours and smooth planes of Precisionism, an interwar art movement vaunting American industry and technology (factories, silos, skyscrapers, suspension bridges) in a crisply geometric style. Rourke authored the first biography of Precisionist painter and photographer Charles Sheeler (1883–1965), published in 1938 with the subtitle "An Artist in

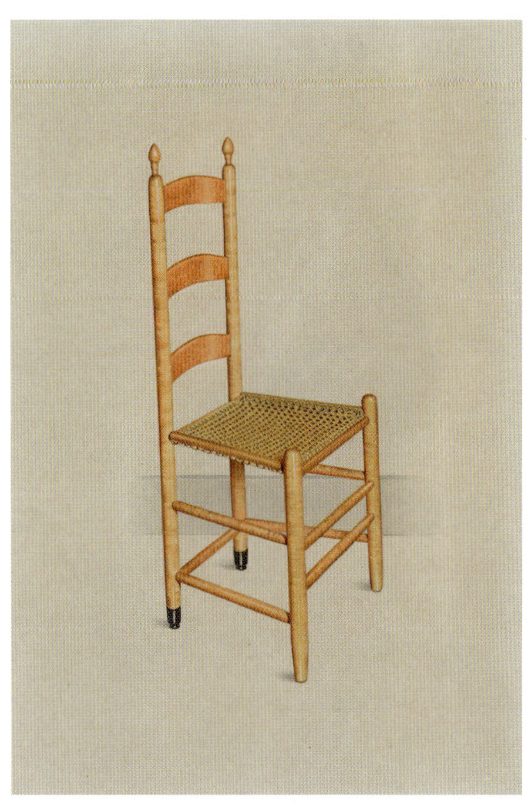

154 John W. Kelleher,
Shaker Tilting Chair, c. 1937

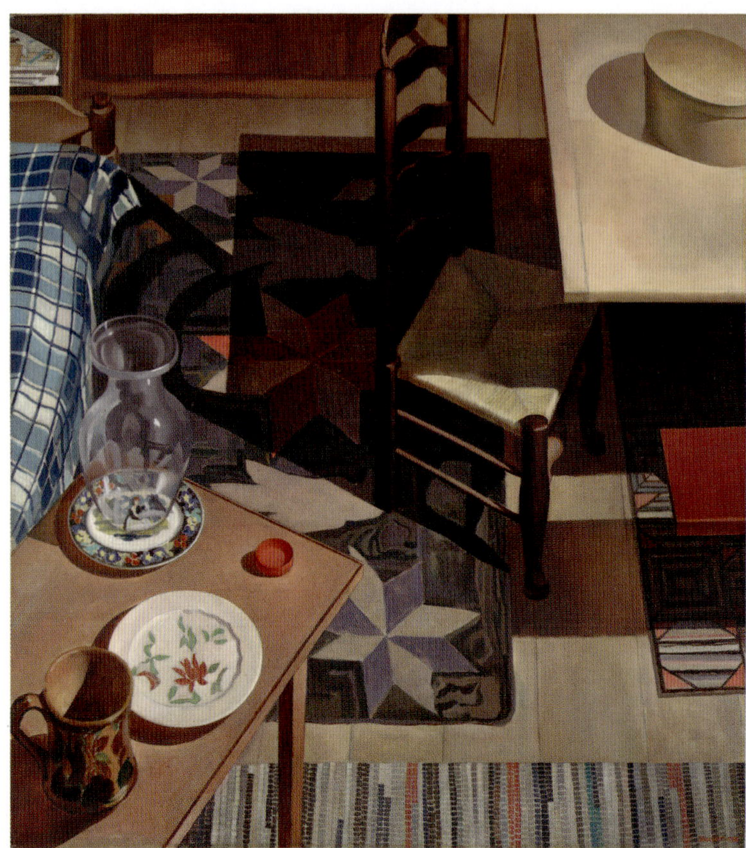

155 the American Tradition." A ladder-backed Shaker chair casts
a long shadow in Sheeler's *An American Interior*, an obliquely
patterned view of a room in his South Salem, New York home.
At Rourke's request, Sheeler made pieces from his Shaker
collection available for Index artists to catalog. This created a
feedback loop: the Shakers inspired Sheeler, whose modernism
informed the Index's "American Tradition."

"Nostalgic modernism": that's how historian Michael
Kammen described the folk art vogue. But the desire to recover
craft history was not only, or simply, about nostalgia. In an
industrial age of assembly lines and mechanized monotony,
Project administrators like Cahill and Rourke looked to
handcraft as a source of social unity and self-fulfillment. In
156 *Shakeress at her Loom*, FAP painter Yvonne Twining Humber
(1907–2004) portrayed a Shaker sister in a bonnet and shawl
weaving at a loom, a basket at her feet and a cupboard behind

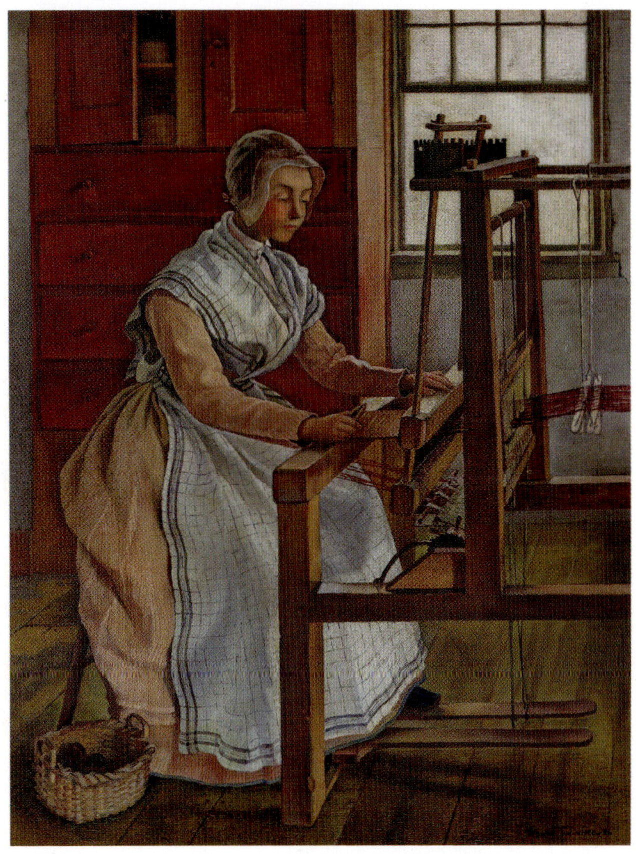

her. She is a Vermeer-esque figure piously absorbed in her task, the opposite of a hurried and harried factory worker or sweatshop seamstress.

The painting would have illustrated a portfolio of the Index's Shaker material, one of a planned series to introduce Americans, especially artists and designers, to their national heritage. Prohibitive costs kept the portfolios, with a few exceptions, from appearing in print. Instead, administrators sent over fifty exhibitions of Index watercolors to department stores, museums, galleries, and community centers. Reproductions of Index plates circulated in publications like *Fortune*, *Town and Country*, and *House Beautiful*. Administrators like Cahill and Rourke hoped viewers would see more than dry records of dusty relics. The Index, they believed, pointed to a cultural democracy where the "common people" might once again craft a fulfilling collective life.

But who were the "people"? As Kay Wells has argued, the Index cherry-picked its definition of "American Design" by largely excising Native, Black, or Asian American contributions, as well as those by immigrants from Southern and Eastern Europe (exceptions like the face jugs by Black potters proved the rule). The Index's free-floating objects bracketed out historical context, obscuring the relations of power, violence, and disenfranchisement that underpin the American paradox: all Americans are equal, but some are more equal than others. The result was less a complete and impartial Index than what literary critic Van Wyck Brooks called in 1918 a "usable past," a way to plunder history for ideological purposes in the present.

Other government projects offered countervailing narratives. Recording Native American objects, for example, came under the purview of the WPA-sponsored Indian Arts Project (IAP) set up in 1935 at the Rochester Museum of Arts and Sciences in western New York. Over a hundred Haudenosaunee artists and artisans, based out of the Tonawanda and Cattaraugus reservations, handcrafted five thousand items: baskets, masks, moccasins, drums, musical instruments, and jewelry, as well as watercolors and oil paintings. "Preserving" Indigenous culture risked reinforcing colonial binaries of traditional and modern by consigning Native artisans to a vanquished and vanishing past. However, as Julia Silverman has shown, IAP artists and craftworkers repurposed as well as preserved traditions by altering designs or adding contemporary references.

Tonawanda Seneca artist Ernest Smith (1907–75) made a series of circuit-breaking paintings inspired by Haudenosaunee history and social life. In *Progress,* a group of Haudenosaunee figures observe the arrival of white settlers via homesteads and steamboats. Smith appropriated a nineteenth-century engraving by a white artist to ironize the idea of "Progress," an ideological alibi for genocide. A painting of Native displacement by a Native artist in the style of the colonizers throws the whole idea of stable traditions (not to mention the meaning of "progress") into provocative doubt.

The IAP belonged to broader government efforts to preserve folk cultures. The National Park Service put unemployed architects and drafters to work documenting the country's architectural heritage through the still-running Historic American Buildings Survey. Federal Music Project employees transcribed or recorded bayou songs of the Mississippi Delta, Appalachian folk, chain gang songs, fiddle reels, spirituals, and lullabies. Blues music inspired the Federal Theatre Project ballet *Frankie and Johnny* (first performed in 1938) while

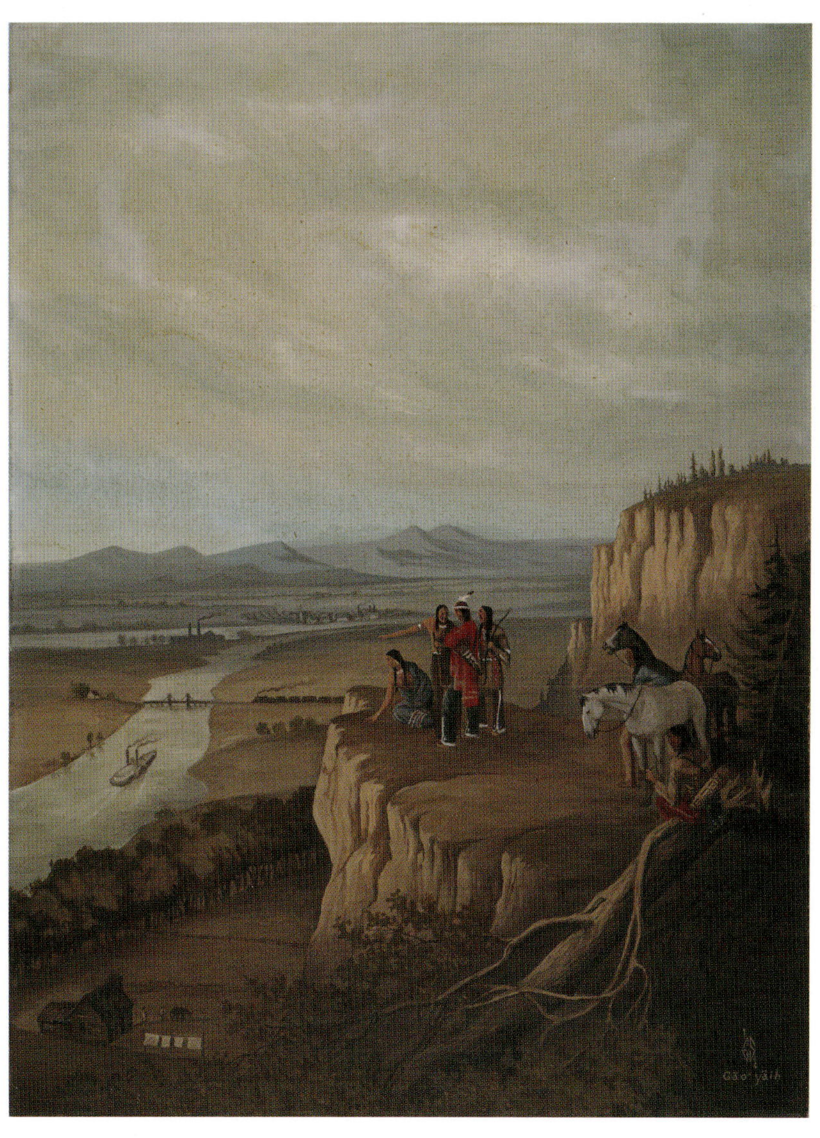

157 Ernest Smith, *Progress*, 1935

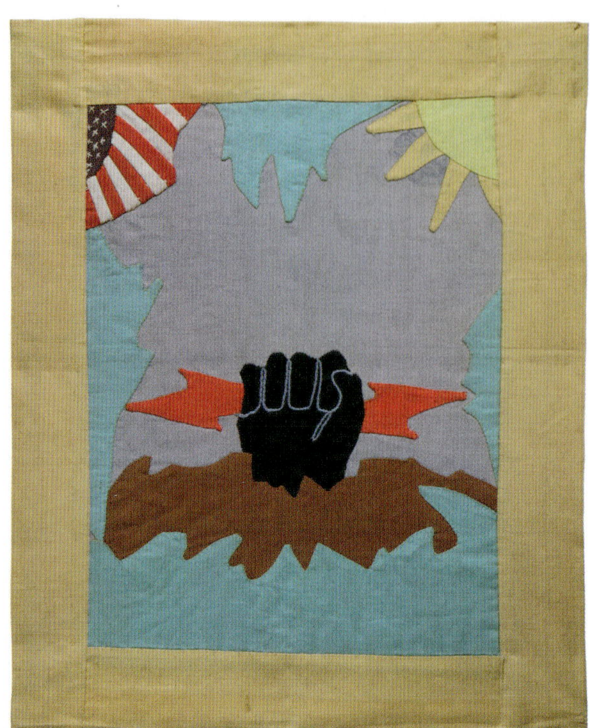

158 Ruth Clement Bond and Rosa Marie Thomas, *Tennessee Valley Authority Appliqué Quilt Design of a Black Fist*, 1934

How Long Brethren?, staged modern dance to a soundtrack of Black spirituals (1935–39). Howard University professor and poet Sterling A. Brown (1901–89) served as Editor of Negro Affairs for the Writers' Project and contributed to surveys of African American history, culture, and folklore.

The government also funded craft as a living tradition. In Ridgeville, Alabama, Ruth Clement Bond (1904–2005) designed quilts to celebrate the Tennessee Valley Authority (TVA), for which her husband served as Director of Negro Personnel and Education on the TVA's Wheeler Dam project. The TVA, which remains the country's largest public power company, built hydroelectric dams and power plants across a region where ninety percent of farms had no electricity. (The end could justify unsavory means: displacing families and offering unfair compensation for flooded farms and homesteads.) Bond collaborated with the wives of the dam's construction workers to fashion inventive modernist quilts. The first, called "Black Power" by Bond and her fellow makers, shows a Black fist gripping a bolt of lightning—a pun on the TVA's logo, which doubled as a symbol of Black agency and strength.

158

Design Laboratory

The Index of American Design was meant to serve as a
sourcebook and stimulus to modern designers. Through its
New York Teaching Division, the FAP sponsored the Design
Laboratory, one of the first schools for modern design in the
US. In the 10 East 39th Street workshop, students realized a
concept—whether for a clock, table, chair, or ashtray—from
sketch through fabrication.

At the Laboratory, sleek design updated Shaker elegance for
the machine age. Such updates could rapture design into the
ether of fine art. In 1934 MoMA's *Machine Art* put on display
industrial items like propellers, pistons, and ball bearings,
selected for their polished, streamlined aesthetic (philosopher
John Dewey and pilot Amelia Earhart judged the objects in a
promotional "beauty contest").

But the Design Laboratory incubated social as well as aesthetic
values, closer to the spirit of the Bauhaus, the fabled German
art school founded in 1919 as a utopian experiment in marrying
traditional craft and modern design. (Several Laboratory
instructors had trained at the Bauhaus before the Nazis closed
it down in 1933, and MoMA would display Laboratory pieces in a
1939 Bauhaus survey.) By offering free education in the synthesis
of art, craft, and design, the Laboratory, like the Bauhaus, held
out the promise of a smoother-functioning, more equitable

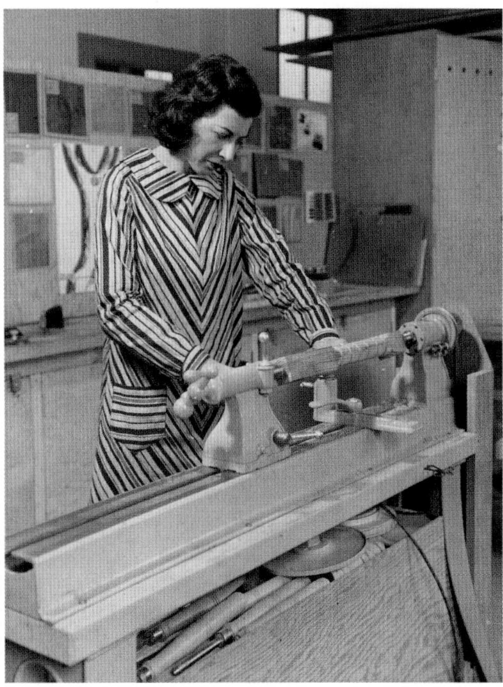

159 The Design
Laboratory, 1937

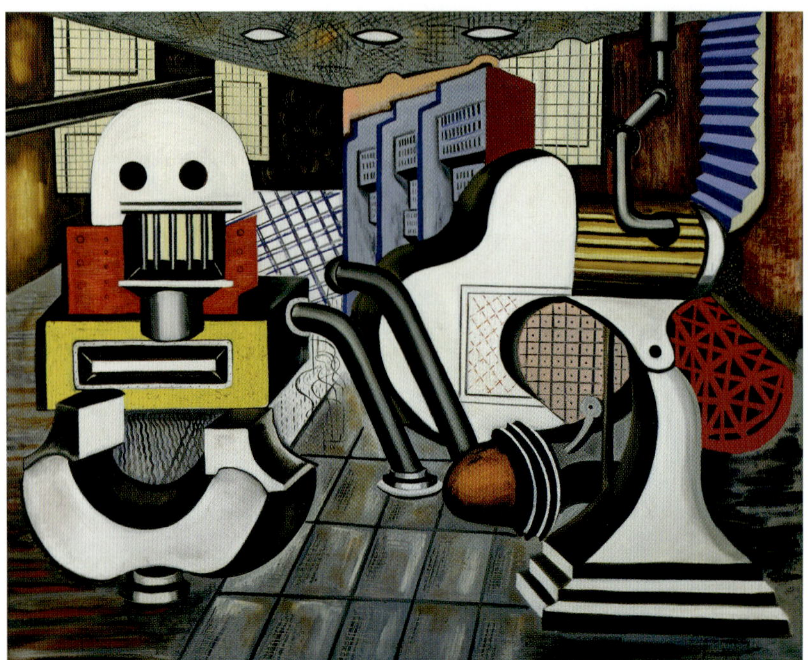

160 Irene Rice Pereira, *Machine Composition #2*, 1937

society engineered through innovative design and the efficient use of industrial materials.

The moment was short-lived: the Design Laboratory lost its WPA funding in a 1937 wave of budget cuts. Irene Rice Pereira (1902–71), a Laboratory instructor and vocal champion of modern art, moved to the FAP easel division. She took with her central Laboratory concerns: to test industrial materials and probe the social effects of technology. *Machine Composition #2*, inspired by a powerhouse visible from her apartment window, alloys the organic and inorganic. Tubes, pipes, grilles, and ventilators assemble into a Frankenstein's monster of heads, limbs, organs, and orifices.

For Pereira, the modern artist should reckon with the everyday dominance of machines, from automobiles and assembly lines to the radio, movies, and appliances. The artist could orient technology to socially positive ends by experimenting with new materials and assimilating scientific discoveries (a fundamental premise of the Bauhaus and the Design Laboratory). But her view of technology is ambivalent, oscillating between the machine's utopian potential and its dehumanizing power.

Community Art Centers

A central plank of the Federal Art Project platform, evident in the Index of American Design and the Design Laboratory, was to restore broken links between art and life. This plank was laid down by John Dewey, whose 1934 book *Art as Experience* called for art to be freed from its captivity in museums and woven "within the texture of the actual," a phrase that Holger Cahill (a onetime student of Dewey's) borrowed in his FAP lectures and writings.

Dewey's fingerprints were visible in the FAP's Community Art Centers (CACs). They redressed a situation Cahill found unacceptable in a democracy: "Fully three-fourths of the population of the United States," he wrote, "is underprivileged in the arts, that is, has never had opportunities to participate to any real extent in the experience of art." (Park and Markowitz 1977, 10) *Experience* shares the same etymology as *experiment*, from the Latin *experiri*, to try, to test. CACs treated art as a process, not a product, part of the trying and testing essential to a participatory democracy.

Between 1936 and 1943 the FAP established over a hundred CACs nationwide, from Harlem to Chicago to remote Gold Beach on the Oregon coast. They provided art education, vocational training, studio space, lectures, performances, and exhibition opportunities to rural communities and under-resourced urban neighborhoods. According to Cahill, the goal was to make art the "property of all, rather than the hobby of the few." (White 1987, 160) By at least one metric (attendance) it worked: some ten to fifteen million people ultimately participated in CAC programs, making them arguably the most successful FAP initiative in cultural democracy.

The success owed to community participation. The FAP provided staff while local partners (such as civic groups, schools, or colleges) raised funds and rented or purchased space—preferably downtown in one of the many storefronts left vacant by the depression. Residents of Sioux City, Iowa, raised eighteen thousand dollars towards an art center. In Salem, Oregon, schoolchildren fundraised through penny campaigns and door-to-door canvassing. In some cases, private donors made substantial contributions, such as a quarter of a million dollars to renovate a church in Greensboro, North Carolina. Volunteers pitched in with carpentry, plumbing, or electricity.

Thousands of people braved subzero temperatures to attend the January 1940 opening of the Walker Art Center in Minneapolis (a still-running and vibrant institution for contemporary art). In nine months over forty-one thousand people attended events at the CAC in Salem, Oregon. Further

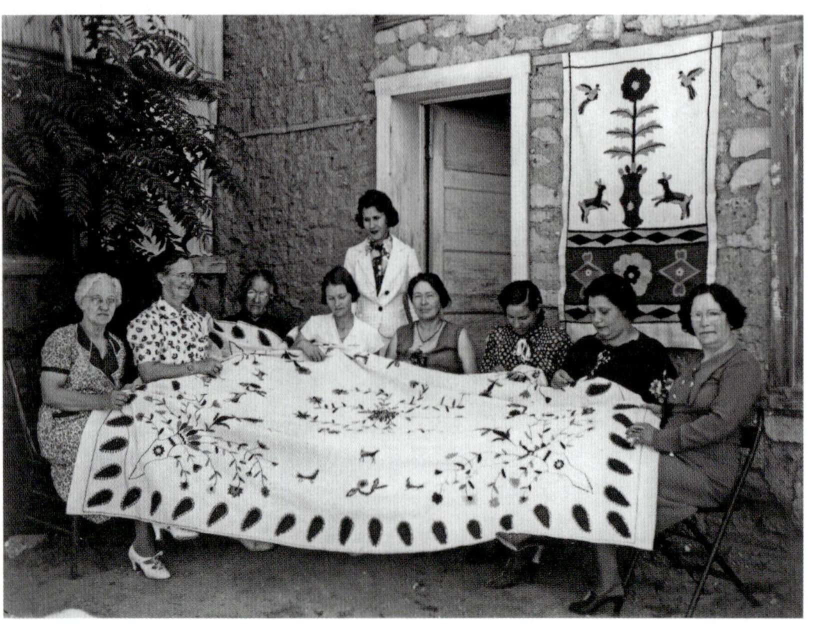

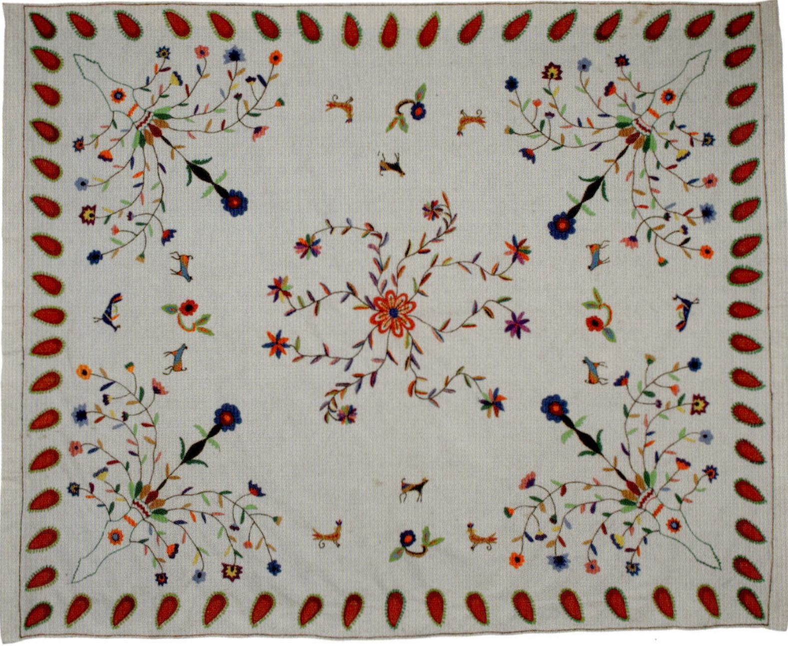

161 TOP Estella García (Standing) and her Colcha Embroidery Class, Melrose, New Mexico
162 ABOVE Estella García, et al., Bordado/Embroidery, c. 1938

south along the Oregon coast, a CAC in Gold Beach supplied art and music classes, studio space, and exhibitions to a population of five hundred. The CAC in Melrose, New Mexico, comparable in size to Gold Beach, hosted lessons by Estella García in *colcha,* a traditional form of wool embroidery practiced in the southwest.

Charles White painted *Five Great American Negroes* at age twenty-one to help raise funds for Chicago's South Side Community Art Center. Readers of the Black biweekly newspaper *Chicago Defender* selected the painting's five protagonists in a poll—itself a form of community engagement. Sojourner Truth leads a column of formerly enslaved people to freedom; bow-tied educator Booker T. Washington holds court at a center podium; abolitionist Frederick Douglass embraces a shirtless and shoeless fugitive; contralto Marian Anderson sings into broadcast microphones (that year she performed to an audience of 75,000 at the Lincoln Memorial in Washington DC); and Tuskegee scientist George Washington Carver hunches over a microscope. The ambitious canvas—which met a better fate than his never-installed (and now lost) FAP library mural, *Struggle for Liberation*—established White's lifelong commitment to celebrating Black history and heroism.

White's portrayal of Marian Anderson would have had special meaning to Eleanor Roosevelt, who cut the ribbon at the SSCAC's December 1940 dedication ceremony. She had resigned the year before from the Daughters of the American Revolution after the group denied Anderson the chance to sing at Constitution Hall, a snub that led Roosevelt to help facilitate the epochal Lincoln Memorial concert on federal property. Dedicating the center was "a most delightful experience," the First Lady reported in her

163 Charles White, *Five Great American Negroes*, 1939

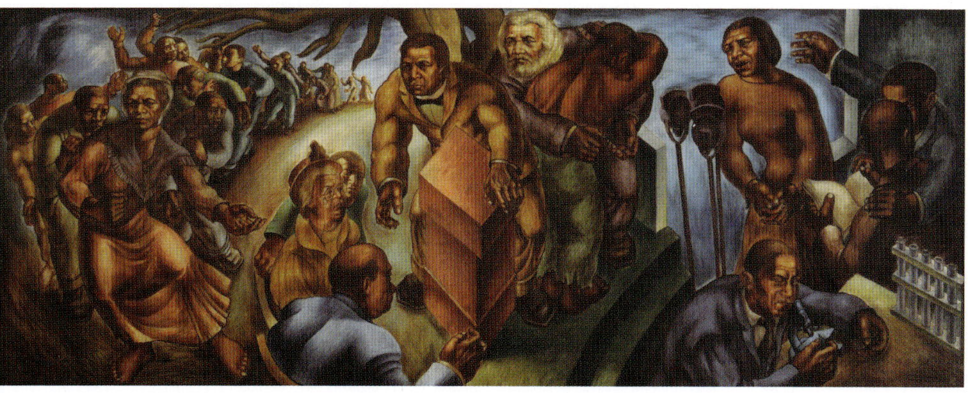

syndicated column, and the SSCAC went on to enjoy a national reputation as a WPA success story. It served as a training ground and social hub for members of the Black Chicago Renaissance: writers Gwendolyn Brooks (1917–2000) and Richard Wright, dancer Katherine Dunham (1909–2006), photographer Gordon Parks, sculptor Marion Perkins (1908–61), and artists Margaret Burroughs (1915–2010), Elizabeth Catlett (1915–2012), and Eldzier Cortor (1916–2015).

Margaret Burroughs called the SSCAC a "beacon of culture" and a significant catalyst for Chicago-based Black creatives. Several Black artists involved in CACs likewise praised FAP efforts to extend art and education to underserved communities. Ceramicist Henry Letcher taught classes in Washington DC, using materials provided by Howard University. The People's Art Center in St. Louis became known for its interracial arts programming. Lawrence Jones taught at the New Orleans CAC, where he embraced, in his words, the opportunity to "create a more democratic America." (Jones 1973, 199)

These successes were hard-won. Art historian Mary Ann Calo has noted that CACs and extension galleries outside big cities, mainly set up in segregated neighborhoods, had little financial or administrative support. (2023, 53–56) Some artists, sent by the FAP to understaffed locales in the South and West, resented "exile" to places they considered cultural backwaters. Some community members, in turn, found the aesthetics and politics of the artists objectionable. Leftist artists ran afoul of conservative residents, and in a few cases communities rejected Jewish and Black applicants. An official in Greensboro, North Carolina, for example, complained that a Black artist failed "to adjust himself to the manners and costumes of the Southern Negro." (Musher 2015, 167)

Overcoming obstacles depended on the energy and initiative of CAC staff. Vertis Hayes, flush from the success of his Harlem Hospital murals in New York (see pp. 97–98), took over the CAC at LeMoyne College in Memphis, Tennessee, one of the most segregated cities in the country. Hayes oversaw an active slate of lectures, exhibitions, free courses in drawing, pottery, printmaking, painting, and Saturday morning children's classes. He supervised a collaborative mural for a faculty lounge on the theme of "progress," tracing a visual arc of African American history from slavery to the Great Migration to professional employment as nurses, doctors, and scientists. Hayes's mural and Ernest Smith's painting of the same name show the concept of progress to be contested and contingent, subject to historical forces and open to competing interpretations.

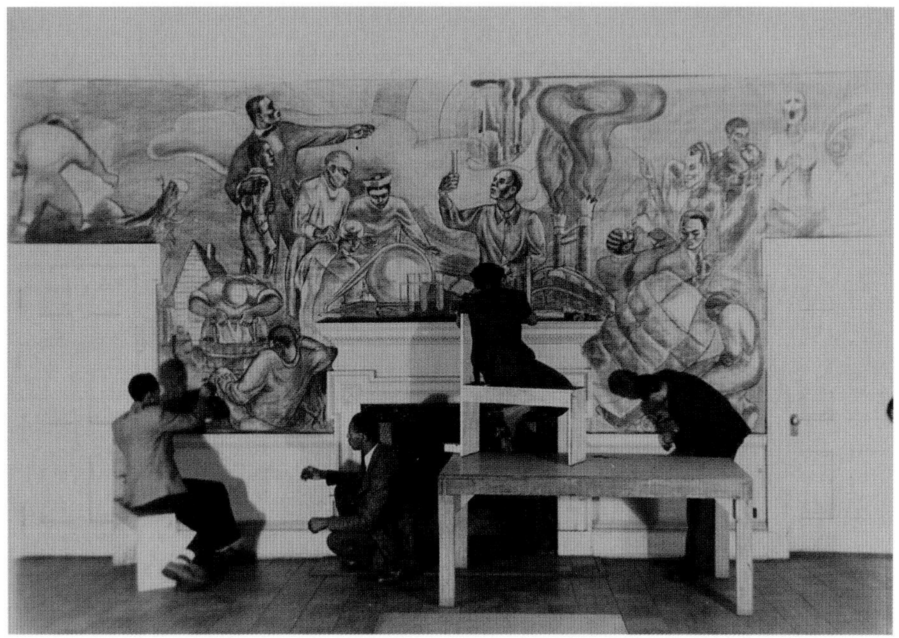

164 Vertis Hayes and students painting *Progress*, LeMoyne Federal Art Center, 1939

Art Therapy and Education

Community art centers expanded the definition of American art beyond its conventional limits. In 1938 the Federal Art Project and Bellevue Hospital (site of a Project mural program) co-sponsored *Art and Psychopathology*, an exhibition of art made by Bellevue psychiatric patients in FAP classes, and the first in the US to present art-making as a form of therapy. As Jackson Davidow has shown, lines between creative inspiration and mental distress were already blurred: in 1936, for example, MoMA exhibited "psychopathic drawings" by institutionalized patients alongside modern artists in *Fantastic Art, Dada, Surrealism.* (2018, 92)

One of the works on view in *Art and Psychopathology* was a watercolor of a monster attacking a naked supine woman. The patient explained the symbolism to her FAP instructor: the nude figure is a self-portrait; the yellow monster is the man who "broke up her home"; the gun-toting figure in a cap is her husband arriving "too late"; the gray shape in the lower right corner is her tombstone. The striking image—modernist in its unshadowed colors, simplified shapes (the woman's yellow hair a mirror to the monster's flaming pelt), and dream symbolism (the husband's stubby arms and wobbly gun are grist for the Freudian

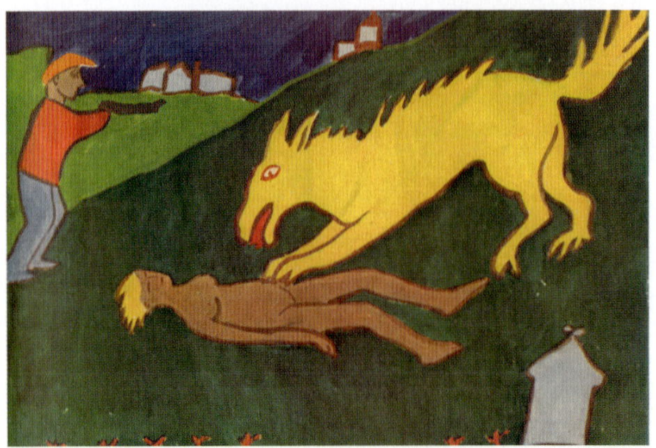

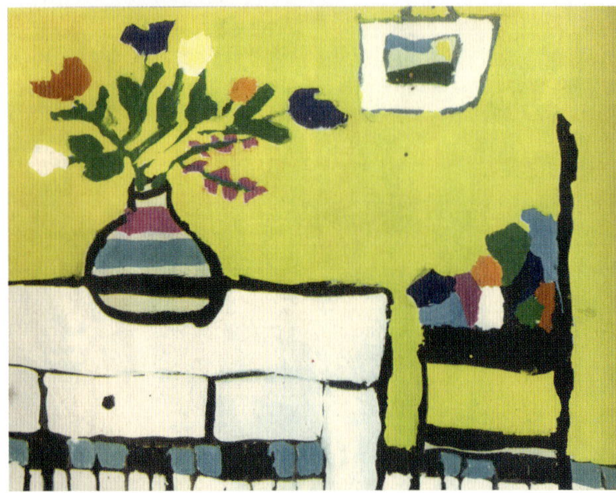

165 TOP LEFT Unnamed Bellevue psychiatric patient, featured in *Life,* 24 October 1938
166 LEFT Joan La Monica, featured in *Fortune,* May 1937

mill)—showed "decided talent," according to *Life* magazine. More importantly, it gave Bellevue psychiatrists "an amazingly clear picture of the artist's mental conflicts."

Art and Psychopathology supported the premise, widely accepted today, that art can have positive mental health benefits. WPA administrators also couched the value of CACs in the language of social improvement and moral hygiene: art classes molded better citizens. This applied to children and young adults as well as the neurodivergent. FAP press releases heralded the decline in "juvenile delinquency" in neighborhoods surrounding community art centers. One teacher called art a "great therapy, which can in many cases turn [delinquent youths] into useful social beings, often into sound craftsmen, and even sometimes into distinguished artists." (Marantz 1973, 198)

For Holger Cahill, children, like his beloved folk artists, were
already "distinguished" for their fresh, untutored approach
to art-making. An estimated two million children attended
FAP art classes, and Cahill considered their work integral to
the program, even exhibiting representative examples in *New
Horizons in American Art*, the 1936 showcase for FAP art. Drawings
and paintings by children of locomotives, steamboats, elevated
trains, butcher shops, and drugstores hung alongside works by
adult artists. *Fortune* magazine reproduced a vibrant still life
by seven-year-old Joan La Monica, painted in a CAC art class,
as evidence that the programs had "tapped a vein of artistic
ability the existence of which no art critic in America had even
suspected." (MacLeish 1937, 114)

The Federal Art Project supported art *for* children as well
as by children. Project artists made child-friendly murals and
sculptures—on themes like animals, fairy tales, and the circus—
for libraries, schools, orphanages, and children's hospitals. The
Astoria Public Library in Queens, New York, commissioned six
of Eugenie Gershoy's (1901–86) whimsical foot-tall figurines—
such as an *Ill-Fated Toreador* skewered by a bull's horn—for the
Children's Reading Room. For Gershoy, the commission was not
fundamentally different from socially informed art made for
adults. "The chaos in the economic and social world in which we
live," Gershoy later wrote, "has emphasized in art the fantastic,
the satirical, and the humorous." (Gershoy 1973, 93) In this sense,
her "ill-fated toreador," a victim of cruel fate and mischance, is as
much a comment on the period's economic "chaos" as any more
high-minded mural or agitational print.

Like folk or self-taught artists, children modeled a form of
nonacademic art-making that appealed to New Deal artists.

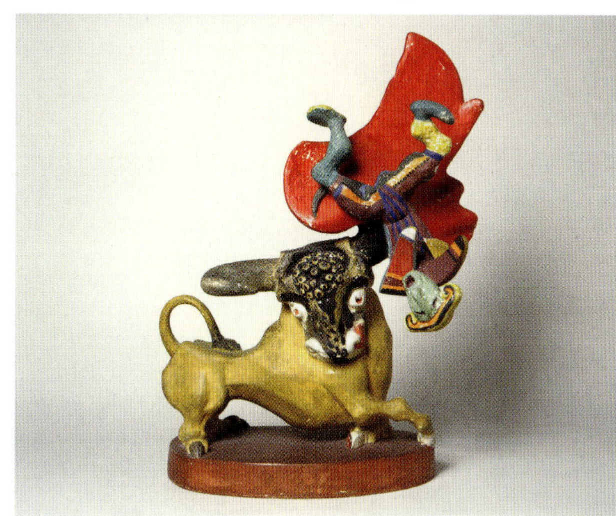

167 Eugenie
Gershoy, *Ill-
Fated Toreador,*
c. 1935–39

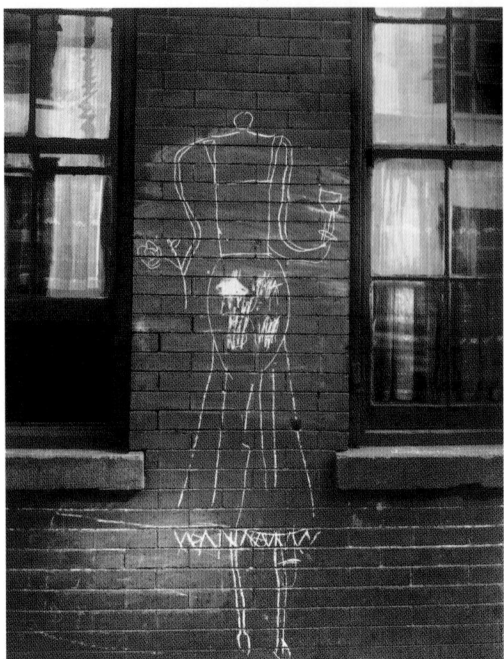

168 Helen Levitt,
New York, c. 1941

Photographer Helen Levitt (1913–2009) taught WPA-sponsored courses at a public school in Spanish East Harlem. With a secondhand Leica she began snapping photographs of children's graffiti on her walks to and from teaching, a project eventually funded by the FAP. Levitt discovered in the chalk drawings a feisty streetwise theater of imagination. Children sketched on brick walls and cement sidewalks a pictographic world of cops and cowboys, speeding trains and sinking ships, budding romances, crude insults, and secret passages. These "ancient, essential and ephemeral forms of art," wrote Levitt's friend, writer James Agee, "have set forth in chalk and crayon the names and images of their pride, love, preying, scorn, desire." (Coles 1987)

Harlem Community Art Center

Like Levitt, William H. Johnson (1901–70) tapped the wellspring of children's art. After early training at the National Academy of Design and a long sojourn in Europe, Johnson joined in May 1939 the teaching staff of the Harlem Community Art Center (HCAC). Hundreds of students attended classes weekly— students like the two girls at their drawing boards in Johnson's *Art Class*. White FAP officials touted CAC classes as a healthy

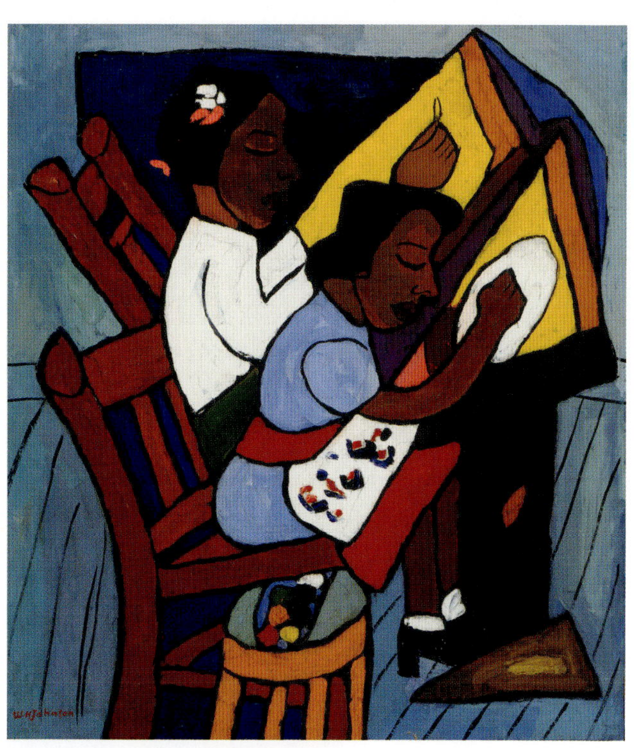

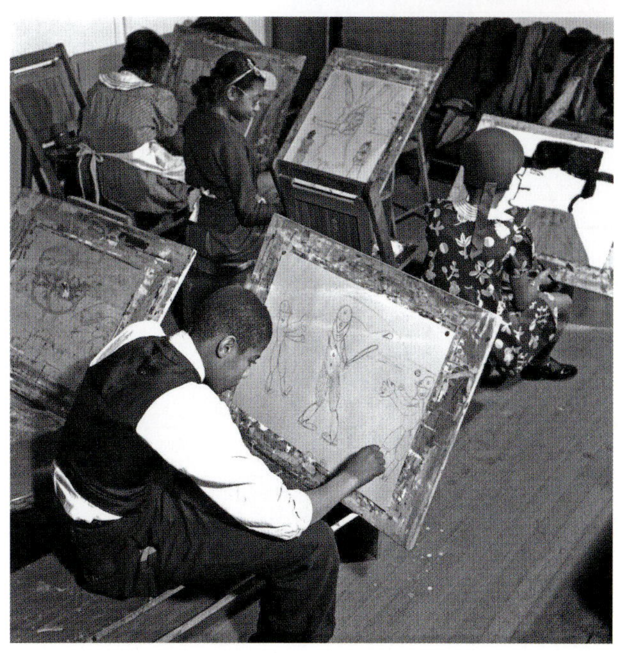

169 TOP William H. Johnson, *Art Class*, c. 1939–40
170 ABOVE Genevieve Naylor, Harlem Arts Center, 1938

outlet for Black children's "instinct" for art, another flash of the program's double-edged sword: it expanded educational opportunities while perpetuating racist stereotypes. (The rhetoric of "instinctual" creativity smacked of the FAP's paternalistic attitude to self-taught artists like Patrociño Barela; see pp. 119–20).

Johnson inverted the classroom's power dynamic: he is the student in this art class, not the teacher. His painting's faux-naive style—thick outlines, shadowless colors, wonky perspective—takes its cue from children's blithe disregard for conventional picture-making. Johnson, like fellow modernists Paul Klee and Joan Miró, drew on children's art as a resource to unlearn outworn formulas and reinvent his artistic identity.

The HCAC, where Johnson worked, had been set up in 1937 in Central Harlem, a culturally vibrant neighborhood of theaters, nightclubs, and music halls still reverberating from the previous decade's Harlem Renaissance. It grew out of an active arts ecosystem: the Harlem Branch Library (where Aaron Douglas's mural cycle *Aspects of Negro Life* was on view), the Harlem YMCA, and the studios of artists Charles Alston and Augusta Savage (1892–1962).

Savage, organizer of the leftwing Vanguard Club salon and the Savage Studio of Arts and Crafts, served as the HCAC's first director. She counted among her students and colleagues Romare Bearden (1911–88), Roy DeCarava (1919–2009), and Jacob Lawrence. Selma Burke taught at the HCAC and described herself as the "people's sculptor," portraying prominent figures from

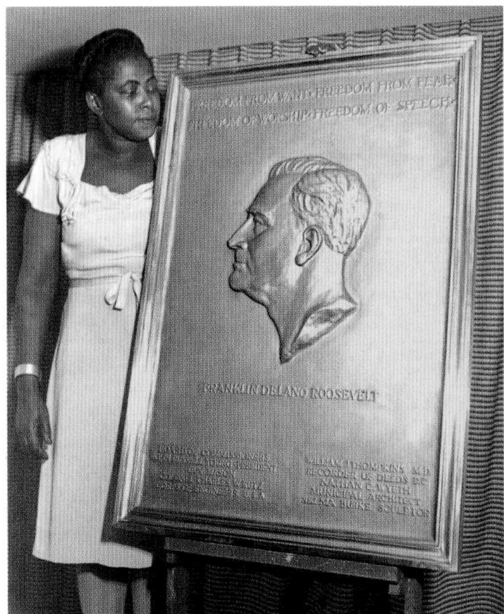

171 LEFT Selma Burke with her portrait of FDR, 1945
172 OPPOSITE Jacob Lawrence, *Blind Beggars*, 1938

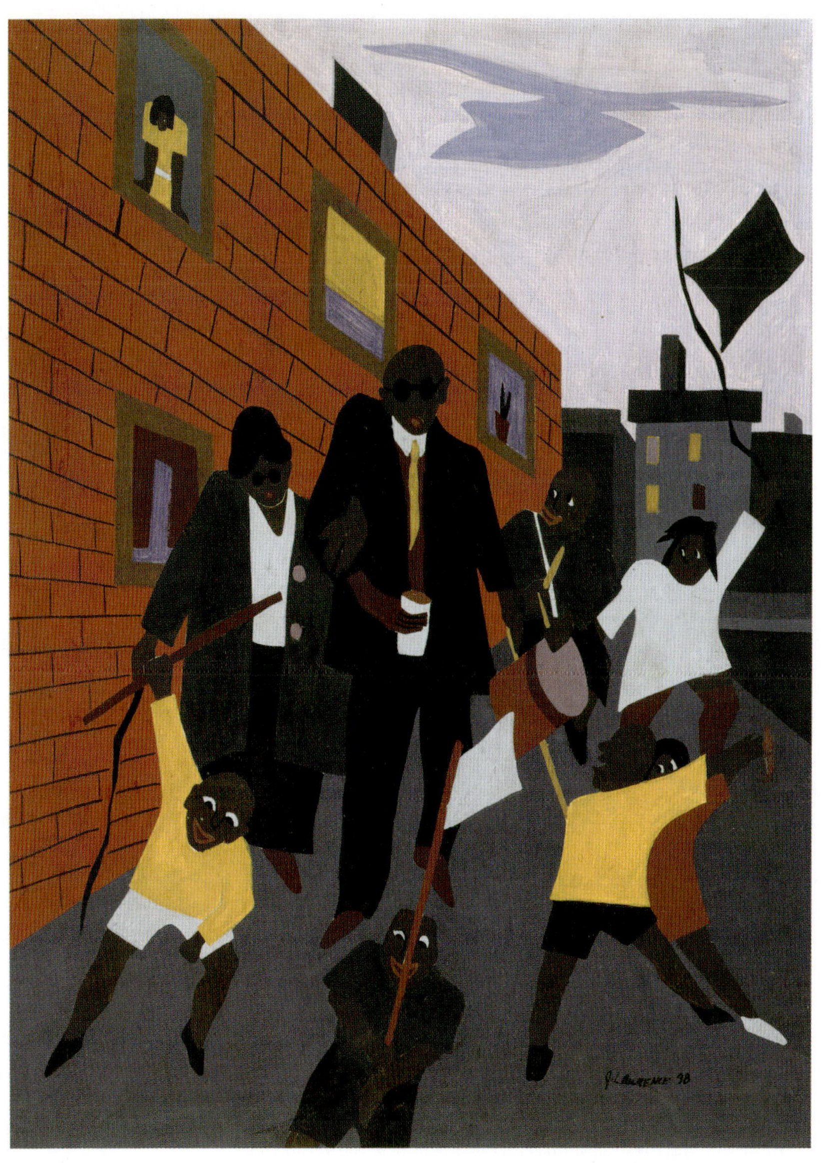

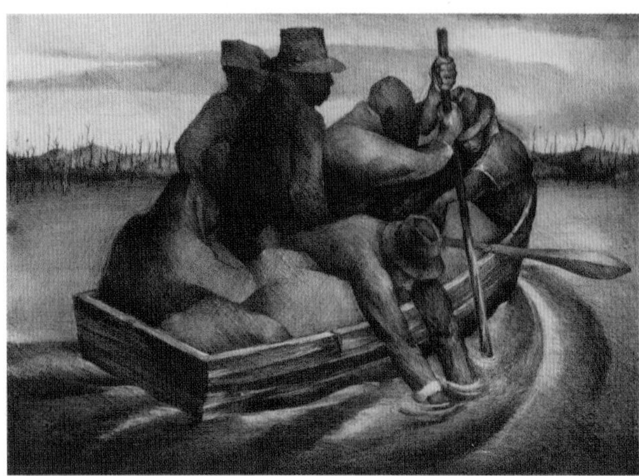

173 Robert Blackburn, *People in a Boat*, c. 1937–39

Black history. Her dedicatory low-relief bronze of FDR, for which the President sat over two days in 1944, may have served as the uncredited basis for his profile on the US dime.

Eleanor Roosevelt attended the HCAC's opening and in its first six months over seventy thousand people participated in the center's programs and events. The HCAC hosted lectures, exhibitions (such as *Art and Psychopathology*), and free classes in easel and mural painting, sculpture, printmaking, and ceramics. Visitors included Albert Einstein and activist singer-actor Paul Robeson, and the center became a lively hub of the city's music, dance, and theater projects.

Jacob Lawrence, barely out of his teens, took classes at HCAC before joining New York's Federal Art Project easel division in 1938. *Blind Beggars* features his signature angular shapes, stylized figures, plunging perspective, and limited palette of bright, smooth colors. A dapper couple in dark glasses, carrying guide canes, walk arm-in-arm down a sidewalk. A boisterous band of children—the same kids likely to throng classes at HCAC— flutters around them dancing, banging on drums, flying a kite, and waving banners. Lawrence treated the common period theme of the downtrodden with undaunted exuberance; painter Charles Alston, an HCAC instructor, admired Lawrence for his sensitivity to "the joy, the suffering, the weakness, the strength of the people he sees every day." (Hills 2019, 36)

Robert Blackburn (1920–2003) was likewise a precocious teenager whose gifts were nurtured at the HCAC. His lithography instructor Riva Helfond (1910–2002), taught her students "the sensuality of stone," he recalled. This sensuality lends *People in a Boat* sculptural mass through sensitive shading and assured

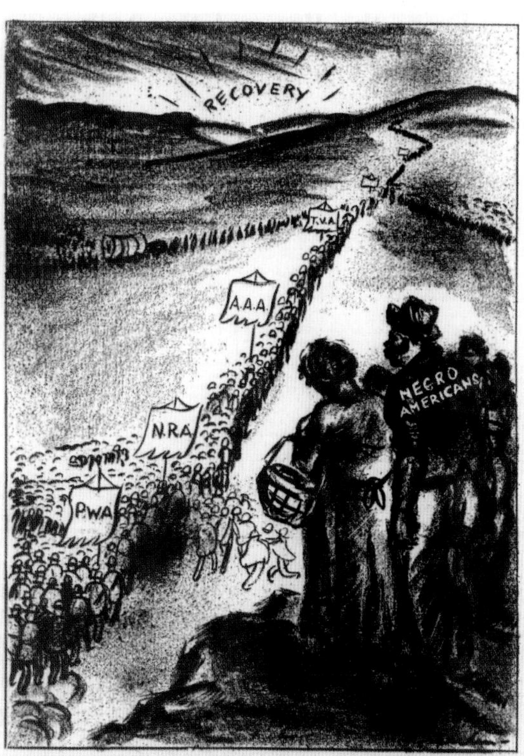

"MARCHING ALONG TOGETHER" (Popular National Recovery "Pep" Song)

174 Romare Bearden, *Marching Along Together*, 1935

drawing. A hatted man rows at the head of the boat, another man dredges with a pole, and a third dips his hands into the water. The far shore, lined with barren trees, appears desolate and forbidding. The composition alludes to Raphael's tapestry design, *The Miraculous Draught of Fishes*, a scene of Christ instructing his hungry and tired disciples to cast out into the sea. Blackburn reimagined the biblical story with Depression-era refugees, whether victims of the Great Flood of the Ohio River in 1937 or allegorical Black Americans navigating hostile environments. Blackburn's massed figures suggest power in unity, despite straitened circumstances, honoring the spirit of the HCAC. His lessons there would have a lasting impact: in 1948 Blackburn opened the Printmaking Workshop, which quickly became one of the country's foremost print studios.

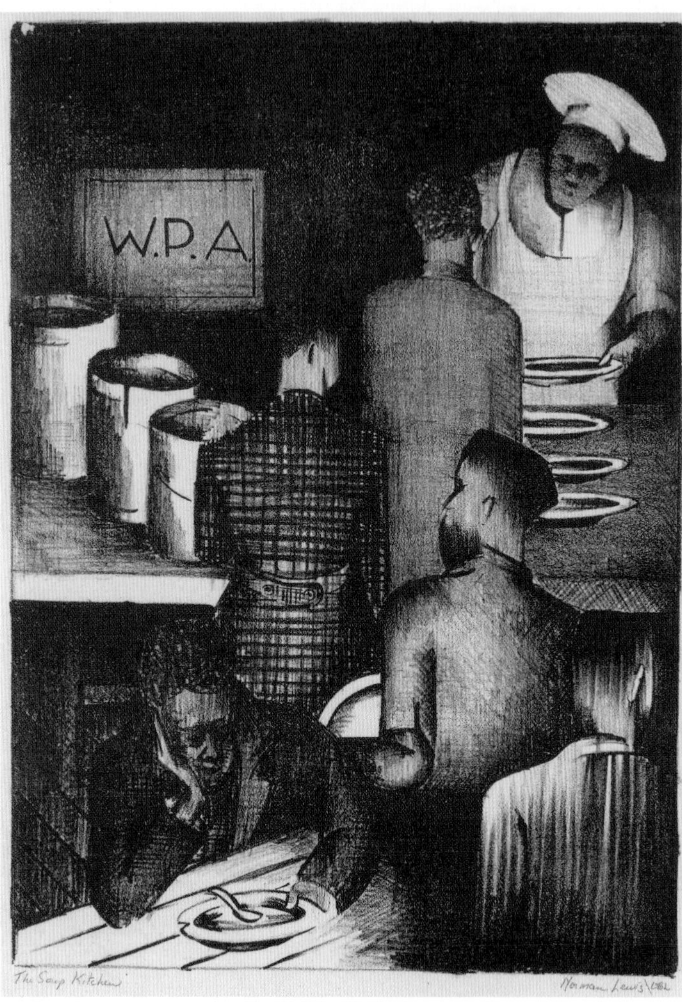

175 Norman Lewis, *The Soup Kitchen*, c. 1937

Harlem Artists Guild

Gwendolyn Bennett (1902–81), author and artist who took over as HCAC director from Augusta Savage in 1939, believed the Center offered a vision of "a new and better world." (Bennett 1973, 215) It was a vision born of struggle. The HCAC was established through the efforts of the Harlem Artists Guild (HAG), founded in 1935 as an advocacy organization by a cohort of Black artists, including Charles Alston, Aaron Douglas, Augusta Savage, and Romare Bearden. Later celebrated for innovative collages on themes of Black history and identity, Bearden was astonished to see almost fifty Black artists at the first HAG meeting; he had no idea there were that many in the whole country.

That year Bearden contributed biting illustrations to *The Crisis*, the journal of the NAACP, indicting the racial politics of the New Deal. In one scene a group labeled "Negro Americans" stands on a promontory overlooking marchers on the road to "Recovery" just over the horizon line. (They resemble Ernest Smith's Haudenosaunee figures observing the arrival of white settlers—both make vivid policies of exclusion.) The marchers carry banners lettered with New Deal acronyms—PWA, NRA, AAA—suggesting these agencies left African Americans behind.

Although over a quarter of a million Black Americans worked for the WPA—a contributing factor in the Black electorate's historic transfer of loyalty in the 1930s from the Republican "Party of Lincoln" to Democrats—they faced discrimination: "Last hired, first fired," the saying went. They were also assigned, in many cases, the most menial and lowest-paid jobs. The New Deal's housing programs, moreover, helped create the racist system of redlining that denied Black families mortgage loans. While Eleanor Roosevelt championed civil rights and FDR relied on a so-called "Black Cabinet" of African American advisors, the President downplayed civil rights legislation to avoid antagonizing southern Democrats.

These prejudices extended to the art projects. It took a concerted pressure campaign by the Harlem Artists Guild for the Graphic Arts Division to hire Black artists. Norman Lewis, co-founder of the HAG and a teacher at the HCAC, was among the first. Better known as a postwar abstract expressionist, Lewis in the 1930s worked in a social realist vein. *The Soup Kitchen* is a somber treatment of the Depression's economic toll on the Black community, which aggravated the effects of redlining, high rents, and unemployment. A line of men, as anonymous as the nearby row of pots, wait to receive soup in a WPA-sponsored kitchen, part of government initiatives to redirect surplus farm crops to the food insecure. A seated melancholic, head propped on palm, faces the opposite direction; with his bowl empty, he seems doubtful about where the next meal will come from.

The Struggle

At a time when demeaning images of African Americans were ubiquitous in popular culture, the Federal Art Project offered a platform for Black artists to portray themselves, their history, and their communities. It provided a living wage, access to training and materials, exhibition opportunities, and a sense of solidarity with other artists. Alain Locke, "dean" of the Harlem Renaissance and author of the influential 1940 study *The Negro in Art,* credited the FAP for the "present flowering of the younger Negro art."

Black artist and scholar James Porter (1905–70) was less impressed: efforts to involve Black artists on the FAP were both "insincerely attempted," he wrote in 1939, and "never achieved the fullness of its possibilities." (Scholar Mary Ann Calo chose this quote as the epigraph to her 2023 study of African American artists and the New Deal.) Few Black Americans featured in the national touring exhibitions meant to be representative of the Project. Even fewer held supervisory positions, and none could be found at the upper levels of administration.

The Harlem Artists Guild, carrying forward the neighborhood's legacy of arts advocacy, challenged these forms of discrimination. Members fought FAP budget cutbacks, lobbied for more Black artists and supervisors, and greater visibility through exhibitions. Their activism gave rise to the Harlem Community Art Center, where the HAG held meetings and displays of its members' work, and leveraged Charles Alston into his supervisory role for the Harlem Hospital mural program (see pp. 97–98). The Guild envisioned and worked for a vital role for African American art in a democratic society, beginning with fostering young talent (like Blackburn and Lawrence, who regularly attended HAG meetings), organizing exhibitions, and applying pressure on the FAP.

The Guild was joined in the struggle by the Artists' Union, a formidable force on behalf of New Deal artists. Printmaker Boris Gorelick (1911–84) went so far as to claim that "Every improvement of the economic condition of the artist on government projects has been obtained through the existence, guidance, and mass actions of the organizations of artists." (Park and Markowitz 1977, 9)

What drove artists out of their studios and into the streets?

Chapter 7
The Artists' Union

Philip Evergood (1901–73), bloodied and beaten, survived a
harrowing night in a packed jail cell. The evening before, the
first of December 1936, he had joined hundreds of artists in
storming New York's Federal Art Project offices to protest steep
budget cuts and layoffs. The building superintendent demanded
that the artists leave, but they refused, locking arms in a human
chain. Reporters and photographers scented a story and rushed
to the offices, notepads and cameras ready. "We came here
peacefully and without disorder," announced sculptor Paul
Block, "and will stay until the dismissals are rescinded."

The police weren't having it. Seventy-five "hot, angry and
excited" officers, Evergood recalled, breached the defenses of
filing cabinets and piled-up chairs. Artists resisted arrest in a
flurry of fists and nightsticks, kicking and shoving, punching
and biting. Police carried and dragged them out as strikers
chanted, "Stop police brutality!" They were hauled off in eleven
patrol wagons to the East 35th Street station and booked
on charges of disorderly conduct. An artist remembered
the antic scene: "'Your name!' bellowed an officer, pad and
pencil in hand. 'Jim Picasso' came the first response. That
was a sufficient cue. Cezanne, Da Vinci, and Peter Breughel
followed." (Solman 1972, 120)

It was the largest mass arrest in New York history. The melee
made the *New York Times* front page the next day: reported
injuries included skull fractures, cuts, bruises, and internal
bleeding. Although the court found the artists guilty and
issued suspended sentences, the gambit may have worked.
While overall WPA employment fell nearly twelve percent
in the first six months of 1937, employment on Federal One
actually increased.

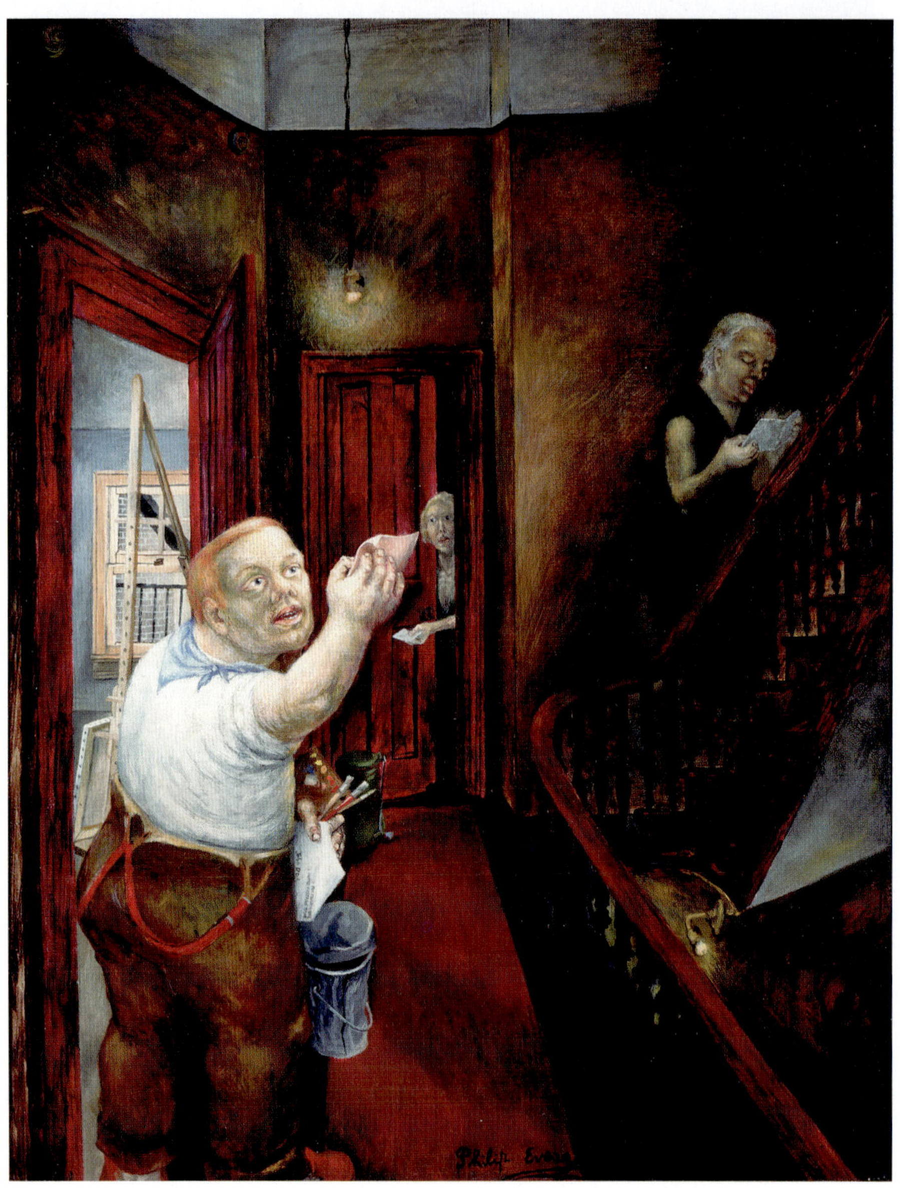

176 Philip Evergood, *The Pink Dismissal Slip*, 1937

What drove artists to band together, risking injury and arrest? Evergood's painting *The Pink Dismissal Slip* gives an idea. It shows "some poor little artist in his crummy cold-water flat," as Evergood put it, getting the notorious pink slip issued to laid-off government workers. He holds the slip aloft as if to curse the heavens, the clutch of brushes in his other hand suddenly useless. The envelope is addressed to John Doe, the artist-as-Everyman subject to the state's caprices. The violent notes of red—in the doors, the carpet, the railing, the suspenders—hint at a barely contained fury. Evergood, by his own account, painted "dangerous bums, discontented bums," far from the resigned "forgotten men" brooding through so much Depression-era imagery. His pink slip-waving artist will soon join the ranks of Union members on the picket lines.

Solitude to Solidarity

The effects of the Great Depression pushed artists like "John Doe" out of the studio into the streets as part of organized struggle. Over the decade, artists moved from solitude to solidarity, taking inspiration from the rising labor movement for a new vision of the artist's role in society. They self-identified as "workers with a brush" and stood shoulder-to-shoulder in the Artists' Union (AU), the first in the country's history. "Art has turned militant," wrote FAP printmaker Mabel Dwight, summing up the mood: "It forms unions, carries banners, sits down uninvited and gets underfoot. Social justice is its battle cry." (Dwight 1973, 152)

The Artists' Union formed part of the pro-labor, antifascist movement retroactively labeled the "Cultural Front" by historian Michael Denning. The Cultural Front charged from all sides, in all media: Woody Guthrie's Dust Bowl ballads, Aaron Copland's "Fanfare for the Common Man," Clifford Odets's one-act play *Waiting for Lefty* about a taxi drivers strike, the antifascist films of Orson Welles and Charlie Chaplin, the proletarian novels of Erskine Caldwell and H.T. Tsiang, the poetry of Langston Hughes and Muriel Rukeyser, the modern dance of Martha Graham and Katherine Dunham, the photography of Aaron Siskind and Gordon Parks. The biggest hits on Broadway? In the 1930s it was *Tobacco Road*, a melodrama about Georgia sharecroppers, and *Pins and Needles,* a musical comedy produced by a labor union and starring garment trade workers.

The US government, wittingly or unwittingly, subsidized key works of the Cultural Front. The Federal Theatre Project, in particular, staged several pro-labor plays through its Living Newspaper Unit. Most famously, Marc Blitzstein's FTP opera,

The Cradle Will Rock, openly supported unionizing the steel
industry. The WPA, fearing blowback, canceled the opening.
What followed has entered the realm of myth: Encountering a
padlocked theater on opening night, the play's director, Orson
Welles, led a six hundred-strong audience twenty blocks north
to Venice Theatre, whose owners agreed last-minute to host the
production. Blitzstein played the score on a borrowed piano
while actors—who risked the WPA's wrath if they took the
stage—shouted and sang their lines from the audience.

Where did this pro-labor energy come from? According to
artist Harry Sternberg, "The Depression, with its attendant
suffering, stirred in most artists a social consciousness and a
left-of-center political orientation." (Langa 2004, 103) This held
true for Sternberg, whose social consciousness is on display in
paintings like *Coal Miner and Family*—with its exploited miner
underground as if consigned to an early grave—a politicized
pendant to his more optimistic Ambler, Pennsylvania, Post
Office mural.

Many turned to the Communist Party USA (CPUSA) to
account for capitalism's failures and its oppressive structures
of class, race, and gender, even as pro-Soviet creatives
overlooked the state's purges and show trials. A significant
number joined the John Reed Club (JRC)—named for the
Communist journalist who covered the Mexican and Russian
revolutions—set up in 1929 as the cultural arm of the CPUSA.
The JRC manifesto, published in the June 1932 issue of *New
Masses*, called on artists to abandon the "treacherous" illusion
"that the artist can remain remote from the historic conflicts"
in which they must take sides.

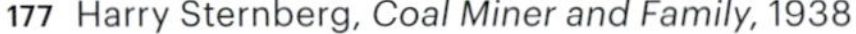

177 Harry Sternberg, *Coal Miner and Family*, 1938

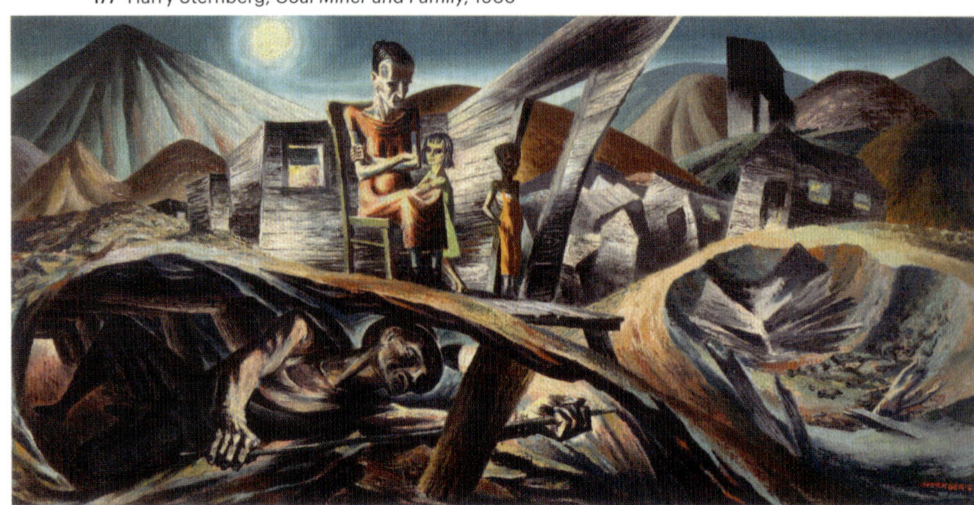

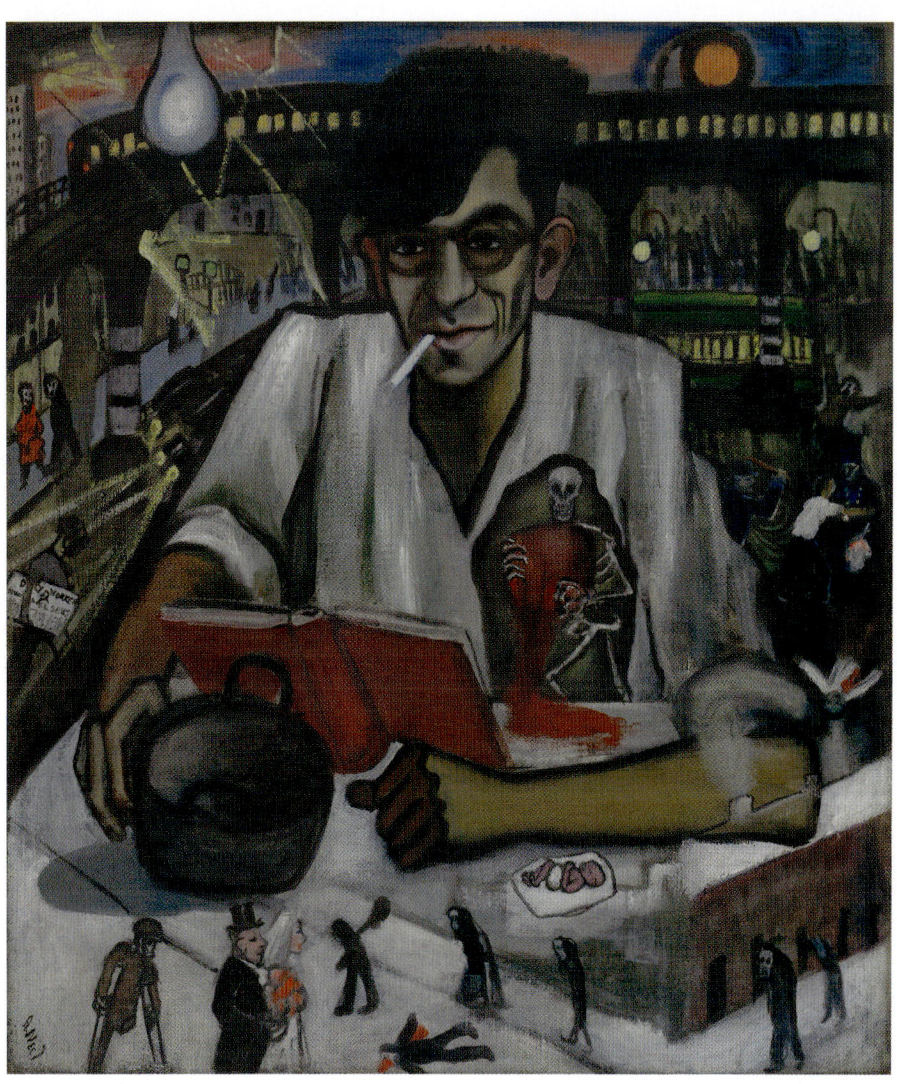

178 Alice Neel, *Kenneth Fearing*, 1935

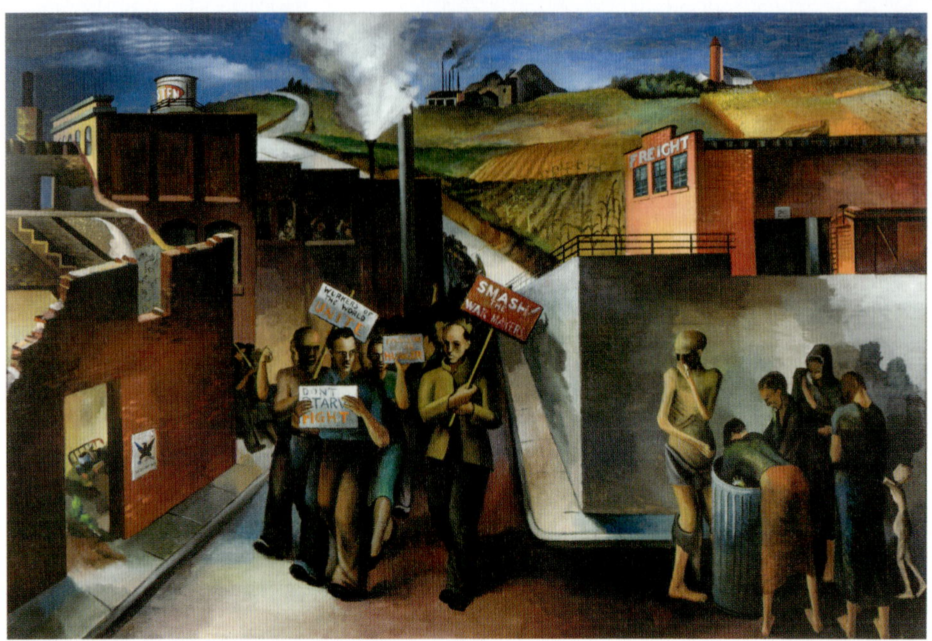

179 Joe Jones, *Demonstration*, 1934

Alice Neel lived near the CPUSA headquarters in Greenwich Village and honored her friend and neighbor, Kenneth Fearing, in an arresting portrait. Fearing was a founding member of the John Reed Club and later worked on the Federal Writers' Project. Seated beneath a bare lightbulb, a symbol of inspiration, he is a hardboiled proletarian poet in horn-rimmed glasses and rolled-up shirtsleeves, cigarette dangling from his lips, and a red book propped on an empty pot. The city buzzes with motifs snatched from his writing: the Sixth Avenue El, a veteran on crutches, a bride and bridegroom, a murder victim, cops clubbing a white-shirted protester, a man striding with a copy of the *Daily Worker*, death's head specters stalking the sidewalks. An open cavity in Fearing's chest reveals a skeleton pumping blood from his heart, the color of his book. Neel explained: Fearing's "heart bled for the grief of the world." (Hoban 2010, 132)

Unemployed Artists Group

John Reed Club artists, nearly all of whom later drew government checks, began the decade openly hostile to FDR and the New Deal. Joe Jones's 1934 painting *Demonstration* is typical of the moment. Marchers stream out of a factory brandishing placards with slogans like "Workers of the World

178

179

Unite" and "Don't Starve, Fight"—the last an invitation to a huddle of scavengers in the right foreground. A poster with the blue eagle, the emblem of the National Recovery Administration (NRA), is posted on a nearby hovel's brick wall. The NRA was a cornerstone of the New Deal effort to regulate industry through price-fixing, codes of fair practice, and protecting labor's right to collective bargaining. Despite the last clause, communists like Jones saw New Deal policies as tools of finance capital, bailing out businesses and banks at taxpayer expense while using public works as an alibi for war mobilization (hence a sign urging "Smash the War Makers").

It became expedient, however, for the far left to tether its goals to the New Deal. The CPUSA backed work relief for the unemployed, including artists, and made a marriage of convenience with Democrats as the threat of fascism loomed ever larger (see Chapter 9). The appeal of federal arts funding to leftists was clear, given the resemblance to the state-sponsored programs in Mexico and the Soviet Union. (Joe Jones, in fact, would celebrate farmers and field hands in Midwestern post office murals for the Section of Fine Arts.)

In the fall of 1933, a cohort of about twenty-five John Reed Club artists based in New York—including Phil Bard, Bernarda Bryson, Boris Gorelick, James Meikle Guy (1909–83), and Joseph Vogel (1911–95)—founded the Unemployed Artists Group (UAG). They met in a shabby loft on West 18th Street, which also served as a gallery, lecture hall, studio, and hub for rowdy parties. The UAG manifesto declared that the "state can eliminate once and for all the unfortunate dependence of American artists upon the caprice of private patronage." (Monroe 1974, 7)

But when the Public Works of Art Project began operating in December, UAG members found it wanting. They objected to the PWAP policy of limited hiring based on perceived merit rather than need. Moreover, Juliana Force, director of the Whitney Museum and head of the PWAP's New York region, played favorites and disapproved of artist activism. In early January 1934 the UAG picketed outside the Whitney's PWAP headquarters to force concessions. A month later the UAG changed its name to the Artists' Union.

Art Front

Art Front, the organ of the Artists' Union, appeared in November 1934 with the stated goal of uniting all artists "in their struggle for economic security and to encourage a wider distribution and understanding of art...[The Union] demands that the Government fulfill its responsibilities towards unemployed artists, as part

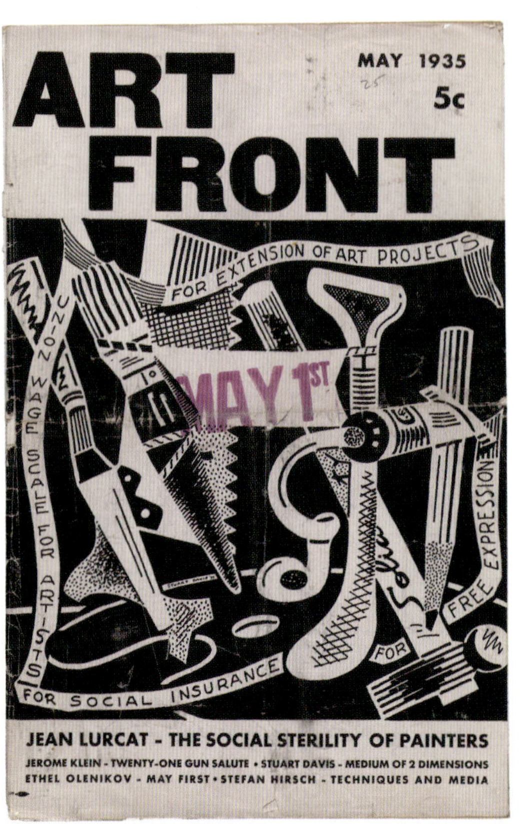

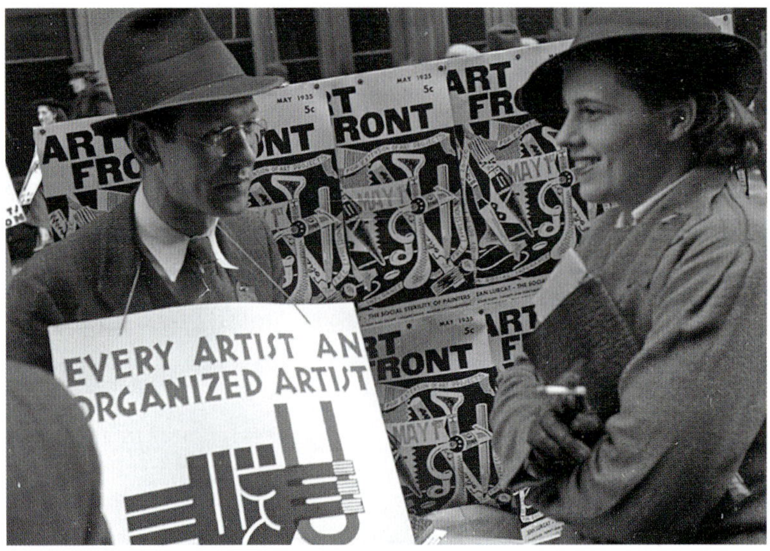

180 TOP Stuart Davis, Cover of *Art Front*, May 1935
181 ABOVE Ben Shahn, *Artists' Union Demonstrators*, 1935

of the Government responsibility toward providing for all
unemployed workers."

83 180 *Art Front* broadcast the Union's activities, goals, and
grievances. Stuart Davis (painter of modernist FAP mural *Swing
Landscape*) edited the journal for a time and designed the May
1935 cover featuring abstracted tools of the trade: palette knives,
brushes, pencils, and paint tubes. Banners proclaim the Union's
demands: "For Extension of Art Projects"; "For Social Insurance";
"For Free Expression"; with May 1st (International Workers' Day)
stamped in purple. Union members hawked copies during street
181 demonstrations and wore placards announcing "Every Artist an
Organized Artist" emblazoned with the AU logo: a closed fist
gripping three paintbrushes.

Art Front became a leading venue for debates over art
and politics. Exhibition and book reviews took stock of art
movements, global trends, and hot-button issues. Isamu Noguchi
asked, "What's the Matter with Sculpture"; Berenice Abbott
(1898–1991) proclaimed "Photography as Art and Document";
painter and writer Charmion von Wiegand (1896–1983) connected
"Expressionism and Social Change"; art historian Meyer Schapiro
(1904–96) advocated for the "Public Use of Art"; James Porter
analyzed "The Negro Artist and Racial Bias." Disputes were
spirited. Attacks could be personal and vicious. Davis, for example,
got into a dustup with regionalist Thomas Hart Benton (who was
given to denouncing modern art in xeno- and homophobic terms)
over the Missourian's "jingoism and racial chauvinism."

The Artists' Union served as the de facto bargaining agent
once the WPA's Federal Art Project got underway in 1935. Goals
included higher wages, paid sick leave, vacation time, securing
larger quotas for Project workers, and freedom from censorship.
A Grievance Committee protested layoffs (Alice Neel barely survived
a round of cuts thanks to an intervention), a Defense Committee
posted bail for artists arrested during demonstrations, a
Cultural Committee organized lectures and seminars, and an
Entertainment Committee hosted Saturday night dances and
annual balls. Wednesday night meetings regularly stretched past
midnight, when the lively debates and discussions might carry
over to all-night diners or bars.

Art Front estimated some sixteen hundred Union members
across affiliates from Boston to Chicago to Los Angeles and in
smaller towns like Springfield, Massachusetts, and Woodstock,
New York. Members came from various FAP divisions including
the Index of American Design and the Design Laboratory.
Organized artists won serious concessions from city, state,
and federal officials. They curtailed wage cuts and negotiated
increases. They got fired artists reinstated. They championed

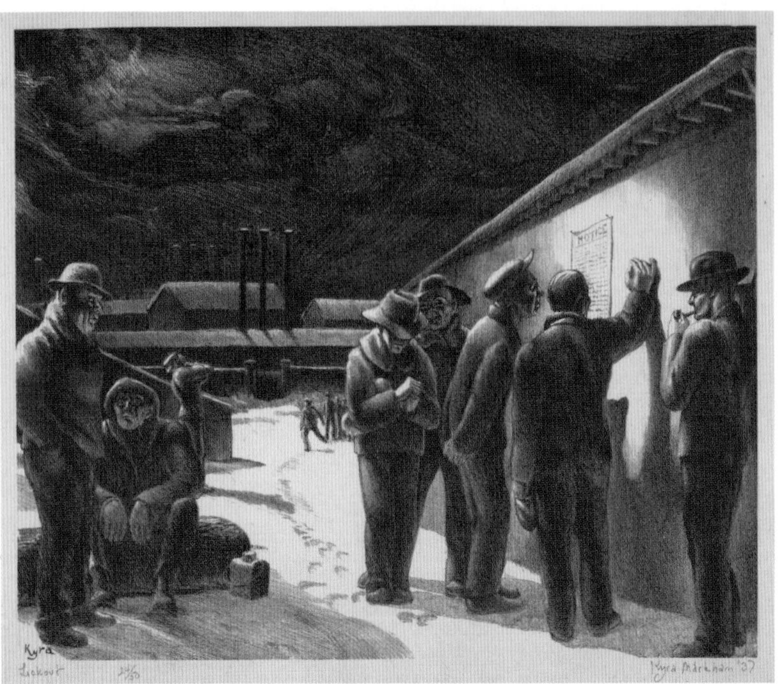

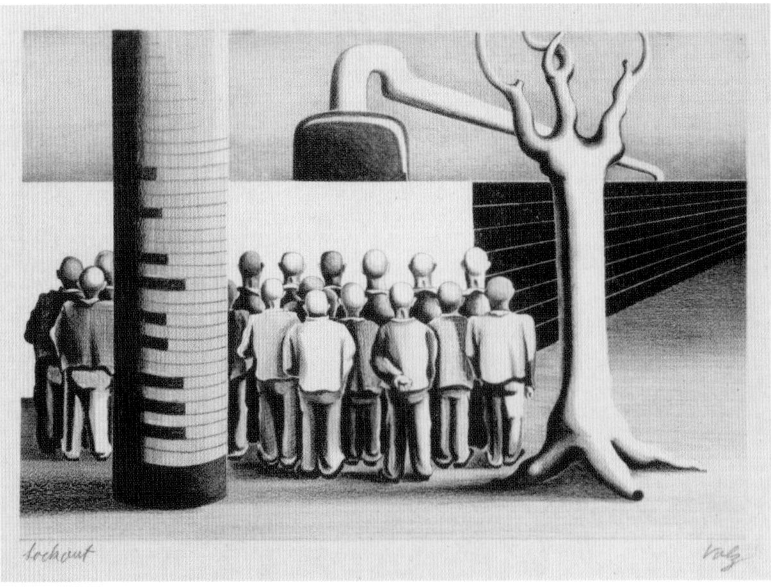

182 TOP Kyra Markham, *Lockout*, 1937
183 ABOVE Herman Volz, *Lockout*, c. 1937

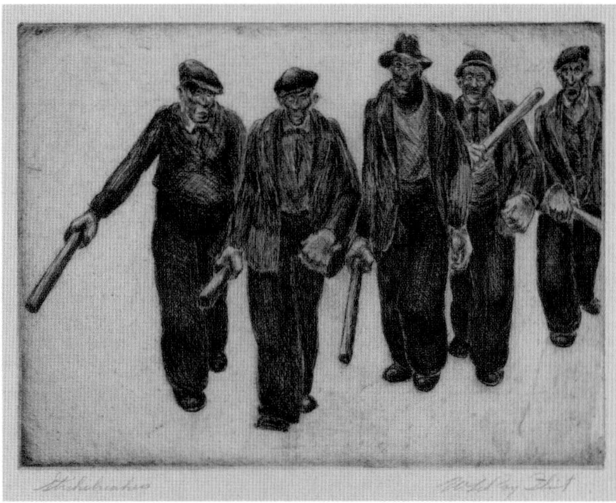

184 LeRoy Flint,
Strikebreakers, 1937

freedom of expression and equality for artists of color. Stuart
Davis credited this activist energy to the recognition that
artists, like other workers, "could only protect their basic
interests through powerful organizations." (Davis 1936, 66)

Pro-Labor

Depression-era artists identified with the working class
based on their shared experience of economic hardship and
unemployment. Artists' Union members earned the nickname
the "fire brigade" for their full-throated participation in
demonstrations and eagerness to show up at rallies or on the
picket lines for other unions. This fellow feeling found outlet in
paintings, prints, and sculptures. Artists portrayed the cycle from
unemployment to breadlines and bowery missions. They exposed
the cruel conditions—mine cave-ins, industrial accidents,
overwork—that led to strikes, protests, and clashes with the
police.

Solidarity assumed different styles. Kyra Markham's (1891–
1967) nocturnal *Lockout* finds a group of men in freshly fallen
snow half-circled around an announcement that the plant is
closing, a tactic employers used to punish workers during labor
disputes. Swiss-born Herman Volz (1904–90), active in the San
Francisco Artists' Union, gave the same theme a surrealist spin:
a featureless factory without entrances or exits bars access to a
crowd of interchangeable worker units.

The year artists formed the Union saw a surge of labor
militancy. From San Francisco to New York the workers'
movement took hold in auto plants, steel mills, coal mines,

and garment sweatshops. Powerful companies enforced anti-
union countermeasures: spy systems, firing workers suspected
of union activity, and hiring thugs to intimidate organizers and
break up strikes. LeRoy Flint (1909–91), executive secretary of the
Cleveland Artists' Union, massed a phalanx of *Strikebreakers* for
his 1937 etching. They stride with threatening purpose, beefy fists
brandishing batons in a field of negative space: a scrum of pent-
up violence ready to be unleashed.

One of the most significant strikes in US labor history began
on 30 December 1936 when autoworkers in Flint, Michigan,
occupied General Motors' Fisher Body No. 1—the world's largest
auto body plant—demanding better pay, job security, and an
end to the exhausting and inhumane assembly line "speed up."
The strike lasted forty-four days as the workers endured bitter
cold (GM cut heat to the plant) and physical threats from private
security, the police, and the National Guard.

Vienna-born Joseph Vavak (1891–1969), a Chicago Artists' Union
member, honored the women of Flint in a 1937 painting made on
the Federal Art Project. A skilled musician, Vavak set the scene
in a minor key. Anguished-looking women in overcoats—workers
themselves or the wives, mothers, sisters, or daughters of workers
connected with the strike—wander on a barren, shallow stage.
A broken gear lies on the ground, a talisman of defeated hope. A
woman in a red beret, feet firmly planted, represents the militant
Women's Emergency Brigade, a faction who put themselves in

185 Joseph Vavak, *Women of Flint*, 1937

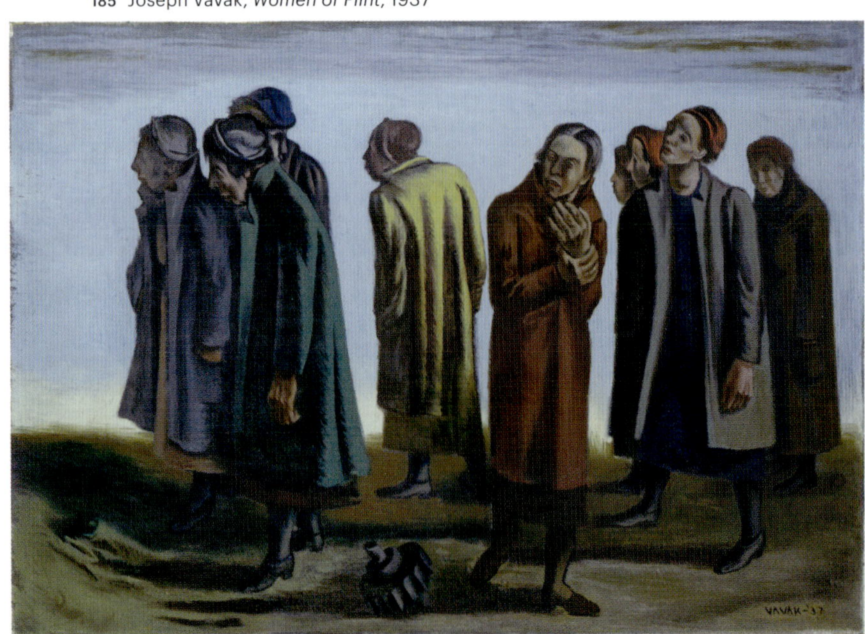

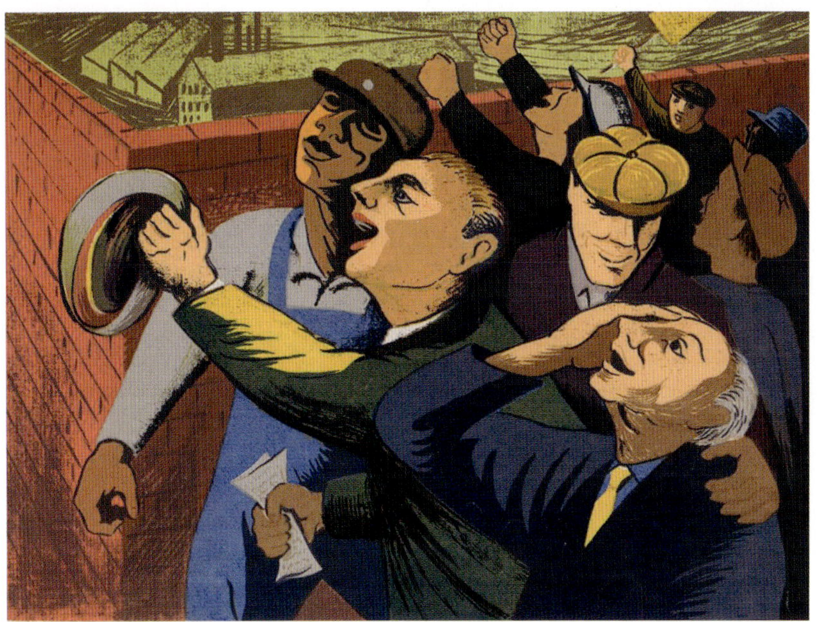

186 Harry Gottlieb, *The Strike is Won*, 1940

physical danger on the picket lines. But the strike is not yet won in this netherworld of anxious endurance.

In mid-February 1937 GM, soon followed by Ford and Chrysler, ceded to the strikers' demands and recognized the United Auto Workers as the negotiator for labor contracts. Harry Gottlieb (1895–1992), president of the Artists' Union, evoked press images of the triumphant workers in his screenprint *The Strike is Won*. An interracial and intergenerational crowd of exultant factory hands swell in the foreground, enlisting the viewer as a participant. The vibrant colors and exuberant gestures express the union members' relief and joy as they bask in the glow of a hard-won victory.

The Union and Art Projects

The Artists' Union was only possible because artists could bargain collectively with a shared employer: the US government. The Union preferred the Federal Art Project to the Treasury Section as the model for government-sponsored art. The FAP's stress on cultural democracy, through initiatives like the community art centers, aligned with leftist goals of worker education and art for the masses. The FAP, less narrowly focused on the American scene, also accommodated a wider range of styles and media than the Section. *Art Front* reviewed Project

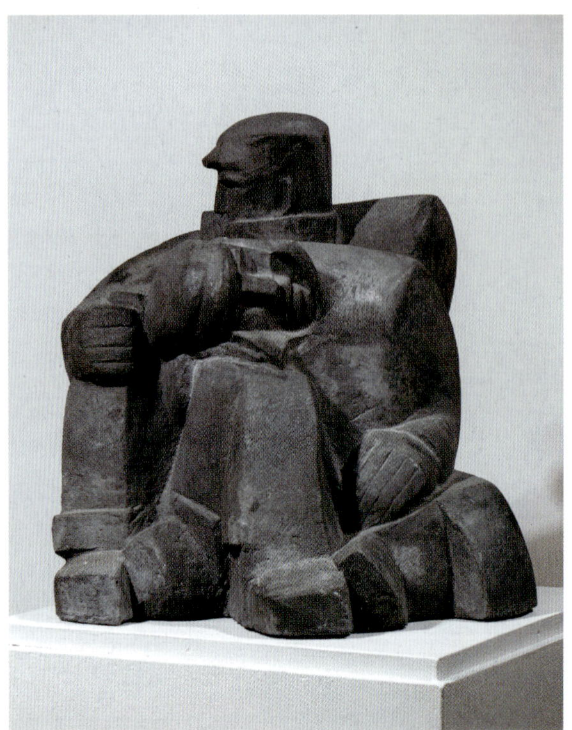

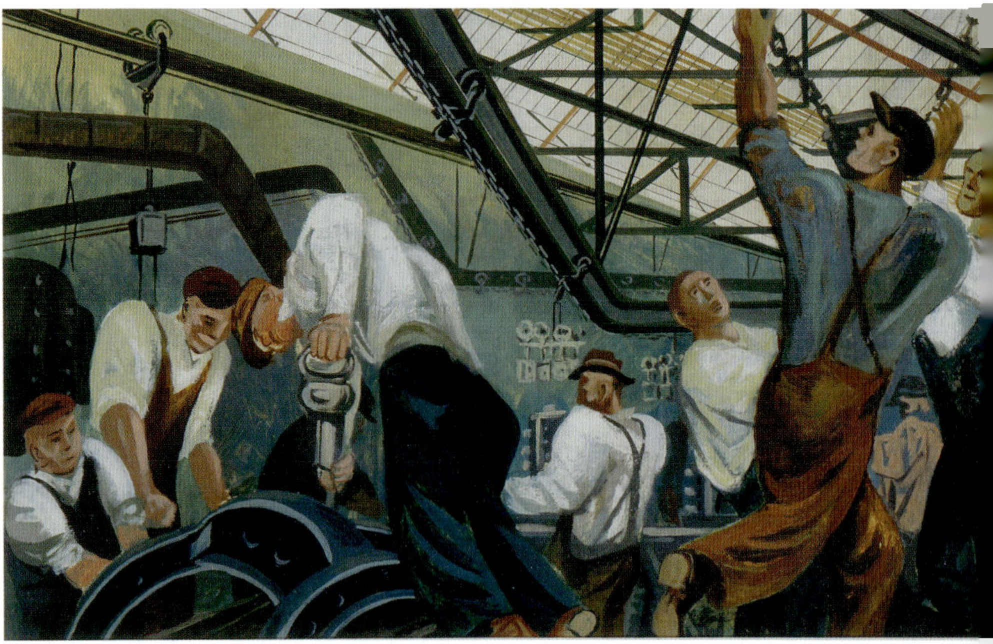

187 LEFT Aaron Goodelman,
Homeless, 1936
188 BELOW William Gropper,
*Study for Automobile
Industry*, 1940–41

exhibitions and reproduced socially-conscious FAP artwork such as Aaron Goodelman's sculpture *Homeless*.

The Section of Fine Arts, by contrast, came in for regular drubbing. Artists' Union members objected to the limited number of Section commissions, which they saw as incommensurate with need. The Section never employed more than 356 artists at once, compared to the 5,000 artists employed at the peak of the FAP. The Union protested the lack of artists represented on selection committees, the unpaid time spent designing murals for open competitions, and the out-of-pocket costs artists spent on materials. Above all, as one *Art Front* contributor wrote, Union members objected that "the personal convictions and ideas of an extremely small group" set policy for a significant federal art program. (Vane 1937, 6)

Even so, Union members—among them Ida Abelman (1910–2002), Philip Evergood, William Gropper, Joe Jones, and Anton Refregier (1905–79)—were hardly in a financial position to pass up Section commissions. Moreover, large-scale public art offered irresistible opportunities to celebrate the working class for a broad audience. Section murals, after all, treated just about every kind of manual labor. As AU member Edward Laning remembered, painting for the Section meant "learning how

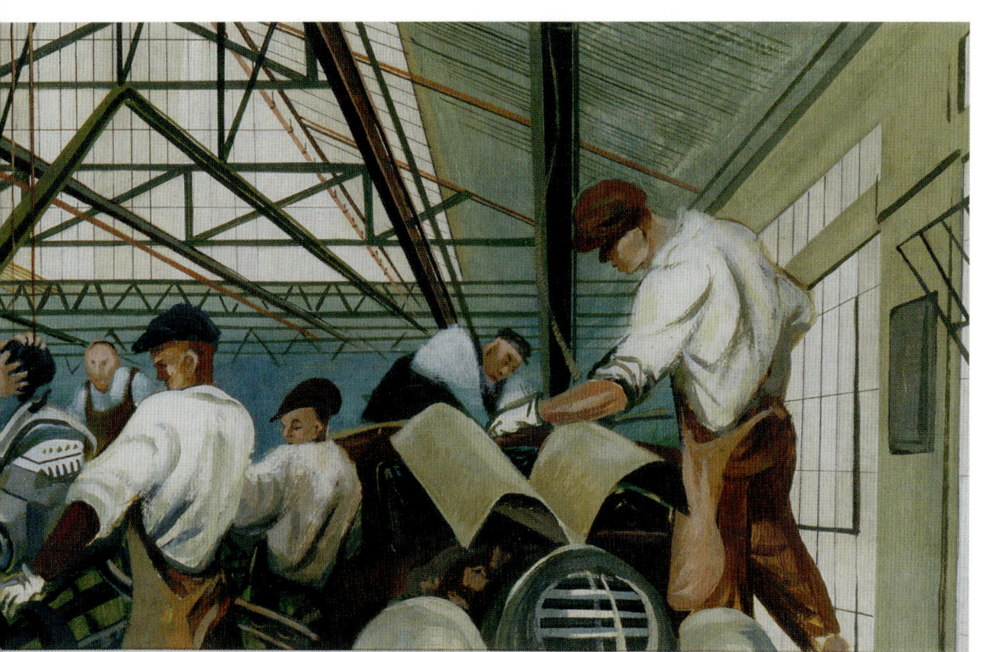

railroads were built and sawmills were operated and coal was mined and steel was manufactured." (Laning 1972, 93)

188 Leftist artists were in a bind, however, as Section murals also boosted capitalist industries. Take, for example, William Gropper's mural study for a post office in Detroit, Michigan. Detroit was the nerve center of the US automobile industry, and no theme was riper for leftist scorn. In 1915 Henry Ford introduced the assembly line to drive down labor costs by increasing the speed and efficiency of production. Workers performed repetitive, mind-numbing tasks as standardized parts sped along a conveyor belt. (A process lampooned by Charlie Chaplin in his silent comedy *Modern Times*.) On 7 March 1932 the police opened fire on a demonstration of unemployed auto workers, killing five and wounding dozens in what became known as the Ford Massacre. The following year

189 Hugo Gellert (1892–1985), in a portfolio translating Marx's *Capital* into lithographs, villainized Ford as a top-hatted monopolist wrapping his arms around a manufacturing plant, confronted by a hulking worker in overalls.

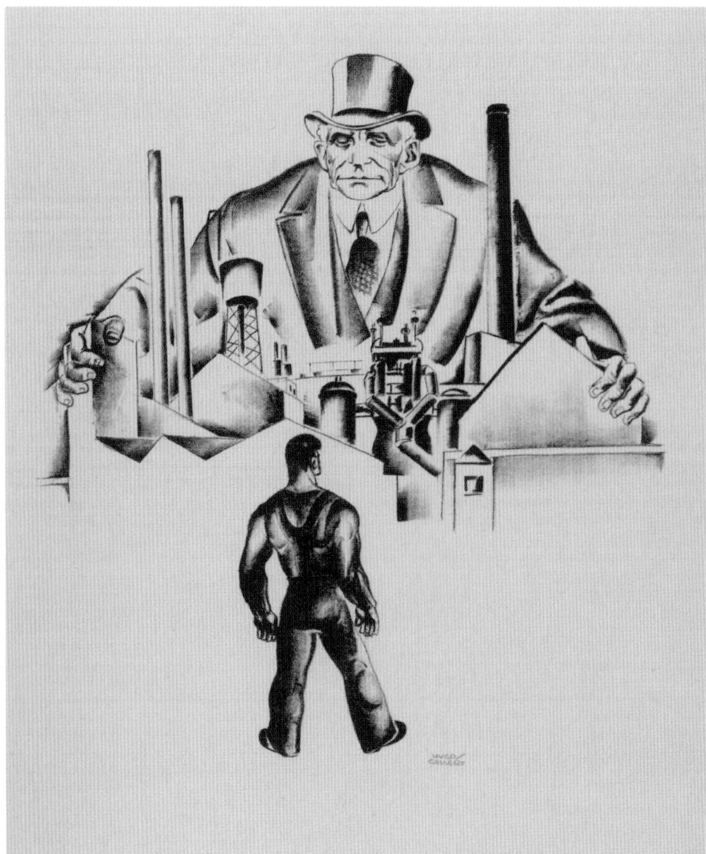

189 Hugo Gellert, *Secret of Primary Accumulation*, 1933

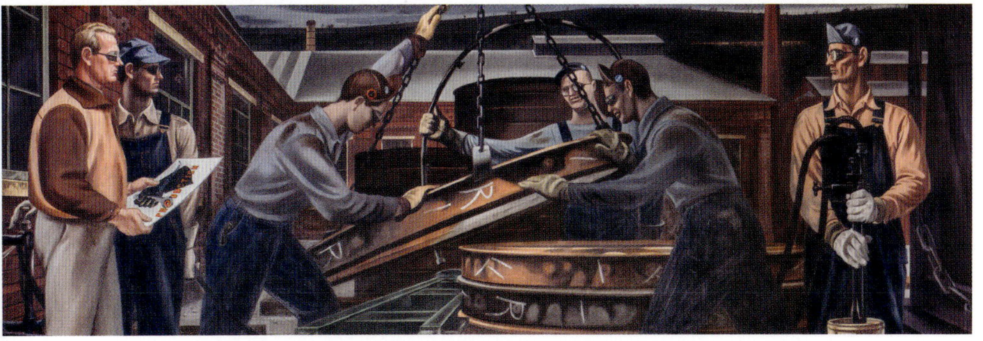

190 Harold Lehman, *Railroad Repair*, 1943

Gropper, who shared Gellert's Marxist convictions, took
a different tack in his Section mural. His assembly line of
autoworkers forms a serpentine chain of linked muscles, tools,
limbs. The upward angle gives the workers dramatic scale
and frames their cyclopean shoulders and forearms against
the soaring beams and girders. The Detroit mural shares the
expressive lines and descriptive shorthand of Gropper's political
cartoons for the Marxist journal *New Masses*, minus the explicit
critique—his workers are hardly alienated cogs in a capitalist
machine. But depending on the audience, the brawny workers
of Gropper's Section murals represented the productive forces
of capitalism *or* proletarian power ready to assume their control.

Pro-Union

Some muralists made their pro-union sympathies explicit.
Harold Lehman's (1913–2006) 1943 post office mural for Renovo,
a small railroad town in north central Pennsylvania, appears
at first glance a prototypical New Deal scene. A trio of denim-
clad workers remove steel tires from the locomotives' wheels.
The foreman at left in a sweater vest and safety goggles holds a
poster encouraging productivity. Management and labor work
together harmoniously, as they so often do in New Deal murals.
But Lehman, an Artists' Union member, managed to slip small
but telling details past the Section gatekeepers: round union
buttons in the workers' caps. Such open union support flouted
Section policy, but the small Brotherhood of Railroad Trainmen
buttons went unnoticed in the sketches submitted for approval.

Prints could be more openly partisan than murals. The lives
of coal miners and the hardships they faced—long hours, low
wages, black lung, the threats of cave-ins and explosions—came
to dominate pro-labor prints in the 1930s, likely due to the
influence and visibility of the United Mine Workers union. In

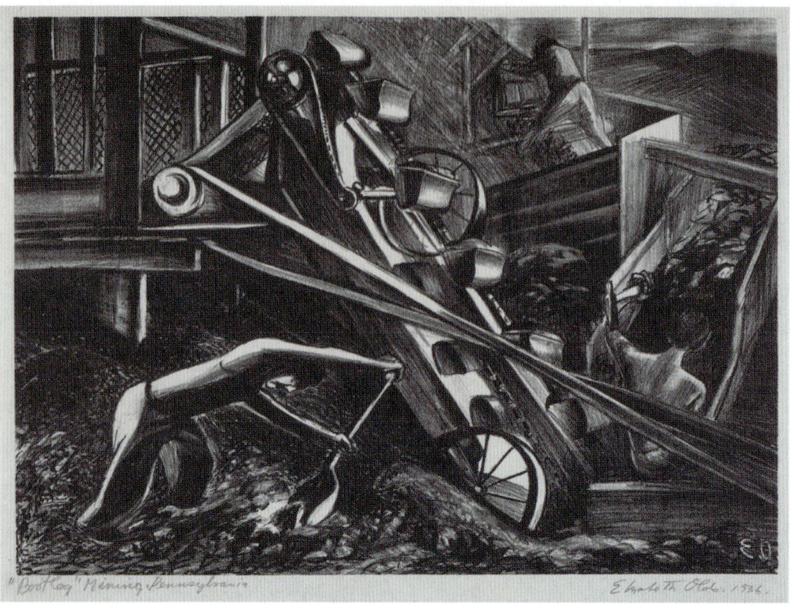

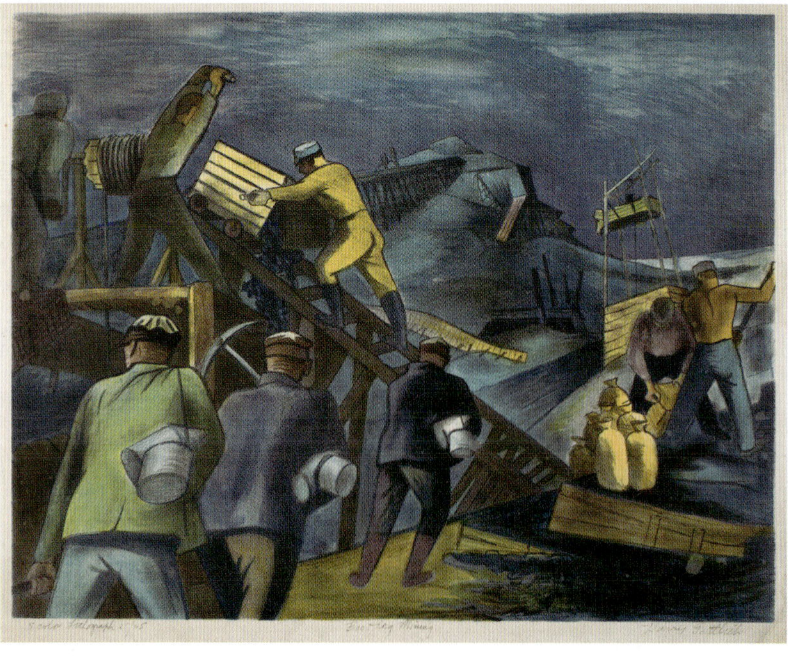

191 TOP Elizabeth Olds, *Bootleg Mining, Pennsylvania*, 1936
192 ABOVE Harry Gottlieb, *Bootleg Mining*, c. 1937–38

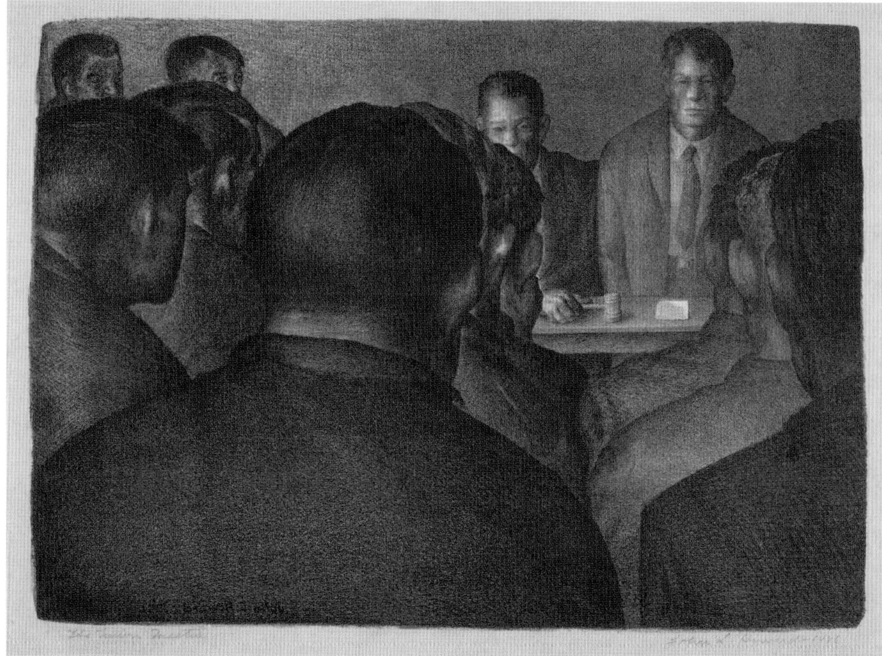

193 John Langley Howard, *The Union Meeting*, 1936

the spring of 1936 Elizabeth Olds and Harry Gottlieb traveled to a northeastern Pennsylvania coal town where striking miners had resorted to bootleg mining, digging coal illegally from surface seams. (The miners insisted that Olds and Gottlieb join their union before giving them access to an active site.) In Olds's lithograph the taut body of a bent-over miner digging into a slag heap mirrors the belt's tension. In Gottlieb's color lithograph, a row of men arrives with lunch pails and thermoses to a mining site of improvised conveyors, pulleys, rails, and winches.

John Langley Howard, whose Coit Tower murals drew controversy in 1934, made a pro-union lithograph in Monterey on the California coast where he joined the local chapter of the John Reed Club. A topography of short hair and broad shoulders mass around a table where the leader strikes a gavel, concentrating the collective will. Their ill-fitting suits and ties imply a new political clout: shed of blue-collar uniforms, they appear ready to take on the halls of Congress.

Howard's cheerless print suggests the costs as well as benefits of union resources. In 1938 the Artists' Union joined the Congress of Industrial Organizations (CIO) as a local of the United Office and Professional Workers of America. The

CIO's militant drive in the 1930s to organize workers gave the labor movement its proudly defiant character—so much so that historian Michael Denning called the Cultural Front the "Age of the CIO." But there were downsides: The headquarters of the New York AU moved from the Village to dreary offices uptown where a bureaucracy supplanted the more freewheeling downtown gatherings.

Public Use of Art

One of the main goals of the Artists' Union, consistent with the Federal Art Project more broadly, was to get art out of museums and into places where people lived and worked. Some fifty or so AU members set up the Public Use of Art Committee (PUAC) to open up new avenues for art. The Committee quickly identified subway stations as a promising location, with New York having completed construction on its first city-owned subway in 1932 (the subject of Lily Furedi's PWAP painting).

34

AU members experimented with various media—glazed tiles, silicon paint, colored cement—able to withstand the subway's fluctuating temperatures and humidity, vibrations and vandalism, dirt and grime. The Museum of Modern Art displayed the results, ranging from geometric abstractions to Elizabeth Olds's satirical contrast between white- and blue-collar commuters, in the 1938 exhibition *Subway Art.* Despite lobbying efforts, congressional cuts to WPA budgets doomed the proposals.

194

The PUAC was more successful in circulating prints to union halls, securing tacit approval from New York's FAP Director, Audrey McMahon—a significant concession given the administration's caution around perceived political bias. Members canvassed national unions for themes and subjects. This way, a PUAC member explained in *Art Front*, artists "need no longer paint what the administration considers appropriate for its mythical public but what the real public of hundreds of thousands of trade unionists thinks appropriate for itself." (Weinstock 1936, 8)

194 Elizabeth Olds, *Study for Subway Mural*, 1938

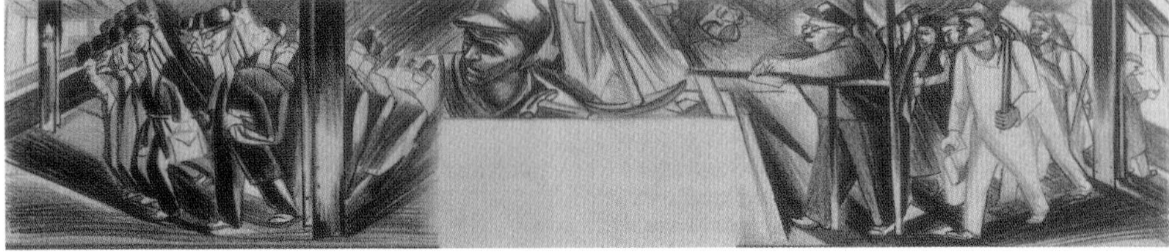

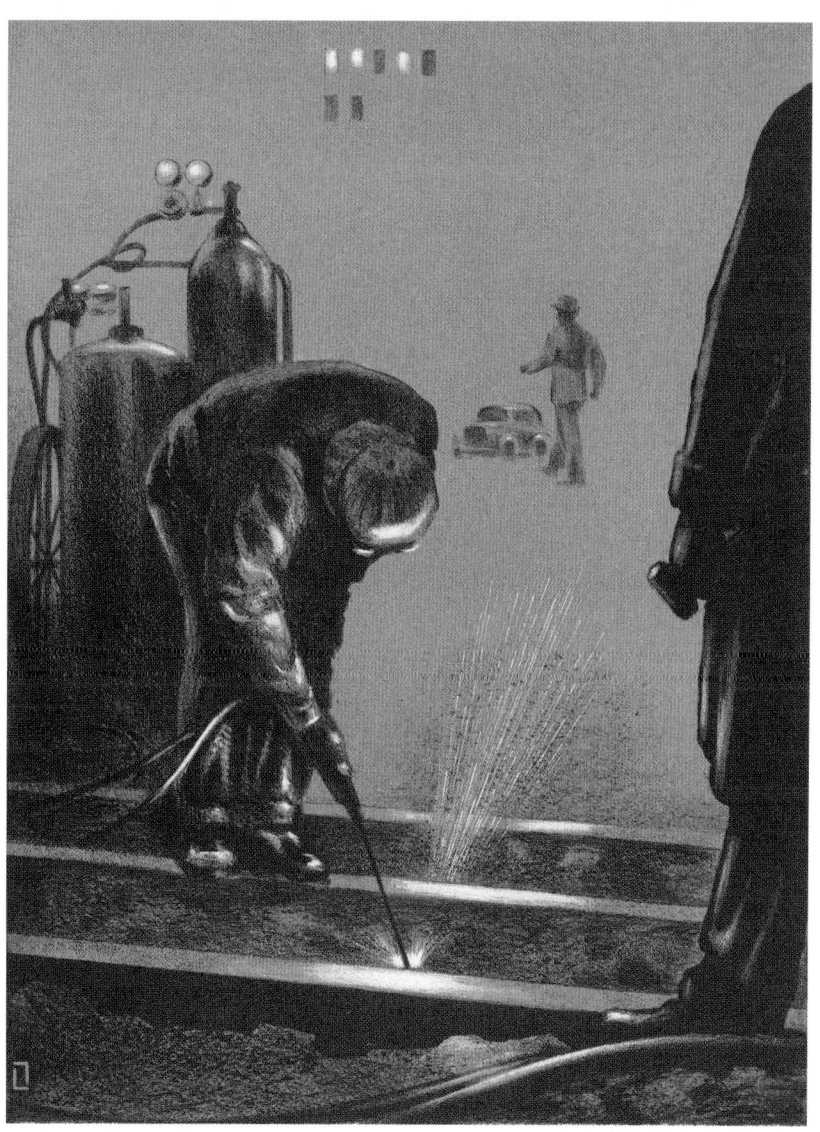

195 Louis Lozowick, *Night Repairs*, 1939

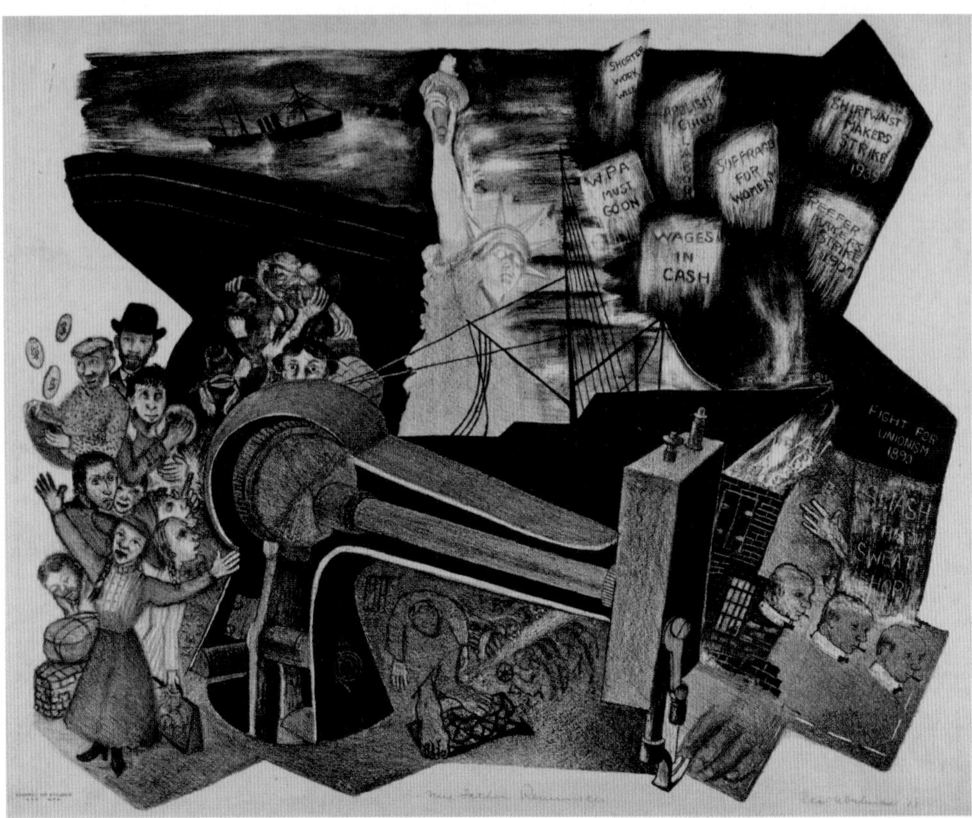

196 Ida Abelman, *My Father Reminisces*, 1937

195 Louis Lozowick contributed *Night Repairs* to a Transport Workers Union exhibition. A welder repairs a length of trolley track, showering sparks from an acetylene torch. The composition winds from the dark silhouette at right to the bent-over worker to a suited man striding toward his car in the fogbound distance. Ukraine-born Lozowick, whose family fled the antisemitic pogroms following the 1905 Russian Revolution, mediated the Soviet and American art worlds. He published *Modern Russian Art* in 1925, a study of the Russian avant-garde and served as the international secretary for the John Reed Clubs. *Night Repairs* honors the unseen labor that keeps the metropolis running.

196 Ida Abelman's *My Father Reminisces*, a FAP print designed for union distribution and reproduced in *Art Front*, spoke to the history and activism of the International Ladies' Garment Workers' Union (ILGWU). On the left a joyful crowd of immigrants disembark at Ellis Island after crossing stormy seas. The Statue of Liberty bisects the composition, a misty form like a dream. The reality is the oversized industrial sewing machine bearing down on a sweatshop seamstress. In the bottom right a burning building alludes to the Triangle Shirtwaist Factory fire of 1911, one of worst industrial disasters in US history when 146 mostly immigrant women garment workers perished in a Greenwich Village building, unable to escape because the exits had been locked by supervisors to prevent theft. Placards shimmer with feminist and pro-union messages: "Shorter Work Week"; "Suffrage for Women"; and "WPA Must Go On."

Women's Work

Abelman's print is rare for the time in dealing with women's wage labor. During the Depression women entered the workforce in increasing numbers to support themselves or their families. They worked long hours for little pay sewing clothes, doing laundry, cleaning homes, teaching or caring for children. At the same time, their presence in the workforce was viewed with suspicion, if not hostility. A male journalist for *Current History*, for example, proposed a sexist solution to unemployment: "Simply fire the women, who shouldn't be working anyway, and hire the men."

The WPA stipulated that only one member per household could hold a WPA job (some married women used their maiden names to get around the policy). Despite these obstacles, women made up a higher percentage of the Federal Art Project's workforce than on the WPA overall. The program offered training and exhibition opportunities, equal pay for equal work, and the support of the Artists' Union, which advocated for fair treatment for all government employees. Even so, women faced structural discrimination: workplace harassment, fewer supervisory roles and high-profile commissions than men, underrepresentation in exhibitions, and sexist media and critical coverage.

As Helen Langa has noted, few of the challenges wage-earning women faced appear in New Deal art. (Langa 2004, 122–27) The garment industry proved an exception, owing to its ubiquity: over half the women employed on the WPA worked in sewing rooms. ("For unskilled men we have the shovel," observed a female WPA official, "for unskilled women we have only the needle.") The activism of the ILGWU and the textile workers strike of 1934—later known as the Uprising of '34, the largest single industry strike to that point in US history—also brought visibility to the trade.

197   In *Custom Made* Riva Helfond, who taught lithography at the Harlem Community Art Center (see p. 200) conveyed the

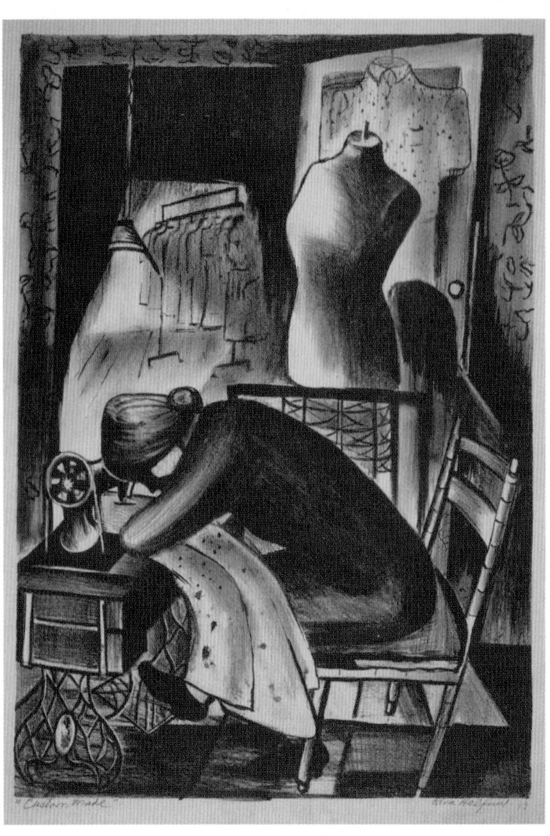

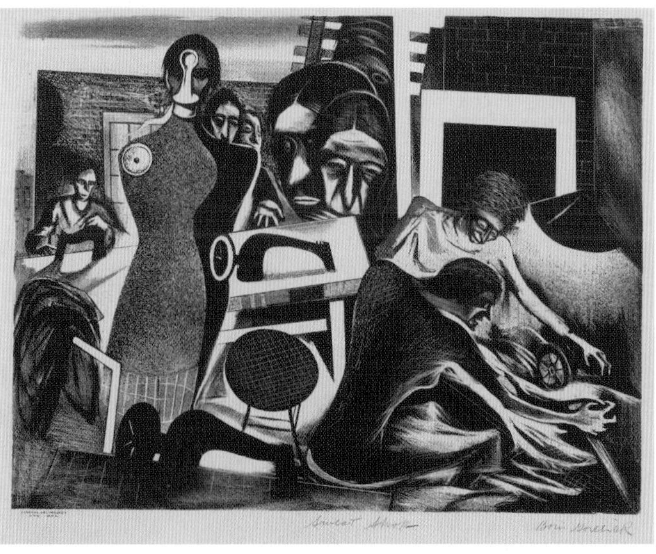

197 TOP Riva Helfond, *Custom Made*, 1939
198 ABOVE Boris Gorelick, *Sweat Shop*, c. 1938
199 OPPOSITE Elizabeth Olds, *Burlesque*, 1936

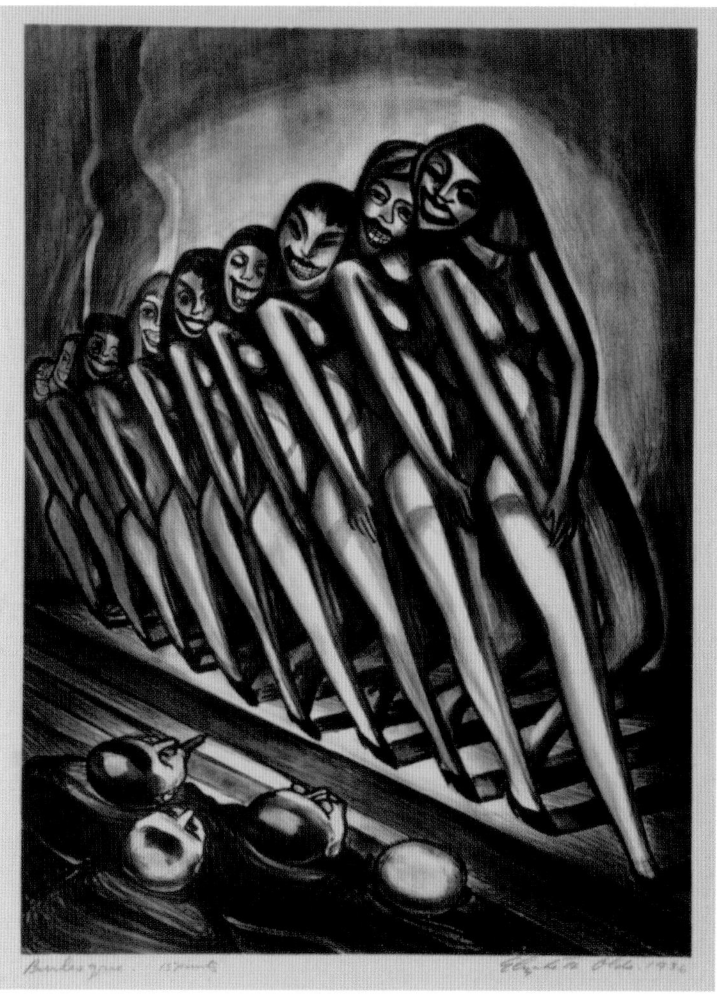

profession's late-night eyestrain and crushing fatigue. (She knew her subject, having paid the bills as an art student with gigs in New York garment factories.) A seamstress, hair twisted in a bun, folds over her sewing machine, her foot operating the pedal. A dress form looms over her, the silent weight of unfinished work. A dress form also looms in Boris Gorelick's surrealist *Sweat Shop* where pieceworkers toil under a nocturnal lamp, their haggard features outward signs of a sweatshop's long hours, low pay, and unhealthy conditions.

In *Burlesque*, Elizabeth Olds staged a maenad-like revenge on the patriarchal conditions faced by women. A raking row

of spotlit dancers perform for a leering audience of bald men,
one chomping on a phallic cigar. The dancers' heads skew at
an angle and their faces wear grimacing masks of forced glee.
While male artists treated the same theme with lusty relish,
Olds de-eroticized the dancers' repetitively robotic bodies
and tubular limbs—more firing line than chorus line. In a
power reversal, the women form a series of slashing diagonals,
like artillery shells, cornering and crushing the passive male
spectators.

Civil Rights

The Great Migration of Black Americans from the Jim Crow
South to industrial cities in the North constituted the largest
internal migration in US history. The ranks of Black workers
swelled in the shipyards and factories of cities like New
York, Chicago, Detroit, and Philadelphia, where they still
encountered discrimination in housing, employment, and
education. In the 1930s, the CPUSA actively recruited Black
workers, including artists. For example, Norman Lewis, Jacob
Lawrence, and Charles White were all affiliated with John Reed
Clubs and the Artists' Union.

The Artists' Union co-sponsored the 1935 exhibition *Struggle
for Negro Rights,* to which Louis Lozowick contributed a
lithograph of a Black protester, one hand holding a placard and
the other gripping a cop's forearm, protecting a fallen comrade
from attack. The exhibition rallied support for the Costigan-
Wagner Bill to make lynching a federal crime. (*Liberty Deferred,*
a Living Newspaper by Black writers Abram Hill and John
Silvera advocating passage of the bill, never reached the stage—
white administrators deemed it insufficiently "objective.")
Roosevelt, fearing the defection of southern Democrats, refused
to support the bill. (Similar legislation to make lynching a
federal offense would not pass until 2022.)

James Meikle Guy, an Artists' Union member, supplied a
striking icon of solidarity in his screenprint *Workers.* The family
unit familiar from New Deal iconography—male breadwinner,
mother and child—encircle a seated worker in overalls. Binaries
break down in a visual fusion of male and female, Black and
white, blue collar and white collar, agricultural and industrial.
The interlaced fingers recall author Richard Wright's lines—
"I am black and I have seen black hands / Raised in fists of
revolt, side by side with the white fists of white workers"—
published in Chicago's John Reed Club journal, *Left Front.*

Chicago-based Charles White painted four Black marchers
with pickaxes and placards, their foreshortened arms and
torsos pressing against the picture plane. As a Chicago Artists'

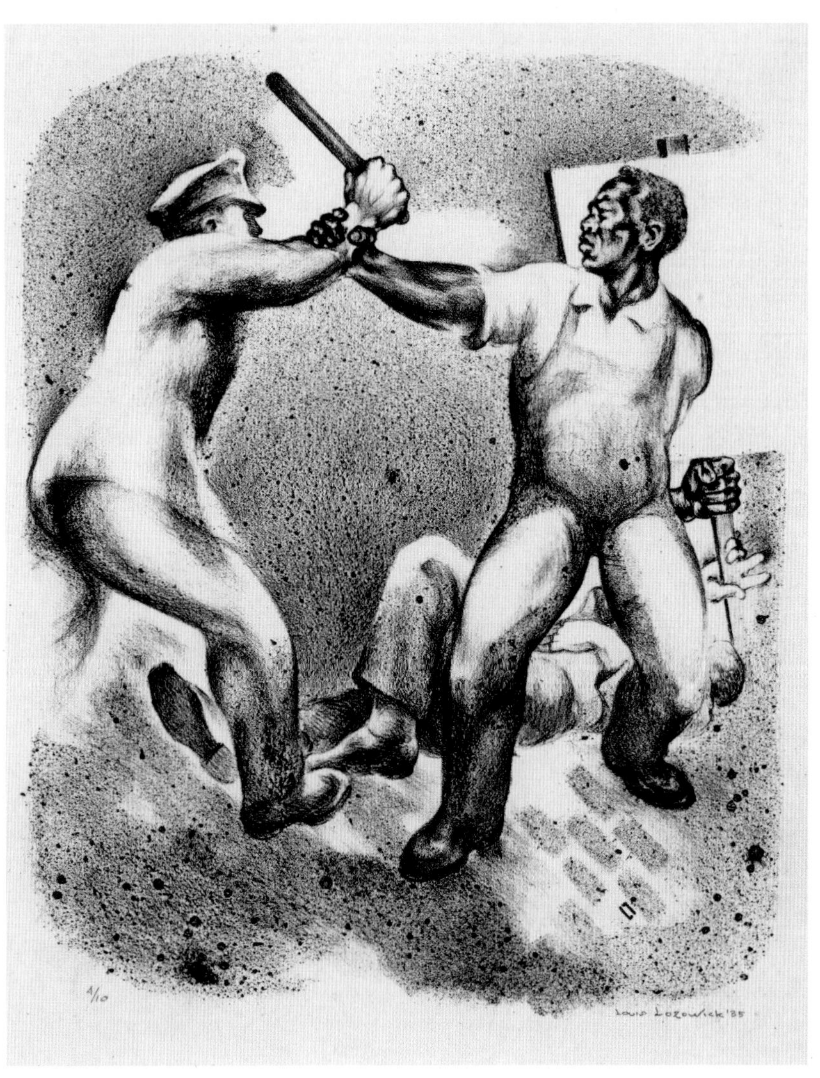

200 Louis Lozowick, *Strike Scene*, 1935

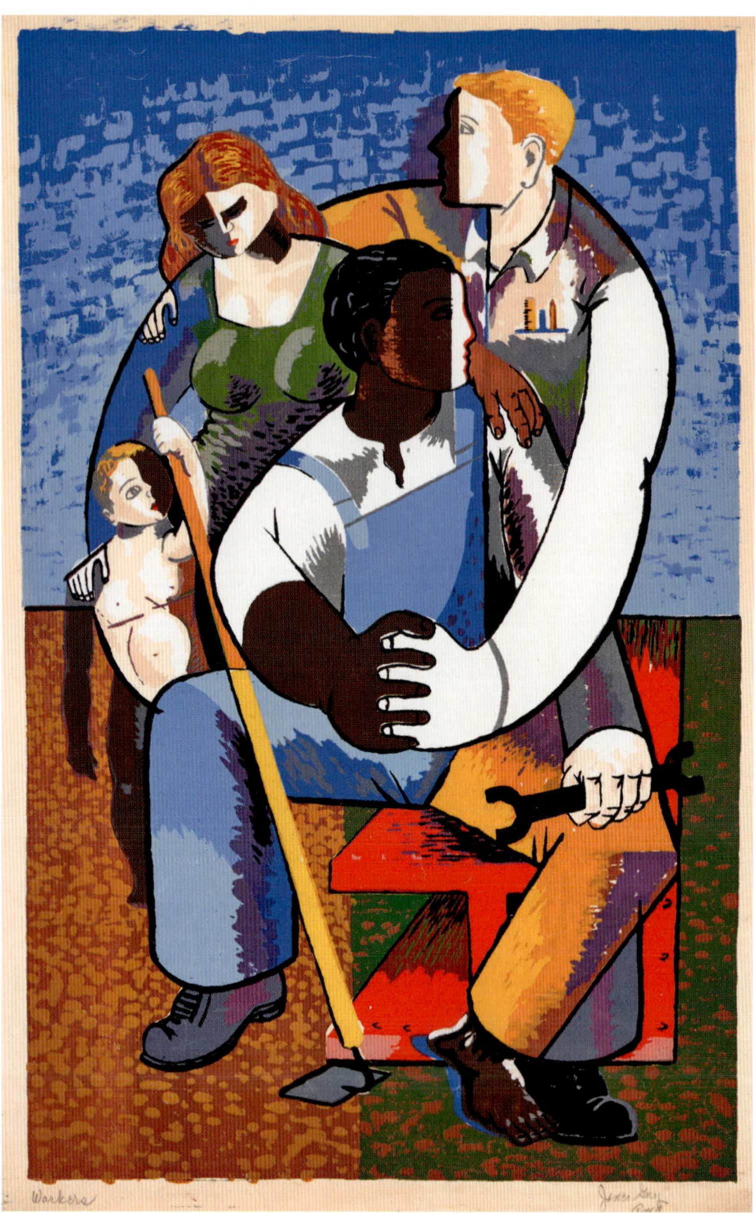

201 James Meikle Guy, *Workers*, 1938

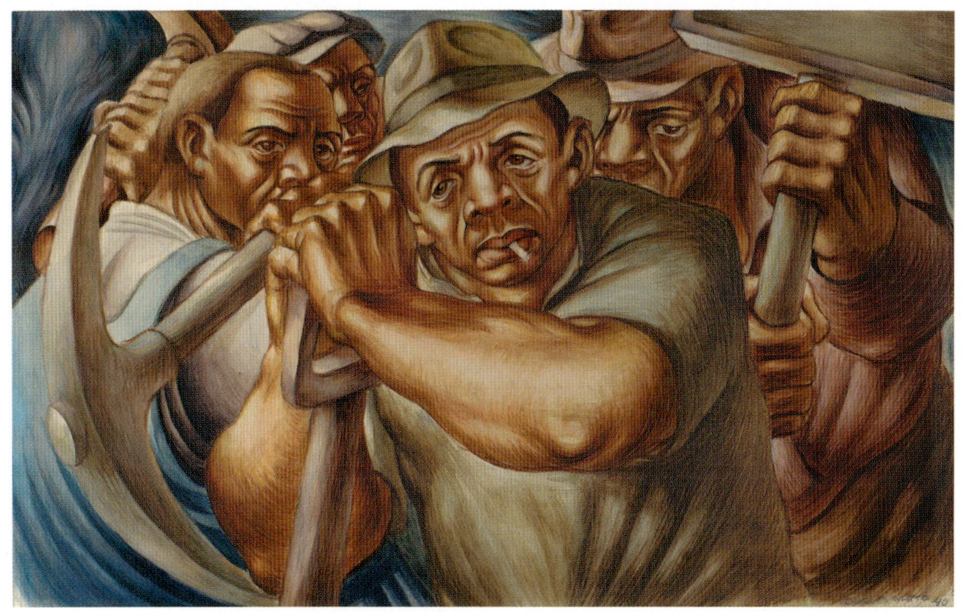

202 Charles White, *Untitled (Four Workers)*, 1940

Union member, White participated in a sit-down strike at
the Illinois Art Project's administrative offices, protesting
low quotas and discriminatory hiring practices. The AU
also orchestrated the ouster of an elitist state director who
consistently hired below the government quotas, blacklisted
union members, and played favorites. "My first lesson on the
[Illinois Art Project] dealt not so much with paint," White later
wrote, "as with the role of unions in fighting for the rights of
working people." (White 1955, 38)

Stop Those Cuts!

Roosevelt won reelection in 1936 with nearly sixty-one percent
of the popular vote, the largest margin ever recorded, buoyed
by an energized coalition of liberals, union members, urban
voters, and racial and ethnic minorities. Overconfident,
Roosevelt made uncharacteristic political missteps, starting
with an abortive scheme to pack the Supreme Court with more
sympathetic Justices. (The year before, the Court gutted key
New Deal legislation by ruling aspects unconstitutional.) He
also cut government spending in a premature bid to balance
the federal budget. The move cratered industrial production,
stock prices plummeted, and four million workers lost their
jobs in what critics labeled the Roosevelt Recession.

The spring of 1937 saw hot-blooded confrontations between unionized artists and the government. In April, Congress slashed WPA funding by nearly a quarter. Over six hundred culture workers descended on the FAP offices in New York and effectively took the administration hostage. Union members forced Harold Stein, a recently appointed administrator (who certainly got more than he bargained for), to relay their demands for an appeals board to Washington. Stein, who refused to call the police out of fear the ensuing fracas would collapse the floor, was held hostage for over fifteen hours until WPA higher-ups agreed to terms on which they would later renege.

Further budget cuts that summer liquidated several divisions of the FAP, including the Design Laboratory, gallery tours, and teaching. More ominously, the US government issued new provisions requiring all WPA workers to be legal US citizens. "Though we live like other Americans—have been educated here, pay taxes, and have the same stomachs as American citizens," protested Eitaro Ishigaki, targeted in the wave of layoffs, "we are not allowed to become naturalized. [The US government offered no pathways to citizenship for Asian immigrants.] You can see how unfair the whole thing is." (Wang 2017, 60) Artists like Mark Rothko (Latvian) and Arshile Gorky (Armenian) continued to work at their own risk; others such as Willem de Kooning (Dutch) opted to resign rather than face deportation.

The Artists' Union opposed the clause and interpreted it as a sign of creeping fascism. "From the exclusion of aliens on the WPA," warned an *Art Front* editorial in October 1937, "it becomes easier to exclude non-Aryans, Jews, Negroes....The method of reaction is to create a precedent and then to quote it."

The fragility of art program funding, combined with regressive new policies, convinced artists to open a bold new front: a campaign to make their vision of a Federal Art Project permanent.

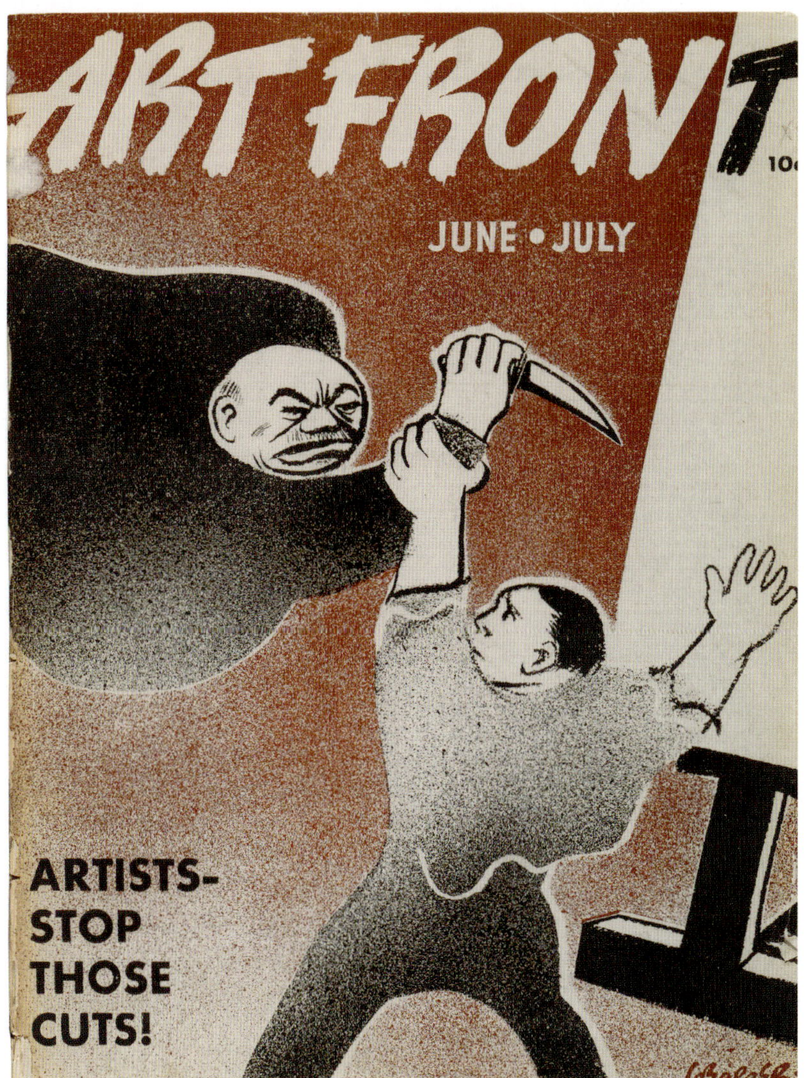

203 William Gropper, "Artists—Stop Those Cuts!," *Art Front*, June–July 1937

Chapter 8
For a Permanent Federal Art Project

"Should the Nation Support Its Art?"
Philip Evergood, one of the 219 artists arrested for occupying
Federal Art Project (FAP) headquarters, posed this question
to readers of the art journal *Direction* in April 1938. Elected
president of the Artists' Union the year before, Evergood gave
a resounding "yes," arguing that the FAP had contributed to
"fuller, happier and better lives."

Evergood was in the middle of a campaign to make the art
projects permanent. Part of the campaign involved a group show
at New York's progressive ACA Gallery titled *1938—Dedicated
to the New Deal*. Joe Jones—Artists' Union member, Section
muralist, and erstwhile critic of the New Deal—contributed
A Worker Again on WPA, a half-length self-portrait as an
artist-laborer (no palettes or brushes in view). The low angle
emphasizes his arms and shoulders, consistent with union
solidarity and New Deal work relief. Evergood contributed
The Artist in the New Deal, a busy composition with marching
workers, led by an artist, striding over the bones of the Old
World. The artist as worker, both paintings insisted, represented
the future of cultural democracy. That future would be secured
through permanent government funding for the arts.

For a Permanent Federal Art Project

The very first November 1934 issue of *Art Front*, and nearly every
issue following, called for permanent federal arts funding.
Before the WPA had even begun, the Artists' Union proposed
a public role for art in *Art Front's* July 1935 issue:

*The Artists' Union holds that the artist is a vital part of the life and
culture of his community. There are public buildings to be decorated;
there are children eager to be taught; there are libraries, schools,*

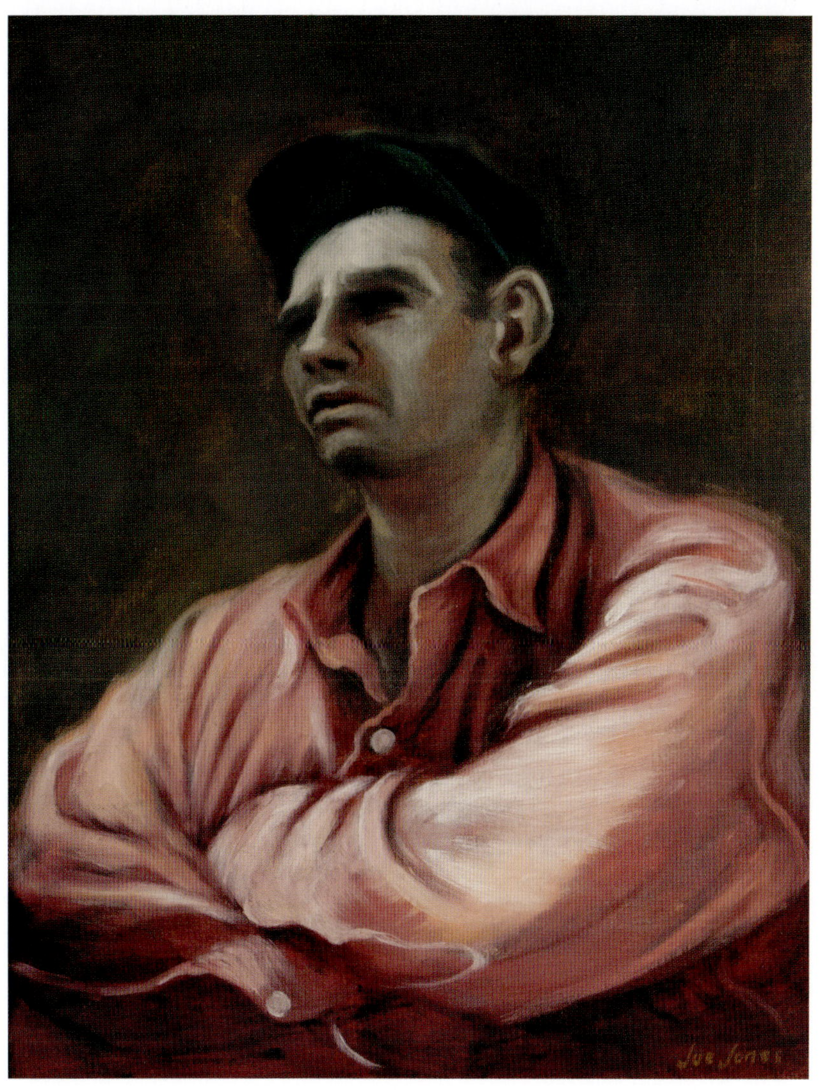

204 Joe Jones, *Self-Portrait: A Worker Again on WPA*, c. 1935

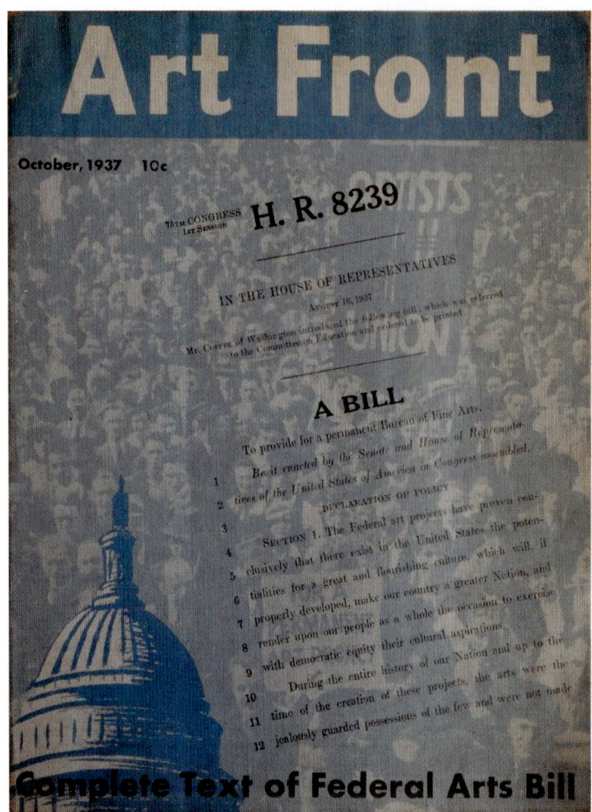

205 *Art Front,*
October 1937

hospitals that want pictures of all sorts for their walls; there is a need for new books with illustrations for schools. These and many more needs of the community can be filled by the artists.

Once the Federal Art Project got underway a month later, artists seized the chance to enshrine permanent state subsidy for art. The FAP Supervisors' Association (a kind of union for supervisors) published "Art as a Function of Government" to help make the case. The pamphlet outlined a history of state-sponsored art stretching back to the pharaohs of Egypt, the age of Pericles, and the Medici popes in Renaissance Italy. The pamphlet looked south to Mexico for a model of popular public art. Soviet Russia organized art production through trade unions and cooperative associations. The authors noted the regulation of culture in Italy and Germany through Ministries of Propaganda—an implicit warning that the US should not fall behind in an art as well as arms race with fascist foes.

The goal of permanent arts funding faced stiff headwinds. Anti-New Dealers intent on discrediting the programs relied on rote claims: 1) Artists on the payrolls were not real artists; 2) The quality of government-funded art was generally low; 3) The projects were communist hotbeds; and 4) Art patronage is not the government's proper role. The neologism "boondoggle" went into circulation when a New Deal detractor complained that the WPA trained educators in braiding lanyards, known as boondoggles, on the government's dime. The word stuck and has since become synonymous with government waste and mismanagement. William Randolph Hearst's tabloid the *Sunday Mirror,* for example, smeared WPA artists in September 1935 as "hobohemian chiselers" who clamor "for additional boons for their boondogglings, the while they bite the hand that is feeding them."

In January 1938 Washington representative John Coffee and Florida Senator Claude Pepper introduced the Coffee-Pepper Bill (the name itself ripe for mockery) to establish a Bureau of Fine Arts. (*Art Front*, a few months earlier, had published the draft legislation in a show of support.) In remarks to Congress quoted in the *New York Times* (3 April 1938), Representative Coffee compared art to a natural resource that should be protected: "We spend seemingly limitless sums in this Congress for the preservation of birds in the sky, beasts in the forests and insects in the ground. But so far we are adamant in our resistance to attempts to subsidize the theater, artists and intellectuals in these United States."

The bill met fierce pushback. In the pages of the *American Magazine of Art*, museum director Francis Henry Taylor reviled it as "one of the most dangerous pieces of class legislation that an organized minority has ever succeeded in introducing into the Congress." (Taylor 1938, 157) In February 1938 seventeen art societies, prominent among them the National Academy of Design and the National Society of Mural Painters, locked arms in opposition to the bill. Conservative artists and politicians argued that state-sponsored art limited freedom of expression and resulted in standardized mediocrity. Genuine artists "would prefer the chains of poverty," insisted one congressman, to the "sycophancy" of government patronage. (Musher 2015, 186)

Artists gave as good as they got. William Gropper's *The Senate* conjures the spirit of nineteenth-century French satirist Honoré Daumier in puncturing congressional windbags who held the fate of the art programs in their hands. A paunchy senator bellows and embraces air in a mostly empty chamber, ignored by the few scattered colleagues napping, reading the papers, and propping their feet on a desk. Gropper, a recipient of prestigious Treasury Section mural commissions, had sharpened his gift for satirical shorthand on cartooning assignments, like the one for *Vanity Fair* that inspired the painting. For Gropper, the leftist son of Romanian and Ukrainian Jewish immigrants, the US Senate is "the best show in the world," as he put it—a stage for empty grandstanding rather than meaningful action.

The Artists' Union, however, strategically engaged the legislative process and threw its support behind the proposed Bureau of Fine Arts. Representatives debated the Coffee-Pepper bill, revised with the support of New York congressman William Sirovich, on the floor of the House on 15 June 1938. A South Dakota congressman fumed that the time would have been better spent on the arms race or Japan's invasion of China. Missouri congressman Dewey Short insisted "subsidized art is no art at all" and mocked the bill by striking ballet poses and mincing around the House floor. The display so discombobulated Sirovich that he supposedly voted both for and against his own bill, which failed ignobly 195 votes to 35.

More trouble lay ahead. Although Federal One comprised a small portion of the WPA's overall budget (roughly 2.5 percent of the total), it attracted outsize controversy. In 1938 Texas representative Martin Dies, chairman of the newly-formed House Committee on Un-American Activities (predating its 1950s association with Senator Joseph McCarthy and the anticommunist "blacklist"), set Federal One in his sights.

206 William Gropper, *The Senate*, 1935

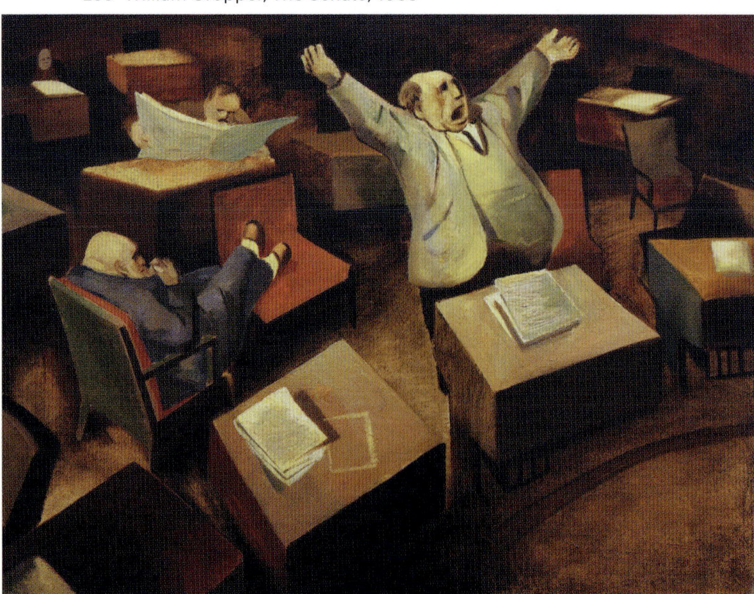

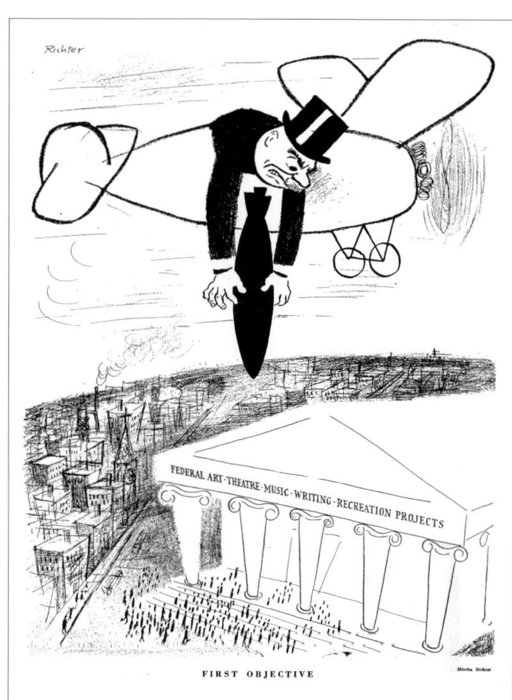

207 Mischa Richter,
First Objective, 1939

The Dies Committee relied on hearsay, false and partial evidence, and unfounded accusations to insinuate that Federal One, especially the Writers' and Theatre Projects, operated as Communist fronts.

Dies exploited the media's appetite for controversy; print and radio news outlets gave airtime and column inches to parroting the partisan hearings. When the 1938 midterm elections swung to conservatives, an emboldened coalition of anti-New Deal legislators—skewered by Mischa Richter in a *New Masses* cartoon as oligarchs torpedoing Federal One—built on the momentum of the Dies hearings in calls to eliminate arts funding.

World of Tomorrow

The embattled WPA art projects, facing media scrutiny and congressional cutbacks, desperately needed a public relations boost. The 1939–40 New York World's Fair supplied the perfect opportunity. Some forty-four million visitors ultimately passed through the Flushing Meadows fairgrounds in Queens, New York. They were greeted by the monumental Trylon and Perisphere, an obelisk and globe, as symbols of the Fair's theme: Building the World of Tomorrow. Inside the Perisphere,

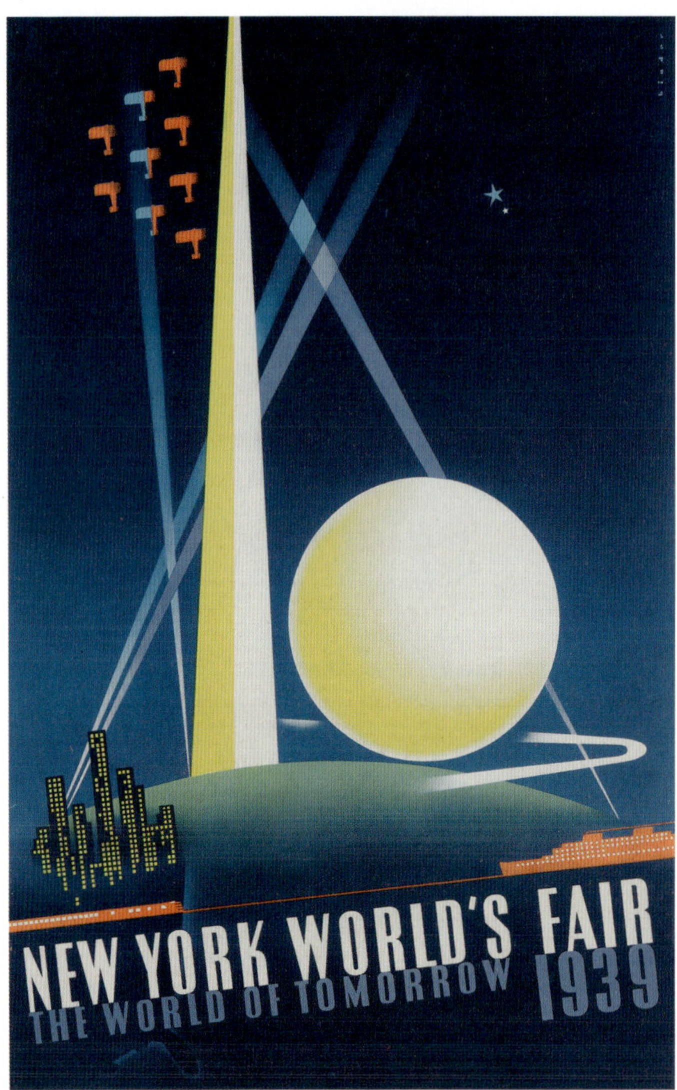

208 Joseph Binder, *New York World's Fair*, 1939

visitors on a moving sidewalk took in a diorama of an imagined "Democracity" in the year 2039 complete with superhighways, soaring skyscrapers, and social harmony.

The Fair was a consumer utopia. Corporations set up pavilions sprawled over twelve hundred acres stocked with the latest consumer goods and gadgets: fluorescent lighting, air conditioning, the fax machine, a prototype television. These newfangled products forecast a thriving future. But whose future? On the eve of the Second World War, spectacular international pavilions—including Italy, Japan, and the Soviet Union (though not Germany)—put forward competing visions.

Artists were enlisted to shore up the New Deal vision of material abundance, progressive government, and cultural democracy. Philip Guston won the coveted commission to paint the outdoor mural over the entry to the WPA pavilion. He treated the theme "Maintaining America's Skills" with monumental simplicity—the workers have sculptural mass inspired by Guston's love of Renaissance art—made more impressive given the technical challenges of painting with new rubber-based paint on a curving 25 × 24-foot exterior wall.

Maintaining skills had been a priority for the FAP, which considered the skills of artists a collective resource threatened by widespread unemployment. (It was true in Guston's case: the FAP "kept me alive and working," he recalled, "It was my education.") To show those skills in action (and tax dollars at work) the FAP set up a makeshift community art center to host live painting, drawing, sculpting, and printmaking demonstrations for fair audiences.

Inside the WPA building, Guston's friend, Anton Refregier, designed eight 30 × 8-foot murals representing the accomplishments of Federal One. For the FAP design, he resolved the tricky tall and narrow format with a composition

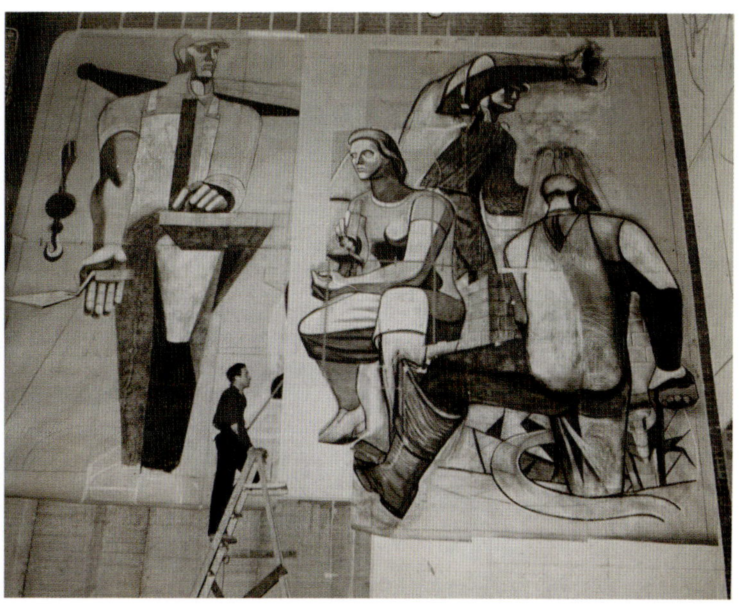
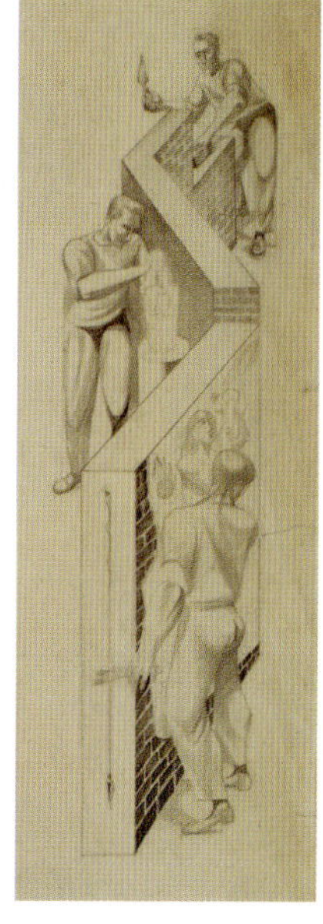

209 ABOVE LEFT Philip Guston working on *Maintaining America's Skills*, 1939
210 ABOVE RIGHT Anton Refregier, *Cultural Activities of the WPA*, 1939

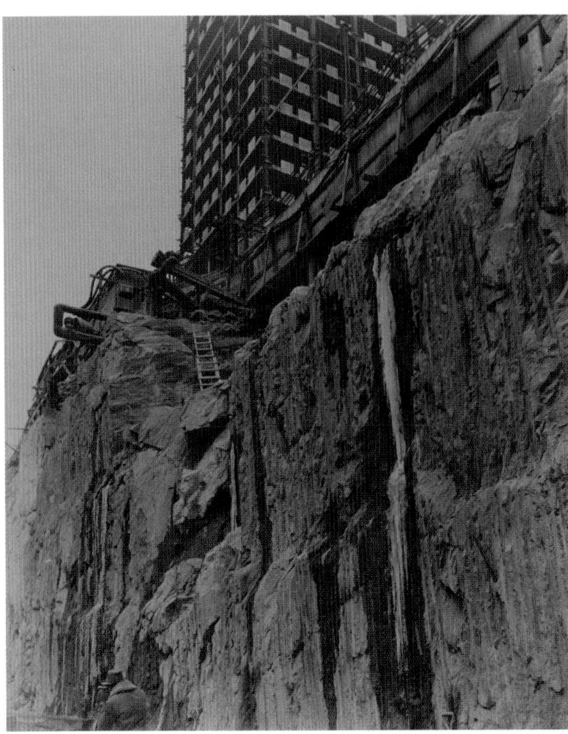

that zig-zags upwards from a muralist painting to a sculptor
chiseling to a mason bricklaying. The continuity between
artist and bricklayer shows their New Deal efforts as mutually
reinforcing—artist as a worker, worker as artist. The brick wall
had another significance: Refregier wanted to show that the
federal art projects "are aimed at the people, out in the streets,
in their daily lives unlike the museums, art galleries or lecture
halls where most simple people never go for this is out of the
pattern of their lives." (Park and Markowitz 1977, 113)

World's Fair visitors could pick up a copy of Berenice Abbott's
Changing New York, a classic of documentary photography.
Abbott had spent the 1920s in Paris, where she trained as a
darkroom assistant to Man Ray (1890–1976), established herself
as a sought-after portraitist, and bought the archive (later sold
to MoMA) of photographer Eugène Atget, chronicler of Parisian
streets in elegant, melancholy black-and-white.

Stateside, Abbott found that "Old New York is fast disappearing."
Working with her life partner, writer Elizabeth McCausland,
Abbott embarked on a decade-long text-image dig into New
York's layered strata of past and present. She photographed

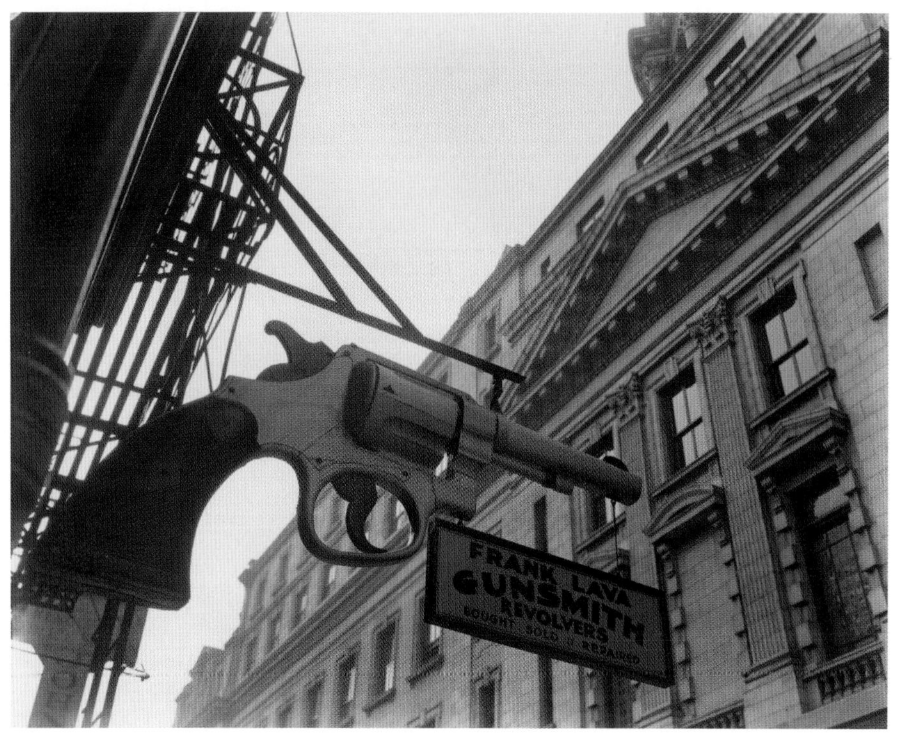

barbershops, pawnshops, brownstones, elevated railroads, bus and train stations, firetraps and antique shops, and buildings slated for demolition. Her camera cranes upwards at sheer cliff walls of the Rockefeller Center excavation to the neat geometric floors of Radio City Music Hall above, conjoined by a comically dwarfed ladder. The daily uncanny—what Abbott called the "bizarre happenings of everyday existence"—is a trademark of the series; in another photograph a gunsmith's sign points across the street at police headquarters.

In 1935 the Federal Art Project hired Abbott as a supervisor in the Photography Division. (When an older male official saw her photographs of the Bowery district, he advised her that "nice girls" shouldn't go to such dangerous neighborhoods. "I'm not a nice girl," she fired back, "I'm a photographer. I go anywhere.") The FAP funded Abbott's ongoing project, but the boon had a catch: WPA administrators bowdlerized the published version of *Changing New York*, rewriting McCausland's captions and retitling and rearranging the photographs. Fair tourists bought it as a guidebook, unaware officials had blunted its critical edge.

American Art Today

The fair's Contemporary Arts Building housed *American Art Today,* the largest survey of work by living artists in US history—with 550 paintings, 250 sculptures, and 400 drawings and prints selected from over 25,000 submissions. The exhibition came about through pressure from organized artists, who also negotiated seats on the selections committee. Co-organized by Federal Art Project director Holger Cahill, the exhibition featured a "who's who" of Project and Treasury Section artists, among them Gertrude Abercrombie, Stuart Davis, Philip Evergood, William Gropper, O. Louis Guglielmi, Joe Jones, Doris Lee, Jack Levine, Concetta Scaravaglione, and Hale Woodruff. In the catalogue introduction, Cahill applauded the exhibition's stylistic range and geographic scope, evidence that a vital and regionally various American art would be part of the "World of Tomorrow."

Robert Gwathmey's (1903–88) *The Hitchhiker*, on display, found contemporary art at a crossroads. The down-on-his-luck hitchhiker, cocking his thumb in hopes of catching a ride to a better future, belongs to the Depression-era realm of social realism. But what will the future hold? The painting points to a society dominated by consumerism and mass media (the fair introduced broadcast television to the public). Across the street an accordion of billboards with smiling lipsticked models announces a new regime of glamor and consumer

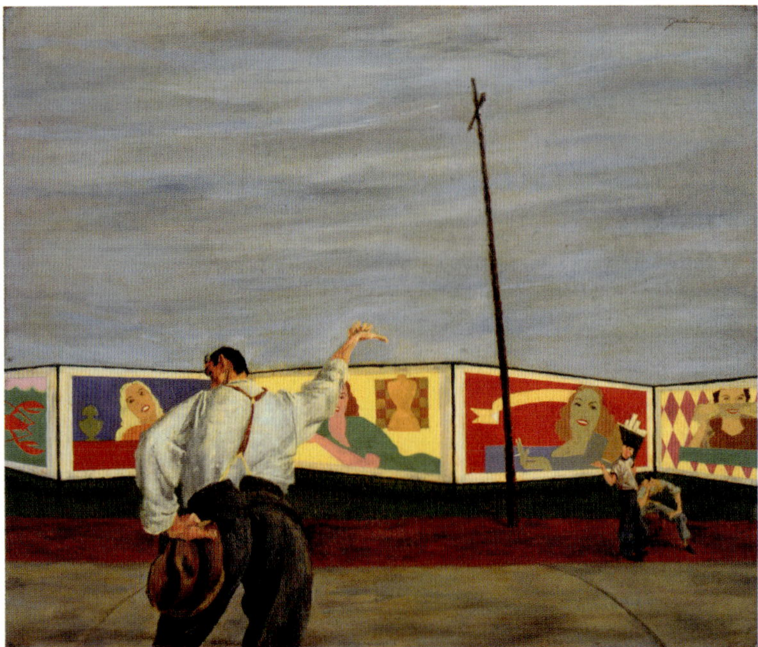

213 Robert Gwathmey, *The Hitchhiker*, 1936

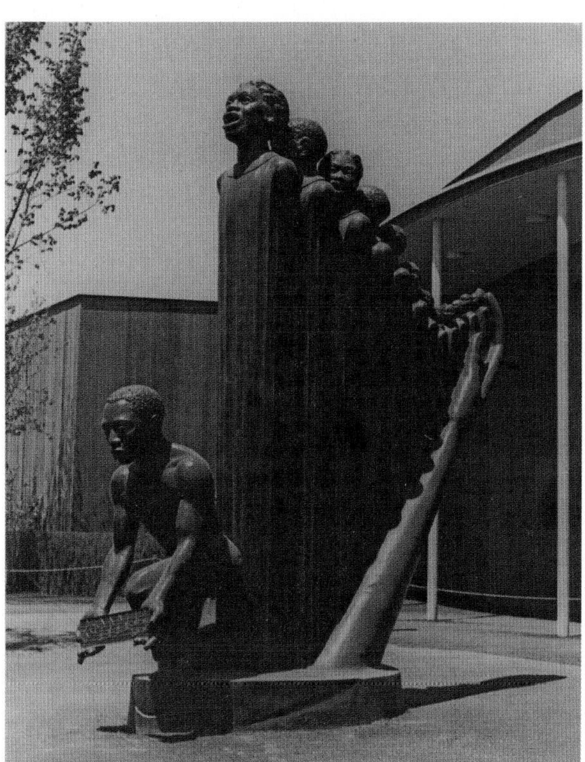

214 Augusta Savage, *Lift Every Voice and Sing (The Harp)*, 1939

bliss. Gwathmey anticipated Andy Warhol's Marilyn Monroe screenprints in the 1960s—the serial lacquered sameness of beauty sold as a product. (As it happened, FAP screenprinter Max Cohn introduced the medium to a fledgling Warhol in the 1950s.)

When the fair closed the organizers bulldozed Augusta Savage's sixteen-foot-tall plaster sculpture *Lift Every Voice and Sing* (from the song considered the "Black National Anthem") and carted it away. Savage had stepped down from directing the Harlem Community Art Center (see pp. 198–204) to focus on the sculpture, commissioned by fair organizers to celebrate African American achievement in the field of music. Twelve Black singers in increasing size, with robes like fluted columns, form the strings of a harp; an arm and hand the sounding board. A young man, like a ship's figurehead, crouches on one knee holding sheet music. The sculpture was popular— miniature bronze versions were sold as souvenirs—but Savage did not have the funds or the space to adequately store the original so it was demolished like one of the old buildings Abbott had recorded in *Changing New York*.

It Can Happen Here

As the curtain came down on the first season of the World's Fair in October 1939, the Section of Fine Arts trumpeted its sweeping "48 States Competition" with a publicity blitz. A post office in each state (Alaska and Hawaii became the 49th and 50th states in 1959) would receive a mural selected from a pool of fifteen hundred entries. The winning designs were reproduced in *Life* magazine and displayed at the Corcoran Gallery of Art in Washington DC. The catalogue for the Corcoran show reprinted a letter of support from FDR: "Art is an added enjoyment of life and an enrichment of the spirit," he wrote, "and history has taught us that the art a people produces is perhaps the most permanent record of its civilization."

Not all that was recorded was flattering. The competition's largest single award of $29,000 went to Chicago-based Edward Millman (1907–64) and Mitchell Siporin (1910–76) for a series of murals for the post office in St. Louis, Missouri. It also proved the most controversial. Disciples of the Mexican muralists, the artists learned from "our Mexican teachers," Siporin wrote, how to apply modernism toward "a socially moving epic of our time and place." (Siporin 1973, 64) Over nine murals and nearly three thousand square feet, Millman and Siporin confronted Missouri's fraught past from early settlement to Reconstruction, registering along the way the Supreme Court's infamous 1857 Dred Scott decision (denying Black Americans

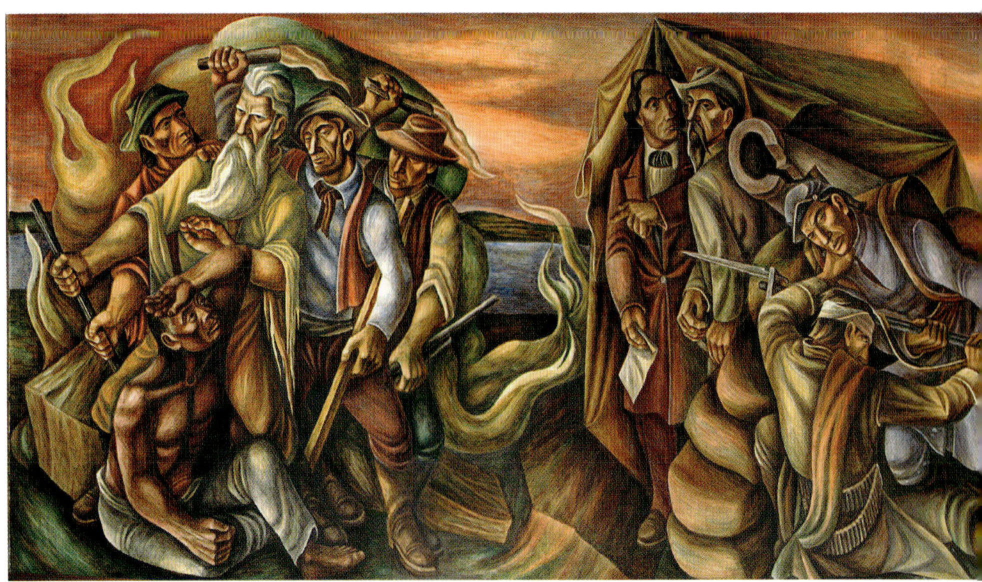

the rights of citizenship), John Brown's anti-slavery revolt, and the Civil War. Departing from the Section's whitewashing tendencies, Siporin and Millman presented Missouri's history as one of bloody conquest, religious persecution, slavery, war, and labor strife.

The St. Louis murals predictably drew the ire of conservative media; not the sort of publicity the Section hoped for. The 48 States Competition was, in fact, a desperate bid to rally popular support for federal art as its future hung in the balance. In one of the *12 Cartoons Defending WPA* William Gropper sketched Uncle Sam approving the work of a WPA painter at his easel. Directly above, two top-hatted conspirators shove a boulder over the cliff's edge.

In summer 1939 Congress had moved to liquidate the Federal One programs and claimed its first victim by defunding the Federal Theatre Project. That year the Section and the surviving Federal One programs came under the administration of the new Federal Works Agency (FWA) as part of the Reorganization Act. The Act stripped Edward Bruce and Holger Cahill of administrative control and transferred power to state offices. Roosevelt, catching wind that Bruce planned to resign, wrote him a letter:

What is all this nonsense about your contemplated resignation? When a fellow turns up in Washington and proves that he can make

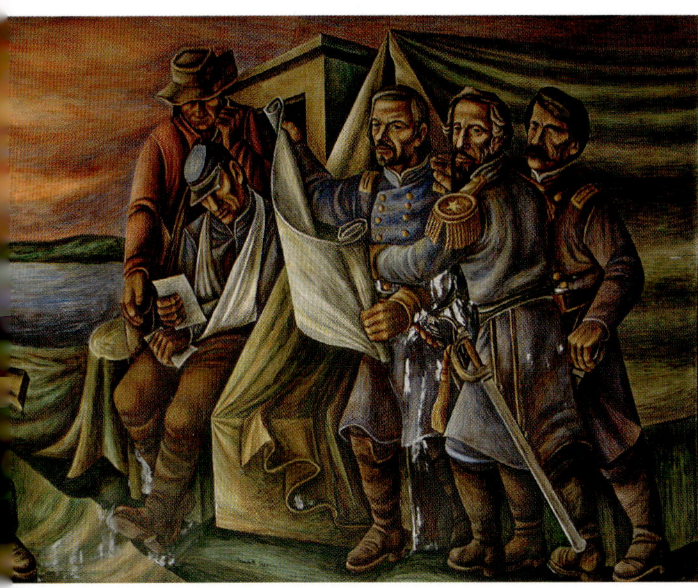

215 Mitchell Siporin, *The Civil War*, 1942

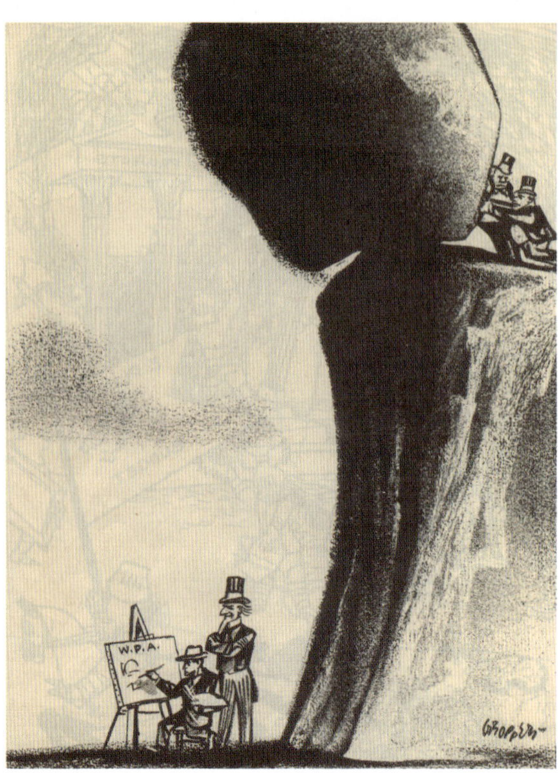

216 William Gropper, from *12 Cartoons Defending WPA*, 1939

bricks out of straw, that the bricks are durable and artistic and that nobody else can make them, the President puts a Marine Guard around him and does not let him leave. Do be a good fellow and write to Paul Manship [sculptor and member of the US Commission of Fine Arts] that you have been chained to the Government of the United States and cannot get away even if you want to. (Contreras 1983, 221)

It was a moving tribute to the artist turned civil servant who had effectively sacrificed his painting career and health to the Section. Bruce remained in his post and soldiered on. The Act, however, did irreparable damage to the programs by instituting mandatory loyalty oaths and compulsory furlough after eighteen months of employment (to prevent so-called "career New Dealers"). Power shifted from federal officers in Washington to local administrators such as New York supervisor Lieutenant Colonel Brehon Somervell, a hardheaded engineer eager to purge the FAP rolls of suspected communists.

Ad Reinhardt (1913–67), renowned postwar for all-black paintings, had a lesser-known talent for swashbuckling satire.

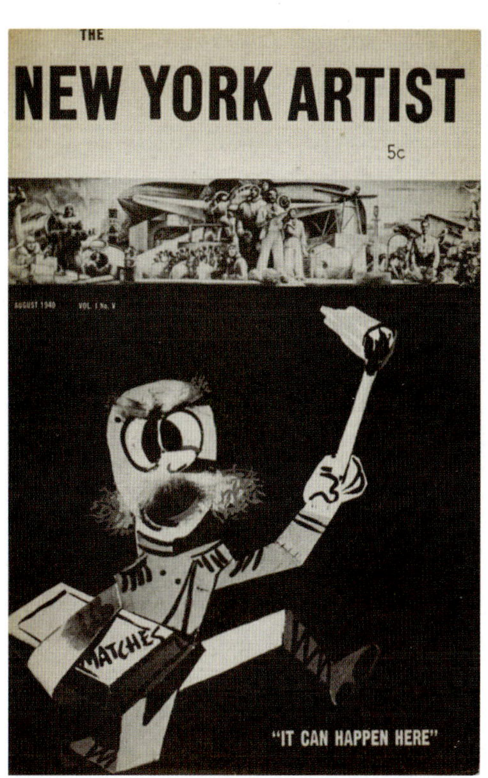

217 Ad Reinhardt, "It Can
Happen Here," 1940

217 For the cover of the *New York Artist* (successor to *Art Front*),
Reinhardt lampooned a goose-stepping, cross-eyed Col.
Somervell wielding a lit match ready to torch a mural painted
for Brooklyn's Floyd Bennett Airport. The mural by August
Henkel (1880–1961) had been denounced by the Chamber of
Commerce and American Legion for purporting to show
Joseph Stalin, a Russian airplane, and a Red Star painted on
a hangar—none in fact the case. Somervell fired Henkel for
refusing to sign a loyalty oath and had the mural destroyed.

The legend "It Can Happen Here" alluded to Sinclair Lewis's
1935 dystopian novel, *It Can't Happen Here*, which was adapted
into a popular Federal Theatre production and warned of a
fascist takeover in the United States.

The threat of fascism, domestic as well as foreign, consumed
the energies of New Deal artists as war loomed on the horizon.

Chapter 9
Artists Against War and Fascism

The fascist threat lurked in the wings as the United States focused on domestic recovery. As early as 1933, when Adolf Hitler assumed power in Germany, Mabel Dwight staged a morbid commentary on world events. In *Danse Macabre* a helmeted, gas-masked skeleton, bayonet propped on its shoulder, takes in a hellish marionette show. An armor-plated Hitler *sieg heils* while brandishing a decapitated head. Beside him, Benito Mussolini gives the Roman salute while John Bull, representing England, wipes nervous sweat from his brow. Marianne, symbol of the French Republic, swoops towards Hitler in front of an allegorical Japan (which had invaded Manchuria in 1931) subjugating China. Uncle Sam, aghast, looks on from the wings.

How long could Uncle Sam keep out of the fray? In October 1935 Mussolini's forces led a brutal invasion of Ethiopia, the subject of a censored Federal Theatre Project play. (The State Department, fearing a diplomatic backlash, objected to its negative portrayals of foreign heads of state.) In March 1936 Nazi Germany reoccupied the Rhineland in violation of the Versailles treaty. The Axis alliance of Germany, Italy, and Japan posed a clear and present danger.

In response to fascist aggression, the Communist Party USA, following the Soviet line, abandoned militant anticapitalism in favor of a detente with the Democratic Party—a Popular Front. "We must hang together," wrote *New Republic* editor Malcolm Cowley to the novelist John Dos Passos, "or else we will hang separately." (Bak 2014, 220)

The Popular Front

Carlos Anderson (1904–78), who worked on the Federal Art Project in Utah and New York, made the threat palpable with his watercolor *Day's End.* Fighter planes fly in formation over

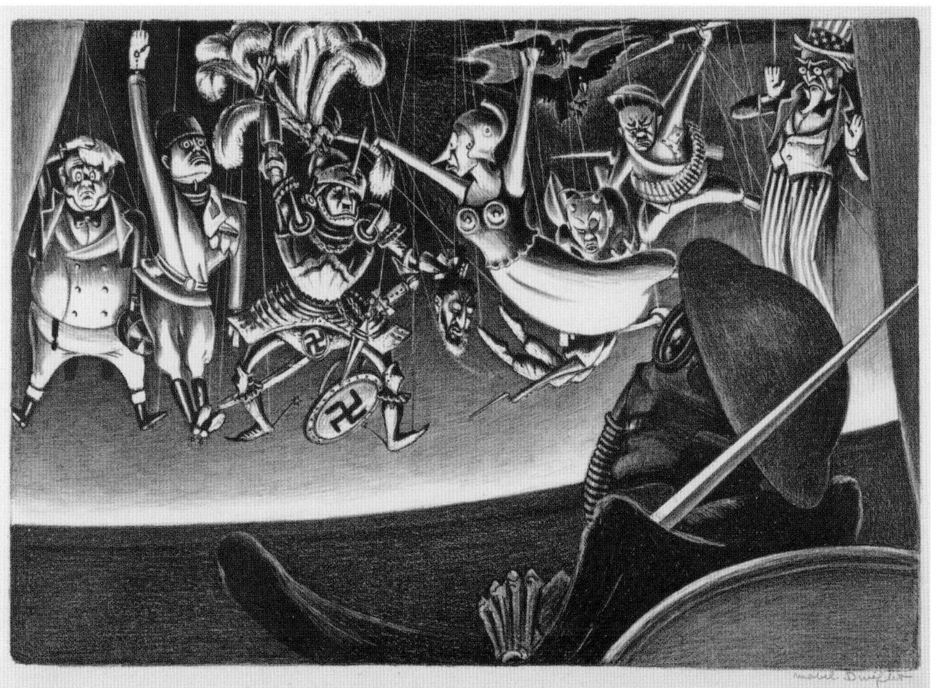

218 Mabel Dwight, *Danse Macabre (Dance of Death)*, 1933

the war-torn landscape of bombed-out buildings and starving animals, a smoky yellow pall in the air. A composer slumps over a piano in roofless ruins surrounded by the desecration of art and culture: scattered sheet music, a torn painting, and a mother-and-child statue heaped in the corner. The message was clear: war and fascism destroyed culture, the lifeblood of civilization, as well as human lives.

Artists joined the Popular Front by forming the American Artists' Congress (AAC). While the Artists' Union advocated for artists as government employees, the AAC took on the threat of fascism, both foreign and domestic. The Call for a Congress rang out in the December 1935 pages of *Art Front*: "We artists must act. Individually we are powerless....We must ally ourselves with all groups engaged in the common struggle against war and fascism." Over four hundred artists signed the call, including many employed by the federal art programs: Paul Cadmus, Aaron Douglas, Harry Gottlieb, Eitaro Ishigaki, Isamu Noguchi, and Elizabeth Olds, to name a few. Stuart Davis served as the AAC's Executive Secretary.

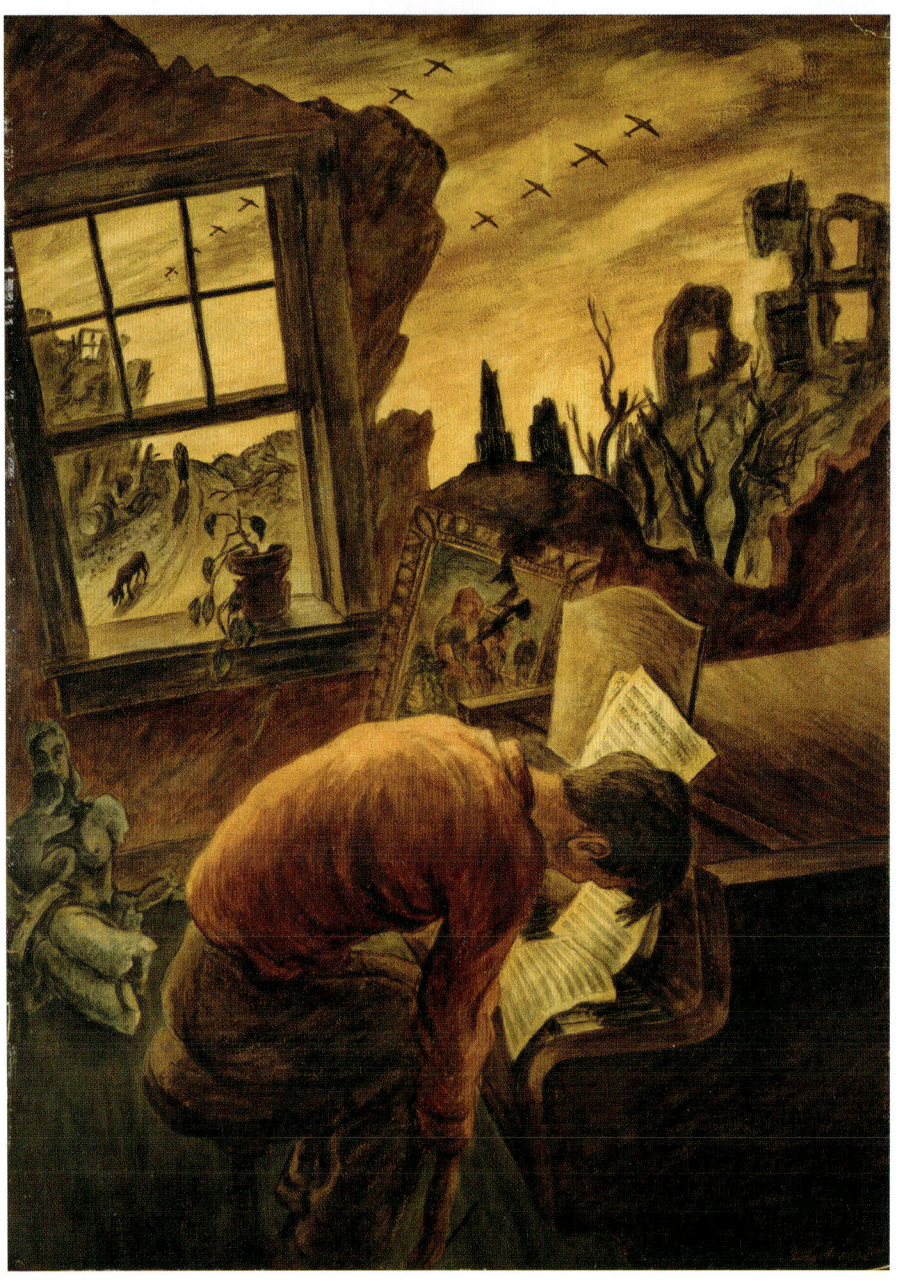

219 Carlos Anderson, *Day's End*, 1939

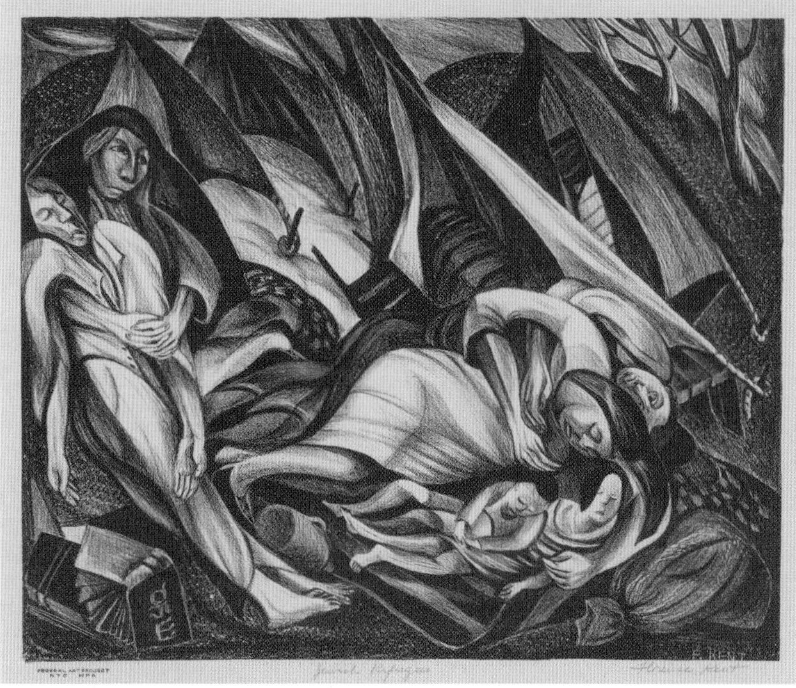

220 Florence Kent, *Jewish Refugees*, c. 1939

The first American Artists' Congress Against War and Fascism convened in mid-February 1936 in New York. Over three days, thirty-four speakers delivered talks to nearly four hundred delegates, all on hand to strategize how to advance the Popular Front. In his opening address, historian and public intellectual Lewis Mumford pronounced that "dictatorships fear artists because they fear criticism... The irrepressible impulse of Art may upset the whole Fascist program." (Mumford 1986, 64)

A German artist and refugee spoke on the Nazi policy of tarring modern art "degenerate" and purging museums of works by non-Aryans. Many German Jews tried to flee to the US in the wake of Germany's 1935 Nuremberg Laws, which legally enshrined antisemitic persecution. However, the strict immigration quotas in the US barred access. Florence Kent (1917–89), whose Jewish parents migrated from Poland before the strict quotas took effect, made a Federal Art Project lithograph of Jewish refugees clinging to each other, buffeted by stormy winds in a makeshift camp. The mood is apocalyptic. A woman at left cradles a lifeless figure in a pietà pose; below

220

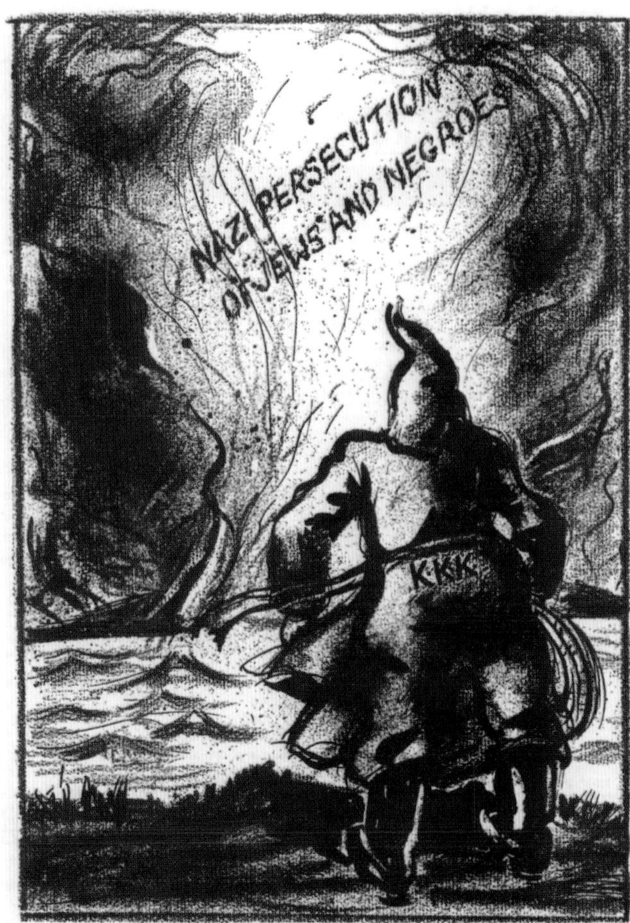

Giving Him Some Fresh Ideas

221 Romare Bearden, *Giving Him Some Fresh Ideas*, 1934

them the cover of an overturned book reads *shlus,* Yiddish for "the end."

Black artists such as Aaron Douglas drew a direct comparison between antisemitism and the racism they experienced. Douglas, addressing the Artists' Congress, warned that fascism built on racism (of the kind vividly depicted in his PWAP mural cycle, *Aspects of Negro Life*). "One of the most vital blows the artists of this congress can deliver to the threat of Fascism," he argued, "is to refuse to discriminate against any man because of nationality, race or creed." (Douglas 1986, 84) His argument resonated with artists such as Romare Bearden, whose June 1934 political cartoon for *The Crisis* sketched a

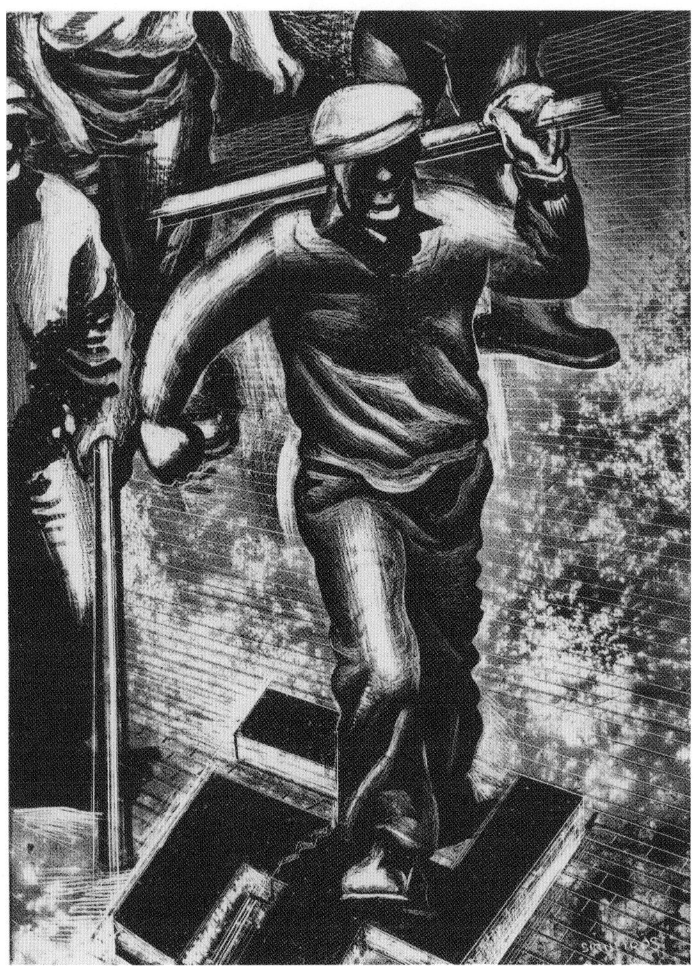

hooded Klansman, lasso in hand, taking his cue from the
overseas "Nazi Persecution of Jews and Negroes."

David Alfaro Siqueiros and José Clemente Orozco presented
papers to the Artists' Congress as part of a twelve-person
delegation from Mexico. Siqueiros called for artists to abandon
mural painting and embrace printmaking as the best way
to reach the masses and respond quickly to shifting world
events. His lithograph *Militant* was a case in point: pro-
labor activism and antifascism merged in his depiction of a
worker stomping on a swastika. The innovative print shows
the fruits of an Experimental Workshop that Siqueiros ran
in New York; he introduced a young Jackson Pollock, among

others, to heterodox techniques of pouring, airbrushing, and dripping. Revolutionary content, Siqueiros believed, required revolutionary forms.

America Today

The AAC took up Siqueiros's charge to deploy prints as art for the masses. It organized *America Today,* an ambitious and innovative exhibition of a hundred prints that opened simultaneously, like a movie release, in thirty cities nationwide in December 1936. The "America Today" of the title was a country plagued by unemployment, drought, lynching, and labor unrest. Many of the prints were openly critical of Roosevelt for failing to live up to the promises of the New Deal.

Several dealt with the domestic fascist threat. The original call for an Artists' Congress listed "daily reminders of fascist growth in the United States": "Oaths of allegiance of teachers, investigations of colleges for radicalism, sedition bills aimed at the suppression of civil liberties, discrimination against the foreign-born, against Negroes, the reactionary Liberty League and similar organizations, Hearst journalism, etc." The "etc." could have included the German American Bund,

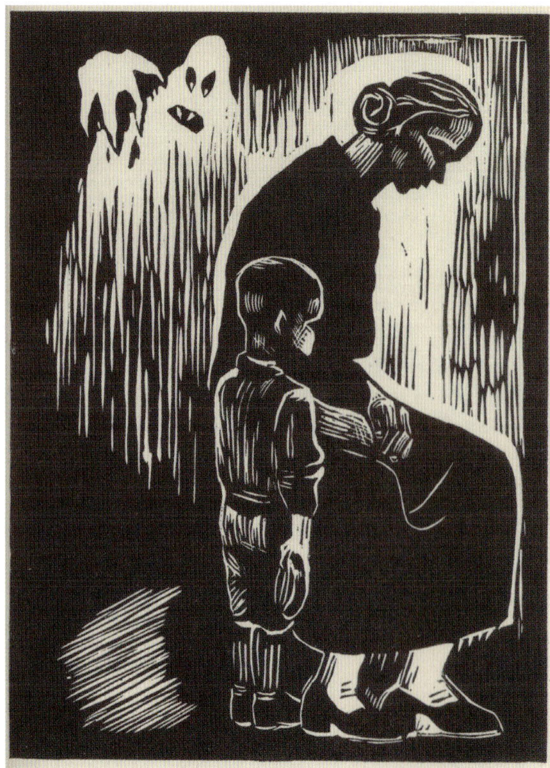

223 Maurice Merlin, *Black Legion Widow,* 1936

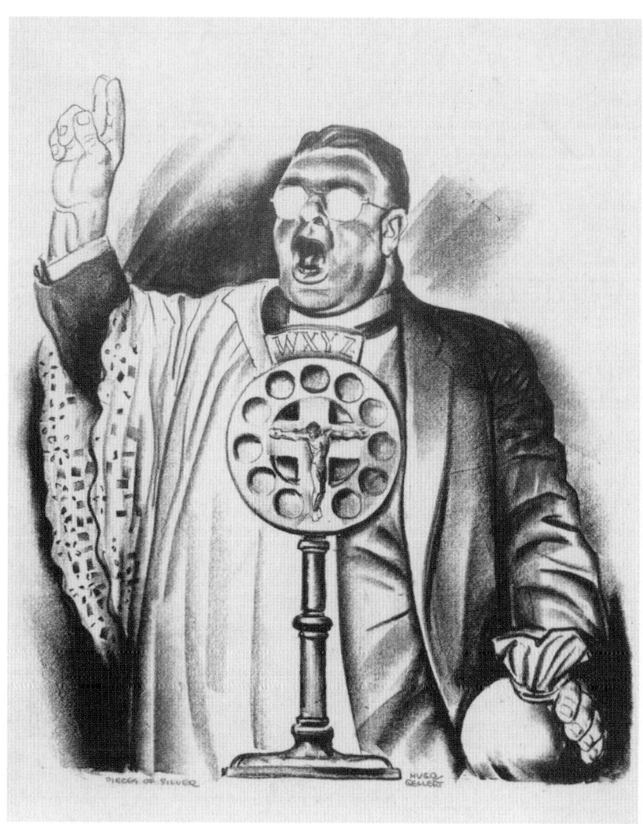

224 Hugo Gellert,
Pieces of Silver,
c. 1935

the Ku Klux Klan, or the Black Legion, a white supremacist
terror organization. In Maurice Merlin's (1909–47) *Black Legion
Widow,* a hooded specter reaches out with a clawed hand
toward a grieving mother and child. The linocut transposed a
contemporary event—the 1936 murder of a WPA employee by
a Black Legionnaire—into the realm of allegory, evoking the
haunting prints of Käthe Kollwitz.

The list of reminders could also have included "radio
priest" Father Charles Coughlin, host of a hugely popular
radio program broadcast from his Detroit parish. At its peak it
attracted some thirty million listeners—supposedly a sidewalk
stroller wouldn't miss a word of a Coughlin sermon floating
through the open windows of every house on the block. Initially
a New Deal supporter, by the end of the 1930s Coughlin served
up a toxic brew of anti-government populism, redbaiting, and
antisemitism, with language in one article cribbed from Nazi
Propaganda Minister Joseph Goebbels. Hungarian-born activist

223

189, 224 and AAC member Hugo Gellert (illustrator of Karl Marx's *Capital* in lithographs) caricatured Coughlin pontificating into a monstrance-microphone. Exhibited in *America Today*, the lithograph skewers Coughlin as a jowly, two-faced blowhard: half priest (a lacy alb and right hand lifted in a gesture of benediction) and half shady businessman (a suit jacket and left hand resting on a moneybag).

The Spanish Civil War

The Spanish Civil War (1936–39) galvanized antifascist energy. In July 1936 General Francisco Franco led a far-right rebellion against Spain's democratically elected government. Mussolini and Hitler supported the mutiny, the latter providing air support from Germany's Luftwaffe in firebombing the ancient Basque village of Guernica. The city was reduced to rubble, and over a thousand defenseless civilians lost their lives.

In response, the American Artists' Congress helped tour Pablo Picasso's (1881–1973) mural-sized *Guernica*, almost instantly an antiwar icon, to various US cities as a fundraiser for the Spanish Republic. Picasso addressed the 1937 Artists' Congress via telephone, insisting that artists "should not remain indifferent" to the fascist threat with so much at stake. It was a coup for the cultural left: the world's most famous artist, catnip to tabloids for his lovers and lavish lifestyle, announced his conversion to the cause of political art.

44, 209
225 Philip Guston, a mainstay of the Section and FAP, answered the Guernica atrocity with *Bombardment*, a febrile painting of civilians rushing from an aerial attack; the sense of horror heightened through Guston's use of extreme foreshortening and fisheye-lens distortion. The civilians—a prone victim, a mother and child, a man thrown violently through the air—seem simultaneously sucked into and hurled away from the explosion. The Renaissance tondo format barely contains the painting's surging, nightmarish intensity.

Bombardment displayed in the AAC-organized *An Exhibition in Defense of World Democracy, Dedicated to the Peoples of Spain and China*. The AAC raised funds for medical supplies and sponsored ambulances. Some members, like FAP artist Joseph Vogel, even joined the 2,800-strong Abraham Lincoln Battalion of US volunteers (part of the XV International Brigade) fighting alongside Spanish Republican forces. Phil Bard returned wounded (he had to relearn to draw with his other hand) and Paul Block, leader of the "219" raid on the FAP offices (see p. 205), 226 was killed in action. Vogel's FAP lithograph, *The Innocents*, pushed Guston's conceit to the edge of abstraction, as if the crimes of war had distorted humanity beyond recognition.

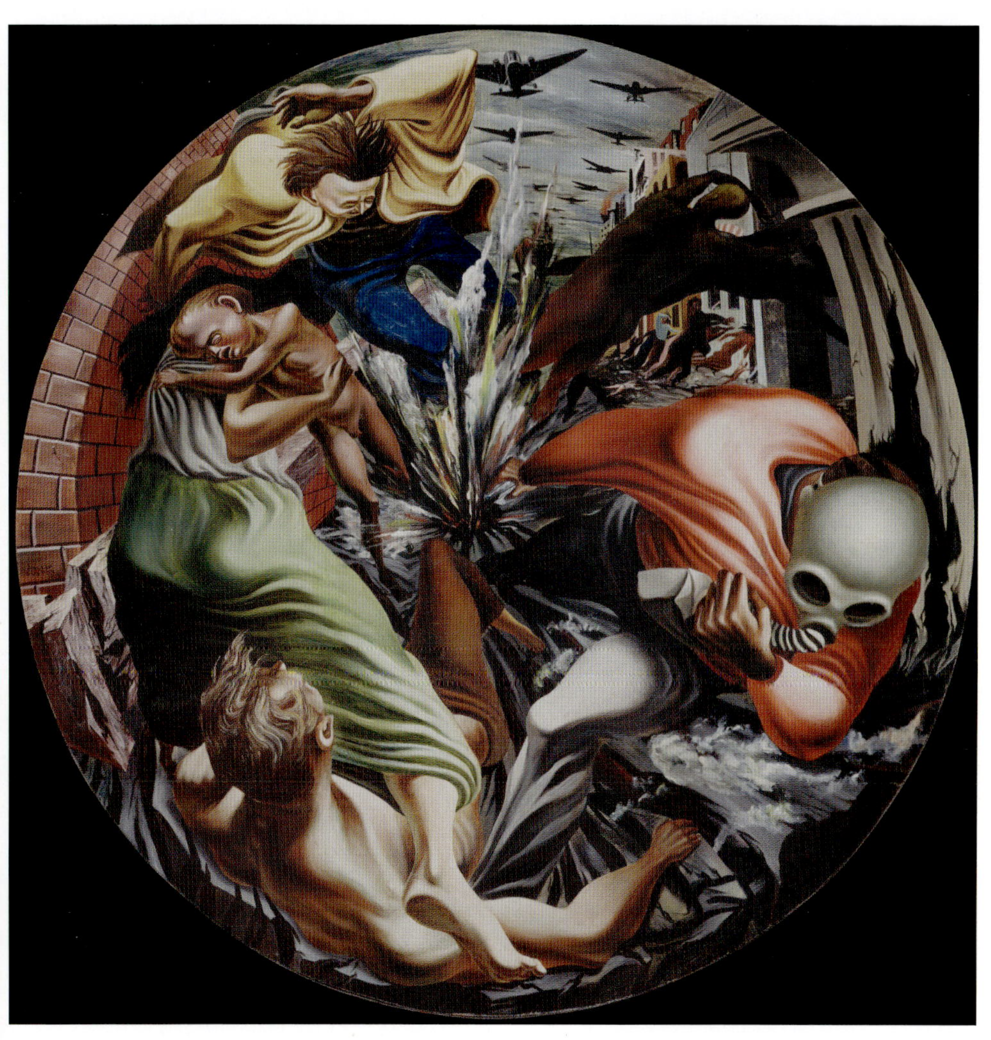

225 Philip Guston, *Bombardment*, 1937–38

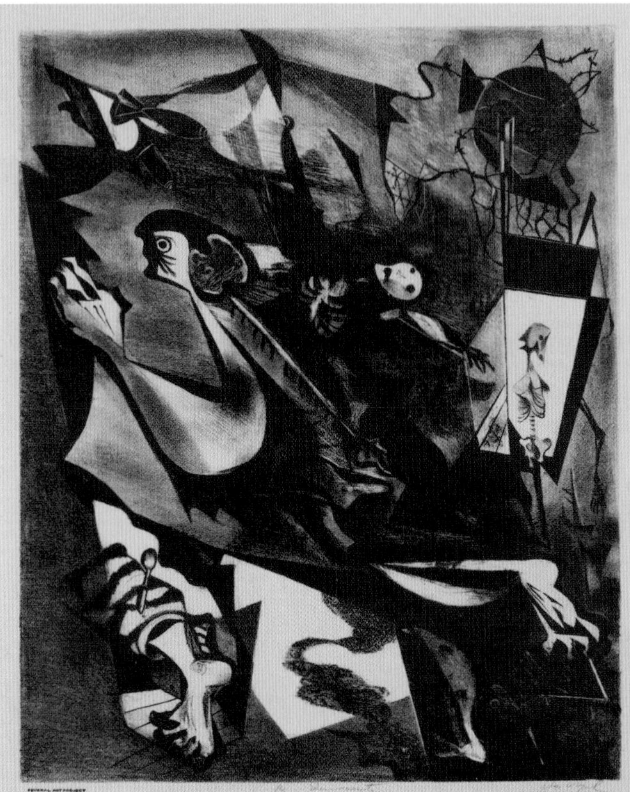

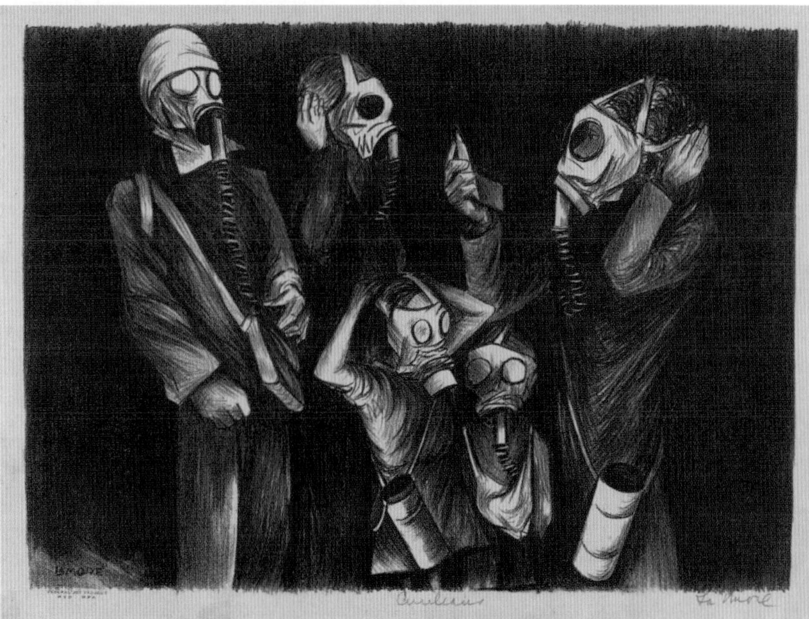

226 LEFT Joseph Vogel,
The Innocents, c. 1937–39
227 BELOW Chet La More,
Civilians, c. 1938

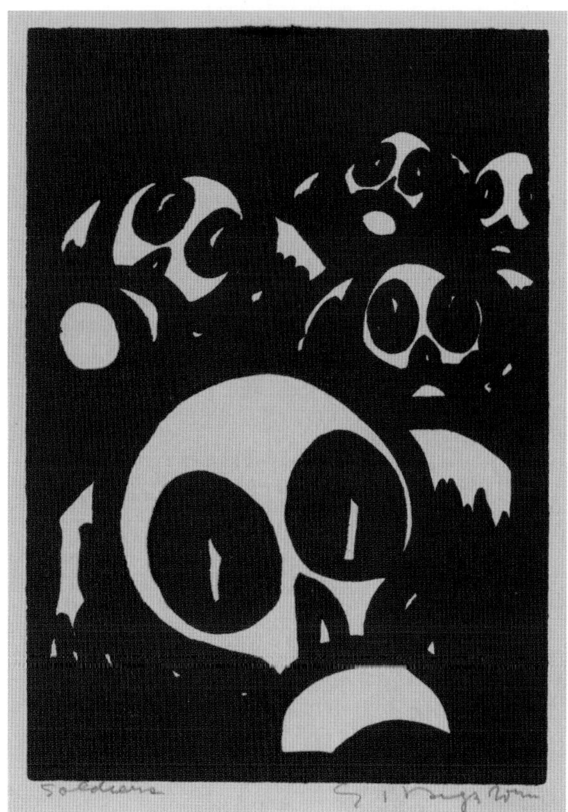

228 Edward Hagedorn,
Soldiers in Gas Masks,
c. 1939

Because the United States remained officially neutral in
the conflict, pro-Republican artists on the federal payroll
had to proceed with caution. They emphasized the suffering
of victims rather than the crimes of perpetrators, relying on
oblique symbolism instead of direct critique. Chet La More
opted for black humor in his group portrait of a gasmasked
family, air canisters slung around their waists, a child
adjusting the mask's harness while a teenager primps with a
handheld mirror. A sea of gas masks float ominously in Edward
Hagedorn's *Soldiers in Gas Masks,* made on the San Francisco
FAP, the large round lenses and filters turning humans into
insectoid apparitions. Each print throws the gasmasked figures
in relief against a dark void—the abyss of modern warfare,
which increasingly unleashed terror against civilians.

Charles Surendorf (1906–79), working alongside Hagedorn
on the San Francisco FAP, spun antiwar messaging into antic
allegory. In *God Comes Down to Inspect his Creations*, a haloed

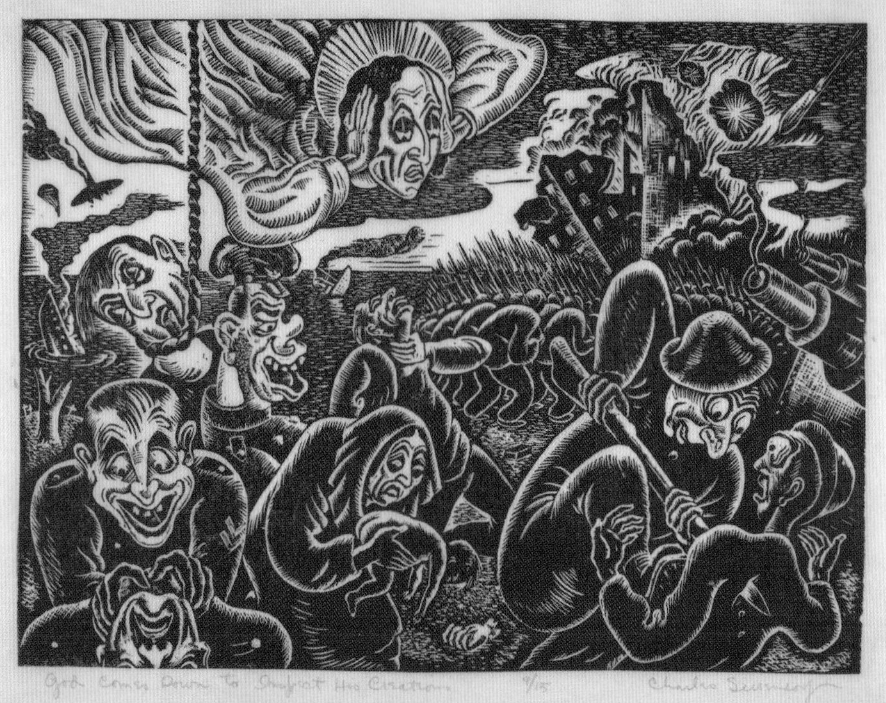

229 Charles Surendorf, *God Comes Down to Inspect his Creations*, late 1930s

deity vices his head in dismay at an orgy of violence and
destruction. (An inversion of the Book of Genesis: "And God
saw all that He had made, and behold, it was very good.") The
cartoonish style belongs to the 1930s craze for comic books,
with the first issues of *Superman* and *Batman* published in 1939
and 1940, respectively. But Surendorf anticipates the anarchic
spirit of underground Sixties comics: Rubbery limbs twist in
nightmarish vignettes of strangling, lynching, and bayoneting.
The pimply, snaggle-toothed combatants, faces contorted by
bloodlust, could hardly be further from the solemn heroes of
most New Deal public art.

David Smith, an AAC member who worked on the FAP's
New York sculpture division, similarly saw humanity plunged
into the Dark Ages. Famed postwar for abstract sculptures,
he made fifteen bronze *Medals for Dishonor* in a bitterly ironic
twist on the tradition of commemorative military medallions.
Cast in shallow relief, about the size of dinner plates, they serve
up a surrealist horrorshow of wartime atrocities: bombing
civilians, sinking refugee ships, biological warfare, human

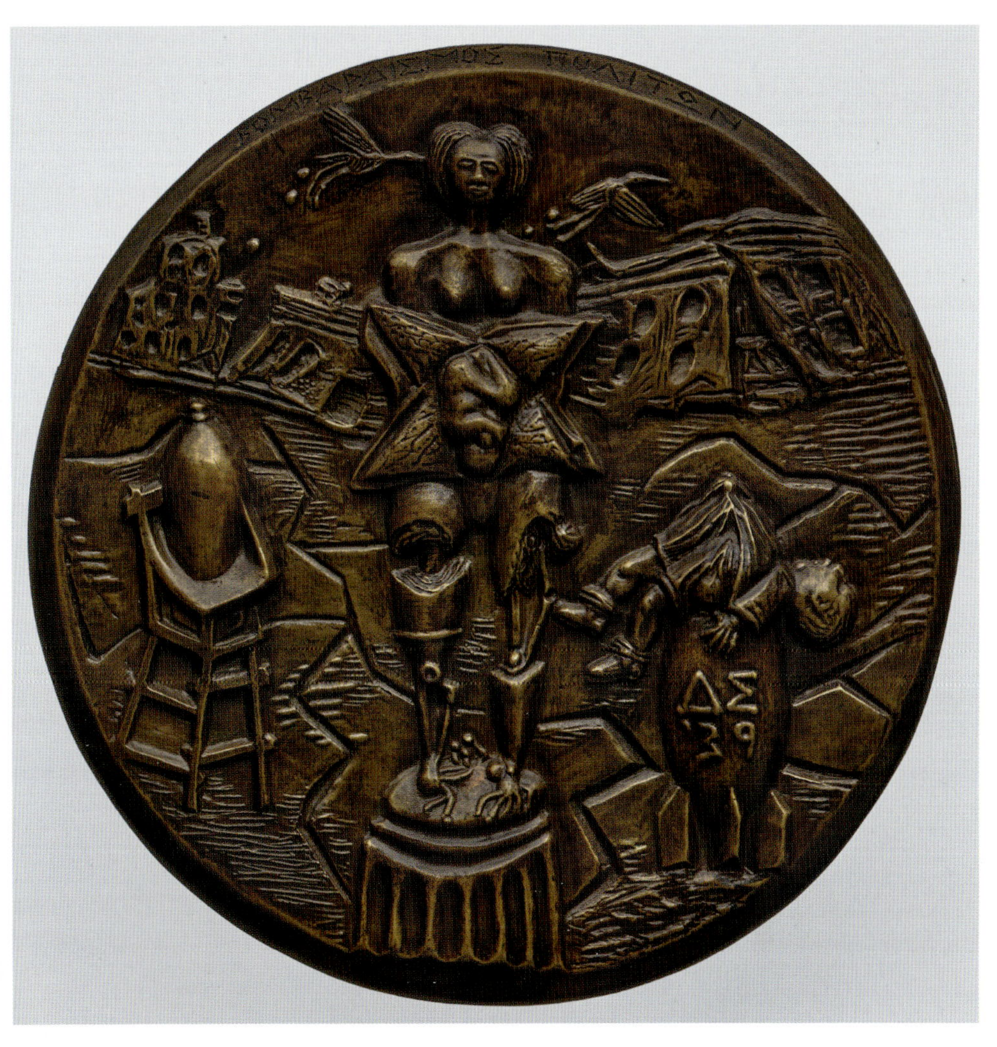

230 David Smith, *Bombing Civilian Populations*, from *Medals for Dishonor*, 1939

medical experiments. During a 1935–36 year abroad, Smith
heard firsthand accounts of Nazi atrocities from German
refugees. But his series did not spare the US: the Ku Klux Klan,
the German American Bund, and American war profiteers all
appear as symptoms of the same disease that gave rise to Hitler.

Towards War

The Spanish Civil War ended in 1939 with General Franco's
victory. The Artists' Congress's hope that art might help check
the slide to world war appeared increasingly feeble. Another
blow came the same year in August when the Soviet Union,
defender of the Spanish Republic and putative leader of global
antifascism, signed a nonaggression pact with Nazi Germany
(which held until the German invasion of Russia in June 1941)
and two months later invaded Finland.

The whiplash caused chaos and dissension among the
American left. A significant number broke ranks with the
pro-Soviet faction. The month Stalin signed the pact with
Hitler, critic Clement Greenberg published his influential essay
"Avant-Garde and Kitsch" in *Partisan Review*, founded as a John
Reed Club journal but reconstituted in 1937 as an anti-Stalinist
publication. Since figurative and narrative art too easily curdled
into totalitarian propaganda or capitalist kitsch, Greenberg
argued, only an avant-garde elite committed to modernist
innovation could "keep culture moving." He would later say
this anti-Stalinist turn, stressing formal experimentation and
artistic freedom, "cleared the way, heroically" for postwar
abstract expressionism.

Although the American Artists' Congress claimed to be
non-partisan, many of its members had placed utopian hopes
in the Soviet Union as a viable alternative to capitalism and
fascism. An April 1940 statement by the AAC's Executive Board
in support of US neutrality—claiming any US involvement in a
foreign war would be a form of imperialism—triggered a wave
of resignations. Sentiment had shifted from art *against* war and
fascism to art *supporting* war against fascism.

Artists turned to the final front of New Deal art: mobilizing
for war.

Chapter 10
Artists for Victory

In the 1930s, United States citizens had little appetite for war. More than 110,000 American soldiers perished in the First World War, a horrific bloodletting in the fields and trenches of France and Flanders. Insulated from threats by two oceans, the Roosevelt administration focused on domestic recovery. The government shrank the armed forces, limited immigration, and passed neutrality acts barring arms sales. In September 1939, as German tanks rolled across the Polish border, the US military ranked seventeenth in the world, just behind Romania, in size and combat readiness.

In the spring of 1940 Nazi Germany launched its blitzkrieg invasions of Belgium, the Netherlands, Luxembourg, and France. All were overrun in less than six weeks. Great Britain stood alone against the Axis powers. Prime Minister Winston Churchill admitted to Roosevelt in secret correspondence that the country could not hold out for long.

National Art Week

It was an inauspicious time for the art programs. The same spring opened the second season of the New York World's Fair, featuring a survey of over eight hundred Federal Art Project works: murals, sculptures, paintings, prints, crafts, and Index of American Design plates. Meant to showcase the Project's vitality, it came across more as a final report.

Project administrators hoped public murals, traveling exhibitions, and community art centers would stimulate a wide demand for contemporary art. Their hope was put to the test in late November 1940 when the WPA sponsored National Art Week with a splashy campaign advertising "A Work of Art for Every American Home." Across the country, art centers, galleries, and museums hosted programs, demonstrations, and exhibitions.

Visitors could buy original prints and paintings for prices starting at one dollar. The goal, clearly, was to wean artists off government dependence and return them to the private market. It didn't work: Although attendance was high, sales proved lackluster.

With tempered expectations, a second National Art Week took place in November 1941. The same month, in a dedicatory address for the National Gallery of Art in Washington DC, President Roosevelt, having won an unprecedented third term the year before, took a victory lap on behalf of the New Deal art programs. Americans had come to learn, he said, that "art is not a treasure in the past or an importation from another country, but part of the present life of all the living and creating peoples—all you make and build." (Musher 2015, 146)

But Roosevelt, in effect, had come to bury the programs, not to praise them. Less than a month later, on 7 December 1941— a "date which will live in infamy"—a Japanese strike force hit the US Naval base at Pearl Harbor, Hawaii. Four days later Hitler and Mussolini declared war on the United States.

Roosevelt was "Dr. Win-the-War" now, he said; no longer "Dr. New Deal."

Mobilizing Art

The Second World War in many ways fulfilled the New Deal dream of mobilizing the country into a great collective effort. Congress gave Roosevelt broad latitude to oversee the coordination of labor, capital, and resources through the War Production Board. Idle factories geared back up. New factories were built. Soon tanks, ships, airplanes, firearms, and ammunition came rolling off the assembly lines. Unemployment dropped from 14.6 to 1.2 percent, the lowest in history. In becoming the "arsenal of democracy," in FDR's phrase, the Depression ended, and the military-industrial complex took shape.

Edward Bruce looked for ways the Section of Fine Arts could contribute. Willem de Kooning, although dismissed from the Federal Art Project in 1937 due to his non-citizen status, won a Section competition to paint a four-panel mural for the troop carrier USS *President Jackson* under the auspices of the US Maritime Commission. From the far right a ship's figurehead, a woman in a long dress, appears to stride forward on a dusky stretch of beach scattered with the flotsam of a shipwreck: an anchor, nautical instruments, a torn-up book, and heavy rope. The wings given to her by the ship's broken prow conjure Nike, goddess of victory, but the mural is more haunting tone poem than jingoist rallying cry.

232

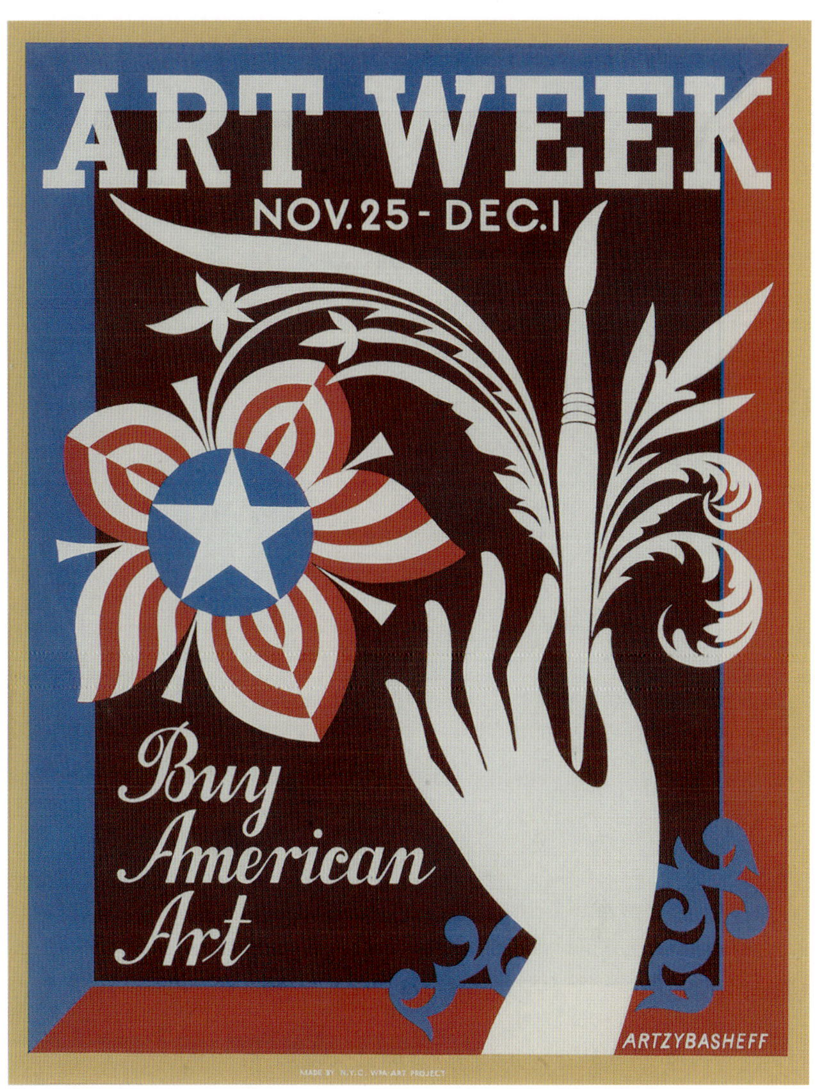

231 Boris Artzybasheff, *Buy American Art*, c. 1940

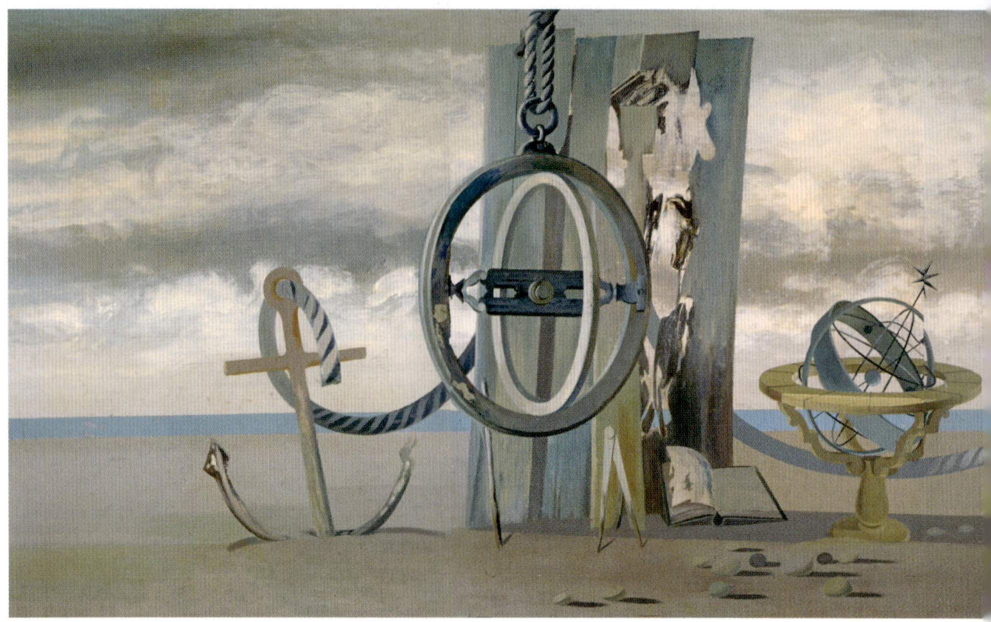

Bruce's hopes of sustaining the Section by decorating newly
built ships for the Maritime Commission did not pan out. The
secretaries of the Navy and War departments rebuffed his offer
to hire artists to work on their behalf. He also had to deal with
local resistance. When the Section planned to move forward
in December 1941 with a post office sculpture in Yakima,
Washington, civic groups protested the waste of public money.
The Section backed down, a pattern that repeated elsewhere.

The Federal Art Project could more easily pivot given its prior
emphasis on practical arts. As early as the spring of 1940 the FAP,
now the WPA Art Program, had started repurposing its spaces,
equipment, and personnel. Holger Cahill directed artists to
make scenes related to the defense industry and military heroics.
Some artists, such as Patrociño Barela (the FAP's "discovery
of the year," see pp. 119–20), translated war themes into their
distinct sensibility. *War* is a frieze nearly six feet wide, carved
into vignettes of flagbearers, fighter planes, armored trucks and
tanks, blitz bombing, and heavy artillery. Such personal works
(the bas-relief format evokes ancient hieroglyphs, as if dooming
humanity to cycles of violence and bloodshed) found little favor
in the glut of airbrushed propaganda.

By spring 1942 the WPA had reallocated its energies and
resources to the war effort. The agency put artists to work

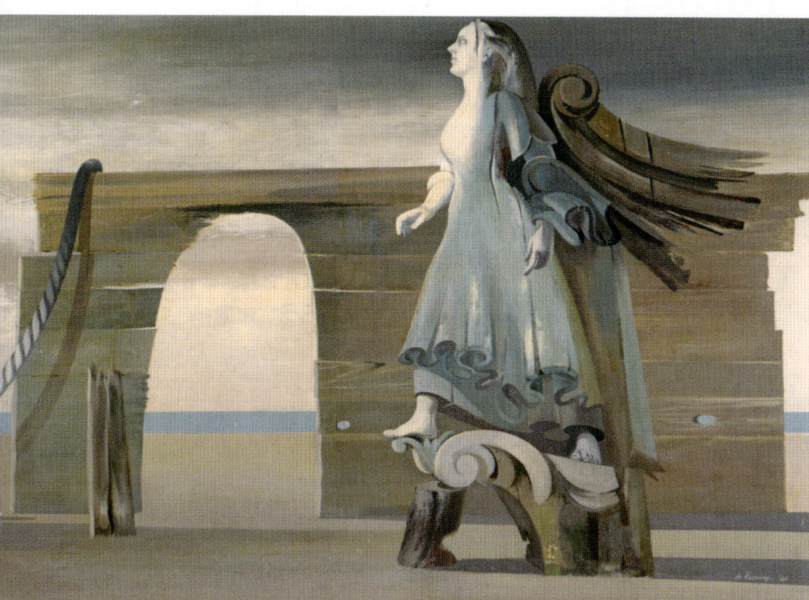

decorating service clubs, painting camouflage on tanks and ships, and producing graphs and models as instructional aids. (Jackson Pollock, supervised by Lee Krasner, added abstract curlicues to the borders of window displays publicizing college war-training courses.) The remaining community art centers hosted poster-making workshops and exhibitions like *America Builds for Defense* and *Strategic Elements of Naval Warfare*. The Graphic Arts studios printed military posters, nautical maps, manuals, and charts. The art projects were now an "Artsenal for Defense," cracked one worker.

Many artists enlisted, were drafted, or took jobs in the defense industry. Artists for Victory brought together several artists groups under one banner, sponsoring a national poster competition and displaying over fifteen hundred works at the

233 Patrociño Barela, *War*, 1942

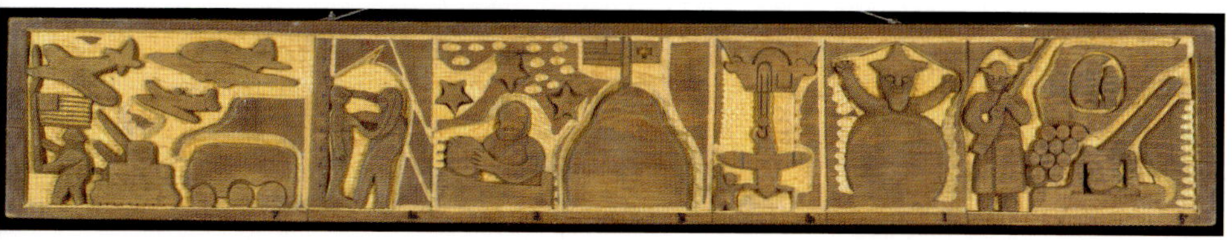

Metropolitan Museum of Art on the first anniversary of the
Pearl Harbor attack. The American Artists' Congress and the
Artists' Union joined forces as the Artists League of America
(ALA). Union mainstays like Philip Evergood, William Gropper,
and Lynd Ward exhibited in ALA group shows with titles like
Artists in the War (1942) and *This Is Our War* (1943). The ALA
called on artists to join the "titanic struggle" pitting "the forces
of humanity and civilization against the forces of darkness,
obscurantism, and medievalism." (McCarthy 2015, 30)

Double V

Black artists made visible the fundamental contradiction of
the fight for freedom abroad—with nearly one million Black
men in the Armed Forces—as discrimination persisted at home
and in the military. Charles White, for example, contracted
tuberculosis after sandbagging flooded rivers in a segregated
Army division in the southern United States. His *Soldier* is
hardly heroic or idealized (a far cry from the powerful figures
in his South Side Community Art Center mural); he stands
paralyzed, clutching his bayoneted rifle and gazing forlornly
upwards, framed against a desolate landscape.

Black newspaper the *Pittsburgh Courier* launched the "Double
V" campaign for victory over fascism abroad and racism at
home. When civil rights leader A. Philip Randolph, head of the
predominantly Black labor union the Brotherhood of Sleeping
Car Porters, threatened in early 1941 a march on Washington
to demand an end to segregation in the defense industries,
Roosevelt relented. He signed Executive Order 8802, one of
the first federal actions on civil rights since Reconstruction,
creating a Fair Employment Practices Commission to
investigate complaints of discrimination and to monitor hiring
practices. These pressure campaigns compelled the military to
slowly and begrudgingly desegregate.

In a twist of art historical fate, Jacob Lawrence (who got his
start at the Harlem Community Art Center) served on the US
Navy's first fully integrated ship, the USS *Sea Cloud.* He had
been drafted into a segregated regiment of the Coast Guard
in October 1943 as Steward's Mate, one of the lowly ranks
available to Black servicemen. His New York gallerist and a
sympathetic commanding officer helped get him reassigned
as a Coast Guard Artist, able to buy materials and dedicate
time to painting. Lawrence left an indelible visual record in his
signature high-key colors and stylized contours of the everyday
routines, assignments, and activities of the sailors at sea and
on shore—washing the deck, operating control panels, playing
cards, and so on.

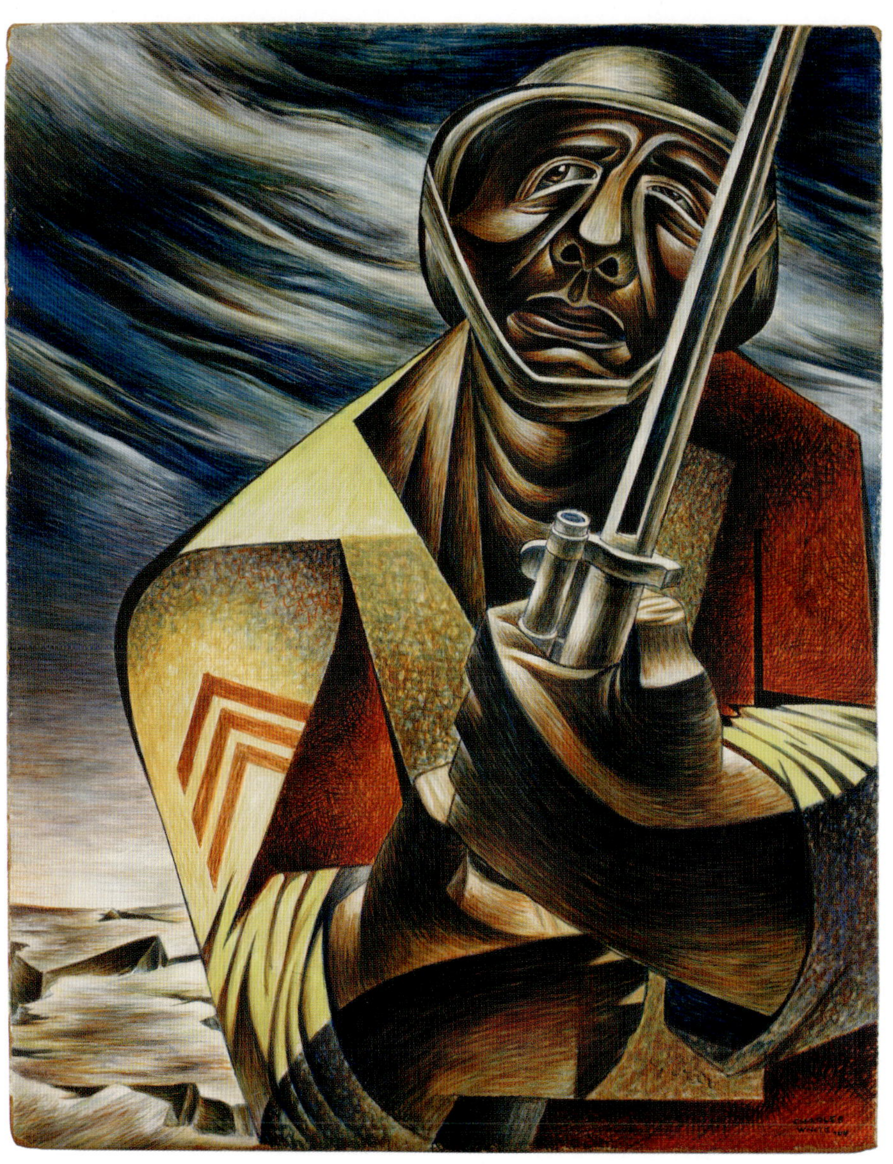

234   Charles White, *Soldier*, 1944

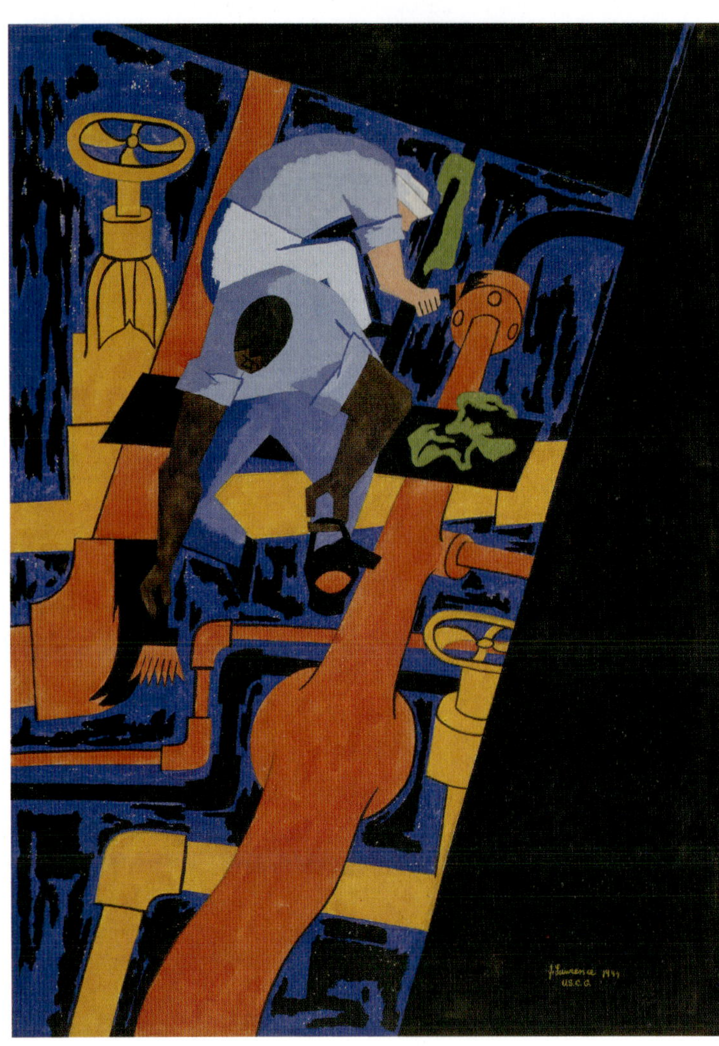

235 Jacob Lawrence, *Painting the Bilges*, 1944

235   In *Painting the Bilges,* white and Black sailors work back-to-back refinishing pipes at the bilge, the part of the ship below the waterline. The high viewpoint reinforces the tight quarters, further compressed by the diagonal swathes of black across the top and right. Lawrence ennobles the menial activity through a sense of mutual effort and coordination between the two seamen, as well as a meta-commentary: it's a painting about painting. Lawrence's series debuted at MoMA in 1944, establishing him as one of the premier artists of his generation. Sculptor Elizabeth Catlett, reviewing the MoMA exhibition, saw

in his paintings a "powerful weapon against those who would divide us race against race." (Catlett 1944, 14)

The Office of War Information

Formed in 1942, the Office of War Information (OWI) was created to manage the flow of propaganda and war-related messaging. The OWI recruited artists, writers, and academics to marshal the resources of the culture industry—movies, radio, newspapers, posters, etc.—to win the hearts and minds of the American public. It launched a blitz campaign to promote the hiring of women in the industrial sector. With men drafted and sent to train or fight, women filled the gap in the workforce, taking on traditionally male-dominated jobs in shipyards, factories, and manufacturing plants.

Alfred T. Palmer (1906–93), the OWI's official photographer, scouted the country's aircraft factories for stirring shots of women at work. In aviation plants from coast to coast, Palmer photographed women operating hand drills and riveting

236 Alfred T. Palmer, *Woman Working on an Airplane Motor*, 1942

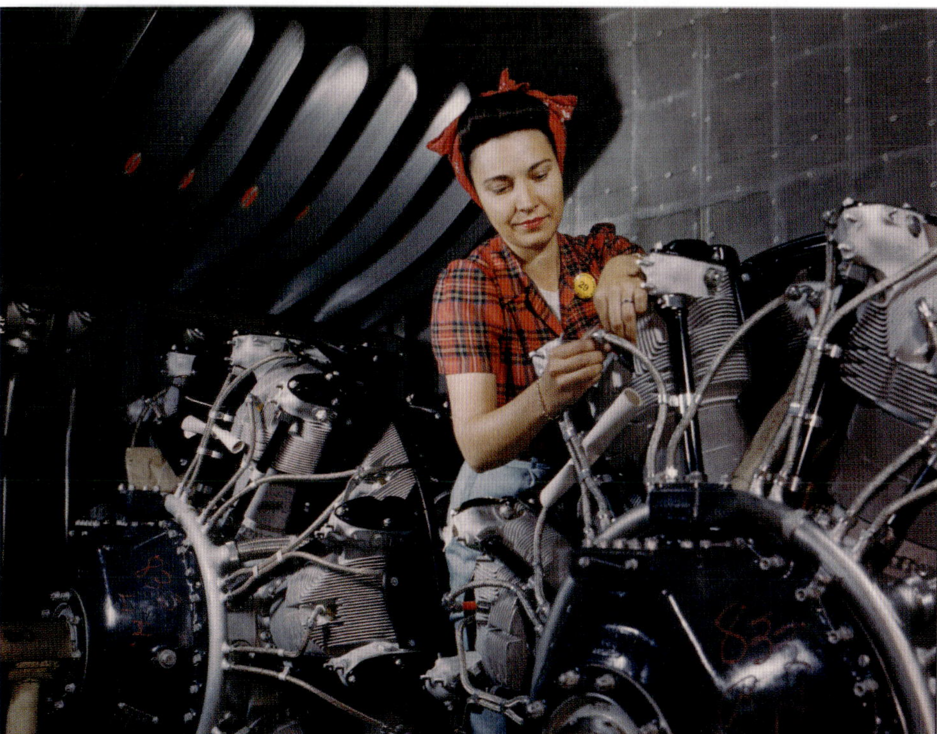

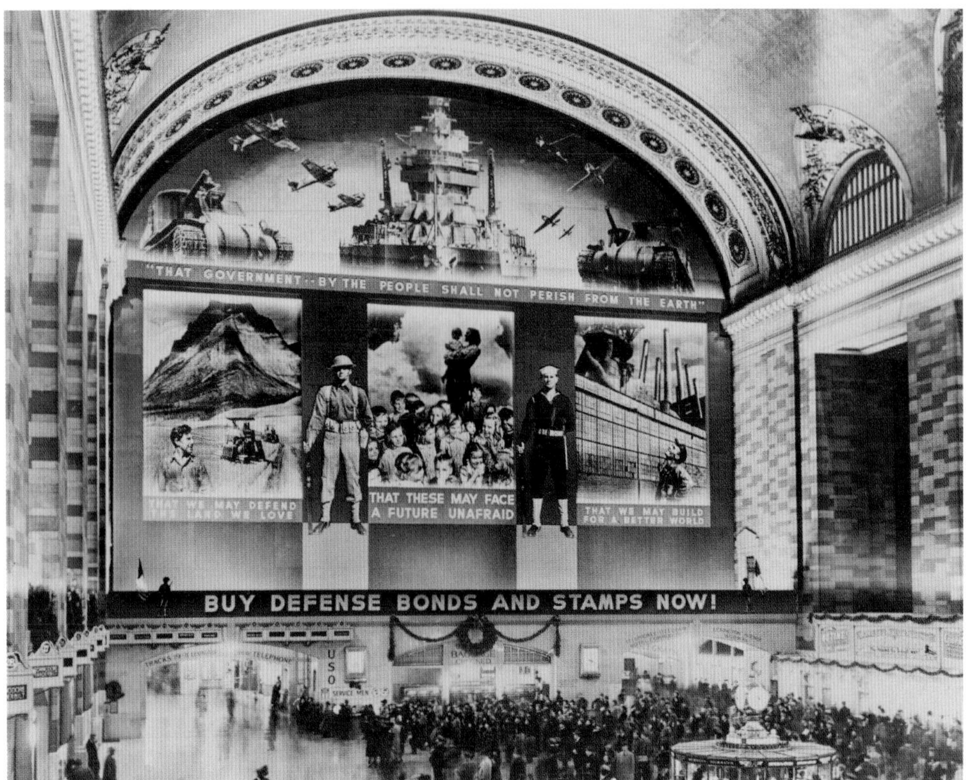

237 Arthur Rothstein, Photomural to promote the sale of defense bonds, 1942

machines, installing gears and fixtures, assembling wing and tail sections. At a plant in Inglewood, California, a woman in a short-sleeved plaid shirt and red bandana works on an airplane motor, seen from below for heightened visual power. At the same time, these "Rosie the Riveter" type images took care to preserve the coiffed "femininity" of the subjects to ease anxieties about traditional gender roles.

Farm Security Administration photographs, originally meant to document economic and environmental hardships, were repurposed as paeans to the country's fertile farms, productive industries, and patriotic citizens. Every day a hundred thousand people walked under a hundred-foot-tall photomural in New York's Grand Central Terminal. The ten-story high photomural (the world's largest according to *US Camera*) covered the eastern wall of the terminal's main concourse in a collage of blown-up FSA images: chugging tractors, smiling children, towering smokestacks. Lit with floodlights, the photomural served as a "constant reminder of the things we are fighting for," as a US Treasury news bulletin put it, and a constant reminder to buy US stamps and war bonds.

The OWI's Bureau of Graphics designed eye-catching posters meant to boost morale, support the war effort, and spur enlistment. Posters exhorted the public to plant Victory gardens, buy war bonds, ration resources, volunteer with the Red Cross, and join in scrap drives. They encouraged healthy living (bad habits caused sluggish production), thrift, and resourcefulness. They instructed on the proper response to air raids and blackouts. They warned viewers not to share sensitive information ("Loose Lips Might Sink Ships") and to stay vigilant. A helmeted German soldier narrows his shadowed eyes: He's Watching You.

Yasuo Kuniyoshi, born in Japan in 1889, designed over a dozen anti-Japanese posters for the OWI to prove his loyalty. According to art historian ShiPu Wang, this series found Kuniyoshi

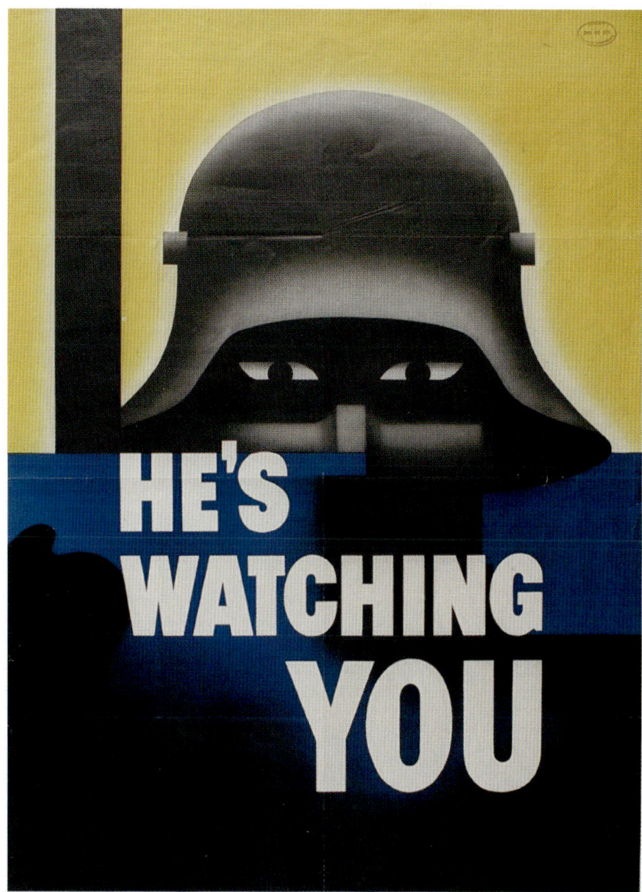

238 Glenn Grohe, *He's Watching You,* 1942

confronting a "ruptured identity" as an assimilated American
who virtually overnight became an enemy "other." Four days
after the Pearl Harbor attack Kuniyoshi penned an agonized
letter to his friend George Biddle: "A few short days has [sic]
changed my status in this country," he wrote, "although I myself
have not changed at all....At hear[t] I am an American and I see
and feel everything that way." (Wang 2008, 30)

Although Kuniyoshi had lived in the US for decades,
achieving commercial and critical success as an artist, the
Justice Department placed him for a time under house arrest.
His bank accounts were frozen and his camera confiscated.
As Wang notes, Kuniyoshi's OWI designs—unlike many by

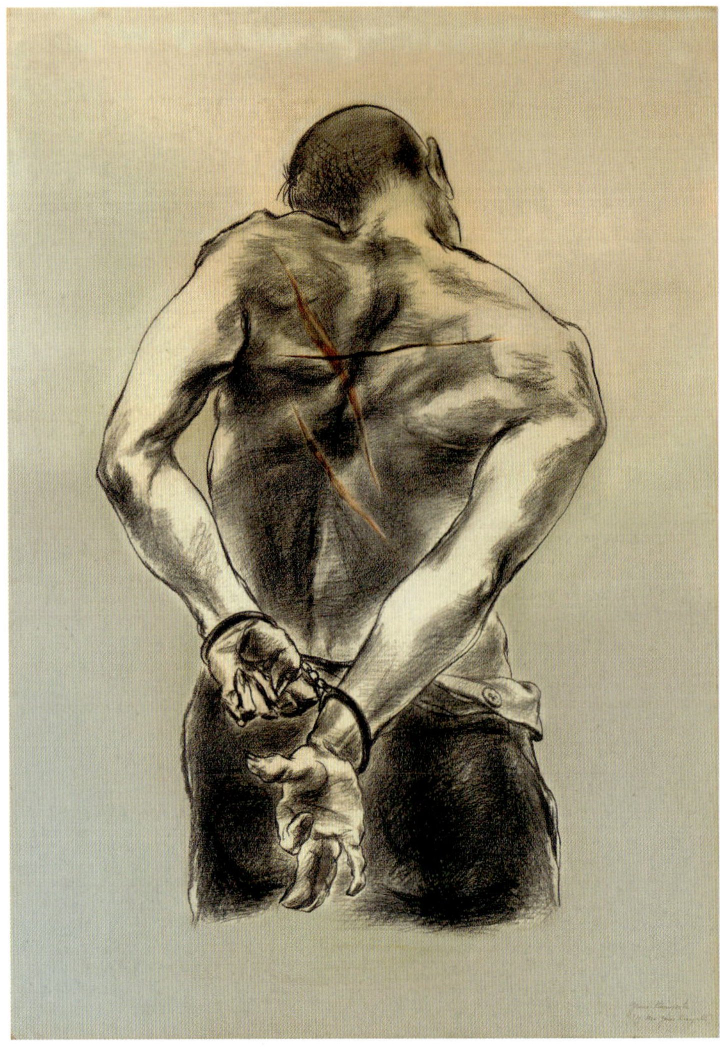

239 Yasuo
Kuniyoshi,
Torture, 1942

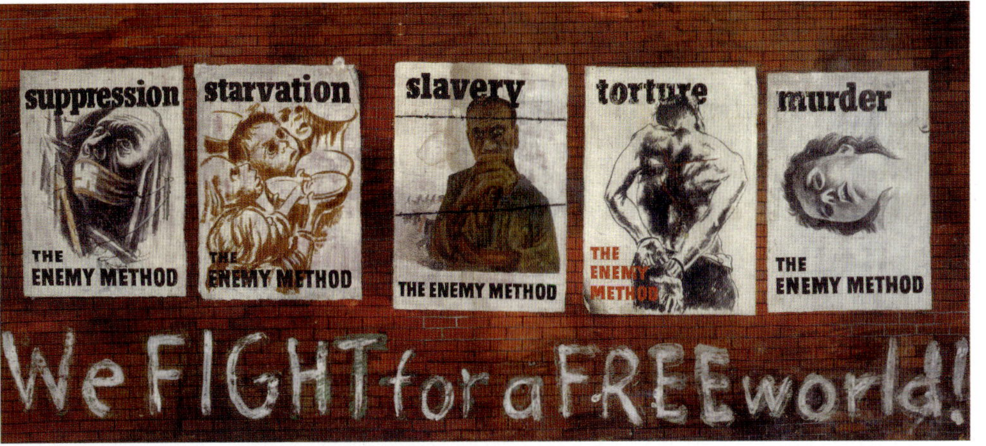

240 Ben Shahn, *We Fight for a Free World!*, c. 1942

white artists that resorted to racist caricature—attended to victims rather than perpetrators. *Torture*, for example, depicts a prisoner stripped to the waist, hands bound, head bowed, with deep scars crisscrossing his back.

Ben Shahn incorporated Kuniyoshi's design into a proposed series of OWI posters cataloging "The Enemy Method"—suppression, starvation, slavery, torture, and murder. Higher-ups rejected Shahn's concept along with most of his others. He lasted only a year in the department, a bad fit for the mandate to churn out slick and derivative imagery.

Shahn repurposed the designs for a tempera painting where the five rejected posters appear wheatpasted in a row on a red brick wall. His own concept for "slavery," with a pensive prisoner behind a barbed wire fence, is flanked by Käthe Kollwitz's "starvation" and Kuniyoshi's "torture." The message *We FIGHT for a FREE World!* is scrawled in white paint "as if graffitied by a member of the resistance," as Christof Decker put it. (Decker 2019, 102) It is a mini-survey of socially conscious art by a collective "We" of German, Jewish, and Japanese artists—a vision of global antifascist solidarity rather than mutual enmity.

Executive Order 9066

Yasuo Kuniyoshi did not suffer the worst of anti-Japanese hysteria. Citing national security concerns, FDR issued Executive Order 9066 in February 1942, suspending the constitutional rights of over 110,000 Japanese Americans living on the West Coast. The War Relocation Authority (WRA) oversaw their forced displacement from homes in Washington, Oregon, and California to remote internment camps where they were detained for up to three years without legal recourse.

The WRA hired Dorothea Lange to document the relocation process, which they expected to be portrayed as orderly, humane, and efficient. Lange strongly opposed the policy and wanted to make "a true record" of the evacuation for posterity. Weeks before, she photographed an elementary school class reciting the Pledge of Allegiance. A nine-year-old girl holds her hand over her heart to say the lines "one nation, indivisible, with liberty and justice for all." Her patriotism haunts Lange's Bay Area photographs of the chaotic, dehumanizing process of Japanese families tagged with registration numbers and packed into trains and buses, carrying all they owned in one or two suitcases.

Lange traveled to the internment camp of Manzanar, a barren desert in eastern California on the edge of Death Valley. Her photographs show families and individuals wresting a sense of normalcy from the cruel conditions. The incarcerated cut hair, cook meals in mess halls, clear brush, and make camouflage nets for the War Department. A grandfather teaches a grandson to walk. A professional landscaper creates a desert garden from the materials at hand. The WRA withheld the nearly eight hundred photographs Lange took which remained largely unseen in her lifetime. "They had wanted a record," Lange remembered, "but not a public record." (Gordon 2006, 21)

Another photographer worked at Manzanar, one not officially sanctioned by the WRA: the prisoner Tōyō Miyatake (1895–1979). Photography had been his livelihood: renowned for poetic landscapes, he ran a successful portrait studio in Los Angeles's Little Tokyo. At great risk, he smuggled a camera lens and film plate holder into Manzanar, where he was held prisoner along with his wife and four children. ("As a photographer, I have a responsibility," he told his teenage son.) He rigged up a makeshift camera with scrap wood and drain piping, and a former client helped him get film. To be able to photograph special occasions like weddings, Miyatake eventually sought and was granted permission to serve as the camp's official photographer (though a proviso prohibited him, for awhile, from physically releasing the camera shutter—an operation performed by a white assistant). Beyond the mundane activities he photographed—baseball, hairdressing, food deliveries, marching bands—a watchtower rises stark against the Sierra Nevada mountains and rising moon, a forbidding monument to impersonal surveillance and state power.

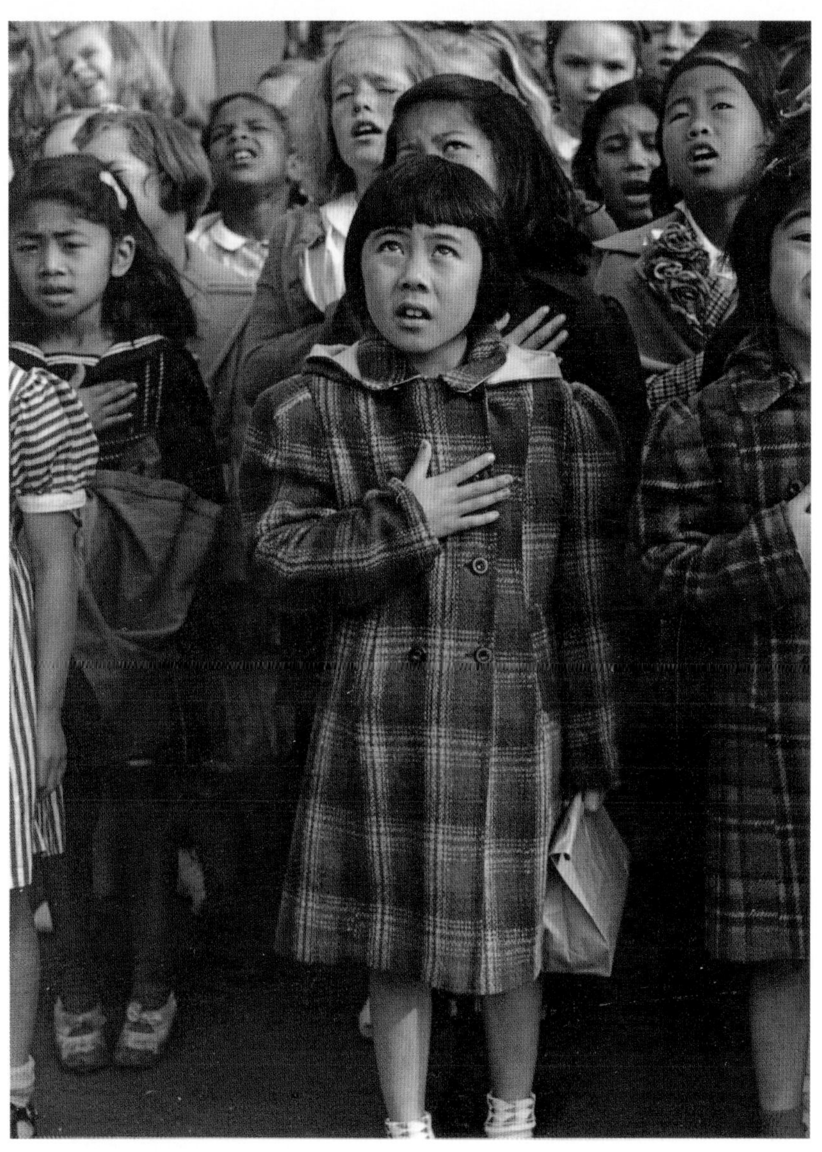

241 Dorothea Lange, *One Nation Indivisible*, San Francisco, 1942

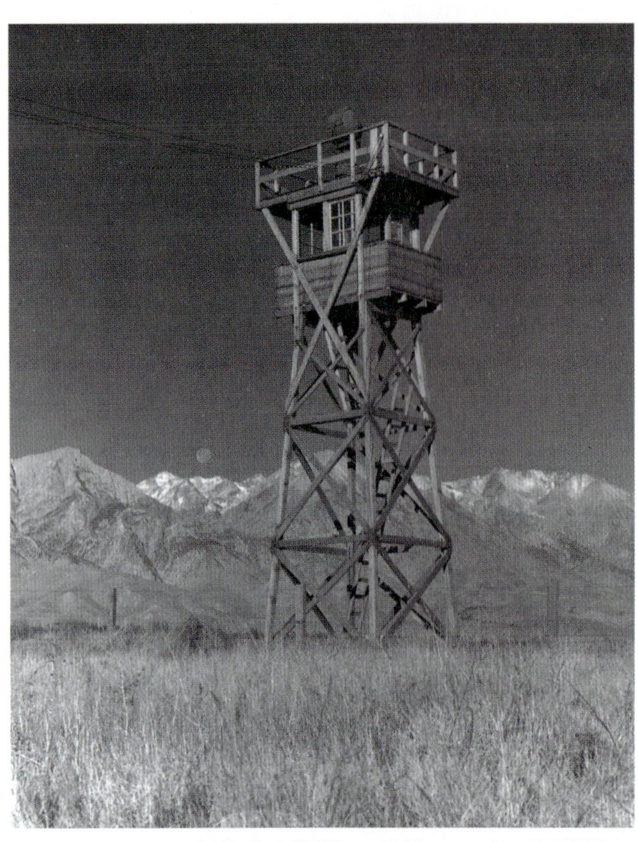

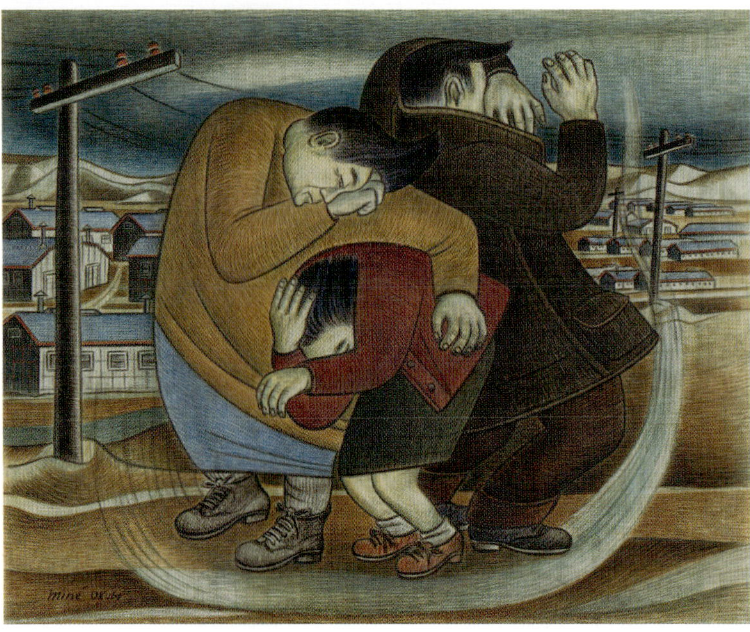

242 LEFT Tōyō Miyatake,
Watchtower, c. 1943
243 BELOW Miné Okubo,
Wind and Dust, 1943

Miné Okubo, who had experimented with screenprinting on the San Francisco FAP, did not have a camera but she had her sketchbook. She made nearly two thousand drawings of life in the Tanforan Assembly Center outside San Francisco and the Topaz Relocation Center in Utah, where she was held prisoner from 1942 to 1944. (Before her incarceration, she had been working on WPA murals for a military building in Oakland.)

Two hundred drawings were reproduced in 1946 as *Citizen 13660*, the first published account of the internment camps by an eyewitness. The series mixes humor and heartbreak in its wry inventory of the accumulating indignities—boredom, bad weather, lack of privacy, foul-smelling latrines—that add up to the grave injustice of violated civil rights.

At Topaz, Okubo taught art classes alongside artist Chiura Obata (1885–1975) and edited the arts magazine *Trek*. She was one of many Japanese American artists who continued to find creative outlets during internment—others include Hideo Date (1907–2005), Hisako Hibi (1907–91), Henry Sugimoto (1900–90)—along with internees who crafted toys, teapots, furniture, and musical instruments. Scholar Delphine Hirasuna identified these objects as the art of *gaman*, a Japanese word for "enduring the unbearable with patience and dignity." The arts, crafts, and photographs of the internment camps remain the New Deal era's strongest argument for art as a necessity, not a luxury—an essential human right to bear witness, process trauma, protest injustice, or endure the unbearable.

Honorable Discharge

On Monday morning, 26 May 1941, a representative of the Citizens' Committee for Government Art Projects appeared before Congress. The Citizens' Committee comprised prominent artists, museum directors, academics, critics, curators, and filmmakers (such as Orson Welles, who had a film opening that month: *Citizen Kane*), all of whom hoped to prevent the dissolution of the art projects. "What the projects have brought into American life," the representative argued, "are among the best things we can defend."

Congress was unmoved. That summer saw art program personnel cut by half. After the Pearl Harbor attack in December, creative efforts effectively ceased. Arts administrators and supporters were quickly disabused of the notion that the US government saw art as a necessity in times of war. "I am thinking that one battleship," growled a Tennessee Senator in a congressional hearing, "will increase the morale more than all the arts in America." (McKinzie 1973, 48)

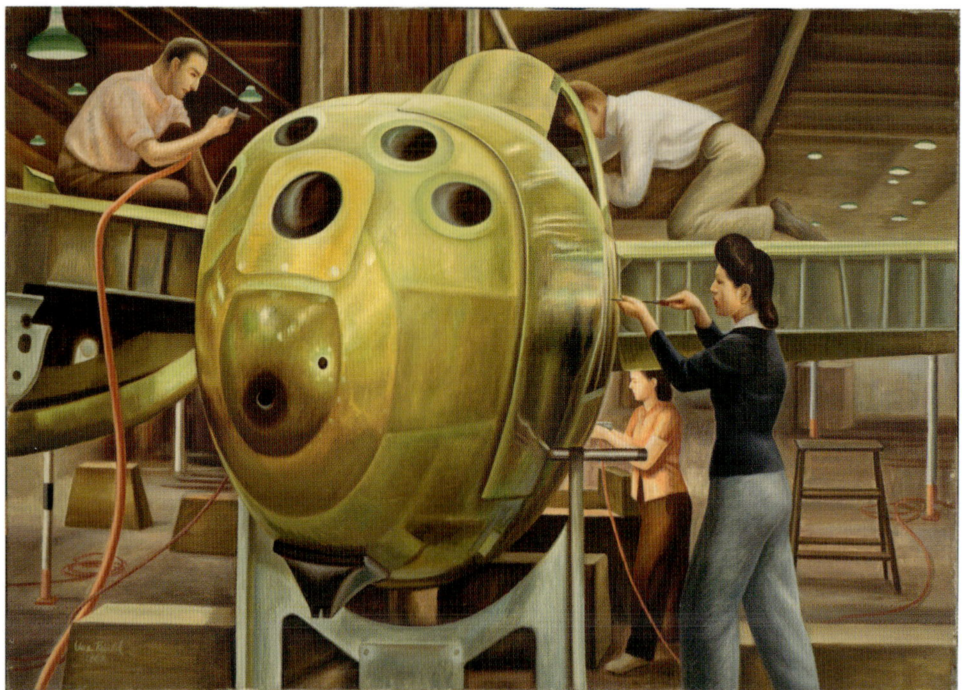

244 Edna Reindel, *Riveter at Lockheed*, 1942

The federal art programs came full circle when George
Biddle, who in 1933 had spurred his former schoolmate
Franklin Roosevelt to fund public art, chaired an Art Advisory
Committee set up in the War Department. The government
launched a short-lived US Army Art Program, and Biddle helped
enlist artists like Joe Jones, Jack Levine, and Mitchell Siporin
to document frontline engagements in the Pacific. Congress
stopped funding the program in the summer of 1943, and
sponsorship shifted to private sector patrons like *Life* magazine
and pharmaceutical company Abbott Laboratories.

In June 1944 *Life* magazine reproduced nine paintings by
Edna Reindel (1894–1990) for a "Women at War" spread based
on her visits to the Lockheed aircraft plant near Los Angeles.
Reindel was an archetypal New Deal artist: she cut her teeth
on the Federal Art Project and painted a post office mural for
the Section. *Riveter at Lockheed* arranges two women and two
men around the unfinished cockpit of a P-38 fighter plane.
They resemble Moses Soyer's *Artists on WPA*—men and women
working together towards a common goal. The man crouched
on the wing is painting the hood with a pneumatic nozzle spray.

A woman in slacks and a dark blue sweater tightens screws on the gun hood—she might be a painter adding finishing touches to a canvas. Instead of a mural cycle for a children's hospital, however, they are making a weapon of war, as gleaming as any modernist sculpture.

Program chiefs Edward Bruce and Holger Cahill had rallied around the banner of art as a bulwark against fascism. "The power that will draw the people together in the end," Cahill hoped, "will not be the power of bayonets or high explosives. It will be this conception of the unity and attraction of culture." (Musher 2015, 169) Yet after ten years the "new horizons" for American art that Cahill imagined turned out to be a mirage. What came into view instead were fighter jets and nuclear submarines, part of the military-industrial complex that would dominate the Cold War economy and beyond. The US government would never again invest in art at anything like the scale it had during the New Deal.

Edward Bruce suffered a stroke in early 1942 and died 26 January 1943. His faithful lieutenant Olin Dows believed that Bruce had "killed himself" in service to the Section, a martyr to the New Deal cause. Bruce's death marked a symbolic, and in some ways literal, end to the decade-long experiment in federal arts funding. While Bruce hoped the Section would become a permanent part of the Treasury, it followed him into the grave.

Roosevelt ordered all federal projects to wind down by mid-1943. He used a timely metaphor: the WPA had served with distinction and had "earned its honorable discharge."

Conclusion
The New New Deal

If in January 1944 you had frequented the Roberts Book
Company, a secondhand bookstore and bric-a-brac shop
on Canal Street in Manhattan's Lower West Side, you could
have bought canvases by Alice Neel, Jackson Pollock, and
Mark Rothko for mere dollars, along with some crockery and
phonograph records. The story hit the pages of *Life* magazine
in April 1944 with the scathing headline: "End of WPA Art:
Canvases which cost government \$35,000,000 are sold for junk."
Look closely, and you can see Eitaro Ishigaki's Abraham Lincoln
looming in the background.

As the programs phased out in the early 1940s, government
officials periodically auctioned or destroyed tranches of
unallocated artwork. No national agency took responsibility
for recording or conserving New Deal art. Virtually none of the
posters remain, and few surviving easel paintings or sculptures
are on view in public collections. Landlords and building
superintendents had murals painted or plastered over during
renovations and retrofits. The ones still visible, mainly in
post offices, are vulnerable to building closures or selloffs to
private developers.

The Section of Fine Art's largest commission also sounded
the death knell of New Deal art: Anton Refregier's sweeping
History of California, a cycle of twenty-seven panels painted
for the Rincon Annex Post Office in San Francisco. Refregier
refused to varnish the state's fraught past, incorporating scenes
such as the 1877 anti-Chinese pogroms, the framing of labor
leader Tom Mooney for the Preparedness Day bombing in 1916,
and the longshoremen's 1934 waterfront strike.

Commissioned in 1941 but not completed until 1948 (it
had been put on hold during the War), *History of California*
drew swift condemnation from the Catholic Church, the

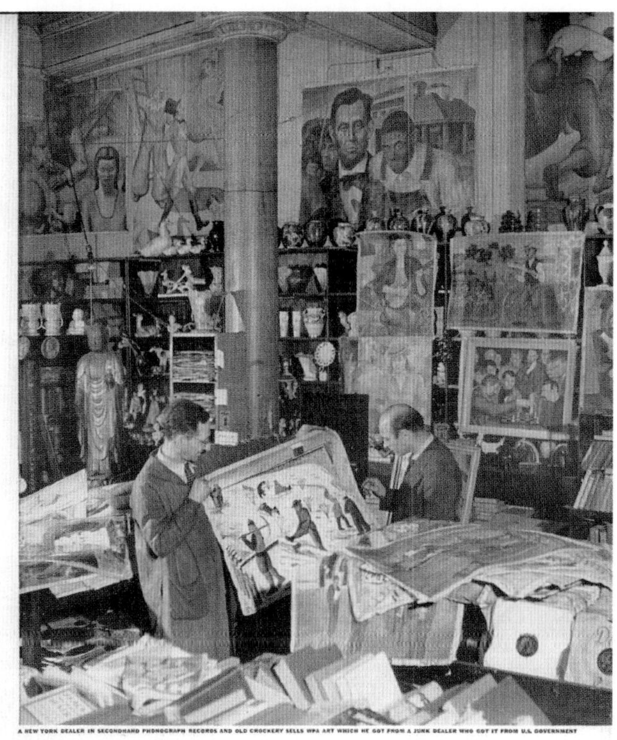

CONTINUED ON NEXT PAGE 85

245 "End of WPA Art," *Life*, 17 April 1944

American Legion, and the Sons and Daughters of the American Revolution. An ambitious California congressman, Richard Nixon, proposed an investigative committee to root out art in government buildings "found to be inconsistent," in his words, "with American ideals and principles." (Eldredge 2021, 34) Although the murals survived thanks to activist efforts, their near-destruction was a fitting bookend to the federal art projects that had begun with the controversial Coit Tower murals in the same city fourteen years earlier.

25, 27–29

As the art projects drew to a close in early 1943, Jackson Pollock started working as a janitor and handyman at New York's Museum of Non-Objective Art, later renamed the Solomon R. Guggenheim Museum. He was introduced to art patron and gallerist Peggy Guggenheim (niece of Solomon), who commissioned a painting from the struggling artist for

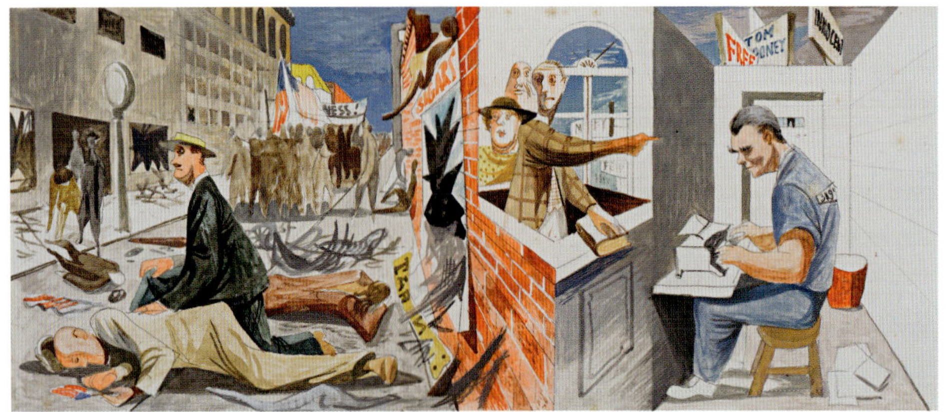

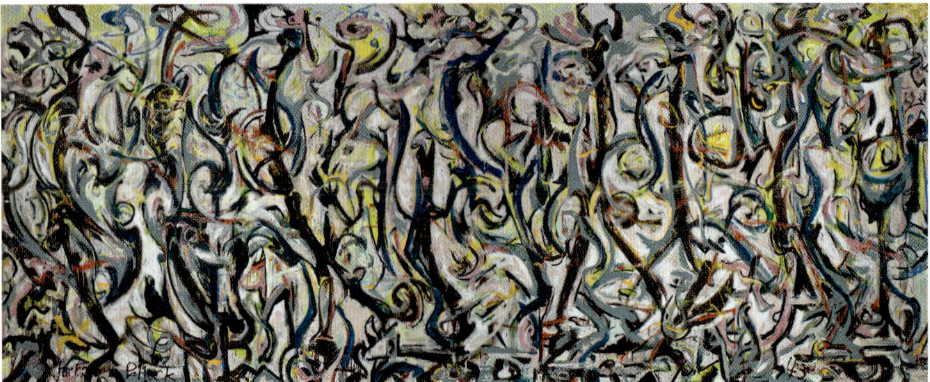

246 TOP Anton Refregier, *Study for 1916, Preparedness Day*, c. 1941
247 ABOVE Jackson Pollock, *Mural*, 1943

247   her townhouse. As Jody Patterson has argued, the result
(Pollock's largest painting) marked a turning point from
the large-scale public art of the 1930s to postwar abstract
expressionism. (2020, 1) Its flowing arabesques and writhing
almost-figures resemble a New Deal mural left too long in the
rain. Even the title, *Mural*, transposed the scale and ambition
of New Deal public art onto a vehicle for formal experiment and
personal expression.

    Pollock, in his jeans and T-shirts, soft-shoeing around huge
canvases with an insouciant cigarette dangling from his lips,
came to embody postwar American swagger. During the Cold
War, the State Department and the CIA tacitly funded abstract
expressionism—identified with creative freedom, innovation,
dynamism—as a weapon in the ideological battle against the
Soviet Union.

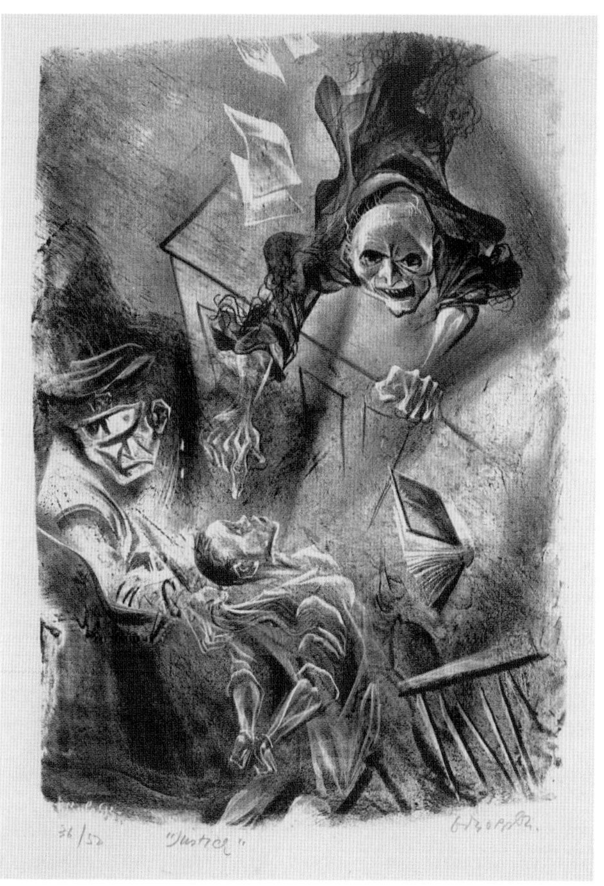

248 William Gropper, *Justice,* from *Capriccios,* 1953–57

Artists like Jack Levine, Alice Neel, Ben Shahn, and Charles White continued to exhibit socially conscious work, but it was risky in the Red Scare atmosphere of the 1950s. Senator Joseph McCarthy carried on the anticommunist witch hunts begun in 1938 by Martin Dies and the House Un-American Activities Committee. In 1951 Eitaro Ishigaki was deported to Japan, and two years later William Gropper was blacklisted, one of the many artists, actors, writers, and musicians whose careers were destroyed for having communist ties. During the hearings Senator McCarthy, perhaps feeling personally attacked, pointed to Gropper's *The Senate* and demanded, "Were you under orders of the Communist Party at the time you did [this painting]?" Gropper refused to answer, but later responded with fifty Goya-inspired lithographs, the *Capriccios,* an anguished reckoning with what he called the "Inquisition of our times."

The figurative realism and social concern of New Deal art
fell into disrepute, politically and aesthetically. Pollock scorned
the "absurd" idea "of an isolated American painting, so popular
in this country during the thirties." Arshile Gorky didn't
mince words: New Deal art was "poor art for poor people."
The history of modern American art retroactively became a
trail of mostly New York-based white male artists on the royal
road to abstraction.

The New Deal Legacy

Yet the "abstract expressionist movement is unthinkable,"
insisted modernist painter Joseph Solman (1909–2008), "without
the encouragement to survive and experiment that was given
by these artists on the WPA." (Park and Markowitz 1977, 63)
The federal art programs kept an entire generation of once-
and-future abstract painters—including Lee Krasner, Norman
Lewis, Ad Reinhardt, and Mark Rothko—fed, clothed, and
housed during the Depression. (Philip Guston, after an abstract
interlude, returned to 1930s themes and imagery in the late
1960s, avowing, "I got sick and tired of all that purity! I wanted
to tell stories.")
  While some artists dismissed the works they made on the
federal programs, few dismissed the programs themselves.
Many remembered the decade as a kind of golden age; others
were simply grateful to have been kept working. A regular
paycheck and sense of public service, as well as the esprit de
corps of the Artists' Union, fostered a spirit of cooperation
rather than competition, of social solidarity and aesthetic
experiment. Unbeholden to private patrons or the art market,
artists painted American scenes, dabbled in abstraction and
surrealism, experimented with new media and techniques,
attempted mosaics and murals, and absorbed the lessons of the
Ashcan School, European modernism, and Mexican muralism.
Artists' Union president Boris Gorelick remembered: "There
was ferment; there was curiosity; there was agitation; there was
activity; there was interest; and there was freedom of thought."
(Gorelick 1964, Archives of American Art interview)
  There was plenty of frustration, too: the humiliations
of applying for work relief, the bureaucratic red tape, the
nagging controversies and negative publicity. The Section's
subjective emphasis on "quality" left many employable
artists languishing. Other challenges were more ominous:
red-baiting, censorship, systemic discrimination, mandatory
loyalty oaths, and the mass layoffs of non-citizens. These
actions foreshadowed the Roosevelt administration's wartime
willingness to suspend civil rights.

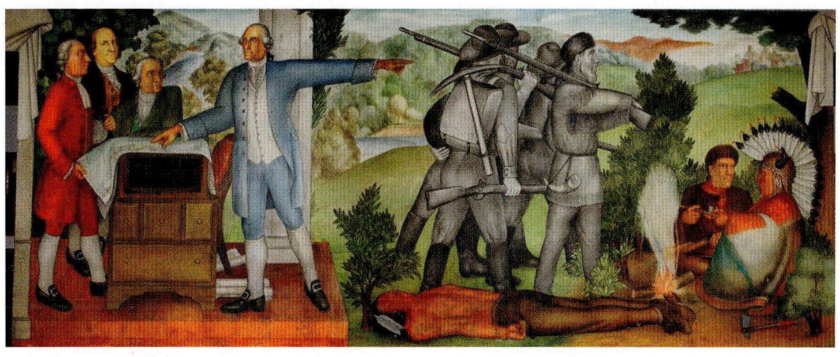

249 Victor Arnautoff, *Westward Vision*, 1936

Fundamental tensions were never resolved: What did cultural democracy look like and how should it be implemented? How should a country—its history, citizens, society—be portrayed? By whom? Those tensions continue to surface. Victor Arnautoff's FAP murals on the life of George Washington for a San Francisco high school sparked a national firestorm in 2019 when the city's Board of Education voted unanimously to paint them over. Arnautoff, having scandalized conservatives with his Coit Tower murals, departed from textbook hagiographies in portraying Washington as a slaveowner whose push for westward expansion made him complicit in Native genocide. Black and Indigenous students, however, saw harmful imagery by a white artist that made for a hostile learning environment.

America Seen

As the Arnautoff controversy suggests, New Deal art continues to pose thorny questions about power and representation, monuments and memory, civics and censorship. The American scene was America seen: the picture depended on the point of view. Many New Deal artists painted encomia to the white Anglo-Protestant vision of US history. They painted pioneers displacing Native tribes, cast women as frontier Madonnas, trafficked in racial and ethnic stereotypes, and boasted human power over the environment.

At the same time, diverse artists challenged as much as enshrined this vision. Women like Riva Helfond, Marion Post, and Augusta Savage made their mark as artists, teachers, photographers, and administrators. Paul Cadmus and Jared French queered the American scene with same-sex desire, overt and covert. Artists such as Selma Burke, Jacob Lawrence, and Charles White foregrounded the Black experience, past and

present. Native artists asserted tribal sovereignty in seats of
political power, from New Mexico to Washington DC. Latino
artists came to national prominence through personally
expressive and formally sophisticated paintings and sculptures.
Jewish artists, often from immigrant families, portrayed the
migrant struggle and protested social injustice. Asian American
artists like Miné Okubo bore witness to a country failing to live
up to its principles.

One of those principles is crystallized in the country's motto:
e pluribus unum, out of many one. For all their shortcomings,
the federal art programs promoted an ideal of human creativity
that found varied expression, whether in the watercolors
of children, the paintings of Alice Neel or self-taught artist
Pedro Cervántez, the sculptures of William Edmondson and
Patrociño Barela, the prints of Fay Chong and Julius Twohy, or
the photographs of Berenice Abbott and Gordon Parks. Cultural
democracy meant, for the first time, genuine if circumscribed
opportunities for aspiring artists from disparate backgrounds
to hone their skills, build community, honor their histories
and lived experiences, and exhibit their work. This expansive,
multicultural vision of American art remains one of New Deal
art's enduring aspirations, however faltering or unrealized.

"Looking back at my three years on the project," Charles
White remembered, "the most wonderful thing for me was
the feeling of cooperation with other artists, of mutual help
instead of competitiveness, and of cooperation between the
artist and the people." (White 1955, pp. 38–39) White, along with
like-minded New Deal artists and administrators, saw his work
as part of collective and cumulative progress towards a more
perfect union: more creative, pluralistic, and egalitarian.

Crises and Callbacks

United States citizens live in a world shaped by the New Deal.
They have likely studied in schools and libraries, convalesced in
hospitals, sent mail in post offices, strolled through parks, and
driven across highways and bridges built in the 1930s. They rely
on a minimum wage, the right to unionize, unemployment and
deposit insurance, and Social Security benefits. During periods
of economic downturn, they expect the government to turn on
the taps of deficit spending to spur the economy.

These permanent shifts only partially extended to culture.
In the 1960s, the Johnson administration established the
National Endowment for the Arts (NEA) as part of its
progressive Great Society legislation. States like New York
offered grants and fellowships to artists as public policy. Faith
Ringgold (1930–2024), for example, used the funds from a state

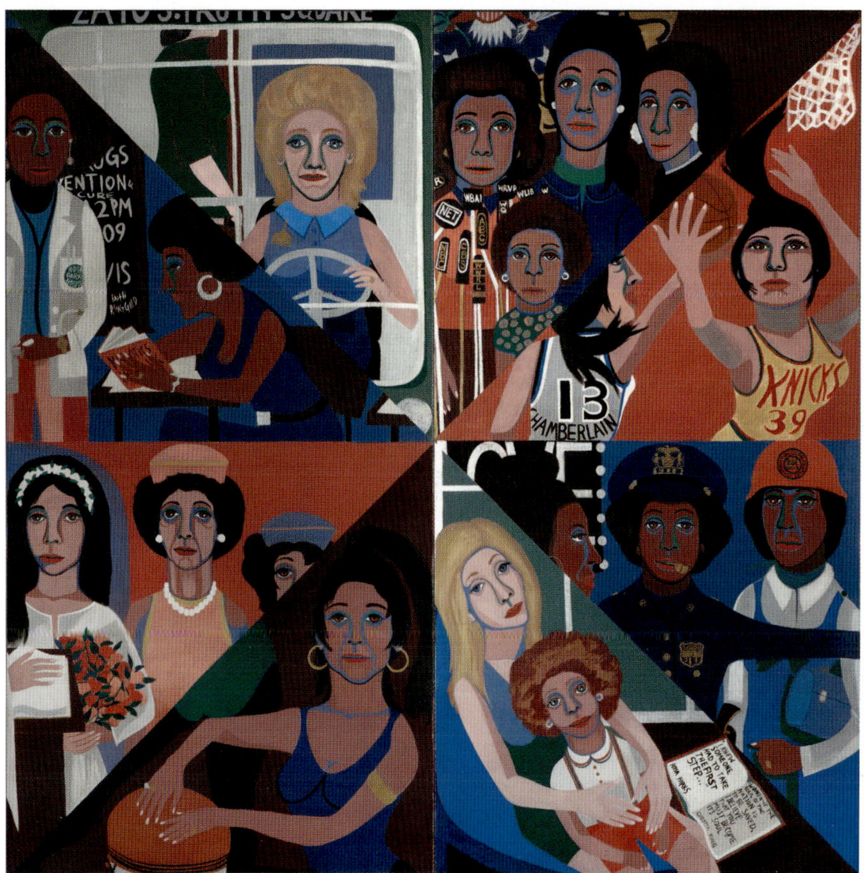

250 Faith Ringgold, *For the Women's House*, 1971

grant in 1971 to paint *For the Women's House* for the Correctional Institution for Women on Rikers Island. Following the precedent of Lucienne Bloch's 1935 mural for the same institution (which had relocated from Greenwich Village), Ringgold based her painting, now on long term loan to the Brooklyn Museum, on interviews with inmates and depicted aspirations beyond the prison walls: careers in ministry, medicine, politics, construction, and sports.

In response to a severe economic downturn in the mid-1970s, the Comprehensive Employment and Training Act (CETA) harkened back to the New Deal in providing employment and job training for millions of Americans, including artists like Judy Baca, Dawoud Bey, and Fred Wilson, all of whom worked on CETA-funded community art projects. In the same decade, the Nixon administration revived the Art in Architecture program of the General Services Administration (GSA), which still commissions original art for new federal buildings. The program, modeled after the Section of Fine Arts, sets aside about one-half of one percent of new construction costs for art. Commissioned artists include Louise Nevelson (who got her start as a sculptor on the Federal Art Project, which she called a "highlight of our American history"), Jenny Holzer (b. 1950), Maya Lin (b. 1959), and Martin Puryear (b. 1941). The GSA has also assumed responsibility for locating and cataloging New Deal art.

These government initiatives have been partial and precarious. Unlike many other countries, the US has no Ministry of Culture, and the arts rely on a patronage patchwork of state agencies, foundations, nonprofits, private and corporate funds. Funding for the NEA and the National Endowment for the Humanities varies based on which party holds the purse strings and rarely amounts to more than .004 percent of the federal budget. State art budgets shrink with falling tax revenues or can be sacrificed on the altar of the culture wars. As in the 1930s, conservative lawmakers tend to view taxpayer-funded art with suspicion, if not hostility, and take opportunities to slash cultural subsidies and funding to agencies like the GSA.

Art fares little better on the private market, despite being a major economic and tourism driver. The contemporary art world's exclusive, high-altitude atmosphere supports a sparse population of celebrity artists, blue-chip gallerists, wealthy collectors, and highly educated curators working in increasingly cost-prohibitive museums (unfrequented, for the most part, by any but college-educated audiences). At the same time, while chatter abounds of the "creative economy," virtually no artists today earn a living from making and selling art.

Burning Embers

New Deal embers still burn. The Great Recession of 2007–09, the worst downturn for the US economy since the Great Depression, conjured memories of the 1930s. The iconography of Occupy Wall Street revived the decade's anti-capitalist prints and political cartoons. Recent years have seen a wave of union activism in art museums and schools supporting higher pay, better conditions, and a voice in institutional policy. As authoritarianism flares up around the globe, contemporary artists like Sue Coe (b. 1951) have taken up the cudgel of antifascism.

In 2020, at the height of the global COVID-19 pandemic, US Congress appropriated seventy-five million dollars through

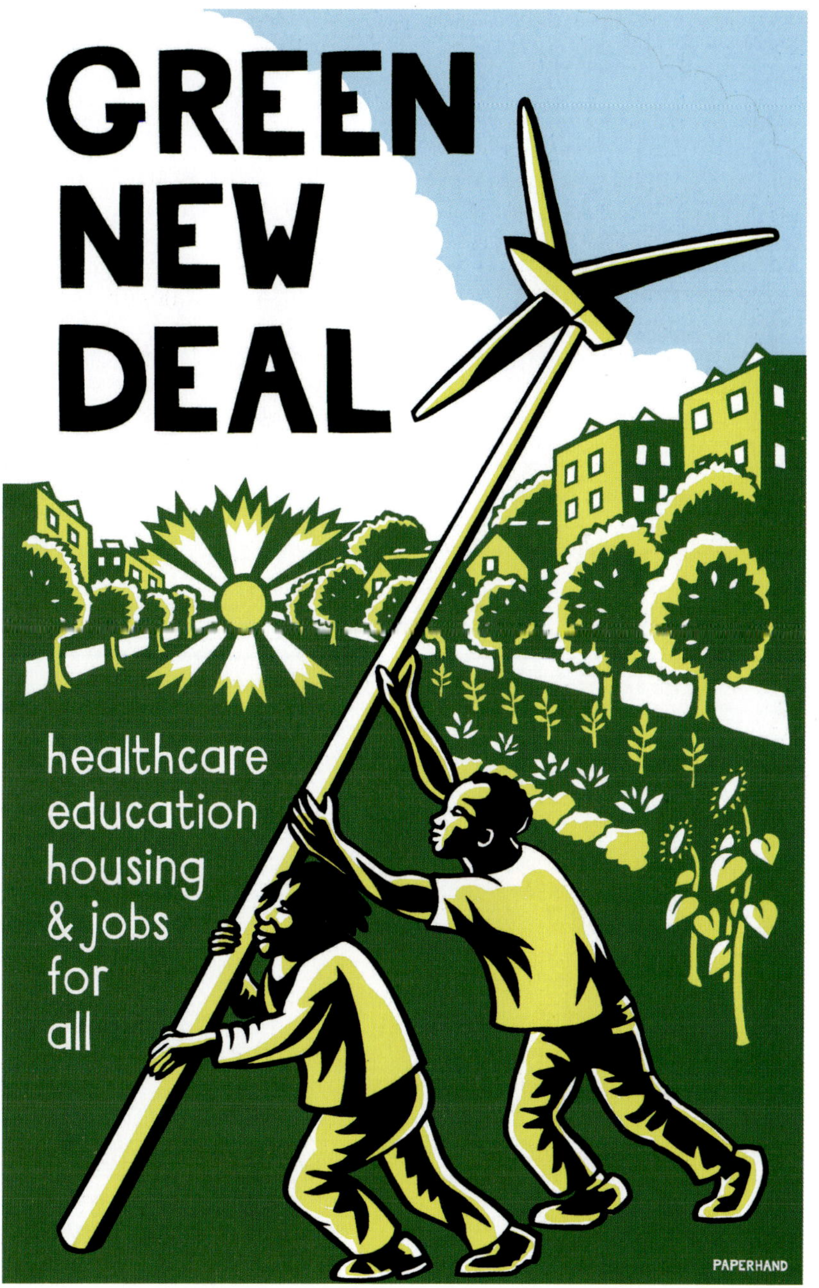

251 Jan Burger, *Green New Deal*, 2019

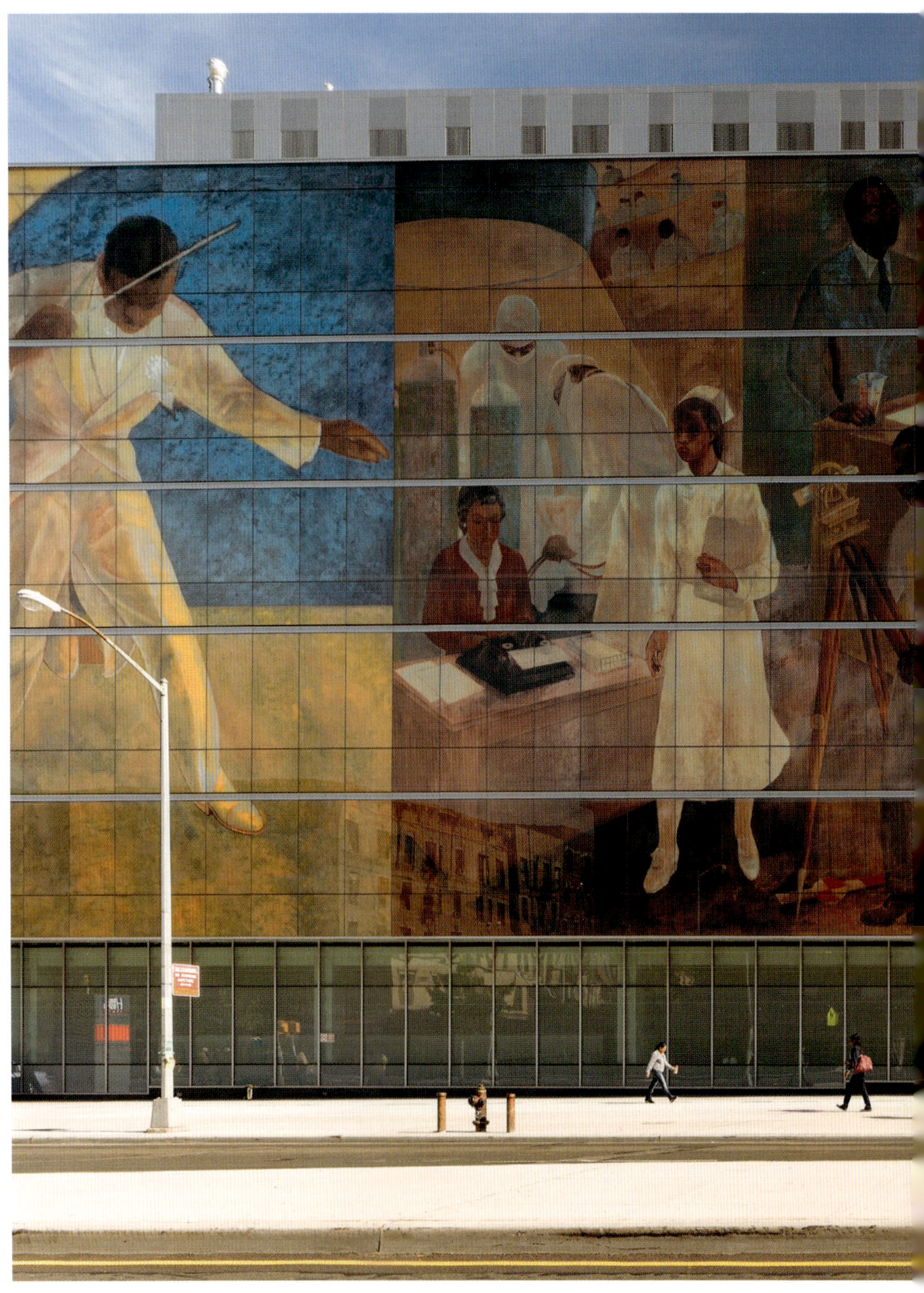

252 Vertis Hayes, *Pursuit of Happiness*, Harlem Hospital Center, New York

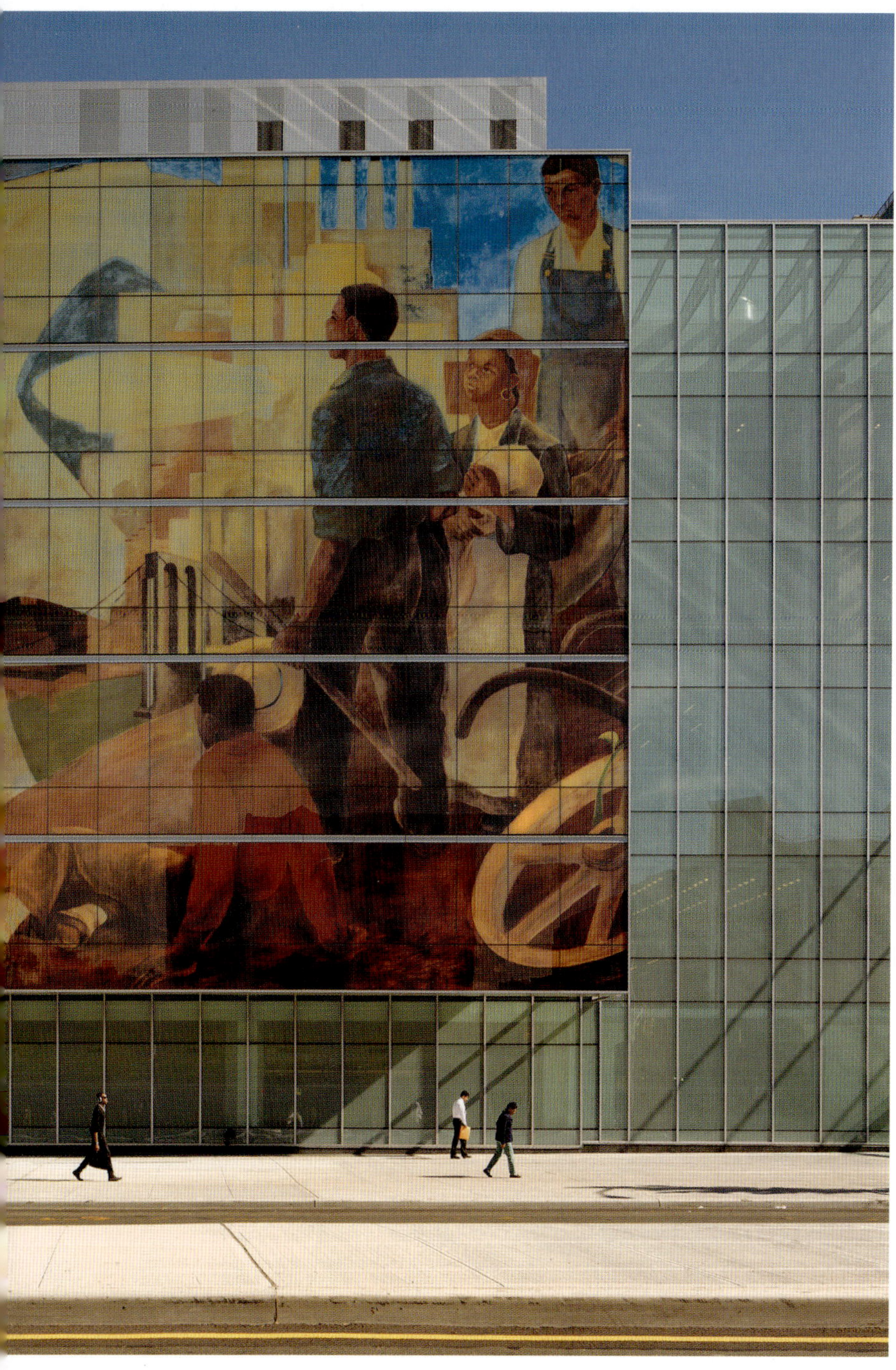

the Coronavirus Aid, Relief, and Economic Security (CARES)
Act to aid struggling artists and arts organizations. It was a
callback to the New Deal, though paltry by comparison. From
2020 to 2024, federal pandemic relief funds to individual artists
and arts nonprofits totaled $17 billion—a desperately needed
infusion, if equivalent to the cost of a single aircraft carrier.
Campaigns for a Green New Deal, sweeping public investment
in renewable energy and green infrastructure, have deployed
WPA-style posters with their saturated colors, bold contours,
and graphic lettering.

The New Deal lives on in public art. The Harlem Hospital
Center has undertaken a multiyear restoration of its WPA
murals, enlarged details of which fill the glass facade of the
Mural Pavilion, five stories high and the width of a city block.
Below ground, the Metropolitan Transportation Authority
(MTA) fulfilled the promise of the Artists' Union's Public Use
of Art Committee by commissioning art for New York subways.
Jacob Lawrence, whose professional career began on the FAP,
designed his last major work for the Times Square station: a
sparkling mosaic celebrating public transit. Three times as
many people see Lawrence's mural in a given year than visit the
Louvre, the Metropolitan, and the British Museum combined.

Kerry James Marshall (b. 1955), once a student of Charles
White, represents a direct lineage from the New Deal era. His
monumental *Rushmore,* painted on the west facade of the
Chicago Cultural Center, celebrates twenty women who shaped
the city's history and culture, including New Deal-era poet
Gwendolyn Brooks and artist Margaret Burroughs. Further
south in Chicago, the Southside Community Art Center, the
longest-running FAP center in existence, continues as a vibrant
cultural hub and was recently added to the register of national
historic places.

Audiences are discovering New Deal artists such as Sargent
Johnson, Norman Lewis, Alice Neel, and Charles White through
major museum retrospectives. The Library of Congress makes its
FSA photography archive available as part of the public domain.
The National Gallery of Art holds all 18,000 Index of American
Design watercolors. The Smithsonian American Art Museum
rotates its New Deal art collection onto its gallery walls. The
Living New Deal is a crowdsourced online archive dedicated to
documenting and preserving the legacy of the New Deal, from
public works to post office murals. The US Department of Arts
and Culture, despite its name, is not a formal federal agency—
it is a grassroots organization of culture workers reimagining
a "People's WPA" for the twenty-first century.

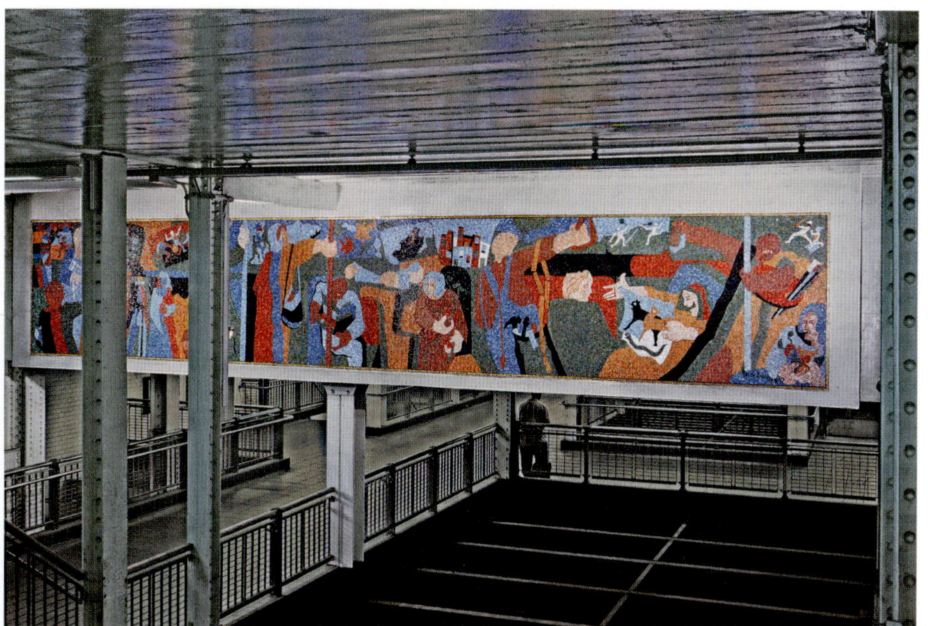

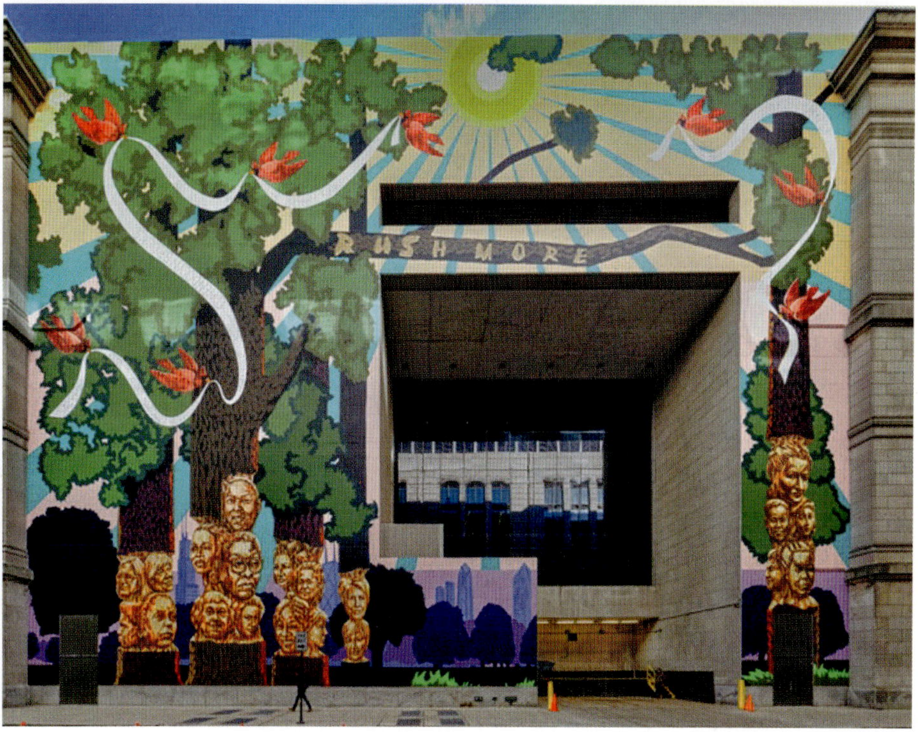

253 TOP Jacob Lawrence, *New York in Transit*, 2001
254 ABOVE Kerry James Marshall, *Rushmore*, 2017

Art as Commons

In November 1940, with Europe in flames and the US on the brink of war, reporters asked Eleanor Roosevelt if the world's "critical conditions" allowed time for art.

If not, she answered, "life would hardly be worth living."

For a decade between 1933 and 1943 the US government supported art as a necessity, not a luxury. A living wage for artists meant cultural enrichment for more of the country than ever before. New channels for art making and appreciating flowed through community art centers, traveling exhibitions, affordable prints and posters, and murals in public buildings. Culture meant something made and built together—art by the people, for the people—not passively received or reserved for the elite.

The federal art programs hired artists of great talent, even genius, who made indelible works: Berenice Abbott's *Changing New York,* Lester Beall's REA posters, Suzanne Chapman's Index of American Design watercolors, Stuart Davis's *Swing Landscape*, Aaron Douglas's *Aspects of Negro Life*, Dorothea Lange's *Migrant Mother*, Maria Martínez's blackware pottery, Gordon Parks's *American Gothic*, Ben Shahn's Social Security murals, Dox Thrash's carborundum prints, and so many more. None would have been possible without the New Deal art programs.

Yet the legacy of the programs goes beyond "rare occasional masterpieces," in Holger Cahill's phrase. It is the ongoing effort to reimagine the relationship between art and society. New Deal artists and administrators worked to make art and culture available to as many people as possible as a shared resource like electricity, clean air and water, or free public education. Representative John Coffee, trying to secure permanent arts funding in 1938, argued before Congress that art should be the "common possession of every citizen in America."

The aspiration for art to be part of the commons, essential to a more "abundant life" for all, remains unfulfilled. In this sense, the New Deal's vision of cultural democracy may not be behind us but ahead of us.

The Living New Deal

The Living New Deal is an organization dedicated to raising awareness of the New Deal's history and legacy. As part of its mission, the Advocating for New Deal Art Initiative was established to broaden public interest in New Deal art and to serve as a resource for its study, care, and teaching. Additionally, the Art Initiative acts as a watchdog group for federal artworks threatened by the ravages of time, censorship, neglect, building selloffs, or budget cuts. By safeguarding the past in all its complexity, the Living New Deal helps preserve a model of cultural democracy for the future. To learn more or find out how to support this mission, visit livingnewdeal.org.

Glossary

Abraham Lincoln Brigade An international volunteer force, including 2,500 Americans, that went to Spain to fight fascism during the Spanish Civil War.

Abstract Expressionism A postwar movement of painters such as Willem de Kooning and Jackson Pollock, whose gestural, intuitive process drew from notions of the unconscious and "truth" to the canvas's flat surface.

Agricultural Adjustment Act A part of the Roosevelt administration's flurry of First Hundred Days legislation that aimed to raise crop prices by subsidizing farmers to reduce crop production.

American Artists' Congress A Popular Front organization set up in 1936 to combat fascism through art, exhibitions, conferences, and fundraising.

American Scene An umbrella term, inclusive of regionalism and social realism, for representational views of everyday American lives and landscapes.

Art Front Magazine published by the New York Artists' Union between November 1934 and December 1937.

Artists' Union An organization formed in 1934, inspired by the labor movement, to advocate for workers' rights in the New Deal art programs.

Ashcan School A New York-based movement of artists (such as George Bellows, Robert Henri, and John Sloan) in the first decades of the twentieth century who portrayed the grittier sides of urban life in a realist style.

Associated American Artists A company founded in 1934 to mass market affordably-priced prints by American Scene artists like Thomas Hart Benton and Grant Wood through mail-order catalogs and department stores.

Avant-garde A French term for the "advance guard" of soldiers first to enter battle; applied since the late nineteenth century to artists and movements that aim to overthrow existing cultural or political order or are otherwise considered ahead of their time.

Bauhaus Founded in Germany in 1919, the school aimed to unite fine art, craft, and industrial design in building a more egalitarian future. The Nazis closed the school in 1933, and many of its key figures emigrated to the US and Mexico.

Black Chicago Renaissance A period of cultural flourishing in Chicago in the 1930s connected to the South Side Community Art Center and often compared to the Harlem Renaissance.

Bonus March In the summer of 1932, an estimated twenty thousand First World War veterans descended on Washington, DC, to petition Congress for advances on war bonuses not scheduled for payment until 1945.

Civilian Conservation Corps A New Deal program to employ young men (ages 18–25) in outdoor projects like planting trees, building parks, and fighting fires.

Community Art Centers The FAP established over a hundred community art centers nationwide to offer free classes, programs, and exhibitions to underserved communities.

Congress of Industrial Organizations A federation of unions founded in 1935 to organize semi- or unskilled workers across industries such as steel, coal, and auto manufacturing.

Cubism An early twentieth-century avant-garde movement associated with Pablo Picasso and Georges Braque that challenged illusionism and realism in art through deconstructing and reassembling forms as if seen from multiple perspectives.

Cultural Democracy The belief, expressed in New Deal policies and programs, that the opportunity to make and experience art and culture should be distributed as widely as possible.

Cultural Front A term coined by historian Michael Denning to account for the wave of pro-union, antifascist cultural energy in the 1930s.

Design Laboratory A short-lived, Bauhaus-inspired school sponsored by the Federal Art Project in New York for free instruction in fine art, industrial design, and craft.

Direct Carving A "truth to materials" method of carving directly into stone or wood, honoring its inherent properties, instead of casting from a preconceived model.

Documentary A nonfiction genre that surged in popularity during the Great Depression as writers, filmmakers, and photographers sought to represent the impact of economic hardship in a straightforward, realistic style.

Double V A campaign launched by African American newspaper the *Pittsburgh Courier* to achieve a "double victory" over fascism abroad and racism at home.

Dust Bowl The region of the southern Great Plains devastated in the 1930s by severe droughts and dust storms exacerbated by unsustainable farming practices.

Executive Order 9066 A 1942 presidential decree designating certain parts of the western US as "military zones," leading to the internment of over a hundred thousand Japanese Americans in remote camps.

Expressionism A style of art (often traced to German avant-garde groups such as Die Brücke and Blaue Reiter) that prioritized intense subjective emotion and experience through non-naturalistic distortions of form and color.

Farm Security Administration A New Deal agency that followed the Resettlement Administration, set up to aid struggling farmers through resettlement, low-interest loans, and education in sustainable farming practices.

Fascism A mass political movement emphasizing ethnocentric nationalism, militarism, territorial expansion, centralized state power, and the cult of an authoritarian leader.

Federal Art Project The WPA-funded program that provided some ten thousand artists with employment during the Great Depression.

Federal Project Number One Aka, Federal One, this umbrella term encompassed the cultural arm of the WPA: the Federal Theatre, Art, Music, and Writers' Projects, and later the Historical Records Survey.

Federal Works Agency Established in 1939 to consolidate and coordinate several agencies and public works initiatives. The WPA art programs and the Section of Fine Arts were merged under the FWA umbrella.

First Hundred Days A flurry of bold legislation passed in the first hundred days of FDR's presidency to address the Great Depression, including bills to stabilize the banks, increase crop prices, assist homeowners, and fund public works.

Forty-Eight States Competition In 1939 the largest competition sponsored by the Section of Fine Arts with the goal of placing a mural in a new post office building in every state in the Union.

Fresco A mural painting technique applying water-based pigment to wet plaster, chemically bonding the two.

Great Depression The most severe and sustained economic downturn in modern US history, lasting from the stock market crash of 1929 until war mobilization a decade later.

Great Migration The movement of millions of Black Americans from the South to states in the Northeast, Midwest, and West between 1910 and 1970 to escape Jim Crow racism and pursue educational and economic opportunities.

Harlem Artists Guild An organization founded in 1935 to advocate for Black artists on the government art programs.

Harlem Community Art Center A cultural institution set up in 1937 by the Federal Art Project after pressure from the Harlem Artists Guild to provide art classes, workshops, and exhibitions to Harlem residents.

Harlem Renaissance An interwar cultural flourishing in the predominantly Black upper Manhattan neighborhood of Harlem marked by Afrocentric pride, political activism, and artistic experimentation.

House Un-American Activities Committee A congressional committee formed in 1938 to investigate alleged disloyalty and subversive activities in American government and society.

Immigration Act of 1924 A federal law setting strict immigration quotas, especially from Africa, Asia, and Southern and Eastern Europe. The law effectively barred European Jews fleeing fascism and would-be immigrants from Asia.

Index of American Design A Federal Art Project initiative to hire unemployed commercial artists and illustrators to make detailed watercolors of pre-1900 American folk and decorative art objects.

Indian Arts Project An initiative set up at the Rochester Museum of Arts and Sciences in western New York to employ Haudenosaunee workers in recording and preserving Native arts and crafts.

Indian Reorganization Act Legislation passed in 1934 that restored a measure of sovereignty to Native American tribes and reversed the policy of breaking up tribal lands into privately owned plots. At the same time, the Act imposed Western democratic models and maintained considerable federal control in tribal affairs.

Jazz Age A period (aka the "Roaring Twenties") marked by unevenly distributed postwar prosperity, the popularity of jazz music and nightclubs, flapper culture, and cultural movements such as the Harlem Renaissance.

Jim Crow The post-Civil War system of white supremacy, particularly in the Southern states, enforced through voter suppression, segregated public spaces, and discrimination in housing, education, and employment.

John Reed Club The cultural arm of the Communist Party USA that enlisted artists and writers to commit to "art as a weapon" in the class struggle.

Kiowa Six A group of six Kiowa artists involved in an arts program at the University of Oklahoma who portrayed Native themes in a signature style based on traditional painting.

Kodachrome A popular brand of color film used by some FSA photographers, first made available in 1935.

Living Newspaper A unit of the Federal Theatre Project that dramatized current issues and events such as affordable housing, public utilities, farm crises, and union organizing.

Los Tres Grandes (The Three Greats) An honorific bestowed on the three major artists of the Mexican mural movement: José Clemente Orozco, Diego Rivera, and David Alfaro Siqueiros.

Machine Age A period of rapid industrialization involving the use of machinery, assembly lines, and mass manufacturing in the production of commodities.

Magic Realism In art, surreal or fantastic themes treated with exacting detail and realism.

Mexican Muralism / Renaissance A movement in the 1920s of government-sponsored public art in Mexico that followed the Mexican Revolution (1910–20).

Milwaukee Handicraft Project A program sponsored by the WPA to employ an integrated workforce of women to make high-quality handcrafted products like books, toys, and textiles.

Modernism In art, a series of interconnected avant-garde movements beginning in the nineteenth century that rejected academic tradition as unsuitable for capturing the modern experience.

Mural A large-scale artwork painted on or affixed to a wall or ceiling.

National Art Week A national event sponsored by the WPA in 1940 and 1941 to encourage the sale of affordable art by living American artists.

National Recovery Administration A New Deal agency (declared unconstitutional by the Supreme Court in 1935) that established codes of fair practice, wage standards, working hours, and prices across various industries.

New Deal An ambitious set of agencies and policies implemented by the FDR administration in response to the Great Depression, focused on economic relief, recovery, and reform.

New York World's Fair An international exposition held in 1939 and 1940 to showcase advancements in science, industry, technology, and consumer goods.

Office of War Information A government agency during World War II charged with creating, coordinating, and disseminating war-related information and propaganda.

Photomural An enlarged photograph mounted to a wall.

Popular Front In the US context, a broad-based antifascist alliance of communists with socialists, liberals, union members, and New Deal Democrats.

Post-Surrealism Perhaps the earliest surrealist movement in the US, based in southern California, which synthesized dream symbolism and formal classicism.

Precisionism An interwar cultural response to the Machine Age that celebrated modern cities and industries using a crisp, geometric style.

Public Use of Art Committee A subset of the Artists' Union that sought public venues for government-funded art, including other unions.

Public Works Administration A New Deal agency that undertook large-scale, material-intensive infrastructure projects such as bridges, dams, highways, and hospitals.

Public Works of Art Project Established in December 1933 as the New Deal's first art program, the PWAP hired 3,750 artists to make artwork for tax-funded buildings before shuttering in June 1934.

Regionalism A movement associated with Midwestern artists Thomas Hart Benton, John Steuart Curry, and Grant Wood, all of whom rejected European modernism and took inspiration from rural lives and landscapes.

Reorganization Act In 1939 a law passed by Congress that restructured government agencies, including bringing the WPA's Federal One and the Section of Fine Arts under the control of the newly-created Federal Works Agency.

Roosevelt Recession An economic downturn in 1937–38 following Roosevelt's cuts to government spending, the introduction of Social Security taxes, and tightening access to credit.

Section of Fine Arts The Section sponsored competitions to hire artists to make murals and sculptures for federal buildings, mostly post offices and courthouses.

Self-Taught Artists with little or no formal training, also known as naive, folk, outlier, or outsider artists.

Serigraph A term coined to designate silkscreens or screenprints as a fine art.

Social Realism A term retroactively applied to representational art of the 1930s in the US that dealt critically with issues of labor, industry, and urban life.

Social Security Act Landmark legislation passed in 1935 that provides social insurance to the elderly, the unemployed, and the disabled.

Social Surrealism A term applied to US artists adapting surrealism to social criticism.

Socialist Realism The state-sponsored "style" of the Soviet Union mandating figurative realism, cult of the leader, and idealized scenes of agriculture and heavy industry.

Spanish Civil War A conflict in Spain between 1936 and 1939, resulting in the overthrow of a democratically elected government by the pro-fascist forces of General Francisco Franco.

Surrealism An international cultural movement that absorbed the lessons of Sigmund Freud and psychoanalysis to unlock the creative and revolutionary power of dreams and the unconscious.

Tennessee Valley Authority A federally owned utility company set up in 1933 to provide electricity and spur economic development in rural parts of the US.

Treasury Relief Art Project Established with funds from the WPA, TRAP operated similarly to the Section: hiring "quality" artists to make artworks for federal buildings.

Usable Past A term coined by literary critic Van Wyck Brooks in 1918 to describe a selective interpretation of history that serves contemporary needs and concerns.

Wagner Act The National Labor Relations Act (or the Wagner Act) of 1935 enshrined the rights of workers to form unions and bargain collectively with employers.

War Relocation Authority A government agency set up in 1942 to manage the relocation and internment of Japanese Americans in the western United States during World War Two.

Work Relief Employment offered through government programs instead of direct cash assistance or the "dole."

Works Progress Administration Government agency that provided over eight million people with jobs between 1935 and 1943.

Select Bibliography

General / Introduction

Richard D. McKinzie's *The New Deal for Artists* (1973) remains the most thorough overview of the federal art programs' bureaucracy and political jockeying. More recent studies, like Joan Saab's *For the Millions* (2004) and Sharon Ann Musher's *Democratic Art* (2015), have stressed the government's efforts to democratize art. Jane De Hart Mathews (1975), Andrew Hemingway (2007), and Helen Langa (2008) examined the concept of "cultural democracy."

Adams, Henry, and Susan M. Anderson, *Art for the People: WPA-Era Paintings from the Dijkstra Collection* (Sacramento, CA: Crocker Art Museum, 2023).

Adams, Katherine H., and Michael L. Keene, *Women, Art and the New Deal* (Jefferson, NC: McFarland & Company, Inc., 2016).

Anreus, Alejandro, Diana L. Linden, and Jonathan Weinberg, eds. *The Social and the Real: Political Art in the 1930s in the Western Hemisphere* (University Park, PA: Penn State University Press, 2006).

Bard, Phil, "The Union Applies for an AFL Charter," *Art Front* (July 1935), 2, 8.

Bustard, Bruce, *A New Deal for the Arts* (Washington, DC: National Archives and Records Administration, 1997).

Contreras, Belisario R., *Tradition and Innovation in New Deal Art* (Lewisburg, PA: Bucknell University Press, 1983).

Dijkstra, Bram, *American Expressionism: Art and Social Change, 1920–1950* (New York: Harry N. Abrams, 2003).

Helfgott, Isadora Anderson, *Framing the Audience: Art and the Politics of Culture in the United States, 1929–1945* (Philadelphia: Temple University Press, 2015).

Hemingway, Andrew, "Cultural Democracy by Default: The Politics of the New Deal Arts Programmes," *Oxford Art Journal* 30:2 (2007), 269–87.

Hills, Patricia, *Social Concern and Urban Realism: American Painting of the 1930s* (Boston University Art Gallery, 1983).

Kalfatovic, Martin R., *The New Deal fine art projects: a bibliography* (Metuchen, NJ: The Scarecrow Press, 1994).

Kammen, Michael, *Mystic Chords of Memory: The Transformation of Tradition in American Culture* (New York: Vintage, 1991).

Kennedy, Roger G., *When Art Worked: The New Deal, Art, and Democracy* (New York: Rizzoli, 2009).

Lampert, Nicolas, *A People's Art History of the United States* (New York and London: The New Press, 2013).

Langa, Helen, "Constructing Cultural Democracy: Ideology, Economics, and Public Art in 1930s America," in *The Political Economy of Art: Making the Nation of Culture*, ed. Julie F. Codell (Madison and Teaneck: Fairleigh Dickinson University Press, 2008), 163–178.

Mathews, Jane De Hart, "Arts and the People: The New Deal Quest for a Cultural Democracy," *The Journal of American History* 62:2 (September 1975), 316–39.

McKinzie, Richard D., *The New Deal for Artists* (Princeton, NJ: Princeton University Press, 1973).

Messinger, Lisa Mintz, Lisa Gail Collins, and Rachel Mustalish, *African-American Artists, 1929–1945: Prints, Drawings, and Paintings at the Metropolitan Museum of Art* (New York: Metropolitan Museum of Art, 2003).

Morgan, Stacy L., *Rethinking Social Realism: African American Art and Literature, 1930–53* (Athens and London: University of Georgia Press, 2004).

Musher, Sharon Ann, *Democratic Art: The New Deal's Influence on American Culture* (Chicago: University of Chicago Press, 2015).

O'Connor, Francis, ed., *The New Deal Art Projects; An Anthology of Memoirs* (Washington, DC: Smithsonian Institution, 1972).

"Organize Against Lay-offs," *Art Front* (July–August, 1936), 3.

Park, Marlene, and Gerald E. Markowitz, *New Deal for Art: The Government Art Projects of the 1930s with Examples from New York City and*

State (Hamilton, NY: Gallery Assocation of
New York State: 1977).

Platt, Susan Noyes, *Art and Politics in the 1930s:
Modernism, Marxism, Americanism* (New York:
Midmarch Arts Press, 1999).

Rudnick, Allison, ed., *Art for the Millions:
American Culture and Politics in the 1930s* (New
York: Metropolitan Museum of Art, 2023).

Saab, A. Joan, *For the Millions: American Art
and Culture between the Wars* (Philadelphia:
University of Pennsylvania Press, 2004).

Shapiro, David, *Social Realism: Art as a Weapon*
(New York: Frederick Ungar, 1973).

Sklaroff, Lauren Rebecca, *Black Culture and the
New Deal: The Quest for Civil Rights in the
Roosevelt Era* (Chapel Hill: University of North
Carolina Press, 2009).

Wang, ShiPu, *The Other American Moderns:
Matsura, Ishigaki, Noda, Hayawaka* (University
Park, PA: Penn State University Press, 2017).

Werckmeister, Otto Karl, *The Political
Confrontation of the Arts in Europe: from the
Great Depression to the Second World War*
(arthistoricum.net, 2020).

Artist Monographs

Appel, Mary Jane, *Russell Lee: A Photographer's
Life and Legacy* (New York: Liveright, 2021).

Bearor, Karen, *Irene Rice Pereira: Her Paintings
and Philosophy* (Austin: University of Texas
Press, 1993).

Biddle, George, *An American Artist's Story* (Boston:
Little, Brown, and Co., 1939).

Breslin, James E.B., *Mark Rothko: A Biography*
(Chicago and London: University of Chicago
Press, 2012).

Carr, Dennis, Jacqueline Francis, and John P.
Bowles, eds. *Sargent Claude Johnson* (San
Marino, CA: Huntington Library, Art Museum,
and Botanical Gardens, 2024).

Cherny, Robert W., *Victor Arnautoff and the Politics
of Art* (Urbana, Chicago, and Springfield:
University of Illinois Press, 2017).

Coles, Robert, *Helen Levitt: In the Street: Chalk
Drawings and Messages: New York City
1938–1948* (Durham, NC: Duke University
Press, 1987).

Earle, Susan, ed., *Aaron Douglas: African American
Modernist* (New Haven: Yale University Press,
2007).

Evans, R. Tripp, *Grant Wood: A Life* (New York:
Alfred A. Knopf, 2010).

Gonzales, Edward, and David L. Witt, *Spirit
Ascendant: The Art and Life of Patrociño Barela*
(Santa Fe, NM: Red Crane Books, 1996).

Greenfield, Howard, *Ben Shahn: An Artist's Life*
(New York: Random House, 1998).

Haaften, Julia Van, *Berenice Abbott, A Life in
Photography* (New York: W.W. Norton & Co.,
2018).

Haskell, Barbara, and Harry Cooper, *Stuart Davis:
In Full Swing* (New York: Whitney Museum of
American Art, 2016).

Heydt, Stephanie Mayer, ed., *Rising Up: Hale
Woodruff's Murals at Talladega College*
(Atlanta, GA: High Museum of Art, 2012).

Hills, Patricia, *Painting Harlem Modern: The Art
of Jacob Lawrence* (Berkeley and Los Angeles:
University of California Press, 2019).

Hoban, Phoebe, *Alice Neel: The Art of Not Sitting
Pretty* (New York: St. Martin's Press, 2010).

Hurley, Jack F., *Marion Post Wolcott: A
Photographic Journey* (Albuquerque: University
of New Mexico Press, 1989).

Ittmann, John, *Dox Thrash: An African American
Master Printmaker Rediscovered* (Philadelphia
Museum of Art, 2001).

Koestenbaum, Wayne, *Alice Neel: Paintings from
the Thirties* (New York: Robert Miller Gallery,
1997).

LeFalle-Collins, Lizzetta, and Judith Wilson,
Sargent Johnson: African American Modernist
(San Francisco Museum of Modern Art, 1998).

Linden, Diana L., *Ben Shahn's New Deal Murals:
Jewish Identity in the American Scene* (Detroit:
Wayne State University Press, 2015).

Oehler, Sarah Kelly, and Esther Adler, eds.,
Charles White: A Retrospective (Chicago: Art
Institute of Chicago, 2018).

Parks, Gordon, *A Hungry Heart: A Memoir* (New
York: Washington Square Press, 2005)

Powell, Richard J., *Homecoming: The Art and Life of
William H. Johnson* (Washington, DC: National
Museum of American Art, Smithsonian
Institution, 1991).

Robinson, Greg, and Elena Tajima Creef, eds.,
Miné Okubo: Following her Own Road (Seattle:
University of Washington Press, 2008).

Rosenberg, James, *Painter's Self-Portrait* (New
York: Crown Publishers, 1958).

Solomon, Deborah, *Jackson Pollock: A Biography*
(New York: Simon and Schuster, 1987)

Spender, Matthew, *From a High Place: A Life of
Arshile Gorky* (New York: Knopf, 1999).

Thompson, Robert Farris, et al., *The Art of William
Edmondson* (Jackson, MS: University Press of
Mississippi, 1999).

Walker, Andrew, ed., *Joe Jones: Radical Painter
of the American Scene* (St. Louis Art Museum,
2010).

Wolf, Tom, *The Artistic Journey of Yasuo Kuniyoshi* (Smithsonian American Art Museum, 2015).
Yochelson, Bonnie, *The Committed Eye: Alexander Alland's Photography* (Museum of the City of New York, 1991).

Public Works of Art Project

This chapter draws on Ann Prentice Wagner's catalogue accompanying the Smithsonian American Art Museum's 2009 exhibition *1934: A New Deal for Artists*. Lea Rosson DeLong (2006), James Dennis (1998), and Lauren Kroiz (2018) discussed regionalism vis-à-vis the New Deal art programs. Anna Indych-López (2009) and Anthony Lee (1999) considered the influence of Mexican muralism on New Deal art. Richard Meyer (2002) unpacked the Paul Cadmus controversy. Robert W. Cherny (2024) exhaustively detailed the Coit Tower controversy. Leah Dickerman (2020) put Aaron Douglas's *Aspects of Negro Life* in context.

Baigell, Matthew, *The American scene: American Painting of the 1930's* (New York and Washington, DC: Praeger Publishers, 1974).
Biddle, George, "The Artist Serves His Community," *American Magazine of Art* 27:9 (September 1934), 31–32.
Bruce, Edward, et al, *National Exhibition of Art by the Public Works of Art Project* (Washington, DC: Corcoran Gallery of Art, 1934).
Cherny, Robert W., *The Coit Tower Murals: New Deal Art and Political Controversy in San Francisco* (Champaign, IL: University of Illinois Press, 2024).
Clark, Lenore, *Forbes Watson: Independent Revolutionary* (Kent, OH: Kent State University Press, 2001).
DeLong, Lea Rosson, *When Tillage Begins, Other Arts Follow: Grant Wood and Christian Petersen Murals* (Ames: Iowa State University, 2006).
Dennis, James M., *Renegade Regionalists: The Modern Independence of Grant Wood, Thomas Hart Benton, and John Steuart Curry* (Madison: University of Wisconsin Press, 1998).
Dickerman, Leah, "Aaron Douglas and *Aspects of Negro Life*," *October* 174 (Fall 2020), 126–62.
"Doors Open on a Stale Tradition," *The Journal of Electrical Workers & Operators* 33:6 (June 1934), 235–38, 276.
Indych-López, Anna, *Muralism Without Walls: Rivera, Orozco, and Siqueiros in the United States, 1927–1940* (Pittsburgh, PA: University of Pittsburgh Press, 2009).
Jewell, Edward Alden, "The Realm of Art: The Public Works of Art Project," *New York Times* (29 April 1934), X7.
Kroiz, Lauren, *Cultivating Citizens: The Regional Work of Art in the New Deal Era* (Berkeley: University of California Press, 2018).
Lee, Anthony W., *Painting on the Left: Diego Rivera, Radical Politics, and San Francisco's Public Murals* (Berkeley: University of California Press, 1999).
Marling, Karal Ann, "Federal Patronage and the Woodstock Colony" (PhD Dissertation, Bryn Mawr College, 1971).
McMahon, Audrey, "May the Artist Live?" *Parnassus* (October 1933), 1–4.
Meyer, Richard, "A Different American Scene: Paul Cadmus and the Satire of Sexuality," in *Outlaw Representation: Censorship and Homosexuality in Twentieth-Century American Art* (Boston: Beacon Press, 2002), 33–56.
Prelinger, Elizabeth, ed. *Scenes of American Life: Treasures from the Smithsonian American Art Museum* (Washington, DC: Smithsonian American Art Museum, 2001).
"The Public Works of Art Project," *Art News* 32:11 (16 December 1933), 10.
Soyer, Moses, "The Second Whitney Biennial," *Art Front* (February 1935), 7–8.
Wagner, Ann Prentice, ed., *1934: A New Deal for Artists* (Washington, DC: Smithsonian American Art Museum, 2009).

The Section of Fine Arts

This chapter draws on three book-length studies of the Section: Karal Ann Marling's *Wall-to-Wall America* (1982), Gerald Markowitz and Marlene Park's *Democratic Vistas* (1984), and Barbara Melosh's *Engendering Culture* (1991). Charles Eldredge (2021) discussed the Section's agriculture-themed murals. Jonathan Weinberg (2006) considered homoeroticism in Section murals. Recent studies by Sara A. Butler (2011), Jennifer McLerran (2009), Denise Neil-Binion (2017), Michaela Elaine Rife (2020), and John Ott (2025) examine the racial politics of Section murals. The Smithsonian's virtual exhibition *Indians at the Post Office* is an indispensable resource for information about Section murals by and about Native Americans.

Bruce, Edward, and Forbes Watson, *Art in Federal Buildings: An Illustrated Record of the Treasury Department's New Program in Painting and Sculpture, Vol. I: Mural Designs, 1934–36* (Washington, DC, 1936).

Bruce, Edward, "Art and Democracy," *Atlantic Monthly* 156 (August 1935), 149–52.

Butler, Sara A., "Ground Breaking in New Deal Washington, DC: Art, Patronage, and Race at the Recorder of Deeds Building," *Winterthur Portfolio* 45:4 (Winter 2011), 277–320.

Carter, Warren, "Figuring the New Deal: Politics and Ideology in Treasury Section Painting and Sculpture in Washington, D.C., 1934–1943" (PhD Dissertation, University College London, 2008).

———. "Structure and Agency in New Deal Art: The Case of William Gropper's 'Construction of a Dam'," *Object* 6 (2003/2004), 5–28.

Dows, Olin, "The New Deal's Treasury Art Program: A Memoir," *The New Deal Art Projects* (1972), 11–50.

Eldredge, Charles C., *We Gather Together: American Artists and the Harvest* (Oakland: University of California Press, 2021).

Fahlman, Betsy, "Louise Emerson Ronnebeck: A New Deal Artist of the American West," *Woman's Art Journal* 22:2 (Autumn 2001), 12–18.

Francis, Jacqueline, "Making History: Malvin Gray Johnson's and Earle Richardson's Studies for 'Negro Achievement,'" in *The Social and the Real* (2006), 135–53.

Lembeck, David, "Rediscovering the People's Art: New Deal Murals in Pennsylvania Post Offices," *Pennsylvania Heritage* (Summer 2008), 28–37.

Marling, Karal Ann, *Wall-to-Wall America: A Cultural History of Post Office Murals in the Great Depression* (Minneapolis: University of Minnesota Press, 1982).

McLerran, Jennifer, *A New Deal for Native Art: Indian Arts and Federal Policy, 1933–1943* (Tucson: University of Arizona Press, 2009).

Mecklenburg, Virginia M., *The Public as Patron: A History of the Treasury Department Mural Program* (College Park: University of Maryland, 1979).

Melosh, Barbara, *Engendering Culture: Manhood and Womanhood in New Deal Public Art and Theater* (Washington, DC: Smithsonian Institution Press, 1991).

Neil-Binion, Denise, "Representation and Misrepresentation: Depictions of Native Americans in Oklahoma Post Office Murals" (PhD Dissertation, University of Oklahoma, 2017).

Ott, John, "'The Whites Do Rule': The New Deal Imagines Racial Integration," in *Mixed Media: The Visual Cultures of Racial Integration, 1931–1954* (forthcoming).

Park, Marlene, and Gerald E. Markowitz, *Democratic Vistas: Post Offices and Public Art in the New Deal* (Philadelphia: Temple University Press, 1984).

Rife, Michaela Elaine, "Public Art, Private Land: Settler Colonialism and Environment in New Deal Murals on the Great Plains" (PhD Dissertation, University of Toronto, 2020).

———. Michigan Post Office Murals Project, University of Michigan, virtual exhibition: https://michiganmurals.hart.lsa.umich.edu/

Starr, Sandra, ed., *Indians at the Post Office: Native Themes in New Deal-Era Murals*, Smithsonian National Museum of the American Indian, virtual exhibition: https://postalmuseum.si.edu/exhibition/indians-at-the-post-office

Vigneault, Marissa, "The Politics of Labor in William Gropper's *Construction of a Dam*," Talk delivered at Sheldon Museum of Art, Lincoln, NE, April 2014. https://www.academia.edu/8167297/_The_Politics_of_Labor_in_William_Gropper_s_Construction_of_a_Dam_Sheldon_Museum_of_Art_Lincoln_NE_April_2014

Weinberg, Jonathan, "I Want Muscle: Male Desire and the Image of the Male Worker in American Art of the 1930s," in *The Social and the Real* (2006), 115–34.

Federal Art Project

Art for the Millions (1973) is a collection of essays by participants in the Federal Art Project (cited essays appear below). Jonathan Harris (1995) interpreted the FAP as a tool of state ideology. Victoria Grieve (2009) dedicated separate chapters to the FAP's Index of American Design and Community Art Centers. Jody Patterson (2020) contextualized abstraction on the New York FAP, with special attention to Arshile Gorky and Stuart Davis. Angela Miller explored self-taught artists (2022) and social surrealism (2007) on the government programs. Stephanie Lewthwaite (2015) and Marianna Tey Nunn (2001) recovered the careers of Patrociño Barela and Pedro Cervántez, respectively. Helen Harrison generously answered queries about Jackson Pollock's FAP career.

Berman, Greta, *The Lost Years: Mural Painting in N.Y. City Under the WPA Federal Art Project, 1935–1943* (New York and London: Garland Publishing, Inc., 1978).

Cahill, Holger, *New Horizons in American Art* (New York: Museum of Modern Art, 1936).

Carlton-Smith, Kim, "A New Deal for Women: Women Artists and the Federal Art Project,

1935–1939" (PhD Dissertation, Rutgers University, 1990).

Fort, Susan Ilene, "American Social Surrealism," *Archives of American Art Journal* 22:3 (January 1982), 8–20.

Grieve, Victoria, *The Federal Art Project and the Creation of Middlebrow Culture* (Urbana and Chicago: University of Illinois Press, 2009).

Harris, Jonathan, *Federal Art and National Culture: The Politics of Identity in New Deal America* (Cambridge: Cambridge University Press, 1995).

Hopkins, Harry, "Aims and Policies of WPA," *Work: A Journal of Progress* 1:1 (September 1936), 1.

Jeffers, Wendy, "Holger Cahill and American Art," *Archives of American Art Journal* 31:4 (1991), 2–11.

Lewthwaite, Stephanie, *A Contested Art: Modernism and Mestizaje in New Mexico* (Norman: University of Oklahoma Press, 2015).

MacLeish, Archibald [unsigned], "Unemployed Arts: WPA's Four Arts Projects: Their Origins, Their Operation," *Fortune* (May 1937), 108–17.

Mavigliano, George J., "The Federal Art Project: Holger Cahill's Program of Action," *Art Education* 37:3 (May 1984), 26–30.

McDonald, William F., *Federal Relief Administration and the Arts: The Origins and Administrative History of the Arts Projects of the Works Progress Administration* (Columbus: Ohio State University Press, 1969).

Miller, Angela, "'The People Looks Upon Its Own Life': Self-Taught Art Between the Wars," in *Boundary Trouble in American Vanguard Art, 1920–2020*, ed. Lynne Cooke (Washington, DC: National Gallery of Art, 2022), 59–78.

———. "With Eyes Wide Open: The American Reception of Surrealism," in *Caught by Politics: Hitler Exiles and American Visual Culture*, ed. Sabine Eckmann and Lutz Koepnick (New York: Palgrave Macmillan, 2007), 61–94.

Miller, Sarah M., *Documentary in Dispute: The Original Manuscript of Changing New York by Berenice Abbott and Elizabeth McCausland* (Cambridge: The MIT Press, 2020).

Mumford, Lewis, "East and West," reprinted in *Mumford on Modern Art in the 1930s* (University of California Press, 2007), 206–208.

Nunn, Tey Marianna. *Sin Nombre: Hispana and Hispano Artists of the New Deal Era* (Albuquerque: University of New Mexico Press, 2001).

O'Connor, Francis V., ed., *Art for the Millions: Essays from the 1930s by Artists and Administrators of the WPA Federal Art Project* (Greenwich, CT: New York Graphic Society, 1973).
Bloch, Lucienne, "Murals for Use," 76–77.
Davis, Stuart, "Abstract Painting Today," 121–27.
Diller, Burgoyne, "Abstract murals," 69–71.
Gorky, Arshile, "My Murals for the Newark Airport: An Interpretation," 72–73.
Guglielmi, O. Louis, "After the Locusts," 113–14.
Hord, Donal, "Symphony in Stone," 104–106.
Hunter, Vernon, "Concerning Patrocinio Barela," 96–99.
Quirt, Walter, "On Mural Painting," 78–81.

Patterson, Jody, *Modernism for the Masses: Painters, Politics, and Public Murals in 1930s New York* (New Haven: Yale University Press, 2020).

Russo, Jillian, "The Works Progress Administration Federal Art Project Reconsidered," *Visual Resources* 34.1–2 (2018), 13–32.

"Ten Crucial Years: The Development of United States Government Sponsored Artists Programs 1933–1943 A Panel Discussion by Six WPA Artists," *The Journal of Decorative and Propaganda Arts* 1 (Spring 1986), 55–56.

Yale, Margot, "'A Healthy Tonic': Lucienne Bloch's 'The Cycle of a Woman's Life' and the Value of the Artist at Work," in *Modernism, Art, Therapy*, eds. Suzanne Hudson and Tanya Sheehan (New Haven: Yale University Press, 2024), Accessed March 8, 2025. https://aaeportal-com.libproxy.vassar.edu/?id=-32159.

FAP Graphic Arts and Poster Divisions

Elizabeth Seaton's dissertation (2000) remains the essential summary and analysis of the FAP's graphic arts division. Helen Langa's *Radical Art* (2004) focused on "social viewpoint" printmakers, including several employed on the FAP in New York. Co-curators Virginia Anderson and Robin Owen Joyce recovered little-known FAP printmakers like Jean Finlayson Holmes for their 2023 Baltimore Museum of Art exhibition *Art/Work: Women Printmakers of the WPA*. LACMA curator Rachel Kaplan generously identified the iconography of Luis Arenal's 1937 *Distribution of Land*. David Martin of Cascadia Art Museum supplied helpful context for the careers of Fay Chong and Julius Twohy. My curatorial assistant Jordana Judd made the connection between FAP prints and Living Newspapers.

Becker, Fred, "The WPA Federal Art Project, New York City: A Reminiscence," *The Massachusetts Review* 39:1 (Spring 1998), 74–92.

Benay, Erin, "Peripheral Prints: Karamu House and the Rise of African American Art in the Midwest," *Panorama* 10:1 (Spring 2024): https://journalpanorama.org/article/peripheral-prints/

Bryson, Bernarda, and Jake Wien, *The Vanishing American Frontier: Bernarda Bryson Shahn and her Historical Lithographs Created for the Resettlement Administration of FDR* (New York: Wien American, 1995).

Carter, Ennis, Christopher DeNoon, and Alexander M. Peltz, eds., *Posters for the People: The Art of the WPA* (Philadelphia: Quirk Books, 2008).

Duncan, Michael, *Post Surrealism* (Logan, Utah: Nora Eccles Harrison Museum of Art, Utah State University, 2002).

Ellis, James W., "Fay Chong and Andrew Chinn: Asian Masters of American Art," *ASJ Occasional Papers* 12 (2017).

Golec, MJ, "Graphic Visualization and Visuality in Lester Beall's Rural Electrification Posters, 1937," *Journal of Design History* 26:4 (2013), 401–15.

Grafly, Dorothy, "The Print—America's Folk Art," *Magazine of Art* 31:1 (January 1938), 32–35, 60.

Kainen, Jacob, "The Graphic Arts Division of the WPA Federal Art Project," in *New Deal Art Projects* (1972), 155–75.

King-Hammond, Leslie, "Black Printmakers and the WPA," in *Alone in a Crowd: Prints of the 1930s–40s by African-American Artists from the Collection of Reba and Dave Williams* (New York: Dave and Reba Williams, 1993).

Langa, Helen, *Radical Art: Printmaking and the Left in 1930s New York* (Berkeley: University of California Press, 2004).

———. "Egalitarian Vision: Gendered Experience: Women Printmakers and the WPA/FAP Graphic Arts Project," in *The Expanding Discourse: Feminism and Art History*, eds. Norma Broude and Mary D. Garrard (New York: IconEditions, 1992), 408–23.

O'Connor, Francis V., ed., *Art for the Millions* (1973).
Floethe, Richard, "Posters," 177–78.
Jacobi, Eli, "Street of Forgotten Men," 157.
Olds, Elizabeth, "Prints for Mass Production," 142–44.

Pillen, Corey, *WPA Posters in an Aesthetic, Social, and Political Context: A New Deal for Design* (New York: Routledge, 2020).

Seaton, Elizabeth, "Federal Prints and Democratic Culture: The Graphic Arts Division of the Works Progress Administration Federal Art Project, 1935–1943" (Ph.D. Dissertation, Northwestern University, 2000).

———. *WPA Federal Art Project: Printmaking in California* (The Book Club of San Francisco, 2005).

———. *Paths to the Press: Printmaking and American Women Artists, 1910–1960* (Marianna Kistler Beach Museum of Art, Kansas State University, 2006).

Wechsler, James, "The Great Depression and the Prints of Blanche Grambs," *Print Quarterly* 13:4 (December 1996), 376–96.

———. "Fred Becker and Experimental Printmaking," *Print Quarterly* 10:4 (December 1993), 373–84.

Williams, Dave and Reba, "The Early History of the Screenprint," *Print Quarterly* 3:4 (December 1986), 287–321.

Farm Security Administration Photography

This chapter is indebted to Melissa A. McEuen's illuminating chapters on Dorothea Lange and Marion Post in *Seeing America* (2000), Gilles Mora and Beverly Brannan's expansive *FSA: The American Vision* (2006), and Cara Finnegan's analysis of the display and reception of FSA photography in *Making Photography Matter* (2015). William Stott's *Documentary Expression and Thirties America* (1973) is a classic study of "documentary" as a Depression-era genre. James Curtis (1989) interpreted FSA photography as an instrument of New Deal ideology. Nicholas Natanson (1992) offered a groundbreaking analysis of race and New Deal photography.

Allred, Jeff, *American Modernism and Depression Documentary* (New York: Oxford University Press, 2009).

Carlebach, Michael L., "Documentary and Propaganda: The Photographs of the Farm Security Administration," *The Journal of Decorative and Propaganda Arts* 8 (Spring 1988), 6–25.

Curtis, James, *Mind's Eye, Mind's Truth: FSA Photography Reconsidered* (Philadelphia: Temple University Press, 1989).

Eisenman, Stephen, "Joe Biden and Dorothea Lange: Politics and Art Revealed," *Counterpunch,* 29 December 2023. https://www.counterpunch.org/2023/12/29/joe-biden-and-dorothea-lange-politics-and-art-revealed/

Finnegan, Cara A., *Picturing Poverty: Print Culture and FSA Photographs* (Washington, DC: Smithsonian Institution, 2003).

———. *Making Photography Matter: A Viewer's History from the Civil War to the Great Depression* (Urbana: University of Illinois Press, 2015), 125–68.

Gilles, Mora, and Beverly W. Brannan, *FSA: The American Vision* (New York: Abrams, 2006).

Goggans, Jan, *California on the Breadlines: Dorothea Lange, Paul Taylor, and the Making of a New Deal Narrative* (Berkeley: The University of California Press, 2010).

Hurley, Jack F., *Portrait of a Decade: Roy Stryker and the Development of Documentary Photography in the Thirties* (Baton Rouge: Louisiana State University Press, 1972).

Kirstein, Lincoln, *Walker Evans: American Photographs* (New York: Museum of Modern Art, 1938).

Lange, Dorothea, "The Assignment I'll Never Forget," *Popular Photography* (February 1960), 42–43.

McEuen, Melissa A., *Seeing America: Women Photographers between the Wars* (Lexington: The University Press of Kentucky, 2000).

Natanson, Nicholas, *The Black Image in the New Deal: The Politics of FSA Photography.* (Knoxville: University of Tennessee Press, 1992).

Stein, Sally, *Migrant Mother, Migrant Gender: Reconsidering Dorthea Lange's Iconic Portrait of Maternity* (London: Mack, 2020).

Stott, William, *Documentary Expression and Thirties America* (New York: Oxford University Press, 1973).

Tagg, John, *The Disciplinary Frame: Photographic Truths and the Capture of Meaning* (Minneapolis: University of Minnesota Press, 2009).

Tormey, Jane, *Photography and Political Aesthetics* (New York: Routledge, 2023).

FAP Index of American Design / Community Art Centers

The most thorough survey of the Index of American Design is the catalogue accompanying the National Gallery of Art's 2002 exhibition, *Drawing on America's Past.* William D. Moore (2013) outlined the Index's "canonization" of Shaker culture and Kay Wells (2022) argued that the Index shaped white American identity. Shannan Clark (2009) recovered the Design Laboratory's radical modernism. Jackson Davidow (2018) entwined the histories of art and therapy through discussions of the Harlem Hospital murals and the FAP exhibition *Art and Psychopathology.* Mary Ann Calo (2023) delved into the racial politics of the New Deal art programs, with particular attention to community art centers.

Brookman, Philip, and Casey Riley, eds. *American Gothic: Gordon Parks and Ella Watson* (Steidl / Gordon Parks Foundation / Minneapolis Institute of Art, 2024).

Burroughs, Margaret Goss, "Chicago's South Side Community Art Center: A Personal Recollection," in John Franklin White, ed., *Art in Action: American Art Centers and the New Deal* (Metuchen, NJ: The Scarecrow Press, Inc., 1987), 131–44.

Calo, Mary Ann, *African American Artists and the New Deal Programs: Opportunity, Access, and Community* (University Park: Penn State University Press, 2023).

Christensen, Erwin O., *The Index of American Design* (New York: The Macmillan Company, 1950).

Clark, Shannan, "When Modernism Was Still Radical: The Design Laboratory and the Cultural Politics of Depression-Era America," *American Studies* 50:3–4 (Fall/Winter, 2009), 35–62.

Clayton, Virginia Tuttle, Elizabeth Stillinger, and Erika Lee Doss, eds. *Drawing on America's Past: Folk Art, Modernism, and the Index of American Design* (Washington, DC: National Gallery of Art, 2002).

Davidow, Jackson, "Art Therapy, Occupational Therapy, and American Modernism," *American Art* 32:2 (June 2018), 80–99.

Jenkins, Earnestine, "Muralist Vertis Hayes and the LeMoyne Federal Art Center: A Legacy of African American Fine Arts in Memphis, Tennessee, 1930s–1950s," *Tennessee Historical Quarterly* 73:2 (Summer 2014), 132–59.

Kirschke, Amy Helene, "Bearden in *The Crisis*: Illustrating Identity and Political Action," *Studies in the History of Art* 71 (2011), 101–17.

Moore, William D., "'You'd Swear They Were Modern': Ruth Reeves, the Index of American Design, and the Canonization of Shaker Material Culture," *Winterthur Portfolio* 47:1 (Spring 2013), 1–34.

O'Connor, Francis V., ed., *Art for the Millions* (1973).
Bennett, Gwendolyn, "The Harlem Community Art Center," 213–15.
Gershoy, Eugenie, "Fantasy and Humor in Sculpture," 92–93.
Jones, Lawrence, "The New Orleans WPA/ FAP," 198–99.

Marantz, Irving J., "The Artist as a Social Worker," 197–98.

Rourke, Constance, "What is American Design," 165–66.

Rourke, Constance, "Artists on Relief," *The New Republic* (15 July 1936), 287.

Rothschild, Lincoln, "The Index of American Design of the WPA Federal Art Project," *The New Deal Art Projects* (1972), 177–98.

Rubin, Joan Shelley, "A Convergence of Vision: Constance Rourke, Charles Sheeler, and American Art," *American Art Quarterly* 42:2 (June 1990), 191–222.

Silverman, Julia, "Haudenosaunee Craft at the Rochester Municipal Museum: A Paradoxical New Deal Project," *The Decorative Arts Trust Bulletin*, published online 22 November 2023: https://decorativeartstrust.org/haudenosaunee-craft-post/

Smucker, Janneken, *A New Deal for Quilts* (Lincoln: University of Nebraska Press, 2023).

Ulbricht, Elsa, "The Story of the Milwaukee Handicraft Project" *Design* 45:6 (February 1944), 6–7.

Wells, KLH, "Indexing Whiteness to American Design," *American Art* 36:3 (Fall 2022), 10–14.

Artists' Union / For a Permanent Federal Art Project

In the 1970s Gerald Monroe published groundbreaking articles on artist activism and organizing. Helen Harrison (1980, 1981), Patricia Hills (1994, 2006), Helen Langa (2002, 2003), and Laura Hapke (2008) have deepened the history and analysis of 1930s art and politics. The indispensable study is Andrew Hemingway's *Artists on the Left* (2002), which tracks the influence of Marxism and the Communist Party USA on artists involved in the Artists' Union, the American Artists' Congress, and the New Deal art projects.

"Artists' Union Constitution," *Art Front* 1:1 (November 1934), 8.

"The Artists' Unions: Builders of a Democratic Culture," *Art Front* 3–4 (May 1937), 3.

Davis, Stuart, "THE ARTIST TODAY: The Standpoint of the Artists' Union," *American Magazine of Art* 28:8 (1935), 476–506.

Denning, Michael, *The Cultural Front: The Laboring of American Culture in the Twentieth Century* (New York: Verso, 1998).

Doss, Erika, "Looking at Labor: Images of Work in 1930s American Art," *The Journal of Decorative and Propaganda Arts* 24 (2002), 231–57.

Dwight, Mabel, "Satire in Art," in *Art for the Millions* (1973), 151–53.

Evergood, Philip, "Should the Nation Support Its Art," *Direction* (April 1938), 2–5.

"Flag-Waving Vs. Art," *Art Front* (October 1937), 3–4.

Hapke, Laura, *Labor's Canvas: American Working-Class History and the WPA Art of the 1930s* (New York: Cambridge University Press, 2008).

Harrison, Helen, "John Reed Club Artists and the New Deal: Radical Responses to Roosevelt's Peaceful Revolution," *Prospects* 5 (1980), 241–68.

———. "Subway Art and the Public Use of Arts Committee," *Archives of American Art Journal* 21:2 (1981), 2–12.

Hemingway, Andrew, *Artists on the Left: American Artists and the Communist Movement, 1926–1956* (New Haven: Yale University Press, 2002).

Hills, Patricia, "1936: Meyer Schapiro, 'Art Front,' and the Popular Front," *Oxford Art Journal* 17:1 (1994), 30–41.

———. "Art and Politics in the Popular Front: The Union Work and Social Realism of Philip Evergood," in *The Social and the Real* (2006), 181–200.

Langa, Helen, "Deep Tunnels and Burning Flues: The Unexpected Political Drama in 1930s Industrial Production Prints," *IA: The Journal of the Society of Industrial Archaeology* 28:1 (2002), 43–58.

Laning, Edward, "The New Deal Mural Projects," in *The New Deal Art Projects* (1972), 79–114.

Marquardt, Virginia Hagelstein, "Art on the Political Front in America: From *The Liberator* to *Art Front*," *Art Journal* 52:1 (1993), 72–81.

McCormick, Fred, "New Greenwich Village Rings with the Wails of Hobo-hemian Chisellers for More 'Filthy Lucre' Via the Dole," *Sunday Mirror* (1 September 1935), 10–11, 19.

Monroe, Gerald, "Artists as Militant Trade Union Workers During the Great Depression," *Archives of American Art* 14:1 (1974), 7–10.

———. "Artists on the Barricades: The Militant Artists Union Treats with the New Deal," *Archives of American Art* 18:3 (1978), 20–23.

Rothschild, Lincoln, "Artists' Organizations of the Depression Decade," *The New Deal Art Projects* (1972), 198–222.

"The Sidewalks of New York," *Art Front* (July 1935), 3.

Siporin, Mitchell, "Mural Art and the Midwestern Myth," in *Art for the Millions* (1973), 64–66.

Solman, Joseph, "The Easel Division of the WPA Federal Art Project," in *The New Deal Art Projects* (1972), 115–32.

Taylor, Francis Henry, "Pork Barrel Renaissance," *American Magazine of Art* 31 (March 1938), 157, 186–87.

Tyler, Francine, "Artists Respond to the Great Depression and the Threat of Fascism: The New York Artists' Union and its magazine 'Art Front'" (PhD Dissertation, New York University, 1991).

Vane, Peter, "Big Words By Bigwigs: What Art Officials Think About While the Artist Fights for a Permanent Project," *Art Front* (May 1937), 5–7, 26–31.

Vitz, Robert C., "Clubs, Congresses, and Unions: American Artists Confront the Thirties," *New York History* 54:4 (October 1973), 424–47.

Weinstock, Clarence, "Public Art in Practice," *Art Front* (December 1936), 8–10.

White, Charles, "Path of a Negro Artist," *Masses and Mainstream* 8:4 (April 1955), 33–44.

Antifascism and World War II

Matthew Baigell and Julia Williams (1986) collated the papers of the first American Artists' Congress and offered an introductory overview of the AAC. Helen Langa (2007) dealt with artists and the Spanish Civil War. ShiPu Wang (2008) and Chrisof Decker (2019) considered OWI designs by Yasuo Kuniyoshi and Ben Shahn, respectively. John Ott (2015) interpreted Jacob Lawrence's Coast Guard paintings in the context of desegregation in the Armed Forces. Melissa McEuen (2010) and Catherine Speck (2014) examined the gender politics of wartime art and photography.

Baigell, Matthew, and Julia Williams, eds., *Artists Against War and Fascism: Papers of the First American Artists' Congress* (New Brunswick: Rutgers University Press, 1986).
    "Call for an American Artists' Congress," 47–48.
    Douglas, Aaron, "The Negro in American Culture," 78–84.
    Mumford, Lewis, "Opening Address," 62–64.

Bak, Hans, ed., *The Long Voyage: Selected Letters of Malcolm Cowley, 1915–1987* (Cambridge, MA: Harvard University Press, 2014).

Catlett, Elizabeth, "Artist with a Message," *The People's Voice* (21 October 1944), 14.

Davidov, Judith Fryer, "The Color of My Skin, The Shape of My Eyes: Photographs of the Japanese American Internment by Dorothea Lange, Ansel Adams and Toyo Miyatake," *The Yale Journal of Criticism* 9:2 (Fall 1996), 223–44.

Decker, Christof, "Fighting for a Free World: Ben Shahn and the Art of the War Poster," *American Art* 33:2 (Summer 2019), 84–105.

Delphine, Hirasuna, *The Art of Gaman: Arts and Crafts from the Japanese Internment Camps, 1942–1946* (Ten Speed Press, 2005).

Gordon, Linda, and Gary Y. Okihiro, eds., *Impounded: Dorothea Lange and the Censored Images of Japanese American Internment* (New York: W.W. Norton and Company, 2006).

Hurlburt, Laurance P., "The Siqueiros Experimental Workshop: New York, 1936," *Art Journal* 35:3 (1976), 237–46.

Langa, Helen, "New York Visual Artists and the Spanish Civil War," in *Facing Fascism: New York and the Spanish Civil War,* eds. Peter N. Carroll and James D. Fernandez (New York: Museum of the City of New York and New York University Press, 2007), 102–19.

McCarthy, David, *American Artists Against War, 1935–2010* (Berkeley: University of California Press, 2015).

McCoy, Garnett, "The Rise and Fall of the American Artists' Congress," *Prospects* 13 (1988), 325–40.

McEuen, Melissa A., *Making War, Making Women: Femininity and Duty on the American Home Front, 1941–1945* (Athens and London: University of Georgia Press, 2011).

Monroe, Gerald, "The American Artists' Congress and the Invasion of Finland," *Archives of American Art Journal*, 15:1 (1975), 14–20.

Ott, John, "Battle Station MoMA: Jacob Lawrence and the Desegregation of the Armed Forces and the Art World," *American Art* 29:3 (Fall 2015), 58–89.

Owen, Robin Joyce, "Prints, Murals, and Radio Waves: Envisioning Networks in an Era of Rising Fascism" (PhD Dissertation, Institute of Fine Arts, New York University, 2023).

Speck, Catherine, *Beyond the Battlefield: Women Artists of the Two World Wars* (London: Reaktion Books, 2014).

Wang, ShiPu, "Japan Against Japan: U.S. Propaganda and Yasuo Kuniyoshi's Identity Crisis," *American Art* 22:1 (Spring 2008), 28–51.

Wang, ShiPu, ed. *Pictures of Belonging: Miki Hayakawa, Hisako Hibi, and Miné Okubo* (Oakland: University of California Press, 2024).

Whiting, Cécile, *Antifascism in American Art* (New Haven: Yale University Press, 1989).

Winkler, Allan M., *The Politics of Propaganda: The Office of War Information, 1942–1945* (New Haven: Yale University Press, 1978).

List of Illustrations

Abbreviations

AAA – Archives of American Art, Smithsonian Institution, Washington DC
AIC – Art Institute of Chicago
BMA – Baltimore Museum of Art
FSA/OWI – Farm Security Administration/Office of War Information
LoC – Library of Congress, Washington DC
MMA – Metropolitan Museum of Art, New York
MoMA – Museum of Modern Art, New York
NGA – National Gallery of Art, Washington DC
NYPL – New York Public Library
PMA – Philadelphia Museum of Art
SAAM – Smithsonian American Art Museum, Washington DC
WMA – Whitney Museum of American Art, New York

Unless otherwise noted, all Farm Security Administration and Office of War Information photographs in Chapter 5 are gelatin silver prints at the Library of Congress, Prints and Photographs Division, FSA/OWI Collection, and identified by reproduction number, e.g., LC-USF34-9058-C.

Post Office™ Murals reprinted with the permission of the United States Postal Service. All Rights Reserved. Written authorization from the Postal Service is required to use, reproduce, post, transmit, distribute, or publicly display these images.

1 Sol Lisbohn, *Philip Guston Working on Mural*, 1940. Photographic print, 20 × 26 (7⅞ × 10¼). AAA. Federal Art Project, Photographic Division collection, *c.* 1920–65, bulk 1935–42. Courtesy The Estate of Philip Guston and Hauser & Wirth
2 James N. Rosenberg, *October 29, Dies Irae*, 1929. Lithograph, 35.0 × 27 (13¾ × 10⅝). PMA. Purchased with the Lola Downin Peck Fund from the Carl and Laura Zigrosser Collection, 1981-115-188. © The estate of James N. Rosenberg
3 Clare Leighton, *Bread Line, New York*, 1932. Wood engraving, 30 × 20 (11¾ × 7⅞). NGA. Reba and Dave Williams Collection, Gift of Reba and Dave Williams, 2008.115.3119. © Estate of Clare Leighton. All Rights Reserved, DACS 2025
4 Margaret Bourke-White, *At the Time of the Louisville Flood*, 1937. Gelatin silver print. Photo Margaret Bourke-White/The LIFE Picture Collection/Shutterstock

(57¾ × 138¼). NYPL, Schomburg Center for Research in Black Culture
31 Aaron Douglas, *Aspects of Negro Life: Song of the Towers*, 1934. Public Works of Art Project. Oil on canvas, 240 × 223.5 (94.2 × 88). NYPL, Schomburg Center for Research in Black Culture
32 Maria and Julián Martínez (Pueblo), *Black-on-Black Bowl*, 1934–36. Ceramic, black matte pottery, 14.61 × 20.32 (5¾ × 8). Frances Lehman Loeb Art Center. Gift of Roberta Brown Rauch, class of 1932, 1990.25.3
33 Ray Strong, *Golden Gate Bridge*, 1934. Oil on canvas, 112 × 182.2 (44⅛ × 71¾). SAAM. Transfer from the US Department of the Interior, National Park Service, 1965.18.50. Photo SAAM/Art Resource/Scala, Florence
34 Lily Furedi, *Subway*, 1934. Oil on canvas, 99.1 × 122.6 (39 × 48¼). SAAM. Transfer from the US Department of the Interior, National Park Service, 1965.18.43. Photo SAAM/Art Resource/Scala, Florence
35 Tyrone Comfort, *Gold Is Where You Find It*, 1934. Oil on canvas, 101.9 × 127.3 (40⅛ × 50⅛). SAAM. Transfer from the US Department of the Interior, National Park Service, 1965.18.49. Photo SAAM/Art Resource/Scala, Florence
36 Maurice Glickman, *Negro Mother and Child*, 1934. Cast bronze, 182.9 × 122 × 50.8 (72 × 48 × 20). US Department of the Interior Courtyard. Courtesy National Archives, Public Works of Art Project (121-PWAP)
37 Isamu Noguchi, *Play Mountain*, 1933. Bronze, 8.6 × 73 × 64.1 (3⅜ × 28¾ × 25¼). Collection of The Isamu Noguchi Foundation and Garden Museum, New York. The Noguchi Museum Archives, 00023. Photo Bill Taylor. © The Isamu Noguchi Foundation and Garden Museum/ARS, New York and DACS, London 2025
38 Paul Cadmus, *The Fleet's In!*, 1934. Tempera on canvas, 94 × 170.2 (37 × 67). Courtesy Navy Art Collection, Naval History and Heritage Command, 34-005-A
39 Douglass Crockwell, *Paper Workers*, 1934. Oil on canvas, 122.4 × 91.7 (48¼ × 36⅛). SAAM. Transfer from the US Department of Labor, 1964.1.152. Photo SAAM/Art Resource/Scala, Florence
40 Louise Emerson Ronnebeck, *The Fertile Land Remembers*, 1938. Oil on canvas, 137.2 × 304.8 (54 × 120). Dick Cheney Federal Building, Casper, Wyoming. Commissioned through the Section of Fine Arts, 1934–43. Fine Arts Collection, US General Services Administration. Photo Carol M. Highsmith/Carol M. Highsmith Archive, LoC, Prints and Photographs Division

41 Joe Cox, *Study for Harvest (mural study, Alma, Michigan Post Office)*, 1939. Oil on fabric, 76.5 × 76.8 (30⅛ × 30¼). SAAM. Transfer from the General Services Administration, 1974.28.55. Photo SAAM/Art Resource/Scala, Florence
42 Isamu Noguchi, *The Letter*, 1939. Tymstone, 81.9 × 162.6 × 22.2 (32¼ × 64 × 8¾). US Post Office, 701 Station Ave, Haddon Heights, NJ. Photo The Noguchi Museum Archives, 152501/Kevin Noble. © The Isamu Noguchi Foundation and Garden Museum/ARS, New York and DACS, London 2025
43 Doris Lee, *Country Post*, 1938. Oil on canvas, 182.9 × 411.5 (72 × 162). William Jefferson Clinton Federal Building, Washington DC. Commissioned through the Section of Fine Arts, 1934–43. Fine Arts Collection, US General Services Administration. Photo Carol M. Highsmith/Carol M. Highsmith Archive, LoC, Prints and Photographs Division
44 Philip Guston, *Study for Early Mail Service and Construction of Railroads (mural study, Commerce, Georgia Post Office)*, 1938. Tempera on fiberboard, 30.5 × 66.1 (12 × 26). SAAM. Transfer from the Internal Revenue Service through the General Services Administration, 1962.8.77. Photo SAAM/Art Resource/Scala, Florence. Courtesy The Estate of Philip Guston and Hauser & Wirth
45 Edward Chávez, *Study for Building a Sod House*, 1941. Courtesy National Archives, Paintings and Sculptures Commissioned by the Section of Fine Arts, 1934–1943, 21-GA-9CHAV(2)4
46 Ward Lockwood, *Daniel Boone's Arrival in Kentucky*, 1938. Oil on canvas, 348 × 246.4 (137 × 97). US Post Office and US Courthouse, Lexington, Kentucky. Commissioned through the Section of Fine Arts, 1934–43. Fine Arts Collection, US General Services Administration. Photo Carol M. Highsmith/Carol M. Highsmith Archive, LoC, Prints and Photographs Division
47 Seymour Fogel, *Wealth of the Nation*, 1942. Buon fresco with secco additions, 292.1 × 442 (115 × 174). Wilbur J. Cohen Federal Building, Washington DC. Commissioned through the Section of Fine Arts, 1935–1943. Fine Arts Collection, US General Services Administration. Photo Carol M. Highsmith
48 Margaret Martin, *Study for Indian Hunters and Rice Gatherers (Study for St. James, Minnesota Post Office Mural)*, 1939. Oil on fiberboard, 42.6 × 92.9 (16¾ × 36⅝). SAAM. Transfer from the General Services Administration, 1985.8.20. Photo SAAM/Art Resource/Scala, Florence
49 Ethel V. Ashton, *Defenders of Wyoming Country–1778*, 1941. Oil on canvas. Tunkhannock

Post Office, Pennsylvania. Photo Michael
Mutmansky/David Lembeck
50 Concetta Maria Scaravaglione, *Agriculture*,
1938. Limestone, 208.3 × 365.8 (82 × 144).
Federal Trade Commission, Washington DC.
Commissioned through the Section of Fine Arts,
1935–1943. Fine Arts Collection, US General
Services Administration. Photo Carol M.
Highsmith/Carol M. Highsmith Archive, LoC,
Prints and Photographs Division
51 Louise Emerson Ronnebeck, *The Harvest*,
1940. Oil on canvas, 179.1 × 236.2 (70½ × 93).
Wayne N. Aspinall Federal Building and
US Courthouse, Grand Junction, Colorado.
Commissioned through the Section of Fine
Arts, 1934–43. Fine Arts Collection, US General
Services Administration. Photo Carol M.
Highsmith/Carol M. Highsmith Archive, LoC,
Prints and Photographs Division
52 Stephen Mopope (Kiowa), *Two Eagle Dancers*,
1936. Oil on plaster. Anadarko Post Office,
Oklahoma
53 Woodrow Crumbo (Citizen Potawatomi
Nation), *Study for Buffalo Hunt (color study for
mural, East Wall, Recreation Room, Department
of the Interior, Washington DC)*, 1939. Gouache,
50.8 × 66.2 (20 × 26⅛). SAAM. Transfer from the
US Department of the Interior, National Park
Service, 1965.18.2. Photo SAAM/Art Resource/
Scala, Florence
54 Gerald Nailor (Navajo), *Untitled (Tourists)*,
1937. Gouache, 35.6 × 32.4 (14 × 12¾). Courtesy
the Museum of Indian Arts and Culture, Santa Fe,
New Mexico. Dorothy Dunn Collection
55 Pablita Velarde (Pueblo), *Guard Turning
Tourists Away*, c. 1940. Casein paint, masonite,
20.5 × 37.8 (8 × 15). Courtesy National Park
Service, Museum Management Program and
Bandelier National Monument, BAND 653
56 Lowell Houser, *The Evolution of Corn*, 1938.
Oil on canvas, 175.3 × 553.7 (69 × 218). Ames
Post Office, Iowa. Photo courtesy Ames History
Museum
57 Joe Jones, *Study for Men and Wheat (mural
study, Seneca, Kansas Post Office)*, 1939. Oil on
canvas, 39.3 × 89.5 (15½ × 35¼). SAAM. Transfer
from the US Department of the Interior,
National Park Service, 1965.18.5. Photo SAAM/Art
Resource/Scala, Florence
58 William Sherrod McCall, *Early Settlers
Weighing Cotton*, 1938. Montevallo Post Office,
Alabama. Photo courtesy Birmingham Historical
Society, Birmingham, AL. Photo Jeff Tombrello
59 William Edouard Scott, *Frederick Douglass
Appealing to President Lincoln*, 1943. Recorder of

Deeds Building, Washington DC. Photo Carol M.
Highsmith/Carol M. Highsmith Archive, LoC,
Prints and Photographs Division
60 Earle Wilton Richardson, *Employment of
Negroes in Agriculture*, 1934. Oil on canvas, 121.8
× 81.6 (48 × 32⅛). SAAM. Transfer from the US
Department of Labor, 1964.1.183. Photo SAAM/Art
Resource/Scala, Florence
61 Harry Sternberg, *The Family, Industry, and
Agriculture*, 1939. Oil on canvas. Ambler Post
Office, Pennsylvania. Photo James Vaughan
62 Jared French, *Mealtime, The Early Coal Miners*,
1936–38. Oil and egg tempera on canvas, 48 × 126
(121.9 × 320). Plymouth Post Office, Pennsylvania.
Photo Michael Mutmansky/David Lembeck
63 Fletcher Martin, *Study for Mine Rescue (mural
study for Kellogg, Idaho Post Office)*, 1939. Tempera
on panel, 40.0 × 92.7 (15¾ × 36½). SAAM. Transfer
from the General Services Administration, 1974.28.
315. Photo SAAM/Art Resource/Scala, Florence
64 William Gropper, *Study for Construction of
a Dam (study for mural, the Department of the
Interior, Washington DC)*, 1938. Oil on canvas,
69.2 × 221.7 (27¼ × 87¼). SAAM. Transfer from
the US Department of the Interior, National Park
Service, 1965.18.11A-C. Photo SAAM/Art Resource/
Scala, Florence
65 Michael Lantz, *Man Controlling Trade*, 1942.
Limestone, 457.2 × 525.8 × 213.4 (180 × 207 × 84).
Federal Trade Commission Building, Washington
DC. Commissioned through the Section of
Fine Arts, 1934–43. Fine Arts Collection, US
General Services Administration. Photo Carol M.
Highsmith/The George F. Landegger Collection
of District of Columbia Photographs in Carol
M. Highsmith's America, LoC, Prints and
Photographs Division
66 Tom Lea, *Stampede*, 1940. Oil on canvas, 167.6
× 487.7 (66 × 192). Odessa Post Office, Texas.
Photo courtesy the Tom Lea Institute
67 Virginia Snedeker, cover illustration for *New
Yorker*, May 17, 1941. © The estate of Virginia
Snedeker
68 Ben Shahn, *The Meaning of Social Security:
Child Labor*, 1940–42. Fresco secco. Wilbur
J. Cohen Federal Building, Washington DC.
Commissioned through the Section of Fine
Arts, 1934–43. Fine Arts Collection, US General
Services Administration. Photo Carol M.
Highsmith/Carol M. Highsmith Archive, LoC,
Prints and Photographs Division
69 Ben Shahn, *The Meaning of Social Security:
Unemployment*, 1940–42. Fresco secco. Wilbur
J. Cohen Federal Building, Washington DC.
Commissioned through the Section of Fine

Arts, 1934–43. Fine Arts Collection, US General Services Administration. Photo Carol M. Highsmith/Carol M. Highsmith Archive, LoC, Prints and Photographs Division

70 Alice Neel, *Investigation of Poverty at the Russell Sage Foundation*, 1933. Oil on canvas, 61.3 × 76.5 (24⅛ × 30⅛). Pennsylvania Academy of the Fine Arts. Art by Women Collection, Gift of Linda Lee Alter, 2010.27.2. © The Estate of Alice Neel. Courtesy The Estate of Alice Neel and David Zwirner

71 Charles Turzak, *Work Relief (Chicago Snowstorm)*, 1935–42. Woodcut, 20.8 × 29.4 (8¼ × 11⅝). AIC. WPA Allocation, 1943.1735. Photo AIC/Art Resource, NY/Scala, Florence

72 Mark Rothko, *Untitled (The Subway)*, 1937. Oil on canvas, 61 × 91.4 (24 × 36). New-York Historical Society. Promised gift of Elie and Sarah Hirschfeld, Scenes of New York City, IL2021.51.80

73 Anthony Velonis, designer, *The WPA Federal Theatre Negro Unit [presents] Macbeth by William Shakespeare*, c. 1936. Screenprint, 55.8 × 35.5 (22 × 14). LoC, Work Progress Administration Poster Collection

74 Employment and Activities poster for the WPA's Federal Art Project, 1936. AAA. Federal Art Project, Photographic Division collection, c. 1920–1965, bulk 1935–1942

75 Lucienne Bloch, *Cycle of a Woman's Life: Childhood*, 1935. Lost mural, original location Woman's House of Detention, Greenwich Village, New York. Photo Nickolas Murray. © Lucienne Allen

76 Walter Quirt, *Study for The Growth of Medicine from Primitive Times*, c. 1935–43. Colored pencil and ink, 50.8 × 107.63 (20 × 42⅜). Courtesy Krannert Art Museum, University of Illinois Urbana-Champaign, 1943-4-354. Allocated by the US Government, commissioned through the New Deal Art projects

77 Georgette Seabrooke, *Recreation in Harlem*, 1936. Oil on plaster wall. Harlem Hospital Center, New York

78 Georgette Seabrooke working on her WPA mural *Recreation in Harlem*, 1936. Photo GBM Historical Images/Shutterstock

79 Eitaro Ishigaki working on *Emancipation of Negro Slaves*, c. 1936. NYPL, Schomburg Center for Research in Black Culture, Photographs and Prints Division, Works Progress Administration Collection

80 Charles White working on *Struggle for Liberation*, c. 1940. Chicago Public Library, Special Collections, Works Progress Administration. Federal Art Project. Illinois Art Project Collection, Photograph 132

81 Arshile Gorky, *Aerial Map* (from *Aviation: Evolution of Forms under Aerodynamic Limitations*), 1935–37. Oil on canvas, 200.7 × 313.7 (79 × 123½). The Port Authority of New York and New Jersey, on loan to the Newark Museum of Art

82 Alexander Alland, *Spirit of Newark*, 1938. Gelatin silver print photomontage, 19.5 × 11.2 (7¾ × 4½). Harvard Art Museums/Fogg Museum. Gift of Bernarda Bryson Shahn, by exchange, P2000.34.2. Photo President and Fellows of Harvard College

83 Stuart Davis, *Swing Landscape*, 1937–38. Oil on canvas, 224.8 × 443.9 (86¾ × 173⅛). Eskenazi Museum of Art, Indiana University. Allocated by the US Government, Commissioned through the New Deal Art Projects

84 Bumpei Usui, *Dahlias*, 1938. Oil on canvas, 76.7 × 61.6 (30¼ × 24¼). SAAM. Transfer from General Services Administration, 1971.447.90. Photo SAAM/Art Resource/Scala, Florence

85 Loren MacIver, *Dune Landscape*, c. 1936. Oil on canvas, 61.3 × 38.4 (24⅛ × 15⅛). Sheldon Museum of Art, University of Nebraska–Lincoln. Allocation of the US Government, Federal Art Project of the Works Progress Administration, WPA-112.1943

86 Jackson Pollock, *Cotton Pickers*, c. 1935. Oil on canvas, 61 × 76.2 (24 × 30). Buffalo AKG Art Museum. The Martha Jackson Collection at the Buffalo AKG Art Museum, 1974. 1974.8.29. Photo Buffalo AKG Art Museum/Art Resource, NY/Scala, Florence

87 Jackson Pollock, *Untitled*, c. 1938–41. Mosaic tesserae in cement with braced wooden frame, 137.2 × 68.6 (54 × 27). Private collection. © The Pollock-Krasner Foundation ARS, NY and DACS, London 2025

88 Samuel Joseph Brown, Jr., *Mrs. Simmons*, c. 1936. Watercolor and pencil, 75.9 × 52.6 (29⅞ × 20¾). SAAM. Transfer from General Services Administration, 1971.447.14. Photo SAAM/Art Resource/Scala, Florence

89 Samuel Joseph Brown, Jr., *The Lynching*, c. 1935. Watercolor over graphite, 77.5 × 52.1 (30½ × 20½). Public Works of Art Project, on long-term loan to the PMA from the Fine Arts Collection, US General Services Administration, 1934, 36-1934-5

90 Jack Levine, *The Feast of Pure Reason*, 1937. Oil on canvas, 106.7 × 121.9 (42 × 48). Extended loan from the United States WPA Art Program to MoMA, New York. Photo MoMA, New York/Scala, Florence

91 O. Louis Guglielmi, *One Third of a Nation*, 1939. Oil and tempera on wood, 76.2 × 61 (30 × 24). MMA. Gift of New York City WPA, 1943. 43.47.10

92 Gertrude Abercrombie, *White Cat*, c. 1935–38. Oil on canvas, 91.5 × 76.5 (36 × 30⅛). SAAM. Transfer from General Services Administration, 1971.447.1. Photo SAAM/Art Resource/Scala, Florence

93 Josephine Joy, *CCC Camp Balboa Park*, c. 1933–37. Oil on canvas, 45.9 × 61.2 (18⅛ × 24⅛). SAAM. Transfer from General Services Administration, 1971.447.41

94 Pedro Cervántez, *Los Privados*, 1937. Oil on fiberboard, 37.5 × 50.2 (14¾ × 19¾). SAAM. Transfer from the General Services Administration, 1985.65.13. Photo SAAM/Art Resource/Scala, Florence

95 Patrociño Barela, *Saint George*, c. 1935–43. Carved juniper, 43.2 × 26.7 × 14.6 (17 × 10½ × 5¾). SAAM. Transfer from the General Services Administration, 1985.65.1. Photo SAAM/Art Resource/Scala, Florence

96 William Edmondson, *Preacher*, c. 1940. Limestone, 45.4 (17⅞). McClung Museum of Natural History and Culture, University of Tennessee. Acquired through US Works Progress Administration (WPA), Federal Arts Project, 1941. 1993.9.1

97 Donal Hord, *Guardian of the Water*, 1939. Granite. San Diego County Administration Center. Photo Max Herman/Alamy Stock Photo

98 Sargent Claude Johnson, *Organ Screen*, 1933–34. Carved, gilded and painted redwood, 274.3 × 365.8 (108 × 144). The Huntington Library, Art Museum, and Botanical Gardens. Purchased with funds from the Art Collectors' Council, the Connie Perkins Endowment, and the Virginia Steele Scott Acquisition Fund for American Art in honor of George Abdo and Roy Ritchie. Photo The Huntington Library, Art Museum, and Botanical Gardens/Bridgeman Images

99 Fred Becker, *John Henry's Hand*, 1935–39. Wood engraving, 15 × 11 (5⅞ × 4⅜). Harvard Art Museums/Fogg Museum, Deknatel Purchase Fund, M22382. Photo President and Fellows of Harvard College

100 Jacob Kainen, *Wood-Block Printer*, 1940. Lithograph on paper, 31.5 × 40.6 (12⅜ × 16). SAAM. Gift of the artist, 1966.69.14. Photo SAAM/Art Resource/Scala, Florence

101 Blanche Lazzell, *My Wharf Studio*, 1937. Color woodcut, 36.83 × 31.75 (14½ × 12½). LoC, Prints and Photographs Division

102 Eli Jacobi, *All Night Mission*, 1936. Linoleum cut, 25.3 × 20.1 (10 × 8). Private collection

103 left Lynd Ward, plate from *Prelude to a Million Years*, 1933. Wood engraving. Vassar College Archives and Special Collections Library. © 1933, 1961 by Lynd Ward

103 right Lynd Ward, plate from *Prelude to a Million Years*, 1933. Wood engraving. PMA. Purchased with the Lola Downin Peck Fund from the Carl and Laura Zigrosser Collection, 1974, 1974-24-234. © 1933, 1961 by Lynd Ward

104 Hughie Lee-Smith, *The Artist's Life, No. 1*, 1939. Lithograph, 27.9 × 21.6 (11 × 8½). MMA. Gift of Reba and Dave Williams, 1999, 1999.529.112. Photo MMA/Art Resource/Scala, Florence

105 Leo J. Meissner, *Civilization AD 1935*, 1935. Wood engraving, 27.3 × 21.1 (10¾ × 8⅜). PMA. Gift of Fern and Hersh Cohen, 2015, 2015-197-111. © The estate of Leo J. Meissner

106 Federal Theatre Project, "Front Page Highlights of 1935," The Living Newspaper, 1935. Screenprint. Hallie Flanagan Papers, Vassar Archives and Special Collections Library. Photo Sharyn Cadogan.

107 Lucienne Bloch, *Land of Plenty*, 1936. Woodcut, 27 × 22.2 (10⅝ × 8¾). NGA. Reba and Dave Williams Collection, Gift of Reba and Dave Williams, 2008.115.944. © Lucienne Allen

108 Luis Arenal, *Distribution of Land*, 1937. Wood engraving, 23.5 × 31.1 (9¼ × 12¼). MMA. Gift of the Work Projects Administration, New York, 1943. 43.33.774

109 Nan Lurie, *Technological Improvements*, 1937. Lithograph, 45.7 × 30.1 (18 × 11⅞). NYPL. The Miriam and Ira D. Wallach Division of Art, Prints and Photographs: Print Collection

110 Blanche Grambs, *Design Steel*, 1937. Etching and aquatint, 35.5 × 27.5 (14 × 10⅞). NGA. Reba and Dave Williams Collection, Gift of Reba and Dave Williams. 2008.115.2217

111 Lewis Rubenstein, *Foundry*, c. 1938. Color lithograph, 52.4 × 37.1 (20⅝ × 14⅝). Photo courtesy Heritage Auctions

112 Dox Thrash, *Mary Lou* (or *Marylou*), c. 1939–40. Carborundum mezzotint, 25.2 × 17.5 (10 × 6⅞). PMA. Gift of E. M. Benson, 1942-86-3. Published by Works Progress Administration (WPA), Federal Art Project, Philadelphia (1935–1943)

113 Fay Chong, *At the Weird Pool*, 1938. Color linoleum cut, 12.8 × 14 (5⅛ × 5½). Sheldon Museum of Art, University of Nebraska–Lincoln. Allocation of the US Government, Federal Art Project of the Works Progress Administration, WPA-334.1943

114 Julius Twohy (Ute), *Blessed Pony*, c. 1939. Lithograph, 36.2 × 43.5 (14¼ × 17⅛). PMA.

Purchased with the Thomas Skelton Harrison Fund, 1942-30-115

115 Helen Lundeberg, *Enigma*, 1937. Lithograph, 40.6 × 29.2 (16 × 11½). PMA. Federal Works Agency, Work Projects Administration, on long-term loan to the PMA from the Fine Arts Collection, US General Services Administration, 1943, 2-1943-59

116 Jean Finlayson Holmes, *Ether*, 1941. Crayon lithograph, 35.1 × 25.5 (13⅞ × 10⅛). The United States General Services Administration, formerly Federal Works Agency, Works Progress Administration, on extended loan to the BMA, L.1943.9.807

117 Chet La More, *Ku Kluxers*, 1939. Color lithograph, 23.5 × 31.8 (9¼ × 12½). PMA. Gift of John W. Ittmann, 2021, 2021-100-8. Published by Works Progress Administration (WPA), Federal Art Project, New York City (1935–1943)

118 Miné Okubo, *Abstraction*, c. 1935–43. Screenprint, 44.6 × 50.5 (17⅝ × 19⅞). MoMA. Extended loan from the United States WPA Art Program. Fine Arts Collection, Public Buildings Service, General Services Administration, EL1957.982. Photo MoMA, New York/Scala, Florence

119 Elizabeth Olds, *Summer People*, c. 1938–39. Screenprint, 24.4 × 44.1 (9⅝ × 17⅜). PMA. Gift of the artist, 1941, 1941-95-1

120 Elizabeth Olds, *Mending Nets*, 1935–42. Wood engraving, 20.3 × 27.6 (8 × 10⅞). Detroit Institute of Arts. Gift of the Works Progress Administration, Federal Art Project, 43.304

121 *Keep Your Teeth Clean*, 1938. Screenprint, 55.8 × 35.3 (22 × 14). Federal Art Project, 1936–38. LoC. Work Projects Administration Poster Collection, Prints and Photographs Division

122 John Wagner, *Don't Kill Our Wild Life*, 1940. Screenprint. Works Progress Administration, Federal Art Project, 1936–40. LoC. Work Projects Administration Poster Collection, Prints and Photographs Division

123 Lester Beall, *Radio*, 1937. Screenprint, 101.6 × 76.5 (40 × 30⅛). Rural Electrification Administration. Collection Merrill C. Berman. Photo Jolie Simpson

124 Bernarda Bryson Shahn, *Cut-Over Land*, 1936. Lithograph, 24.4 × 31.8 (9⅝ × 12½). NGA. Reba and Dave Williams Collection, Gift of Reba and Dave Williams, 2008.115.4356

125 Dorothea Lange, *Migrant Agricultural Worker's Family. Seven hungry children. Mother aged thirty-two. Father is native Californian. Nipomo, California*, 1936. LC-USF34-009098

126 Dorothea Lange, *Migrant Mother, Nipomo, California*, 1936. Gelatin silver print. Frances Lehman Loeb Art Center, Vassar College. Purchase, Horace W. Goldsmith Foundation Fund, 1997.14

127 Arthur Rothstein, *Dr. Rexford Tugwell Confers with Farmer on Lawn of Courthouse. Springfield, Colorado*, 1936. LC-USF34-005243-E

128 Russell Lee, *The Hands of Mrs. Andrew Ostermeyer, Wife of a Homesteader, Woodbury County, Iowa*, 1936. NYPL, The Miriam and Ira D. Wallach Division of Art, Prints and Photographs: Photography Collection, 011121-M1 c.2

129 Marion Post Wolcott, *Mountaineer and Marion Post Wolcott Changing a Tire with a Fencepost as a Jack. Up South Fork of the Kentucky River*, 1940. LC-USF33-031080-M5

130 Walker Evans, *Negro House, Tupelo, Mississippi*, 1936. LC-USF342-008019-A

131 Ben Shahn, *Scotts Run, West Virginia, Miner's Sons*, 1935. LC-USF33-006014-M2

132 Ben Shahn, *A Deputy with a Gun on his Hip during the September 1935 Strike in Morgantown, West Virginia*, 1935. NYPL, The Miriam and Ira D. Wallach Division of Art, Prints and Photographs: Photography Collection, 006121-M3 c.3

133 Arthur Rothstein, *Farmer and Sons walking in the face of a dust storm, Cimarron County, Oklahoma*, 1936. LC-USZ62-11491

134 Dorothea Lange, *Hitch-hiking from Joplin, Missouri, to a sawmill job in Arizona. On US 66 near Weatherford, western Oklahoma*, 1938. NGA. Gift of Daniel Greenberg and Susan Steinhauser, 2016.191.75

135 Dorothea Lange, *Filipinos Cutting Lettuce, Salinas Valley, California*, 1935. LC-USF347-000826-D

136 Dorothea Lange's photograph *Ex-tenant farmer on relief grant in the Imperial Valley, California*, 1937, as featured in "Dust Bowl Farmer Is New Pioneer," *Life*, 21 June 1937

137 Dorothea Lange, *Plantation Overseer and his Field Hands, Mississippi Delta*, 1936. AIC. Purchased with funds provided by Vicki and Thomas Horwich, 2016.341

138 Marion Post Wolcott, *Man Entering a Theater, Belzoni, Mississippi*, 1939. LC-USF33-030577-M2

139 Marion Post Wolcott, *Jitterbugging in Negro Juke Joint, Saturday Evening, Outside Clarksdale, Mississippi*, November 1939. LC-USF34-052594-D

140 Marion Post Wolcott, *Miner Takes Shower, which he Built in the Cellar of his Home. Westover, West Virginia*, 1938. LC-USF34-050289-E

141 Marion Post Wolcott, *June in January, Miami Beach, Florida*, 1939. LC-USF33-030493-M3

Roosevelt in July 1945, at its first public showing. Photo Bettmann/Getty Images
172 Jacob Lawrence, *Blind Beggars*, 1938. Tempera on illustration board, 51.1 × 38.1 (20⅛ × 15). MMA. Gift of New York City WPA, 1943. 43.47.28. Photo MMA/Art Resource/Scala, Florence
173 Robert Blackburn, *People in a Boat, c.* 1937–39. Lithograph, 38.7 × 50.2 (15¼ × 19¾). MMA. Gift of Reba and Dave Williams, 1999.529.9. © The Trust for Robert Blackburn. Used with permission
174 Romare Bearden, *Marching Along Together*, illustration from *The Crisis*, March 1935. © Romare Bearden Foundation/VAGA at ARS, NY and DACS, London 2025
175 Norman Lewis, *The Soup Kitchen, c.* 1937. Lithograph, 39.4 × 28.6 (15½ × 11¼). MMA. Gift of Reba and Dave Williams, 1999.529.118. Photo MMA/Art Resource/Scala, Florence. © Estate of Norman Lewis, Courtesy Michael Rosenfeld Gallery LLC, New York, NY
176 Philip Evergood, *The Pink Dismissal Slip*, 1937. Oil on hardboard, 71 × 56 (28 × 22½). Herbert F. Johnson Museum of Art, Cornell University. Gift of Harry N. Abrams, 57.409. Image courtesy the Johnson Museum. © 2024 Courtesy ACA Galleries, New York
177 Harry Sternberg, *Coal Miner and Family*, 1938. Oil on canvas, 61.0 × 121.9 (24 × 48). Collection of Bram and Sandra Dijkstra. Courtesy the Estate of Harry Sternberg and Susan Teller Gallery, New York, NY
178 Alice Neel, *Kenneth Fearing*, 1935. Oil on canvas, 76.5 × 66 (30⅛ × 26). MoMA. Gift of Hartley S. Neel and Richard Neel, 28.1988. Photo MoMA/Scala, Florence. © The Estate of Alice Neel. Courtesy The Estate of Alice Neel and David Zwirner
179 Joe Jones, *Demonstration*, 1934. Oil on masonite, 122.24 × 183.2 (48⅛ × 72⅛). Private collection. Courtesy Hirschl & Adler Galleries, New York. Photo Eric Baumgartner. © The estate of Joe Jones
180 Stuart Davis, Cover of *Art Front*, May 1935. Beinecke Rare Book and Manuscript Library, New Haven, Connecticut, 1993 Folio S1. © Estate of Stuart Davis/VAGA at ARS, NY and DACS, London 2025
181 Ben Shahn, Untitled (Artists' Union demonstrators, Division IX, May Day Parade, Communist Party route, Twenty-fifth Street between Fifth and Sixth Avenues, New York City), May 1, 1935. Harvard Art Museums/Fogg Museum. Gift of Bernarda Bryson Shahn,

P1970.4003. Photo © President and Fellows of Harvard College
182 Kyra Markham, *Lockout*, 1937. Lithograph, 25.5 × 30.7 (10 × 12). NGA. Reba and Dave Williams Collection, Gift of Reba and Dave Williams, 2008.115.3348. © The estate of Kyra Markham
183 Herman Volz, *Lockout, c.* 1937. Lithograph, 26.7 × 39.1 (10½ × 15⅜). PMA. Purchased with the Lola Downin Peck Fund from the Carl and Laura Zigrosser Collection, 1982-10-517
184 LeRoy Flint, *Strikebreakers*, 1937. Etching, 15.2 × 20.3 (6 × 8). PMA. Purchased with the Lola Downin Peck Fund from the Carl and Laura Zigrosser Collection, 1982-10-541(24). © The estate of LeRoy Walter Flint
185 Joseph Vavak, *Women of Flint*, 1937. Oil on canvas, 63.5 × 91.3 (25 × 36). SAAM. Transfer from General Services Administration, 1971.447.92. Photo SAAM/Art Resource/Scala, Florence
186 Harry Gottlieb, *The Strike is Won*, 1940. Silkscreen, 48 × 64 (19 × 25). Private collection. Courtesy the estate of Harry Gottlieb
187 Aaron Goodelman, *Homeless*, 1936. Cast concrete, 44.4 × 40.6 × 38.1 (17½ × 16 × 15). Roberson Museum and Science Center, 1978R7
188 William Gropper, *Study for Automobile Industry (mural study, Detroit, Michigan Post Office)*, 1940–41. Oil on fiberboard, 48.0 × 118.4 (18⅞ × 46⅝). SAAM. Museum acquisition, 1971.2. Photo SAAM/Art Resource/Scala, Florence
189 Hugo Gellert, *Primary Accumulation 3 (Secret of Primary Accumulation)*, 1933. Offset lithograph, 34.6 × 32.1 (13⅝ × 12⅝). PMA. Gift of Mr and Mrs Michael Egnal, 1967, 1967-232-1(3). © Hugo Gellert; courtesy Mary Ryan Gallery, New York
190 Harold Lehman, *Railroad Repair*, 1943. Oil on canvas. Renovo Post Office, Pennsylvania. Photo Michael Mutmansky/David Lembeck
191 Elizabeth Olds, *Bootleg Mining, Pennsylvania*, 1936. Lithograph, 25 × 35.3 (9⅞ × 14). NGA. Reba and Dave Williams Collection, 2008.115.3787. © Harry Ransom Center, The University of Texas at Austin
192 Harry Gottlieb, *Bootleg Mining, c.* 1937–38. Color lithograph, 35.2 × 45.4 (13⅞ × 17⅞). Amon Carter Museum of American Art, Fort Worth, Texas, 1998.62. Courtesy the estate of Harry Gottlieb
193 John Langley Howard, *The Union Meeting*, 1936. Lithograph, 25.3 × 36 (10 × 14). NGA. Reba and Dave Williams Collection, Gift of Reba and Dave Williams. 2008.115.2601.
194 Elizabeth Olds, Study for porcelain enamel mural, reproduced in *Subway Art*, MoMA, 1938. © Harry Ransom Center, The University of Texas at Austin

195 Louis Lozowick, *Night Repairs*, 1939. Color lithograph, 29.8 × 22.2 (11¾ × 8¾). Published by The Work Progress Administration. MMA. Gift of the Work Projects Administration, New York, 1943, 43.33.1181

196 Ida Abelman, *My Father Reminisces*, 1937. Lithograph, 38.1 × 46.7 (15 × 18⅜). Published by Works Progress Administration (WPA), Federal Art Project (1935–1943). PMA, Purchased with the Thomas Skelton Harrison Fund, 1942, 1942-30-1

197 Riva Helfond, *Custom Made*, 1939. Lithograph, 33 × 24.1 (13 × 9½). NGA. Reba and Dave William Collection, Gift of Reba and Dave Williams, 2008.115.2442. Courtesy the Estate of Riva Helfond and Susan Teller Gallery, New York

198 Boris Gorelick, *Sweat Shop*, c. 1938. Lithograph, 30.2 × 39.4 (11⅞ × 15½). PMA. Federal Works Agency, Work Projects Administration, on long-term loan to the PMA from the Fine Arts Collection, US General Services Administration, 1943. 3-1943-461

199 Elizabeth Olds, *Burlesque*, 1936. Lithograph, 36.8 × 27.4 (14½ × 10⅞). Published by Works Progress Administration (WPA), Federal Art Project (1935–1943). PMA. Purchased with the Lola Downin Peck Fund from the Carl and Laura Zigrosser Collection, 1981, 1981-115-129

200 Louis Lozowick, *Strike Scene*, 1935. Lithograph, 27.9 x 22.9 (11 × 9). SAAM. Gift of Adele Lozowick, 1984.132.27. Photo SAAM/Art Resource/Scala, Florence. © Louis Lozowick; courtesy the estate of the artist and Mary Ryan Gallery, New York

201 James Meikle Guy, *Workers*, 1938. Screenprint, 51 × 33 (20 × 13). The Wolfsonian-Florida International University, Miami, Florida. The Mitchell Wolfson Jr Collection. Published with the permission of The Wolfsonian – Florida International University, Miami, Florida. Photo Lynton Gardiner. © The estate of James Meikle Guy

202 Charles White, *Untitled (Four Workers)*, 1940. Tempera on paperboard, 50.8 × 76.2 (20 × 30). Private collection. © The Charles White Archives

203 William Gropper, "Artists—Stop Those Cuts," *Art Front*, June–July 1937. AAA. Courtesy Craig Gropper

204 Joe Jones, *Self-Portrait: A Worker Again on WPA*, c. 1935. Oil on canvas, 68.6 × 83.8 (27 × 33). From the Collections of the St Louis Mercantile Library at the University of Missouri, St Louis; courtesy the Feldacker Labor Art Collection

205 "Complete Text of Federal Arts Bill," *Art Front*, October 1937. AAA

206 William Gropper, *The Senate*, 1935. Oil on canvas, 63.8 × 84.2 (25⅛ × 33⅛). MoMA. Gift of A. Conger Goodyear, 108.1936. Photo MoMA, New York/Scala, Florence. Courtesy Craig Gropper

207 Mischa Richter, *First Objective*, 1939. Published in *New Masses*, January 24, 1939. Courtesy Dan Richter. © Mischa Richter

208 Joseph Binder, *New York World's Fair, The World of Tomorrow*, 1939. Lithograph, 129.5 × 88.9 (51 × 35). Courtesy Swann Auctions. © designaustria

209 David Robbins, Philip Guston working on *Maintaining America's Skills*, 1939. AAA. Federal Art Project, Photographic Division collection, c. 1920–1965, bulk 1935–1942. Courtesy The Estate of Philip Guston and Hauser & Wirth

210 Anton Refregier, *Study for Cultural Activities of the WPA*, detail, 1939. Graphite, 57.2 × 46.4 (22½ × 18¼). The Wolfsonian–Florida International University, Miami Beach, Florida, The Mitchell Wolfson, Jr Collection, TD1992.157.8. Published with the permission of The Wolfsonian – Florida International University. Photo Lynton Gardiner

211 Berenice Abbott, *Rockefeller Center*, 1932. Gelatin silver print, 29.4 × 23.8 (11⅝ × 9⅜). PMA. 125th Anniversary Acquisition. The Lynne and Harold Honickman Gift of the Julien Levy Collection, 2001, 2001-62-9. Photo © Berenice Abbott/Getty Images

212 Berenice Abbott, *Gunsmith and Police Department, 6 Centre Market Place*, 1937. Gelatin silver print, 20.3 × 25.4 (8 × 10). Federal Art Project. NYPL. The Miriam and Ira D. Wallach Division of Art, Prints and Photographs: Photography Collection

213 Robert Gwathmey, *The Hitchhiker*, 1936. Oil on panel, 76.2 × 91.4 (30 × 36). Brooklyn Museum, New York. Gift of David Teichman, 57.46. Photo Brooklyn Museum/Bridgeman Images. © Estate of Robert Gwathmey/VAGA at ARS, NY and DACS, London 2025

214 Augusta Savage, *Lift Every Voice and Sing (The Harp)*, 1939. Beinecke Rare Book and Manuscript Library. Gift of Carl Van Vechten and Fania Marinoff, 1941–71, JWJ MSS 1050. Photo Carl Van Vechten

215 Mitchell Siporin, *The Civil War*, 1942. Tempera. St Louis Post Office, Missouri

216 William Gropper, *Untitled*, from *12 Cartoons Defending WPA by members of the American Artists Congress*, 1939. Courtesy Craig Gropper

217 Ad Reinhardt, "It Can Happen Here," cover of *New York Artist*, August 1940. AAA. © Anna Reinhardt/Artists Rights Society (ARS), New York and DACS, London 2025

218 Mabel Dwight, *Danse Macabre (Dance of Death)*, 1933. Lithograph, 24.1 × 34.6 (9½ × 13⅝). PMA. Purchased with the Thomas Skelton Harrison Fund, 1942, 1942-30-143. © The estate of Mabel Dwight
219 Carlos Anderson, *Day's End*, 1939. Opaque watercolor, 91.5 × 66 (36 × 26). SAAM. Gift of Serene and Claire Puglisi, 1977.115. Photo SAAM/Art Resource/Scala, Florence. © The estate of Carlos Anderson
220 Florence Kent, *Jewish Refugees*, c. 1939. Lithograph, 25.1 × 30.5 (9⅞ × 12). Federal Works Agency, Work Projects Administration, on long-term loan to the PMA from the Fine Arts Collection, US General Services Administration, 1943, 3-1943-574
221 Romare Bearden, *Giving Him Some Fresh Ideas: Nazi Persecution of Jews and Negroes*, from *The Crisis*, June 1934. © Romare Bearden Foundation/VAGA at ARS, NY and DACS, London 2025
222 David Alfaro Siqueiros, *Militant*, 1936. Lithograph, 30.3 × 22.2 (12 × 8¾). PMA. Purchased with the Thomas Skelton Harrison Fund, 1963. 1963-208-21. Siqueiros © DACS 2025
223 Maurice Merlin, *Black Legion Widow*, 1936. Linocut reproduced in *America Today*, 1936
224 Hugo Gellert, *Pieces of Silver*, c. 1935. Lithograph, 32 × 28.5 (12⅝ × 11¼). Yale University Art Gallery, New Haven, Connecticut. Gift of Judith and Norman Zlotsky, B.S. 1953, 2006.93.6. © Hugo Gellert; courtesy Mary Ryan Gallery, New York
225 Philip Guston, *Bombardment*, 1937–38. Oil on masonite, diameter 106.7 (42). PMA. Gift of Musa and Tom Mayer, 2011. © The Estate of Philip Guston, courtesy Hauser & Wirth
226 Joseph Vogel, *The Innocents*, c. 1937–39. Lithograph printed in black ink on wove paper, 35.6 × 29.2 (14 × 11½). Detroit Institute of Art. Gift of the Works Progress Administration, Federal Art Project, 43.384
227 Chet La More, *Civilians*, c. 1938. Lithograph, 25.7 × 35.9 (10⅛ × 14⅛). Federal Works Agency, Work Projects Administration, on long-term loan to the PMA from the Fine Arts Collection, US General Services Administration, 1943, 3-1943-599
228 Edward Hagedorn, *Soldiers in Gas Masks*, c. 1939. Relief print, 25.4 × 18.1 (10 × 7⅛). Federal Works Agency, Work Projects Administration, on long-term loan to the PMA from the Fine Arts Collection, US General Services Administration, 1943, 3-1943-496
229 Charles Surendorf, *God Comes Down to Inspect his Creations*, late 1930s. Linocut,
23.7 × 30.6 (9 × 12). NGA. Reba and Dave Williams Collection, Gift of Reba and Dave Williams, 2008.115.4680. Courtesy Charles Surendorf II Art Foundation
230 David Smith, *Bombing Civilian Populations (Medals for Dishonor)*, 1939. Cast bronze, 25.4 × 25.4 (10 × 10). Harvard Art Museums/Fogg Museum. Gift of The Estate of David Smith, New York, 2023.472. Photo President and Fellows of Harvard College. © Estate of David Smith/VAGA at ARS, NY and DACS, London 2025
231 Boris Artzybasheff, *Art Week/Buy American Art*, c. 1940. W.P.A. Art Project, NYC. Screenprint, 58.5 × 46.5 (23 × 18¼). Private collection. Courtesy Swann Auction Galleries
232 Willem de Kooning, *Legend and Fact*, 1940. Duco enamel on gypsum board (marinite), overall (four separate panels combined) 152.4 × 483.7 (60 × 190½). NGA. Transferred from the Department of Commerce, Maritime Commission, 1971.52.1.a-d
233 Patrociño Barela, *War*, 1942. Carved and stained pine, 28.8 × 180.4 × 3.2 (11⅜ × 71 × 1¼). SAAM, Transfer from the General Services Administration, 1985.65.9. Photo SAAM/Art Resource/Scala, Florence
234 Charles White, *Soldier*, 1944. Tempera on masonite, 76.2 × 63.5 (30 × 25). The Huntington Library, Art Museum, and Botanical Gardens. Gift of Sandra and Bram Dijkstra, 2013.23. Photo Bridgeman Images. © The Charles White Archives
235 Jacob Lawrence, *Painting the Bilges*, 1944. Opaque paint and pencil on paper, 75.5 × 54.6 (29¾ × 21½). Hirshhorn Museum and Sculpture Garden, Smithsonian Institution, Washington DC. The Joseph H. Hirshhorn Bequest, 1981. Photo Lee Stalsworth. © The Jacob and Gwendolyn Knight Lawrence Foundation, Seattle/Artists Rights Society (ARS), New York and DACS, London 2025
236 Alfred T. Palmer, Woman working on an airplane motor at North American Aviation Inc. plant in Inglewood, June 1942. LoC, Prints and Photographs Division, FSA/OWI Photography Collection, LC-USW36-142
237 Arthur Rothstein, Photomural to promote the sales of defense bonds, 1941, designed by Farm Security Administration, in concourse of Grand Central terminal. LoC, Prints and Photographs Division, FSA/OWI Photography Collection, LC-USF34- 024493-D. Photo Arthur Rothstein
238 Glenn Grohe, *He's Watching You*, 1942. Published by the US Government Printing

Office. Screenprint, 101 × 72 (40 × 28). Courtesy Northwestern University Libraries

239 Yasuo Kuniyoshi, *Torture*, 1942. Graphite, 101.6 × 72.4 (40 × 28½). Collection of John Cassara

240 Ben Shahn, *We Fight for a Free World!*, c. 1942. Gouache and tempera on board, 34.3 × 75.6 (13 × 29). Courtesy Michael Rosenfeld Gallery LLC, New York, NY. © Estate of Ben Shahn/VAGA at ARS, NY and DACS, London 2025

241 Dorothea Lange, *One Nation Indivisible, San Francisco*, 1942. Gelatin silver print. NGA. Gift of Daniel Greenberg and Susan Steinhauser, 2016.191.17

242 Tōyō Miyatake, *Watchtower*, c. 1943. Gelatin silver print, 23.8 × 18.7 (9⅜ × 7 ⅜). Courtesy Toyo Miyatake Studio

243 Miné Okubo, *Wind and Dust*, 1943. Opaque watercolor on paperboard, 58.7 × 74 (23⅛ × 29⅛). SAAM. Museum purchase through the Luisita L. and Franz H. Denghausen Endowment, 2023.46.3. Photo SAAM/Art Resource/Scala, Florence. Courtesy the Miné Okubo Charitable Corporation

244 Edna Reindel, *Riveter at Lockheed*, 1942. Oil on canvas, 71.1 × 101.6 (28 × 40). National Museum of Women in the Arts. Gift of the artist © 1942 Edna Reindel

245 "End of WPA Art," *Life*, 17 April 1944. © The estate of Elizabeth Timberman

246 Anton Refregier, *1916, Preparedness Day*, c. 1941. Color sketch for Rincon Annex, Post Office, San Francisco, California. Tempera, watercolor, and graphite, 17.1 × 41 (6¾ × 16¼). The Frances Lehman Loeb Art Center. Gift of Susan and Steven Hirsch, class of 1971, 2015.23.1.4

247 Jackson Pollock, *Mural*, 1943. Oil and casein on canvas, 241.3 × 604.5 (95 × 238). University of Iowa Stanley Museum of Art. Gift of Peggy Guggenheim, 1959.6. Reproduced with permission from The University of Iowa. © The Pollock-Krasner Foundation ARS, NY and DACS, London 2025

248 William Gropper, *Justice*, from *Capriccios*, 1953–57. Lithograph, 36.5 × 25.8 (14½ × 10). MoMA. Gift of Mrs. William Gropper. 1155.1964.3. Courtesy Craig Gropper

249 Victor Arnautoff, *Westward Vision* from *Life of Washington*, 1936. Fresco. George Washington High School, San Francisco

250 Faith Ringgold, *For the Women's House*, 1971. Oil on canvas, 243.8 × 243.8 (96 × 96). Courtesy NYC Department of Correction, L2022.1. Photo Brooklyn Museum. © 2025 Anyone Can Fly Foundation/DACS

251 Jan Burger, *Green New Deal* poster, 2019. Green New Deal Arts: Signs of the Times, an initiative of art350.org

252 Vertis Hayes' mural *Pursuit of Happiness* (1937) digitally printed on glass, the Mural Pavillion, Harlem Hospital Center, New York, 2017. Photo HOK and Paul Warchol Photography

253 Jacob Lawrence, *New York in Transit*, 2001. Glass mosaic mural. NYCT Times Square–42nd Street Station. Commissioned by Metropolitan Transportation Authority Arts & Design. Photo Rob Wilson. © Jacob Lawrence

254 Kerry James Marshall, *Rushmore*, 2017. Mural, 40 × 30 m (132 × 100 ft). West side of the Chicago Cultural Center. Photo Brian Kay. © Kerry James Marshall. Courtesy the artist and Jack Shainman Gallery, New York

Index

"This kind of book at this kind of price
is what art publishing should be about"
—*New York Times Book Review*

"An extraordinarily rich and varied series"
—Linda Nochlin

The World of Art series is a comprehensive,
accessible, indispensable companion to the history
of art and its latest developments, covering themes,
artists and movements that span centuries and
the gamut of visual culture around the globe.

You may also like:

**American Art and
Architecture**
Michael J. Lewis

Art in California
Jenni Sorkin

**Black Art
A Cultural History**
Richard J. Powell

Caribbean Art
Veerle Poupeye

**Latin American Art
Since 1900**
Edward Lucie-Smith

**North American
Indian Art**
David W. Penney
Foreword by George Horse
Capture

Georgia O'Keeffe
Lisa Mintz Messinger

World of Art